Louisiana Law of Property, A Précis

LOUISIANA CODE SERIES

LOUISIANA POCKET CIVIL CODE
2022

LOUISIANA CIVIL CODE PRÉCIS SERIES

LOUISIANA LAW OF CONTRACTS AND QUASI-CONTRACTS
Alain Levasseur & Nikolaos Davrados
2024

LOUISIANA LAW OF OBLIGATIONS IN GENERAL
Alain Levasseur & Nikolaos Davrados
5th ed. 2024

LOUISIANA LAW OF PROPERTY
John Randall Trahan
2nd ed. 2024

LOUISIANA LAW OF SALE AND LEASE
Alain Levasseur & David Gruning
3rd ed. 2015

LOUISIANA LAW OF SECURITY DEVICES
Michael H. Rubin
2nd ed. 2017

LOUISIANA LAW OF SUCCESSIONS AND DONATIONS
Elizabeth R. Carter
2021

LOUISIANA LAW OF TORTS
Frank Maraist
2010

LOUISIANA LAW OF PERSONS
Forthcoming

Louisiana Law of Property
A Précis

SECOND EDITION

J. Randall Trahan

Saul Litvinoff Distinguished Professor of Law
Newman Trowbridge Distinguished Professorship
in Louisiana Property Rights
Louisiana State University
Paul M. Hebert Law Center

CAROLINA ACADEMIC PRESS
Durham, North Carolina

Library of Congress Cataloging-in-Publication Data

Name: Trahan, J. Randall, author.
Title: Louisiana law of property, a précis / J. Randall Trahan.
Description: Second Edition. | Durham, North Carolina : Carolina Academic Press, 2024. | Includes bibliographical references and index.
Identifiers: LCCN 2024008662 | ISBN 9781531025434 (paperback) | ISBN 9781531025441 (ebook)
Subjects: LCSH: Property—Louisiana.
Classification: LCC KFL110 .T73 2024 | DDC 346.76304—dc23/eng/20240224
LC record available at https://lccn.loc.gov/2024008662

CAROLINA ACADEMIC PRESS
700 Kent Street
Durham, North Carolina 27701
(919) 489-7486
www.cap-press.com

Printed in the United States of America

Contents

About the Author xxxi

Chapter One | Introduction
The Domain of Property Law 3

I. Property 3
A. The Common Meaning 3
B. The Technical Meaning(s) 3
1. Things 4
2. Rights 4
a. Patrimonial Rights 4
b. Real Rights 4
II. Property Law 8

PART I | THINGS

Chapter Two | The "Greater" Classifications 11

Sub-Chapter A. Common, Public, and Private Things 11
Section 1. Common and Noncommon Things 12
I. Definitions and Illustrations 12
II. Significance 12
Section 2. Public Things and Private Things 13
I. Explication 13
A. Definitions 13
1. Public Things 13
a. Preliminary Investigation: Public v. Private Capacity 13
b. Subdivision 14

1) Definitions 14
a) Public Things as a Matter of Law 14
b) Public Things as a Matter of Fact 14
2) Criteria 14
a) Public Things as a Matter of Law 15
b) Public Things as a Matter of Fact 15
3) Illustrations 16
a) Public Things as a Matter of Law 16
1] Running Waters 16
2] Waters and Bottoms of Natural Navigable Water Bodies 16
a] Waters 16
b] "Bottoms" of "Natural Navigable" Water Bodies 16
1} Natural Navigable 16
2} Bottoms 17
a} The Distinction Between Streams/ Rivers and Lakes 17
b} The Definition of "Bottom" 17
1. Of Streams and Rivers 17
2. Of Lakes 18
3] Territorial Sea 18
4] Seashore 18
b) Public Things as a Matter of Fact 18
2. Private Things 19
a. Subclassifications 19
1) Private Things of Public Persons 19
2) Private Things of Private Persons 20
B. Significance 20
1. Significance of the Distinction Between Public and Private Things 20
a. Susceptibility of Private Ownership 20
1) Ease of Disposal 20
2) Susceptibility of (Adverse) Possession 21
3) Vulnerability to Prescription 21
b. Susceptibility of "Public Use" 21
1) Public Things 21

2) Private Things 22
a) Subject to Public Use by Law 22
1] The "General" Servitude of Public Use 22
2] The "Levee" Servitude of Public Use 23
3] The "River Road" Servitude of Public Use 23
b) Subject to Public Use by Dedication 23
2. Significance of the Distinction Between Public Things as a Matter of Law and Public Things as a Matter of Fact: Duration of Insusceptibility of Private Ownership 26

Sub-Chapter B
Immovable and Movable Things 27
I. Definitions 27
A. Immovables 27
B. Movables 27
II. Classifications 28
A. Immovables 28
1. Corporeal Immovables 28
a. Definition 28
b. Varieties 28
1) By "Nature" 28
a) All Tracts of Land 28
b) Certain Man-Made Structures 28
1] The Classifications: Enumeration and Differentiation 28
2] Prerequisites to Immovability 29
a] Buildings 29
b] Other Constructions 30
1} Permanently Attached to the Ground 30
2} Belongs to the Owner of the Ground 30
c) Certain Vegetation 30
1] The Classifications: Enumeration and Differentiation 31
a] Standing Timber 31
1} Timber 31
2} Standing 31
a} Not Cut Down 31
b} Rooted in the Soil 31

b] Unharvested Crops 32
c] Ungathered Fruits 32
2] Prerequisites to Immovability 33
a] Standing Timber 33
b] Unharvested Crops and Ungathered Fruits 33
d) Integral Parts of Tracts of Land, Buildings, or Other Immovables Constructions 35
1] Of Tracts of Land 35
2] Of Buildings or Other Immovable Constructions 37
e) Attachments to Buildings and Other Immovable Constructions 37
1] Definition 37
2] Classifications 38
a] Attachments as a Matter of Fact 38
b] Attachments as a Matter of Law 38
1} To Buildings 38
2} To Other Immovable Constructions 40
2) By Declaration 41
2. Incorporeal Immovables 41
a. Definition 41
b. Illustrations 41
B. Movables 42
1. Corporeal Movables 42
a. Definition 42
b. Illustrations 42
2. Incorporeal Movables 42
a. Definition 42
b. Illustrations 42
III. Significance 43
A. Property Law 43
1. Modes of Acquiring Ownership 43
a. Accession 43
b. Acquisitive Prescription 43
2. Transfer of Ownership: Effectivity vis-à-vis Third Persons 43

3. Servitudes: Objects 44
4. Accessory Real Rights: Mortgage and Pledge 44
B. Other: Obligations 44
1. Formalities 44
a. Sale 44
b. Donation Inter Vivos 45
2. Sales: Lesion 45
Sub-Chapter C. Corporeal and Incorporeal Things 46
I. Definitions 46
A. Corporeals 46
B. Incorporeals 46
II. Significance 47
A. In Property Law 47
B. Outside Property Law 48

Chapter Three | The "Lesser" Classifications 51
I. Consumables and Nonconsumables 51
A. Definitions 51
1. Consumables 51
2. Nonconsumables 51
B. Illustrations 51
1. Consumables 51
2. Nonconsumables 52
C. Nature of the Criterion for Distinction 52
D. Significance 52
1. In Property Law: Nature and Effects of Usufruct 52
2. Outside Property Law: Nominate Contracts 53
II. Fruits and (Mere) Products 53
A. Definitions 53
1. Fruits 53
2. Mere Products 53
B. Illustrations 54
1. Fruits 54
a. Natural Fruits 54
b. Civil Fruits 54

2. Products 54
C. Complications 54
1. Natural Fruits v. Natural Products 54
a. Minerals 54
b. Timber 56
D. Significance 57
1. In Property Law 57
a. Modes of Acquiring Ownership: Accession: Ownership of Unconsented-To Production 57
b. Dismemberments of Ownership: Usufruct: Rights of Usufructuaries 57
2. Matrimonial Regimes Law: Community Property 58
III. Single and Composite 58
A. Definitions and Illustrations 58
1. Single (Simple) Things 58
2. Composite (Complex) Things 58
B. Significance 59
1. Property and Obligations Law: Ownership, Sales and Mortgage: Transfer and Encumbrance of Immovables 59
2. Property Law: Accession: Movables 59
IV. Improvements v. INATs 60
A. Definitions/Illustrations 60
1. Improvements 60
2. INATs 60
B. Nature of the Criterion of Distinction 61
C. Subclassifications: Consented-To and Unconsented-To Improvements and INATs 61
D. Significance: Property Law: Accession with Respect to Immovables 61
1. Ownership 61
2. Remedies 62
a. Unconsented-To Improvements and/or INATs 62
b. Consented-To Improvements and/or INATs 63
1) Consented-To Improvements 63
2) Consented-To INATs 63

PART II | POSSESSION

Chapter Four | Possession in General 67
I. Introduction: Possession and Ownership 67
II. The Concept of Possession 68
A. Definitions 68
III. Scope of Possession: Things Susceptible of Possession 69
A. Public and Private Things 69
B. Corporeal and Incorporeal Things 69
a. Corporeals 69
b. Incorporeals 69
IV. Constitutive Elements of Possession 70
A. Corpus 70
B. Animus 71
1. Substantive Matters 71
2. Procedural Matters: Presumptions and Burden of Proof 72
V. Extent of Possession 73
A. With Title 74
1. Nature of Constructive Possession 74
a. Requisites for Constructive Possession 74
B. Without Title 74
1. Substantive Matters: Definition of Actual Possession 74
2. Procedural Matters: Modes of Proving Actual Possession 75
VI. Acquisition, Conservation and Loss of Possession 75
A. Acquisition of Possession 75
1. Original Possession 76
a. Vicarious Corpus 76
b. Vicarious Animus 76
2. Derivative Possession 77
a. Derivative Possession Via a Universal Succession 78
b. Derivative Possession Via a Particular Succession 79
B. Conservation of Possession 79
1. Substantive Matters 80
a. Animus Domini 80
b. Corpus 80
2. Procedural Matters: Presumption and Burden of Proof 81

C. Loss of Possession 81
1. Loss of Both Corpus and Animus 82
2. Loss of Corpus Alone 82
a. Eviction (Usurpation) 82
b. Destruction 83
c. Escape 83
3. Loss of Animus Alone 83
VII. Vices of Possession 83
A. Violence 83
B. Clandestinity 84
C. Discontinuity 84
D. Equivocation 85
VIII. Detention (Precarious Possession) 85
A. Definition 85
B. Illustrations 86
1. Simple Precarious Possession 86
a. Lease 86
b. Deposit 86
c. Pledge (Possessory Security Right) 86
d. Loan for Use (Commodatum) 87
2. Complex (Compound) Precarious Possession 87
a. Co-Ownership 87
b. Servitude 87
C. Procedural Matters: Presumptions 88
D. Termination 88
1. Co-Owners 88
2. Other Detainers (Lessees, Depositaries, Pledgees, Borrowers, Servitude Holders) 89
IX. Junction of Possessions (Continuation of Possession; Tacking of Possessions) 90
X. Effects of Possession 95
A. Procedural Rights: Presumption of Ownership 95
B. Substantive Rights 96
1. The "Right to Possess" 96
a. Acquisition 96
b. Loss 96

2. Accession 96
a. Rights with Respect to Fruits and Products 97
b. Rights with Respect to Enhancements (Improvements and INATs) 97
3. Others 97

Chapter Five | Judicial Protection of Possession 99
I. Introduction 99
II. The Possessory Action 100
A. Scope 100
III. The Possessory Action 100
A. Prerequisites to the Possessory Action 100
1. Disturbance in Fact or in Law 101
a. Necessity 101
b. Definition and Varieties 101
1) Disturbance in Fact 101
a) Eviction 101
b) Mere Disturbance 101
2) Disturbance in Law 102
2. Possession at the Time of the Disturbance 104
3. Uninterrupted Possession for One Year Prior to the Disturbance 104
a. Elements of the Requirement 104
b. Exception to the Requirement 104
1) Eviction by "Force" 105
2) Eviction by "Fraud" 105
4. Action Within One Year of the Disturbance 105
B. Proper Parties Plaintiff 106
1. True Possessors 106
2. Precarious Possessors 106

Chapter Six | Occupancy 107
I. "Occupancy" Properly So Called 107
A. Definition 107
B. Constitutive Elements 107
1. Possession 107

2. Corporeal Movable 108
3. Thing that has no Owner (Res Nullius) 108
a. Things that Have Never Been Owned 108
1) Constituents of Certain Common Things 108
2) Certain Wild Animals 108
a) Wild Animal 109
1] Definition by Exposition 109
2] Definition by Contrast 109
b) Never Deprived of Natural Liberty 109
1] Wild Animals that Have Been Captured 110
2] Enclosed Wild Animals 110
3] Wild Animals that Have Been Tamed 110
3) Certain Domestic Animals 110
b. Things That, Though Once Owned, Have Ceased to be Owned 110
1) Abandoned Things 110
2) Certain Wild Animals 111
II. "Quasi"-Occupancy 111
A. Definition 111
B. Varieties 113
1. Quasi-Occupancy of Lost Things 113
a. Definition 113
1) By Exposition 113
b. Requirements 113
1) Diligent Effort 113
2) Three Years' Possession 114
2. Quasi-Occupancy of Treasure 114
a. Definition 114
b. Requirements 114
c. Rules of Allocation 114

Chapter Seven | Acquisitive Prescription **115**
Sub-Chapter A. Acquisitive Prescription in General 115
I. Definition 115
A. By Exposition 115
B. By Contrast 115

1. The Varieties of Prescription 115
2. Comparison 116
a. Differences 116
1) Necessity of Possession 116
2) Domain 116
b. Similarities 116
II. Basic Principles 117
A. Calculation of the Lapse of Time 117
1. Commencement 117
2. Accrual 117
B. Interruption of Prescription 118
1. Definition 118
2. Varieties 118
a. Natural Interruption 119
1) Eviction 119
2) Abandonment 119
b. Civil Interruption 120
1) By the Owner (Suit) 120
2) By the Possessor (Acknowledgement) 121
3. Effect of Interruption 121
C. Suspension of Prescription 122
1. Definition 122
2. Causes for Suspension 122
a. General Rule 122
b. Exceptions 122
1) Familial Relationships 122
2) Certain "Fiduciary" Relationships 122
3) Registered Immovables of Municipalities 123
4) Contra Non Valentem, Etc. 123
3. Effect of Suspension 124
D. Renunciation of Prescription 124
1. Definition 124
2. Attributes 124
3. Form 125
a. Immovables 125
b. Movables 125

3. Time of Renunciation 125
4. Effect of Renunciation 126
III. Effects of Acquisitive Prescription 126

Sub-Chapter B. Constitutive Elements of Acquisitive Prescription: *Elements Common to All Modes of Acquisitive Prescription* 127
I. Thing Susceptible of Acquisition by Prescription 127
A. Common Things 128
B. Public Things 128
C. Private Things 128
1. General Rule 128
2. Exception 128
II. Possession 129
III. Delay 130
A. General Principles 130
B. Continuation of Possession and Tacking of Possessions 130
1. In General 130
2. Special Problem: Spatial Extent of Joined Possession 131
a. Universal Successors: Spatially Unrestricted Tacking 132
b. Particular Successors 132
1) General Rule: No Tacking Beyond Title 132
2) Exception: "Boundary Tacking" (Tacking Beyond Title Up to Visible Boundaries on Adjacent Land) 133

Sub-Chapter C. Constitutive Elements of Acquisitive Prescription: *Elements Common to All Modes of Acquisitive Prescription* 135
I. Immovables 135
A. Unabridged Acquisitive Prescription 135
B. Abridged Acquisitive Prescription 135
1. Just Title 135
a. Elements Enumerated in Article 3483 136
1) Juridical Act 136
2) A Translative Act 136
a) Definition 136
b) Distinctions 136

1] Declarative Acts 136
2] Acts Generative of Merely Personal (Credit) Rights 137
3) A Written Title 137
4) In Proper Form 137
5) A Recorded Title 138
b. Elements Derived from General Principles 138
1) Not Absolutely Null 138
2) Not Subject to a Still-Pending Suspensive Condition 139
3) Not Putative (But Real) 139
2. Good Faith 140
a. Substantive Matters 140
1) Definition 140
2) Nature 141
3) Timing 141
b. Procedural Matters 141
1) The Presumption of Good Faith 141
2) Evidence of Bad Faith 142
a) Errors of Fact 142
1] In General 142
2] Special Problems 143
a] Quitclaim Deeds 143
b] Clouds on Title Reflected in the Public Records 144
b) Errors of Law 145
3. Delay 146
a. Length 146
b. Junction of Possessions 146
II. Movables 147
A. Unabridged Acquisitive Prescription 147
B. Abridged Acquisitive Prescription 148
1. Special Kind of Title: Act Translative of Ownership 148
2. Good Faith 148
3. Delay 149
a. Length 149
b. Junction of Possessions 149

PART III | PRINCIPAL REAL RIGHTS

Chapter Eight | Ownership 153

Sub-Chapter A. General Principles 153

I. Definition 153

II. Constitutive Elements 153

A. Usus 154

B. Fructus 154

C. Abusus 154

1. Physical Disposition 154

2. Juridical Disposition 154

C. Characteristics 155

1. Absolute 155

2. Exclusive 155

3. Perpetual 155

Sub-Chapter B. Extent of Ownership: *Accession* 156

I. Explication 156

A. Definition 156

B. Varieties 156

C. Prerequisites 157

D. Types of Rules 157

II. Regimes of Accession 158

A. Accession with Respect to Immovables 158

1. Preliminary Matters 158

a. Distinctive Prerequisites 158

b. Nature of Rules 158

2. The Rules 158

a. Artificial Accession 158

1) Union Accomplished by the Contributor Using Things That Did Not Belong to the Owner of the Original Immovable 159

a) Ownership Rules 159

1] Accession of Improvements 159

2] Accession of INATs 161

b) Remedial Rules 162

1] Where the Owner of the Original Immovable Consented to the Production or Union of the New Thing 162
a] Consented-To Improvements 162
b] Consented-to INATs 163
2] Where the Owner of the Original Immovable Did Not Consent to the Production or Union of the New Thing 165
a] Domain 165
b] Content 166
1} Preliminary Matter: Good Faith v. Bad Faith 166
2} The Rules 168
2) Union Accomplished by the Owner Using Things That Belonged to Another 170
a) Ownership Rules 170
b) Reimbursement Rules 170
b. Natural Accession 171
1) Alluvion and Dereliction 171
a) Along a River or Stream 171
b) Along a Lake or the Seashore 172
2) Avulsion 172
3) Islands From New Channels 172
4) Abandoned Bed 173
5) Islands on Beds 173
B. Accession with Respect to Movables 173
1. Adjunction 173
a. Definition 173
b. Prerequisites 173
1) Principal and Accessory 174
a) Function 174
b) Value 174
c) Bulk 174
2) Whole 175
c. Effects 175
1) Ownership 175

2) Remedies 175
a) Owner of Principal 175
b) Owner of Accessory 176
1] Separation and Return 176
2] Reimbursement 176
3] Damages 176
2. Transformation 176
a. Definition 176
b. Varieties 176
1) "Labor Plus Capital" Transformation 176
a) Definition 176
b) Prerequisites 176
c) Effects 177
1] Ownership 177
2] Remedies 177
a] Reimbursement 177
b] Replacement and Damages 177
2) "Labor Only" Transformation 177
a) Definition 177
b) Prerequisites 177
c) Effects 178
1] Ownership 178
2] Remedies 178
a] Reimbursement 178
b] Replacement and Damages 178
3. Mélange 179
a. Definition 179
b. Prerequisites 179
c. Effects 179
1) Ownership 179
2) Remedies 180
a) Reimbursement 180
b) Replacement and Damages 180
C. Accession of Fruits and (Mere) Products 180
1. Fruits 180
2. Mere Products 181

Chapter Nine | Modified Ownership: Ownership in Indivision **183**
I. Definition 183
A. Ownership 183
B. The Same Thing 184
C. Two or More Persons 184
II. Domain 185
III. Creation 185
A. By Operation of Law 185
1. Intestate Succession 185
2. Commingling or Mixture of Materials 186
3. Termination of Community: Divorce and Separation 186
4. Acquisitive Prescription by Co-Possessors 187
5. Quasi-Occupancy of a Treasure 187
6. Occupancy and Quasi-Occupancy by Co-Possessors 187
B. By Act of Will 188
1. Bilateral Acts: Sales, Exchanges, Donations *Inter Vivos, Dations En Paiement* 188
2. Unilateral Acts: Donations *Mortis Causa* 188
IV. Division of Shares 188
A. General (Default) Rule 188
B. Exceptions 189
1. Division Mandated by Law 189
2. Division Mandated by Juridical Act 189
V. Rights of Co-Owners 189
A. Rights in the Co-Owned Thing Itself 189
1. Fruits 189
2. Use 190
a. General Rule: Equal Use 190
b. Exception: Use Defined by Agreement 191
3. Conservatory Acts 191
4. Ordinary Maintenance and Repair 192
5. Improvements and Alterations 192
B. In the Co-Owner's Share of the Co-Owned Thing 193
1. Disposition 193
a. Alienation 193
b. Creation of Real Rights 193

1) Accessory Real Rights (Security Rights) 193
2) Principal Real Rights Less Than Ownership: Servitudes 193
c. Creation of Personal Rights: Lease 194
VI. Improvements and Alterations: Accession 195
A. Ownership 195
B. Remedies 196
VII. Termination of Co-Ownership 198
A. Loss of the Thing 198
B. Juridical Act of Transfer by the Co-Owners 198
C. Partition 199
1. Availability 199
a. General Rule 199
b. Exceptions 199
1) Contrary Provision in a Juridical Act 199
a) Act Creating Indivision 199
b) Convention Among Co-Owners 200
2) Contrary Provision of Law 200
2. Juridical Nature 200
a. Conventional 200
b. Legal (Judicial) 200
3. Modes 200
a. In Kind 201
b. By Sale 201
4. Effects 204
a. Interests of Co-Owners 204
1) In Kind: Localization 204
2) By Licitation 204
b. Interests of Third Parties 204
1) Third Parties Who had Real Rights in the Formerly Co-Owned Thing 204
2) Third Parties Who Had Real Rights in a Former Co-Owner's Share 205

Chapter Ten | Dismemberments of Ownership: Servitudes and Building Restrictions 207
Sub-Chapter A. Predial Servitudes 207
I. Definitions 207
A. Estate 207
1. Servient 208
2. Dominant Estate 209
B. Charge (on a Servient Estate) 209
C. Benefit (of a Dominant Estate) 211
D. Separate Ownership of Estates 214
II. Nature 215
III. Characteristics 215
A. Inseparability 215
1. From the Servient Estate 215
2. From the Dominant Estate 216
B. Indivisibility 216
IV. Limitations 217
V. Classifications 217
A. Natural Servitudes 218
1. Right of Drain 218
a. Definition 218
b. Rights and Duties 218
2. Right to Use Running Water 218
B. Legal Servitudes 218
1. Legal "Public" Servitudes 218
2. Obligations of Neighborhood 219
3. Encroaching Buildings 220
4. Common Enclosures 221
a. "Common Walls" 221
b. Common Fences 222
c. Common Ditches 222
d. Removal of Plants 222
5. Enclosed Estates (C.C. Arts. 689–696) 223
a. Entitlement to a Right of Passage 223
1) General Rule 223
2) Exception 224

b. Indemnity 224
1) General Rule 224
2) Exception 225
c. Location of the Passage 225
1) General Rule 225
2) Exceptions 226
a) Where the Enclosure Results from a Partition or a Voluntary Alienation 226
b) Other 226
d. Loss of the Right 226
C. Conventional Servitudes 227
1. Subclassification 227
a. Classification Based on Nature of Charge on Servient Estate: Affirmative v. Negative 227
b. Classification Based on Evidence of Charge on Servient Estate: Apparent v. Nonapparent 227
2. Acquisition 228
a. By Title 228
1) Domain 228
2) Requirements 228
a) Substantive Requirements 228
1] Re the Act 228
2] Re the Grantor 229
a] Who Can Grant 229
1} Owner of the Servient Estate 229
2} Co-Owner of a Servient Estate 229
3} Possessor—Prescriber of the Servient Estate (Servitude on After-Acquired Immovable) 230
4} Usufructuary of the Servient Estate 230
b] Capacity to Grant 231
c] Power to Grant 231
3] Re the Grantee 232
a] Who Can Receive 232
b] Capacity 233
b) Formal Requirements 233

1] General Rule 233
2] Exception 233
b. By Acquisitive Prescription 234
1) Domain 234
2) Modes 234
3) Requirements 234
a) Possession 234
1] Quasi-Possession 234
2] Constitutive Elements 235
a] Corpus 235
b] Animus Domini 235
b) Just Title 236
c) Good Faith 236
c. By Destination 237
1) Definition 237
2) Manner of Creation 238
a) Apparent Servitudes 238
b) Nonapparent Servitudes 238
3. Effects: Rights and Duties of the Owners of the Servient and Dominant Estates 238
a. The Owner of the Dominant Estate 238
b. The Owner of the Servient Estate 239
4. Extinction 240
a. Destruction 240
b. Nonuse 241
1) Substantive Elements 241
a) What Is "Use" 241
b) Who Can Use 242
c) Delay 242
1] Commencement of the Delay 242
2] Interruption and Suspension 242
3] Alteration of the Delay by Contract 243
2) Procedural Incidents: Burden of Proof 244
c. Confusion 244
d. Abandonment 244
e. Renunciation 245

Sub-Chapter B. Personal Servitudes 245
I. Usufruct 245
A. Definitions 245
B. Varieties 246
C. Acquisition 247
1. By Juridical Act 247
a. General Exposition 247
1) Particular Questions and Problems 247
a) Contractual and Testamentary Freedom 247
b) Contractual and Testamentary Interpretation 249
2. By Operation of Law 251
a. Spousal Usufruct 251
b. Marital Portion Usufruct 252
3. By Acquisitive Prescription 252
D. Effects of Usufruct 253
1. Rights and Duties of the Usufructuary During the Usufruct 253
a. Rights 253
1) With Respect to the Thing Subject to the Usufruct 253
a) Disposition (Abusus) 253
1] Usufruct of Consumables 253
2] Usufruct of Nonconsumables 253
b) Fruits (Fructus) 253
1] Definition 254
2] Allocation 254
a] Natural Fruits 254
b] Civil Fruits 254
c) Use (Usus) 255
1] In General 255
2] Limitations on Use 255
a] Usufruct of Consumables 255
b] Usufruct of Nonconsumables 255
1} Duty to Act as Prudent Administrator 255
2} Restriction on Improvements and Other Physical Alterations 255
3} Restriction on Changes in Destination 256

2) With Respect to the Usufruct Itself 257
b. Duties 257
1) Inventory 257
2) Security 258
a) Duty to Post 258
1] General Rule 258
2] Exceptions 258
b) Form of Security 259
c) Amount of Security 259
3) Repairs 259
4) Preservation 260
5) Charges 260
6) Prudent Administrator 261
2. Rights and Duties of the Naked Owner During the Usufruct 261
a. Usufruct of Consumables 261
b. Usufruct of Nonconsumables 261
3. "Other" Effect: Partition Powers 262
a. Relative: Partition of Usufruct or of Naked Ownership 262
1) Partition of Usufruct 262
2) Partition of Naked Ownership 263
b. Absolute: Partition of the Underlying Thing 263
E. Termination 264
1. Causes of Termination 264
a. "Death" of the Usufructuary 264
b. Destruction of the Underlying Thing 264
c. The Transformation of the Burdened Thing 266
d. Waste or Abuse 268
e. Forced Sale of the Burdened Thing 269
f. Prescription of Nonuse 269
2. Consequences of Termination 269
a. Usufruct of Nonconsumables 269
b. Usufruct of Consumables 270
II. Habitation 270
III. Right of Use 271

Sub-Chapter C. Building Restrictions 272
I. Definition 272
II. Characterization 273
III. Classification 273
A. By Type of Restricted Activity: Building Standards, 0Specified Uses, Improvements 273
B. By Nature of Duty: Negative vs. Affirmative 274
IV. Creation 274
A. Means 274
B. Special Requirement: General Plan of Development 275
V. Interpretation 276
VI. Enforcement 276
VII. Alteration 277
A. Amendment 277
1. Modes Established by the Juridical Act(s) that Create(s) the Restrictions 277
2. Modes Established by Suppletive Law 277
a. More Than Fifteen Years 277
b. More Than Ten Years 277
B. Termination 278
1. By Juridical Act 278
2. By Prescription of Non-Use 278
3. By Abandonment 279
a. Of the Whole Plan 279
b. Of a Particular Restriction 279

Chapter Eleven | Protection of Ownership **281**
Sub-Chapter A. Immovables 281
I. The Petitory Action 281
A. Burden of Proof 282
1. "Perfect Title" or "Title Good Against the World" 283
a. Acquisition by Acquisitive Prescription 283
b. Acquisition "From a Previous Owner" 283
1) The Possibilities (via "Chains of Title" to Previous Owners) 283
a) Acquisition From a Previous Acquisitive Prescriber 283

b) Acquisition From a Sovereign 284
1] General Rule 284
2] Exception: the "Common Author" Rule 284
c) "Better title" 285
B. Relationship to the Possessory Action 286
1. Against the Plaintiff (the Rule of "Noncumulation") 286
2. Against the Defendant 286
II. The Boundary Action 287
A. Definitions 287
1. Boundaries 287
2. Boundary Markers 288
B. Scope 288
1. Fixing Markers 288
2. Fixing Boundaries 288
C. Prerequisites 288
1. Prerequisites Relative to the Thing 288
2. Prerequisites Relative to the Person 289
D. Rules of Determination 290
1. In General 290
2. For Particular Situations 291
a) Where Both Parties Rely on Title 291
b) Where (at Least) One Party Relies on Acquisitive Prescription 292

Sub-Chapter B. Movables 293
I. Basis for the Action 293
II. Burden of Proof 293

Table of Legislation 295
Mineral Code 427
Revised Statutes 429
Constitution 432

Topical Table of Cases 433

Index 441

About the Author

Professor Trahan received his J.D. with high honors from Louisiana State University's Paul M. Hebert Law Center in 1989, where he was the Articles Editor of the Law Review and a member of The Order of the Coif. Before joining the Law Center faculty in 1995, he served as a law clerk to the late Judge Alvin B. Rubin of the United States Court of Appeals, Fifth Circuit, for one year and then practiced law with the firm Phelps Dunbar in Baton Rouge, Louisiana, for five years. A "civil law" specialist, he has taught, at one time or another, every course in the Law Center's so-called "civil law curriculum", that is, Western Legal Traditions, Obligations, Property, Persons & Family, Matrimonial Regimes, Sales & Leases, Security Devices, Successions & Donations, and Conflict of Laws. He is the author or co-author not only of this Précis, but also of several other books on the civil law of Louisiana, including *Western Legal Traditions & Systems: Louisiana Impact*, *Yiannopoulos' Civil Law Property*, *Louisiana Law of Obligations: A Methodological & Comparative Perspective*, *Family Law in Louisiana*, and *Secured Credit: Louisiana & American Perspectives*. He regularly lectures at the "Recent Developments" seminars put on by the Louisiana Center of Continuing Professional Development in the fields of property, sale, lease, and family law. He participates in law reform work as a member of the Council and of various Committees of the Louisiana State Law Institute and as one of Louisiana's delegates to the Uniform Law Commission.

Louisiana Law of Property, A Précis

Chapter One

Introduction: The Domain of Property Law

I. Property

A. The Common Meaning

Unlike many other terms that one encounters in studying the civil law, "property" is familiar. It is used in everyday speech by the "man (or woman) on the street." As so used, it means the "stuff' that one "has." This "stuff" is understood to include physical objects, such as land, cars, computers, and cash, and, by extension, various kinds of rights, such as "mineral interests" (for example, the right to receive royalties) and those represented by certain kinds of documents, such as a certificate of corporate stock or a United States Treasury bond. The "having" of this stuff is understood to consist of "owning" or "possessing," depending on the circumstances.

B. The Technical Meaning(s)

Though "property" as used in the civil law has a meaning that is not unrelated to the term's everyday meaning, the two are not quite the same. In the civil law, "property" may be used in either of two basic senses.

1. *Things*

The first is that of "things," a term that refers to any and all possible "objects" from which a person might hope to draw some utility or benefit. One example of this use of the term is found in **LSA-C.C. Art. 535**: "Usufruct is a real right of limited duration on the *property* of another. The features of the right vary with the nature of the *things* subject to it as consumables or nonconsumables." **LSA-C.C. Art. 642** offers another example: "A right of use includes the rights contemplated or necessary to enjoyment at the time of its creation as well as rights that may later become necessary, provided that a greater burden is not imposed on the *property* unless otherwise stipulated in the title."

2. *Rights*

Second, the term "property" is sometimes used in the sense of "rights." Under this heading there are two possibilities.

a. Patrimonial Rights

Sometimes "property," understood as "rights," refers to so-called "patrimonial rights." To make sense of this expression, one must, of course, first understand the notion of "patrimony." That term refers to anything that is "susceptible of pecuniary valuation," in other words, to which a "dollar value" can be attached. A patrimonial right, then, is one that can be valued in terms of money. Examples of this use of the term property can be found in **LSA-C.C. Arts. 3182 and 3183**, which provide as follows: "Whoever has bound himself personally is obliged to fulfill his engagements out of all his *property*, movable and immovable, present and future"; and "[t]he *property* of the debtor is the common pledge of his creditors." "Property," in this sense of the word, entails not only the rights that one typically associates with things, such as ownership or servitudes, but also those that have no such association, such as the right to the performance of a contract or to the payment of a "tort" claim.

b. Real Rights

Sometimes, however, "property," understood as "rights," is used in a much narrower sense, namely, to designate only those rights that one typically associates with things, that is, "real rights." According to traditional doctrine, a real right is one that exhibits three characteristics.

First, comment (b) to **LSA-C.C. Art. 476** tells us that it "confer[s] direct and immediate authority over a thing." What that means is that the holder, depending on the nature of his real right, may use that thing, collect the fruits of that thing, or even dispose of that thing, without having to depend on the intervention or permission of anyone else.

Second, comment (b) to **LSA-C.C. Art. 1763** explains that it "can be held against the world," or, to put it another way, it is "opposable" to everyone. That means that everyone—not only the person who granted the right—must respect the right or, to put it in procedural terms, that the holder of the right can obtain judicial relief against anyone who happens to infringe that right.

Third, it confers on its holder a right of "pursuit." The idea here is that if the thing that is subject to the real right should happen to change hands—should come to be possessed by someone other than he who had it to start with—the holder of the right can still assert the right and, further, can "get back" the thing for the purpose of exercising his right on it.

One can question at least one element of this traditional account of real rights, specifically, the supposed first characteristic: direct and immediate authority over a thing. The problem is that this attribute is predicable of only *some* real rights, namely, the "principal" real rights, such as ownership and servitudes. It is not predicable of "accessory" real rights, such as mortgage or pledge. Though an accessory real right does confer special power over a thing, that power hardly qualifies as either direct or immediate: it is the power, first, to cause the thing to be seized by a governmental authority and, afterwards, to be sold at auction and, then, to receive the proceeds of the sale. For these reasons, it would be better, when describing real rights as a whole, to say merely that they confer special authority over a thing and to leave it at that.

The nature of real rights comes into clearer relief when one contrasts them with their counterparts (what is left over when one subtracts "real rights" from the larger category of "patrimonial rights"), namely, "personal rights" or, better yet, "credit rights." It is customary to define a "personal right" as comment (b) to **Art. 476** does, i.e., one that "confer(s) merely authority over the person of a certain debtor." Another definition is this: a personal (credit) right is one that is entailed in the kind of legal relationship known as "obligation." Obligation, according to **LSA-C.C. Art. 1756,**

> ... is a legal relationship whereby a person, called the obligor, is bound to render a performance in favor of another, called the obligee. Performance may consist of giving, doing, or not doing something.

This right to demand a performance from another person, that is, the right to demand that a particular person (or determinate set of persons) give, do, or not do something, is what is meant by personal (credit) right.

How, then, does a personal (credit) right differ from a real right? First, whereas a real right necessarily concerns a thing, a personal right need not. Second, whereas a real right is good against the world, that is, against every conceivable person, a personal right is good against only a single person or a determinate set of persons, that is, the particular obligor or obligors of the obligation in question. Third, whereas a real right entitles the holder to "pursue" the thing to which it is related should it pass into someone else's hands and to reclaim it from that person, a personal right does not.

The first of these points of difference is so obvious that it hardly requires further explication. No matter what real right one might choose to imagine, for example, "ownership" or a "servitude" or a "mortgage," it must, of necessity, be a right *on* or *in* or *to* some *thing*. But there is no shortage of credit rights that have nothing at all to do with any *thing*. Suppose, for example, that A hires B—in more technical terms, A and B enter into a "labor contract"—whereby B, in return for A's promise to pay him a certain sum of money, promises to sing at A's wedding. Thanks to this contract, A now has a credit right against B, specifically, that B show up and sing as promised. This right, clearly enough, has no connection to any *thing*. Or suppose that X, parent of Y, enters into a contract with Y whereby X promises to pay Y a certain sum of money in return for Y's promise to stop "smoking." This contract gives X a credit right against Y, specifically, that Y not smoke and, this credit right, no less than that involved in the first example, is not related to any *thing*.

Of course, to say that a credit right "need not" concern a thing is to admit that it "may" and, in fact, quite a few credit rights "do." To distinguish such credit rights from real rights, one must have recourse to the second and third points of difference between the two.

Consider this illustration: M, the owner of a landlocked tract of land that lies next to another tract owned by N, proposes to N that N "sell" him the "right to pass" over N's land to the public road that lies on the other side, a proposal to which N is amenable. At this point, M and N have a choice to make, namely, whether they will set up N's right to pass as a credit right or a real right. They can do either, and the choice will be dictated by which set of legal effects—those of a credit right or those of a real right—they wish to realize. In weighing the decision, M is worried about two possible future developments. The first is that N might sell N's land to someone else. If that happens, M would still like to be able to pass over N's (now someone else's) land. The second is that some third party, T, might end up blocking the passageway area on N's land, with the result that M will not be able to cross. If that happens, M would like to be able to sue T directly to get a court order enjoining him to move. Given that these are his concerns, M should ask that his right to pass be set up as a real rather than a credit right. Why? Consider M's first concern. If the right to pass were to be set up as a real right, then the right, because it would then entail a right of "pursuit," would enable him to continue to pass across the land, even over the new owner's objection. To say that he has a right of pursuit, it will be recalled, is to say that the right follows the thing—stays on the thing—no matter whose hands it may happen to pass into. But if the right to pass were to be set up as a credit right, then M, lacking any right of pursuit, would not be able to insist that the new owner allow him to pass. A credit right would give M only a right "on" the person N, not a right "on" the thing N's land. As a result, all M could do would be to insist that N allow him to pass, a right that, under the circumstances, would be useless. Next, consider M's second concern. If the right to pass were to be set up as a real right, then the right, because it would then be "opposable" to the "whole world," could be asserted against everyone, including T. But if the right to pass were to be set up as a credit right, then the right would be opposable only against the person N, which means that M's only legal recourse would be to sue and collect damages from N for "breach of contract." Against T, to the contrary, he would have no recourse whatsoever.

II. Property Law

Like Caesar's Gaul, Louisiana's property law, in all, is divided into three parts.[1] They are, first, the law of the classification of things; second, the law of possession; and third, the law of principal real rights.

Of these three parts of property law, we have already made mention of two, namely, things and principal real rights, the connection between which should by now be clear. But the third, possession, we have yet to introduce. Possession, which is defined as physical acts of use, of enjoyment, of detention of a thing, forms something of a link—some would say *the* link—between things, on the one hand, and principal real rights, on the other. It is the means whereby most principal real rights, especially those associated with immovable property (for instance, land), arise in the first place. The mechanisms whereby this occurs, for example, occupancy, quasi-occupancy, and acquisitive prescription, we will study in detail in due course. Suffice it to say, for now, that by means of these mechanisms, one who takes possession of a thing may, be it instantaneously or be it only after the passage of time, end up acquiring a principal real right on the thing, such as ownership or some servitude.

The delimitation of the field of property law to that of "principal real rights" serves to set off this field of the law from two other major fields, namely, the law of "obligations" and the law of "security devices." The former—the law of obligations—concerns the part of the set of patrimonial rights other than real rights, that is, personal (credit) rights. The latter—the law of security devices—concerns the part of the set of real rights other than principal real rights, that is, accessory real rights.

---

1. The reference is to the first line of Julius Caesar's COMMENTARII DE BELLO GALLICO: "*Gallia est omnis divisa in partes tres....*" (Translation: "Gaul is, in all, divided into three parts....").

PART I

Things

Devising a simple intensive[1] definition of the term "things" that, at once, catches everything that the law regards as things and excludes everything that the law does not is no easy task. The term certainly refers to "objects" in the ordinary sense of the word, that is, to *physical* things—those that exist in time and space and can be sensed (seen, touched, etc.)—but the term refers to more than just that. Its referents include certain *non-physical* things that, unlike objects, exist only "in the mind" (as opposed to in time and space) and that cannot be sensed, but that, like objects, can have a certain utility or value for persons, namely, patrimonial "rights," "powers," and "privileges." Perhaps it is too much to ask that a simple intensive definition be fashioned for a term that has so disparate a set of referents.

We shall have to content ourselves, then, with understanding "things" as "that which the legislature says are things." The legislature has addressed itself to this matter in the various so-called "classifications" of things. These classifications are numerous, and some are more import-

1. I invoke an Aristotelean distinction here, namely, that between "intensive" and "extensive" definitions. An intensive definition is one that seeks to express the essence or fundamental properties of that to which the term refers; it is the kind of definition that one typically encounters in a dictionary. An extensive definition, by contrast, consists of the enumeration of examples of that to which the term refers.

ant than others. The law governing the most important classifications (the "greater" classifications) is found where one would expect to find it, namely, at the beginning of Book II of the Civil Code (the book entitled "Things"), beginning with **LSA-C.C. Art. 448.** The law governing the less important classifications (the "lesser" classifications) is scattered elsewhere throughout the Civil Code, the law of each classification forming part of the law with respect to which that classification has the greatest significance. For example, the distinction between "fruits" and "mere products" is treated within the law of "usufruct," the field of law in which that distinction has the most play.

Chapter Two

The "Greater" Classifications

The most important classifications of things, **Art. 448** tells us, are three: (1) common, public, and private things; (2) immovable and movable things; and (3) corporeal and incorporeal things.

SUB-CHAPTER A

Common, Public, and Private Things

The classification of things into "common," "public," and "private" suggests that these three categories are of the same order or rank within the larger taxonomy of things. But that is not correct. In fact, the "classification" of things into common, public, and private represents the conflation of two distinct classifications, to be precise, a primary classification and a secondary classification (that is, a *sub*-classification). The primary classification is this: all things are divided into common and noncommon; and the secondary classification is this: noncommon things are (sub)divided into public and private things.

SECTION 1

Common and Noncommon Things

I. Definitions and Illustrations

"Common" things, according to **LSA-C.C. Art. 449**, are those that "may be freely used by everyone conformably with the use for which nature has intended them." The article itself gives two examples: "the air and the high seas." ***Id.*** By applying the interpretive principle *ejusdem generis* to the text, we can perhaps come up with still more examples, such as sunshine, wind, and rain."

II. Significance

The principal (if not the sole) consequence of classifying a particular thing as "common" is that it may not be owned by anyone." **Art. 449**. The point of distinguishing "common" from "noncommon" things, then, is **to determine what can be owned and what cannot**. Common things are completely insusceptible of ownership; no one can own them, not even the state or its political subdivisions. Noncommon things, by contrast, can in principle be owned by someone, if not by individuals then at least by the state or its political subdivisions.

SECTION 2

Public Things and Private Things

I. Explication

A. Definitions

1. Public Things

According to **LSA-C.C. Art. 450**, "public" things are (noncommon) things that "are owned by the state or its political subdivisions in their capacity as public persons."

a. Preliminary Investigation: Public v. Private Capacity

To understand this classificatory scheme, one must first appreciate the distinction between "public capacity" and, its antithetical correlative, "private capacity." The former, as we have just seen, is referred to in **LSA-C.C. Art. 450**: "Public things are owned by the state or its political subdivisions in their capacity as public persons." The latter is referred to in **LSA-C.C. Art. 453**: "Private things are owned by... the state or its political subdivisions in their capacity as private persons." Taken together, these articles make it clear that state and one of its political subdivisions may own a given thing in either of two capacities: public or private. In addition, these articles make it clear that if the state or political subdivision owns a thing in its public capacity, then the thing is a public thing, but if the state or political subdivision owns a thing in its private capacity, then the thing is a private thing.

But what, precisely, differentiates the one capacity from the other? A complete and detailed answer to this question must await an examination of the subdivision of public things into those that are public as a matter of "law" and those that are public as a matter of "fact," for what "public capacity" means in connection with the one is a bit different from what it means in connection with the other. But we can, at this point, at least say the following. The capacity in which a governmental entity holds a given thing is a function of the use the entity makes of it and the purpose to which the entity puts it. If the entity uses it for the same kind of purpose and in the same way that a private person might use it, in the process restricting public access to it, then the entity holds the thing in the entity's private capacity. But if the entity uses it for a purpose and in a way that is customarily associated with the exercise of distinctively "sovereign" powers or prerogatives or, if not that, at least opens the thing to more or less indiscriminate use by the public at large, then the entity holds the thing in the entity's public capacity.

b. Subdivision

1) Definitions

a) Public Things as a Matter of Law

According to the second paragraph of comment (c) to **LSA-C.C. Art. 450**, certain public things, according to constitutional or legislative provisions, must necessarily be owned by the state or one of its political subdivisions and, further, are inalienable. For convenience, we may refer to such things as "public as a matter of law."

b) Public Things as a Matter of Fact

The same comment explains that other public things, though *by nature* alienable and thus susceptible of ownership by private persons, have been applied to some public purpose and are held by the state or its political subdivisions in their capacity as public persons. These things we will call, again for convenience, "public as a matter of fact."

2) Criteria

We said earlier that the criterion whereby one identifies a public thing, be it public as a matter of law or public as a matter of fact, is that the state or one of its political subdivisions owns the thing in its "public capacity," as opposed to its "private capacity." In the same connection, we noted that the difference between these two capacities, i.e., how one can tell, in any given concrete case, whether a government-owned thing is owned in the governmental entity's "public" or "private" capacity, varies somewhat depending on whether it is a question of a public thing as a matter of law or a question of a public thing as a matter of fact.

a) Public Things as a Matter of Law

The hallmark of a public thing as a matter of law is that there is some constitutional or legislative provision which *requires* that the thing be owned by the state or this or that of the state's political subdivisions. In such a case, the governmental entity holds the thing in its public capacity simply because the law (constitutional or legislative) "says so."

b) Public Things as a Matter of Fact

If a given thing owned by the state or one of its political subdivisions is not public as a matter of law, then whether the governmental entity in question holds it in the entity's public capacity or private capacity is, as the very name of this subcategory of public thing suggests, a question of "fact" (rather than a question of "law"). Inasmuch as the pertinent legislation itself does not identify the "facts" that are relevant to this determination, that task has been fallen to the courts and to scholars.

The jurisprudence and the doctrine, synthesized and systematized, indicates that a two-staged inquiry is required. "Stage one" of the inquiry is this: has the thing been devoted to an "administrative" use? Administrative use refers to a use that is confided exclusively to certain public employees for the execution of some public function. In one celebrated case, the court, finding that a city-owned fire truck had been devoted to "administrative use" by firefighters, concluded that the truck and all its component parts were held by the city in its private capacity and, for that reason, were private things. Analogous examples include the buildings in which the employees of state agencies do their work and the equipment (computers, copiers, etc.) located within those buildings. If the thing in question has not been devoted to an "administrative use," then one proceeds to "stage two." At this stage, one must ask and answer three questions, all of them designed to determine the extent to which, if at all, the governmental owner uses the thing as would a private person. The questions are these: (i) does the thing serve a quasi-proprietary or quasi-commercial purpose, specifically, does it generate revenue; (ii) are all members of the public allowed to use it indiscriminately; and (iii) are those members of the public who use it charged a fee. Employing these criteria, one court concluded that parish-owned airport was held by the parish in its private capacity and, as a consequence, was a private thing. Another court, relying on similar considerations, arrived at the same characterization of a city-owned tract of land that the city had leased to a businessman.

3) Illustrations

a) Public Things as a Matter of Law

Paragraph two of **Art. 450** provides several examples of public things as a matter of law: "running waters, the waters and bottoms of natural navigable water bodies, the territorial sea, and the seashore." Because of their practical importance in Louisiana, these public things merit closer examination.

1] RUNNING WATERS

The expression "running waters" is not defined in the pertinent Civil Code articles, in the comments thereto, in the jurisprudence, or in the doctrine. One might suppose, then, that the expression has its everyday, common meaning, namely, water that is in motion. But that definition is undoubtedly too broad. Understood in context, "running waters" refers to waters that flow through natural water bodies, such as streams, rivers, and lakes, and, under certain circumstances, large man-made water bodies, such as canals.

2] WATERS AND BOTTOMS OF NATURAL NAVIGABLE WATER BODIES

a] Waters

The term "waters," as used in this context, undoubtedly has its ordinary meaning. To a large extent, the category "waters of natural navigable bodies" is redundant of the category "running waters." But it covers more than just running waters, namely, waters of lakes that do not flow.

b] "Bottoms" of "Natural Navigable" Water Bodies

1} NATURAL NAVIGABLE

A water body is "navigable" if it is susceptible of being used in its "ordinary" (natural) condition as a highway of commerce over which trade and travel may be conducted in their customary modes. Because the "ordinary" condition of the waterway is determinative, man-made obstructions or improvements do not affect the navigability of the waterway. Use for commercial purposes in the past when water travel and trade were more customary is usually determinative, but courts will also look to possible future use based upon depth, channel, current, and banks. Because the use must be "commercial," recreational use is insufficient. "Customary modes of trade or travel" may include any watercraft customarily used in commerce.

2} *BOTTOMS*

According to well-established jurisprudence, what constitutes the "bottom" of a naturally navigable water body depends on the type of water body in question, specifically, whether it is (1) a "stream" or "river" or (2) a "lake."

a} The Distinction Between Streams/Rivers and Lakes

The distinction between "streams/rivers," on the one hand, and "lakes" on the other, a jurisprudential distinction, reflects less a difference in kind than a difference in degree. According to the courts, the determination of whether a given water body constitutes one or the other requires the application of a "multiple-factor test," one that takes into account various physical and historical characteristics of the water body. These characteristics include (1) "size," especially the "width" of the water body as compared to those of the water bodies that flow into it (the wider the water body, the more likely it is a lake; the narrower, the more likely a stream or river); (2) "depth" (the shallower the water body, the more likely it is a lake; the deeper, the more likely a stream or river); (3) "banks," more precisely, how steep they are (the more gradual the banks of the water body, the more likely it is a lake; the steeper, the more likely a stream or river); (4) "current," more precisely, the speed with which water flows through the water body, especially as compared to the currents of the water bodies that enter into it (the slower the current, the more likely the water body is a lake; the faster, the more likely a stream or river); and (5) "historical designation" in various official documents, in particular, maps.

b} The Definition of "Bottom"

1. OF STREAMS AND RIVERS

In the case of a river or stream, one distinguishes the "bank" from the "bottom" or, as the bottom is more typically known in the case of a river or stream," the "bed." **LSA-C.C. Art. 456** defines the *bank* of a "navigable river or stream" as "the land lying between the ordinary low and ordinary high stage of the water." This definition has reference to a physical characteristic of rivers and streams of which many people today are unaware, namely, that the level of water in a river or stream fluctuates regularly from one season of the year to the next, that there is a fixed pattern to these fluctuations, and that, over time, it is possible to calculate when the water will be at its highest and when at its lowest and, further, how high or low, on average, it is likely to get at these times. The "bank" is the land that lies between these "average" and "annual" high and low water levels. Take away the bank, and one is left with the "bed," that is, the "bottom," which is the land below the ordinary (average) low water mark of the river or stream.

2. *OF LAKES*

In the case of a lake, one draws no distinction between the "bank" and the "bed" in defining the "bottom." To the contrary, the bottom of a lake is all of the land that lies below the lake's ordinary (average) high water mark. In a sense, then, the bottom of a lake includes what, in the case of a stream or river, would be both the bank and the bed.

3] TERRITORIAL SEA

The term "sea," which refers not only to *water* but also to *the land that lies beneath it* (the "bottom"), includes the "Gulf of Mexico" and of all "arms of the Gulf." **LSA-R.S. 49:3.** These "arms of the Gulf" include (1) all bodies of water located in close proximity to the open Gulf that receive direct overflow from the tides and (2) Lake Pontchartrain.

4] SEASHORE

According to **LSA-C.C. Art. 451**, the "[s]eashore is the space of land over which the waters of the sea spread in the highest tide during the winter season." Though the article does not say so, it is understood that "highest tide" refers to the "ordinary" or "average" high tide. To some degree, then, the definition of seashore parallels that of the bottom of a lake.

b) Public Things as a Matter of Fact

Public things as a matter of fact include everything else that fits into the category of public things, but whose ownership is not specifically restricted by some constitutional or statutory provision to the government. Paragraph three of **LSA-C.C. Art. 450** provides two such examples: "streets and squares." Comment (e) to **Art. 450** further gives the examples of "drainage ditches," "parks," "cemeteries," and "open spaces" which are also public as a matter of fact because their ownership is not specifically restricted constitutionally or statutorily to the government.

2. *Private Things*

"Private things" are those that either are privately owned, that is, owned by private individuals or other private persons,[1] or that, though owned by the state or one of its political subdivisions, are held by this governmental entity in its "private capacity." **LSA-C.C. Art. 453.** Let us now examine each of these subcategories of private things in greater depth.

a. Subclassifications

1) Private Things of Public Persons

Private things of public persons, as we saw earlier, are those owned by the state or one of its political subdivisions in its private capacity. Examples of private things of this kind are numerous. In the explication of the category "private things of public persons" provided above, we encountered a number of them, namely, (1) fire trucks and their components, (2) airports, and (3) lands leased to private persons. Still other examples can be found in comment (b) to **LSA-C.C. Art. 453**: "public offices, police and fire stations, markets, schoolhouses." Finally, and deserving of special mention, are several examples associated with certain water bodies. It will be recalled that some water-related lands belong to the state in its *public* capacity and, for that reason, are *public* things. Examples include the bottoms of natural navigable streams, rivers, and lakes and the seashore. By contrast, certain *other* water-related lands, though they also belong to the state, are held by the state in its *private* capacity and, for that reason, are *private* things. These include certain "islands," "sandbars," "alluvion," and "dereliction."[2] Islands and sandbars that form on the beds (as opposed to the banks) of natural navigable streams and rivers are private

1. The "other private persons" referred to who can also own private things are "juridical persons," such as corporations, partnership, and unincorporated associations.

2. Though the meanings of the first two of these terms are well known, those of the latter two are not. "Alluvion" refers to accretion (deposition of sediment) formed *successively and imperceptibly* on the bank or bed of a stream or river or the shore of a lake (**LSA-C.C. Art. 499, ¶1**); "dereliction," to land that was originally part of the bed or bank of a stream or river or the shore of a lake but that is "left dry" (i.e., ends up *above* the ordinary low water mark) as a result of the water's having *imperceptibly and permanently* receded (**LSA-C.C. Art. 499, ¶2**).

We shall have occasion to say more about these four kinds of water-related lands, first, when we consider examples of private things of private persons and, later, when we consider "natural accession" with respect to immovables.

things of the state. The same is true of alluvion or dereliction that forms along the seashore or along the shore of a natural navigable lake.

2) Private Things of Private Persons

Private things of private persons are those that are owned by private individuals (also known as "natural persons") or other private persons (also known as "juridical persons"), such as a partnership or a corporation. Examples of private things of this kind are legion and ubiquitous. They include your house, car, clothes, textbooks, computers, and telephones. Other important examples include various kinds of lands that are related in one way or another to water bodies. As we have already seen, some water-related lands belong to the state and, of these, some are public things (e.g., the bottoms of natural navigable streams, rivers, and lakes) and some are private things (e.g., alluvion and dereliction that forms along the seashore or lakeshore). But other water-related lands belong to private persons and, as a result, are private things. Examples include the banks and beds of non-navigable streams and rivers; the bottoms of non-navigable lakes; alluvion and dereliction formed along these banks, beds, or bottoms; the banks (as opposed to the beds) of natural navigable streams and rivers; and alluvion and dereliction formed along those banks.

B. Significance

1. Significance of the Distinction Between Public and Private Things

a. Susceptibility of Private Ownership

The principal significance of the classification of things into public and private is this: it determines whether the thing in question is **susceptible of *private* ownership.** Whereas a private thing can be owned by private persons, a public thing cannot. That this is so has a myriad of important consequences.

1) Ease of Disposal

The first has to do with the **disposal** of property. Whereas the owner of a private thing can in principle dispose of it (i.e., sell it, donate it, exchange it) to whomever he wants, whenever he wants, and on whatever terms he wants, the owner of a public thing cannot.

2) Susceptibility of (Adverse) Possession

The second has to do with **possession.** Whereas private things can, in principle, be possessed by private persons, public things cannot. To put it another way, public things, unlike private things, are insusceptible of possession.

3) Vulnerability to Prescription

The third has to do with **prescription.** Whereas private things are, in principle, susceptible of prescription (i.e., can be acquired by private persons via acquisitive prescription), public things are not. This principle, as we shall see, has been modified by the state constitution and by special legislation, but we do not need to worry about that just yet.

b. Susceptibility of "Public Use"

The classification of things into public and private matters for yet another reason: it affects whether and, if so, under what conditions the thing may be "subject to public use." A thing is subject to public use if and to the extent that members of the public may use it, usually free of charge and largely without restriction, for certain limited purposes according to its nature or its destination. Public use is commonly regarded as a "charge" (or burden) on a thing, for the benefit of the public generally or for the state or one of its political subdivisions, that is analogous to a "servitude." For this reason, the public's right of public use is often referred to as the "servitude of public use."

1) Public Things

As a general rule, public things are *per se* subject to public use of one kind or another. **LSA-C.C. Art. 452. Art. 452** offers several examples of such public things and of the public uses to which each may be put:

> Everyone has the right to fish in the rivers, ports, roadsteads, and harbors, and the right to land on the seashore, to fish, to shelter himself, to moor ships, to dry nets, and the like, provided that he does not cause injury to the property of adjoining owners.

The public use of these and other public things is, of course, subject to the "police power" of the governmental entity or entities that have jurisdiction over them.

To the general rule that public things are subject to public use there are a few exceptions. One important example is the "bed" of a navigable stream or river. Though the bed is public, its use is restricted to those individuals, if any, to whom the state has leased or licensed it. Another example is "running water" that flows "naturally" through a private canal or otherwise over privately-owned lands. Though the water is public, members of the public do not have the right to navigate or fish in it.

2) Private Things

As a general rule, private things are *not* subject to public use. By way of exception, however, "[p]rivate things may be[come] subject to public use by law or by dedication." **LSA-C.C. Art. 455.**

a) Subject to Public Use *by Law*

A private thing is subject to public use "by law" if and only if and only to extent that legislation so provides. Examples are relatively few, and most of these have to do with the "banks" of "navigable rivers and streams."

1] THE "GENERAL" SERVITUDE OF PUBLIC USE

According to **LSA-C.C. Art. 456**, "[t]he banks of navigable rivers or streams are private things that are subject to public use." As is noted in comment (b) to this article,

> the servitude of public use under this provision is not "for the use of the public at large for all purposes" but merely for purposes that are "incidental" to the navigable character of the stream and its enjoyment as an avenue of commerce.

At the present day, the purposes that are considered to be "incidental" to the navigable character of waterways and that therefore fall within the scope of the permitted public use of the banks thereof seem to be few and far between. These purposes include fishing from the bank, "passing" along the bank, and, possibly, mooring vessels to the bank, provided that the mooring be "temporary." Public use of the banks does not, however, include the right to hunt or trap, to camp out, to moor vessels indefinitely, to drive pilings into the bank for use in mooring vessels, or to use wharves or other man-made structures that have been added to the banks. Whether and if so to what extent public use of the bank includes the right to unload moored vessels is contested.

2] THE "LEVEE" SERVITUDE OF PUBLIC USE

The "shores" (that is, the banks) of navigable rivers and streams are subject to a "servitude[] imposed for the public or common utility... for the making and repairing of levees." **LSA-C.C. Art. 665.** Thanks to this servitude, the owner of the bank is required to leave some free "space" on the bank sufficient for the construction of a suitable public levee. Issues regarding under what circumstances, to what effect, and by whom the servitude right may be invoked (that is, when a levee may be demanded, what kind of levee may be demanded, and who may demand it) are governed by special legislation, specifically, the legislation that establishes "levee districts."

3] THE "RIVER ROAD" SERVITUDE OF PUBLIC USE

By virtue of the provisions of **LSA-C.C. Arts. 665** and **666**, the banks of navigable rivers and streams are also made subject to a servitude of public use for the construction and maintenance of so-called "river roads." The duty incumbent on the bank owner parallels that which he owes with respect to levees: he must leave free "space" on the bank sufficient for the construction of a suitable public road. "Suitable," in this context, means necessary for "purposes incidental to the navigable character" of the waterway. Once the public road has been constructed, if it should thereafter be destroyed or carried away by the current, the bank owner "must furnish another" elsewhere on the bank. **Art. 666, ¶1.** If, on the contrary, the road is not destroyed or carried away, but is merely "injured or inundated by water" so as to become "impassable" for a time, the bank owner must provide the public a "passage on his lands" that is "as near as possible to the public road." ***Id.*** **at ¶2.**

b) Subject to Public Use *by Dedication*

A private thing is subject to public use "by dedication" if and only if and only to extent that the owner of that thing so provides through some juridical act. The kinds of juridical acts whereby the owner can accomplish this result—commonly called the "modes of dedication to public use"—are many. First and foremost, the owner may resort to a classic, full-blown "donation *inter vivos*," one whereby he donates a servitude of public use for this or that purpose to the public at large. *See* **LSA-C.C. Arts. 1467–1468** and **1526** ***et seq.*** Our courts have, over time, recognized still several other, less formal alternatives. These include "formal dedication," "implied dedication," and "tacit dedication";[3] through each of these "modes," the owner can (or may only) confer upon the public a servitude of public use of one kind or another. Among the kinds of private things that are commonly subjected to public use via dedication are roadways, parks, and cemeteries.

Excursus on Dedication to Public Use

As we just noted, our courts have recognized several "informal" means whereby the owner of a thing may "dedicate" it to "public use." Up to this point, we have considered dedication as a mechanism whereby the public might acquire only a "servitude of public use" over (as opposed to "ownership" of) the thing that is dedicated. But nothing prevents the owner, if he so chooses, from using dedication to confer ownership on the public. In such a case, the thing becomes a public thing and, as such, is *per se* subject to public use.

We have so far mentioned three modes of dedication: formal, implied, and tacit. There is yet one more: statutory. We will now look at each more closely.

A. Formal dedication

A "formal dedication" is one made by a written juridical act. Strict compliance with the form requirements for donations *inter vivos* (i.e., authentic act) is *not* required. It is sufficient, but also necessary, that the writing clearly reflect an intent to dedicate.

What interest is conveyed to the public by the dedicator—full ownership or a mere servitude of public use—depends on the intent of the grantor. The presumption, however, is that he intended to convey full ownership.

3. These three modes of dedication, plus one other—"statutory dedication"—will be examined in detail in the "excursus" that immediately follows this section.

B. Implied dedication

"Implied dedication" takes place when the owner sells land by reference to a map that depicts still other land owned by him and on which this or that part of this other land is designated as some kind of "public" or "common" area, such as a "cemetery," a "park," or a "square." No formalities are required for this mode of dedication except for proof of a positive intent to dedicate on the part of the dedicator and proof of acceptance from actual use on the part of the public. The interest conveyed by the owner to the public through this mode of dedication is a mere servitude of public use.

C. Statutory dedication

"Statutory dedication" refers to a dedication pursuant to **LSA-R.S. 33:5051**. This statute requires of the subdivider of certain lands that he file for recordation a "plat map" of his "subdivision" that contains the following information: (1) the "Section, Range, Township" of the subdivision; (2) the number and dimensions of squares and lots; (3) the names and dimensions of alleys and streets; (4) each square dedicated to public use; (5) a certificate from the parish surveyor or other licensed surveyor as to compliance with § 5051; and (6) a formal dedication of streets, alleys, and squares. Strict compliance with these requirements is not necessary; "substantial compliance" will do. The interest conveyed to the public through this mode of dedication is full ownership.

D. Tacit dedication

Dedication accomplished pursuant to **LSA-R.S. 48:491** is known as "tacit dedication." The only requirements are (1) maintenance of a road for three years by either parish or municipal authorities and (2) actual or constructive knowledge of this maintenance work on the part of the landowners on whose land the road lies. Where these requirements are satisfied, the landowners are said to have "tacitly" dedicated the road to public use. In such a case, the only interest conveyed to the public is a servitude of public use.

2. *Significance of the Distinction Between Public Things as a Matter of Law and Public Things as a Matter of Fact:* Duration *of Insusceptibility of Private Ownership*

The classification of a thing as public as a matter of law or as a matter of fact determines the ***duration* of its insusceptibility to private ownership.** If the thing is public as a matter of law, then it is public once and for all: it can never cease to be public and, therefore, can never become private.[4] If the thing is merely public as a matter of fact, by contrast, then its public status can end if it ceases to be used by the governmental entity in its public capacity. When and if that happens, it becomes private.

---

4. Short of a change in the law, that is. As we have learned, a thing is public as a matter of law if and only if the constitution, legislation, or other provision of law dictates public ownership. Those provisions of law, of course, are not themselves immutable. If the people (in the case of a constitutional provision) or the government (in the case of legislation or other second order provision of law) were to repeal such a law or otherwise change it so that public ownership was no longer required, then the thing to which that law applies would, of course, cease to be public as a matter of law and become, instead, public as a matter of fact or private, depending on the circumstances.

SUB-CHAPTER B

Immovable and Movable Things

I. Definitions

A. Immovables

The Civil Code does not provide us with a definition of the term "immovable." Neither does the doctrine or the jurisprudence. One might be tempted, the, to suppose that the term, as used in the civil law, has its everyday, common meaning, that is, "That [which] cannot be moved physically; firmly fixed; incapable of movement. Often less strictly: Motionless, stationary, fixed," as the Oxford English Dictionary puts it. But this temptation should be resisted, for "construct," which is as much as to say that it is something somebody—in this case, the legislature—simply "made up." And in putting together this construct, the legislature has, on occasion and for reasons of policy, chosen to qualify as immovable some things that can, in fact, be moved (for example, a house) and, by the same token, to qualify as movable some things that cannot, in fact, be moved. For this reason our courts have stated—rightly—that immovability in fact is neither a sufficient nor a necessary condition for immovability in law. In the end, then, an immovable is whatever the legislature has said is an immovable, nothing more and nothing less. As a result, determining whether a particular thing is an immovable entails determining whether it might possibly fit into any of the categories of things that the legislature has chosen to call "immovable."

B. Movables

The category of movables is a residual one. **LSA-C.C. Art.** 475 explains that "[a]ll things ... that the law does not consider as immovables, are movables."

II. Classifications

A. Immovables

1. Corporeal Immovables

a. Definition

Corporeal immovables are corporeals that are not susceptible of being moved from place to place or that, by legislative fiat or by declaration of the owner, have been assimilated to such corporeal things.

b. Varieties

1) By "Nature"

a) All Tracts of Land

LSA-C.C. Art. 462 provides that "Tracts of land... are immovables." Comment (c) to that article tells us that "[l]ands may be defined as portions of the surface of the earth."

b) Certain Man-Made Structures

As a reading of **LSA-C.C. Arts. 463** and **464** reveals, certain man-made structures are immovable, at least under certain circumstances.

1] THE CLASSIFICATIONS:
ENUMERATION AND DIFFERENTIATION

These articles refer to two categories of such man-made structures, namely, "buildings" and "other constructions." The use of the word "other" before the word "constructions" tells us two important things: (1) that a building itself is a kind of construction and (2) that there are some constructions that, for whatever reason, do not qualify as "buildings."

But what marks the dividing line between a "building construction," on the one hand, and an "other, non-building construction," on the other? The Civil Code does not lay down a rule or, for that matter, even enumerate relevant factors or criteria. The comments also fail to provide any help in drawing this distinction.

Stepping in to fill this gap, our courts have concluded that whether something is a "building" or some lesser "other construction" is a function of at least three factors: (i) size, (ii) cost, and (iii) function. Though the first two factors—size and cost—are self-explanatory, the third—function—needs further elaboration. What functions do we typically associate with "buildings" as opposed to the lesser constructions? One is housing humans, providing either dwelling space or work space. As far as housing animals is concerned, though some structures that perform that function (provided they be large and costly enough) may be considered buildings, that function is not associated *exclusively* with buildings. Comment (c) lists as an example of an other construction a "poultry house" (in other words, a large chicken coop). The same would probably be appropriate for a dog house, but a larger, more costly structure for housing animals, e.g., a barn, probably qualifies as a building. As far as housing equipment or goods goes, again, though some structures that perform that function may be considered buildings, that function is not associated *exclusively* with buildings. A shed just big enough to cover a riding lawnmower and/or a few garden supplies is probably just a mere construction. But something like a full-sized warehouse or a massive grain elevator would probably qualify as a building.

Still other helpful illustrations of "other constructions" can be gleaned from various comments to several of the pertinent Civil Code articles. Comment (c) to **Art. 463** gives these additional examples: a tractor engine that has been affixed to the ground, a canal, a cistern, a brick pit, a corn mill, a gas tank, a railroad track. Comment (g) to **LSA-C.C. Art. 466** provides one more: water towers.

2] PREREQUISITES TO IMMOVABILITY

a] Buildings

Strictly speaking, there are no prerequisites for a building to be immovable. That is because *all* buildings *per se* are immovables, regardless of the circumstances. That this is so follows from three Civil Code articles: (i) **Art. 462** ("Tracts of land, with their component parts, are immovables."); (ii) **Art. 463** ("Buildings... are component parts of a tract of land when they belong to the owner of the ground."); (iii) **Art. 464** ("Buildings... are separate immovables when they belong to a person other than the owner of the ground."). These articles, read together, make it clear that *all* buildings are immovables. If a building belongs to the owner of the land on which it sits, then it is a "component part" of the land (**Art. 463**) and, as such, is an immovable (**Art. 462**). If, on the other hand, the building does not belong to the owner of the land on which it sits, then it is a "separate immovable" (**Art. 464**). In either case, however, it is an immovable.

b] Other Constructions

On the other hand, not every "other construction" is an immovable: there are two prerequisites.

1} PERMANENTLY ATTACHED TO THE GROUND

To qualify as an immovable, a construction must be "permanently attached to the ground." There appears to be no hard and fast rule for how one should determine whether a particular construction is "permanently attached" to the ground. In the words of comment (c) to **LSA-C.C. Art. 465**, it is a "question of fact to be determined by the trier of facts." Perhaps one could, by analogy, apply the various definitions of "attachment" that are set forth in **LSA-C.C. Art. 466**, which, as we will see later on, concerns things "attached" in various ways to "buildings" and to "other constructions" that are immovable. If so, then "attachment" could be either a matter of "law" or a matter of "fact." On this hypothesis, another construction could be considered "permanently attached as a matter of law" if, according to "prevailing usages," it "serves to complete" the land or if it "serves the principal use of the land" or could be considered "permanently attached as a matter of fact" if it "cannot be removed without substantial damage" to itself or to the land.

2} BELONGS TO THE OWNER OF THE GROUND

One thing more is required for a construction to be an immovable, i.e., that it belong to the owner of the ground to which it is permanently attached: According to **Art. 463**, other constructions permanently attached to the ground... are component parts of a tract of land when they belong to the owner of the ground." The implication is that a construction which belongs to someone other than the owner of the thing might not be immovable. Comment (d) to **Art. 464** confirms this implication: "[c]onstructions permanently attached to the ground, other than buildings, are component parts of a tract of land when they belong to the owner of the ground. They are *movables* when they belong to another person."

c) Certain Vegetation

As a reading of **Arts. 463** and **464** reveals, certain vegetation is immovable, at least under certain circumstances.

1] THE CLASSIFICATIONS: ENUMERATION AND DIFFERENTIATION

The articles refer to three categories of such vegetation, namely, "standing timber," "unharvested crops," and "ungathered fruits."

a] Standing Timber

Neither the Civil Code articles on immovables nor the comments thereto define "standing timber." We shall, then, have to come up with a definition ourselves. Let us begin by breaking the term down into its component parts: "timber" and "standing."

1} TIMBER

Like "standing timber," "timber" is not defined in either the article of the Civil Code that pertain to immovables or the comments to those articles. But it is defined in a comment to **LSA-C.C. Art. 562**, which concerns the usufruct over "timberlands," namely, comment (c):

> Timber may be defined as tress which, if cut, would produce lumber for building or manufacturing purposes. This includes any trees that could be cut for economic gain, such as pulp wood, pines, hardwoods or building lumber. This would be equivalent to the definition of "merchantable timber" as used in Louisiana law.
>
> Timber, then, consists of vegetation that contains "wood" (dense cellulose) and whose wood can be turned to economic advantage.

This definition, then, corresponds to the narrower of the dictionary definitions.

2} STANDING

To qualify as standing timber, a thing must not only be "timber" as we have just defined it, but it must also be "standing."

a} Not Cut Down

By definition, a tree that has been chopped down is not standing. Paragraph two of comment (d) to **Art. 463** provides that "[t]rees cut down, whether carried off or not, are movables."

b} Rooted in the Soil

The great French civil law scholar Planiol, summarizing unanimous French doctrine, once wrote that "[a]ll vegetation that pushes up onto the earth is immovable, provided that it adheres to the soil." What is true of vegetation in general must be true of timber in particular. The "standing" requirement is designed, among other things, to capture this idea that timber, to be immovable, must "adhere to the soil."

Being "rooted in the soil" is a *necessary* condition for being "standing." But is it as well a *sufficient* condition? It may be possible for a timber-type tree to be "rooted in the soil" and yet, at least for the moment, be considered "not standing" and, therefore, not immovable (i.e., movable). The opinion of some French authors is that trees which, though planted in the ground, are planted only provisionally, that is, with a view to future re-transplantation, are "movables." Though this is the opinion of the majority of French authors, there are some dissenters. Neither the jurisprudence nor the doctrine in Louisiana has yet to take a position on the question.

b] Unharvested Crops

Nowhere in the Civil Code or in any of the comments thereto does one find a definition of "unharvested crops." Nor has one been supplied (at least not yet) by either the jurisprudence of the doctrine. One must assume, then, that the expression has here its common meaning. As for "crop," it means vegetation that can be grown for profit or subsistence. Examples include cotton, rice, soybeans, and sugarcane. "Unharvested" means, depending on the kind of crop, "still on the plant" ("unplucked") or "still in the soil" ("uncut" or "unearthed").

c] Ungathered Fruits

Art. 463 does not define "fruits." But the Civil Code does set forth a definition of that term in **LSA-C.C. Art. 551**: "things that are produced by or derived from another thing without diminution of its substance." The question is whether this definition from the usufruct articles is the same as what is meant as that of "fruits" in **Art. 463.** The answer is "no." The phrase "ungathered fruits" as used in **Art. 463** is an English translation of the French expression *les fruits des arbres non cueillis*, which appeared in the French versions of the predecessors to **Art. 463** in the Code of 1825, the Digest of 1808, and the Code Napoleon. *Les fruits des arbres* means the fruits of trees. Assuming that the meaning of the term has not been changed, what does that tell us about the meaning of the term "fruits" as it is used in **Art. 463**? First, that the term fruits as used in **Art. 463** is much narrower in scope than is the term "fruits" as defined in **Art. 551** and, second, that the meaning of the term fruits as used in **Art. 463** conforms more or less perfectly to its common meaning.

The same seems to be true of "ungathered" as well, that is, the term as used in this context apparently has its common meaning. That common meaning is "unpicked."

2] PREREQUISITES TO IMMOVABILITY

a] Standing Timber

Is standing timber anywhere and always immovable? Or is it movable or immovable depending on the circumstances, such as, for example, who owns it, in particular, whether it belongs to the owner of the ground?

To pose the question in this way presupposes that standing timber can be owned separately from the ground, in other words, one person can own the timber while another owns the ground. This presupposition is correct as **Art. 464** explains: "Buildings and *standing timber* are separate immovables *when they belong to a person other than the owner of the ground.*"

How separately owned standing timber should be classified is found in **Art. 464**: "Buildings and *standing timber* are *separate immovables* when they belong to a person other than the owner of the ground." So, standing timber is *always and under all circumstances* immovable.

b] Unharvested Crops and Ungathered Fruits

In order for unharvested crops or ungathered fruits to be immovable, they must belong to the owner of the ground, **Art. 463** tells us. If they do, then they are immovable. But if they do not, that is, if they belong to someone other than the owner of the ground, comment (e) to **Art. 463** explains, then they are movables, more precisely "movables by anticipation."

Excursus on "Other" Vegetation

The categories "standing timber," "ungathered crops," and "unharvested fruits" hardly exhaust the universe of "vegetation." What conclusions should be reached about the classification of "other" kinds of vegetation? Are they always immovable, always movable, or sometimes one and sometimes the other?

Perhaps an examination of legal history can shed some light on this question. **Arts. 463** and **465**, the only current Civil Code articles that concern "vegetation" of any kind, can be traced back to Article 520 of the Code Napoleon, which provided as follows: "Crops hanging by the stems and fruits of trees not yet gathered are likewise immovables." This article, which seems to have been copied by the redactors of the Digest of 1808 without alteration, does not say anything about trees themselves in general or timber in particular. Even so, the early commentators on the French Civil Code argued that the article was merely illustrative, so that *all* vegetation should be classified as immovable, provided that it is owned by the owner of the ground. If it is not owned by the owner of the ground, the commentators asserted, then the vegetation should be classified as movable. By 1825, this commentary had reached the shores of Louisiana. And so it happened that, when the redactors revised the Digest in that year, they added a new phrase to the article just after the phrase "fruits of trees," namely, "and the trees, provided that they've not been felled." At that point then, "trees" were to be classified as immovables. This rule was not altered in the revision of the Civil Code of 1870. By the end of the 19th century, the Louisiana courts, in derogation of the Civil Code, had begun to recognize that some vegetation, for example, crops grown by and owned by a farm lessee, should be classified as "movables by anticipation." The question then arose, "Well, what about timber?" In 1904, the legislature passed a special statute that addressed this question. Under that statute, so-called "standing timber," a term that had never before been used in any civil law jurisdiction, was to be treated as immovable *regardless of who owned it.* Given the context within which this special statute was adopted, it seems clear that its authors must have considered the category "timber" to be narrower than the category "trees" and, further, that they understood "timber" in its common sense, i.e., as trees that yield wood suitable for commercial exploitation. Then came the revision of the Civil Code in 1978, which produced **Art. 463.** In contrast to its predecessor in the code of 1870, this new article expressly provides for "standing timber," but not for other trees.

It appears, then, that the current legislation makes no express provision for vegetation that is not "standing timber," "unharvested crops," or "ungathered fruits." So, how should such vegetation be classified? There would seem to be several possibilities.

First, we could interpret the new Civil Code articles on immovables, notwithstanding the redactors' failure to provide for non-timber trees expressly, in such a fashion that non-timber trees are immovables if they belong to the owner of the ground, but movables if they belong to someone else. Recall that **Art. 462** provides that "[t]racts of land, with their component parts, are immovables," after which **Art. 463** purports to identify various "component parts" of tracts of lands. Perhaps the enumeration of component parts of land set forth in **Art. 463** is merely illustrative, not exhaustive. And perhaps non-timber trees, by analogy to unharvested crops and ungathered fruits (not to mention other constructions permanently attached to the ground), could be treated as component parts of the land so long as they belong to the owner of the ground.

Second, we might conclude, instead, that non-timber trees, like timber, are always immovable. This conclusion could be reached by following either of two routes. The first involves **Arts. 462 and 463**. Perhaps the better analogue for non-timber trees is not unharvested crops and ungathered fruits (and other constructions, etc.) but rather timber (along with buildings). If so, then non-timber trees should be treated as immovable regardless to whom they belong. The second involves **Arts. 462** and **465**. This latter article, which we will not examine in depth until later on, provides that things that are so "incorporated" into a tract of land so as to become an "integral part" of it are its component parts. As component parts of a tract of land, these **Art. 465** "integral parts" are immovable. Perhaps non-timber trees rooted in the ground qualify as "integral parts" thereof.

d) Integral Parts of Tracts of Land, Buildings, or Other Immovables Constructions

1] OF TRACTS OF LAND

Art. 465 provides that "[t]hings incorporated into a tract of land... so as to become a part of it... are its component parts." The conceptual fulcrum round which this article turns is "integration." But just what "integration" means is left somewhat obscure: neither **Art. 465** nor its comments sheds much light on the subject.

Perhaps we can get some guidance from the pertinent jurisprudence. In an apparent effort to provide a concrete illustration for **Art. 465**, the author of comment (b) to that article cited, apparently with approval, a case in which the court characterized an underground gasoline storage tank as an immovable. To support this characterization of the tank, the court placed heavy reliance on the following facts: (1) removal of the tank from the ground (a) would be difficult, time-consuming, and costly (in no small measure because the tank had been covered over with a cement slab); (b) would cause significant damage to the tank; (c) would cause significant damage to the ground; and (d) would risk causing damage to various above-ground structures and (2) the owner of the ground, when he installed the tank, intended for it to remain there indefinitely. Similar considerations, no doubt, should now be taken into account when deciding whether a man-made structure qualifies as an **Art. 465** "integral part."

Several other cases, though not cited in the comments to **Art. 465**, nevertheless seem to have inspired its authors, to one degree or another. In those cases, the courts, to justify classifying the things before them as immovable, noted that they had become so "integrated" into the underlying immovable that they had "lost their separate identity," had become "part and parcel" of it, and had become "merged" with it. Perhaps these notions, too, should be taken into consideration in determining whether a given thing has become an "integral part" of some underlying immovable, such as land.

As we have noted, it seems to be the case that, at least under some circumstances, it may be appropriate to classify an underground man-made structure as an "integral part" of the ground under **Art. 465.** But could one not, with equal justification, place such a structure into another, different category of things, one that we will study in depth later on: other constructions permanently attached to the ground? And, if that is so, is it not problematic? If we were to classify them in this other way, then their immovability would not be guaranteed, as it would be were we to classify them under **Art. 465.** That is because whether an "other construction permanently attached to the ground" is movable or immovable depends on who owns it, i.e., the owner of the ground or someone else. If it belongs to the owner of the ground, it would still be immovable. But if it does not, then it would be movable. There *is*, then, a problem with these categories, and it is a *big* one: the categories "overlap" and, in at least some circumstances, they will not lead to the same legal effects.

How, then, do we know if this or that thing should be characterized as an integral part of the ground and not a construction permanently attached to the ground? As amazing as it may seem, there is no answer to this question. Some have suggested that the difference is one of *degree* of integration into the ground, not one of *kind*: if the construction is integrated into the ground *a whole lot*, it is an integral part under **Art. 465**; if the construction is integrated into the ground *only a little bit*, then it is an other construction permanently attached to the ground under **Art. 463.** One can question whether this account of the difference is fully satisfactory.

2] OF BUILDINGS OR OTHER IMMOVABLE CONSTRUCTIONS

The subcategory of movables integrated into buildings or other constructions causes the judge, the practitioner, and the legal scholar less trouble than the subcategory of movables integrated into land for two reasons. First, **Art. 465** sets out the principal, if not the only, example of movables of this kind: building materials. That term entails things such as bricks and mortar, paint, caulking, floor tiles, ceiling tiles, and the like. Second, this subcategory overlaps more or less perfectly with another category of immovables, one whose contours are much better defined: component parts of a building or other construction under **Art. 466.** It is almost impossible to think of a movable integrated into a building or other construction that would not, at the same time, be a component part of that building or other construction under **Art. 446.**

e) Attachments to Buildings and Other Immovable Constructions

1] DEFINITION

LSA-C.C. Art. 466 is concerned with things that become so "attached" to a building or other immovable construction as to become a component part of it. The first paragraph of the article addresses certain attachments of buildings; the second, certain attachments of other immovable constructions; and the third, still other attachments of both buildings and immovable constructions. Because the criterion for "attachment" established in the third paragraph is fact-dependent, it may be appropriate to refer to such attachments as "attachments as a matter of *fact*." Lacking any better term whereby we might refer to the kinds of attachments delineated in the first two paragraphs, we may refer to them as "attachments as a matter of *law*."

2] CLASSIFICATIONS

a] Attachments as a Matter of Fact

Paragraph three of **Art. 466** provides that things that become "attached" to a building or other immovable construction "to such a degree that they cannot be removed without substantial damage to themselves or to the building or other construction" are its "component parts." Examples include things that have been affixed to the building or other construction with plaster or mortar. *See* ***id.*** **cmt. (e) (1978)** (quoting **LSA-C.C. Art. 469 (1870)**).

b] Attachments as a Matter of Law

1} TO BUILDINGS

Paragraph one of **Art. 466** provides that "[t]hings attached to a building and that, according to prevailing usages, serve to complete a building of the same general type, without regard to its specific use, are its component parts." The elements crucial to this classification are four in number: (1) "attachment," (2) "serve to complete," (3) "same general type, without regard to... specific use," and (4) "prevailing usages." Let us now examine each of these elements one at a time.

To qualify as an attachment to a building as a matter of law, the thing in question must, first and foremost, be "attached" to the building. As comment (h) (2008) to **Art. 466** makes clear, what is required here is a "modicum of *physical* attachment." To be sure, the degree of attachment need not be as great as that which is required for attachments as a matter of fact (i.e., substantial damage). But the attachment must be "substantial" and it must be more than "ephemeral." ***Id.*** Merely placing the thing "on top of" or "against" some part of the building would certainly not do. Nor would merely inserting an "electrical plug" from the thing into an "electrical outlet" of the building, as one might do with some appliance. ***Id.***

An attachment to a building as a matter of law must "serve to complete" the building. The meaning of this phrase, which is rather vague, is not entirely clear. Since it is not defined in **Art. 466** or in the comments to that article, the phrase should, one must suppose, be understood as a layman would understand it, that is, according to the common and generally prevailing meaning of the words. Comment (e) (2008) to **Art. 466**, though silent in regard to what the phrase *does* mean, nevertheless at least tells us two things that it does *not* mean. First, "completion... is not to be viewed as a discrete and identifiable event beyond which nothing further can be done." A building may be "complete" in some sense of the word and yet, in another sense of the word, still be susceptible of being "further completed" by the attachment to it of some new thing. The comment gives the example of a house that, in its original state, has no gutters, but to which gutters are later added. The addition of the gutters makes the house, which was "complete" to start with in some sense, still "more complete." Second, it is not necessary, in order for a thing to "serve to complete" a building, that it be so important to the building that, without it, the structure would not even qualify as a building. The standard is not "serve to *create*," but rather "serve to *complete*."

Whether a given thing "serves to complete" the building to which it is attached must be determined with reference to a building of the "same general type" without considering the "specific use" to which the particular building in question has been put. What this means is perhaps best explained with the help of an illustration. Comment (f) (2008) to **Art. 466** provides what may now be considered the "classic" illustration, one based on a famous (or infamous) judicial decision. Imagine a large building that might possibly be used for any of a number of different commercial or (light) industrial purposes. At the moment, the building houses a hospital. Among the things that are attached to this building are (1) a light fixture in the lobby and (2) some sophisticated piece of diagnostic medical equipment in one of the back rooms. Which, if any, of these two things "serves to complete" the building? As to the light fixture, the answer is "it does." Why? Because it "serves to complete the building in its quality as a commercial building." ***Id.*** But as to the medical equipment, the answer is "it does not." Why not? Because "though it might be useful in the operation of a *hospital* within the building," it nevertheless "does not serve to complete the building itself" *qua* generic commercial building.

In determining whether a given thing "serves to complete" the building, one must take into account "prevailing usages." According to comment (d) (2008) to **Art. 466**, this expression has here the same meaning as it does in **LSA-C.C. Art. 4**, which directs courts how to proceed in the absence of applicable legislation or custom. Now, "prevailing usages" as used in **Art. 4** has much the same meaning as does "usages" as used in **LSA-C.C. Art. 2053**, which concerns the interpretation of contracts, and as does "practice long repeated" as used in **LSA-C.C. Art. 3**, which defines "custom." In each of these articles—**Arts. 4, 2053**, and **3**—"prevailing usages" or whatever synonym thereof happens to be used has the same connotation: the reference is to what one might call the "standard practice" and the "common understanding" of persons who regularly deal with the kind of matter that is in question.

Several helpful illustrations of things that may, under appropriate circumstances, qualify as attachments to a building as a matter of law are included in the text of the first paragraph of **Art. 466.** They include "doors, shutters, gutters,... cabinetry" and "plumbing, heating, cooling, electrical, and similar systems."

2} TO OTHER IMMOVABLE CONSTRUCTIONS

Paragraph two of **Art. 466** provides that "[t]hings that are attached to a construction other than a building and that serve its principal use are its component parts." The crucial concepts here are "attachment" and "serve its principal use." Let us consider first the one and then the other.

As applied to attachments to *other constructions* as a matter of law, "attached" has the same meaning as it does as applied to attachments to *buildings* as a matter of law. Some minimal degree of *real physical* attachment is required. Mere "placing" or "plugging" of the thing onto or into the construction will not suffice.

To qualify as an attachment to an other construction as a matter of law, the thing in question must "serve" the "principal use" of this other construction. This notion, which is reminiscent to some extent of the notion on which the suppressed category of "immovable by destination" was based, is a bit vague and, beyond that, undefined. As was suggested earlier in our examination of the similarly vague notion of "serving to complete" a building, this notion, too, should perhaps be viewed from the vantage point of a "common sense" layman. A helpful illustration of the notion is provided in comment (g) to **Art. 466**, an illustration that involves various attachments to a "water tower":

> ... valves, piping, and access ladders that are attached to a water tower... further its principal use and are consequently component parts. On the other hand, a cellular telephone antenna which is bolted atop a water tower as a convenient point of elevation... having nothing to do with the water tower itself does not further the water tower's principal use and thus does not constitute its component parts.

2) By Declaration

Immovables by declaration, the subcategory of corporeal immovables correlative to that of corporeal immovables by nature, are addressed in **LSA-C.C. Art. 467.** To declare something immovable, one must satisfy several requirements. First, the thing in question must qualify as "machinery, appliances, and equipment." Second, the underlying immovable must not be a "private residence." Third, there must be "unity of ownership" between the thing and the underlying immovable, in other words, the thing must belong to the owner of that immovable. From this it follows that immobilization by declaration is available only to the owner of the immovable. Fourth, the thing must be "placed on the immovable." Fifth, the thing must be used for the "service and improvement of the immovable." Finally, the owner must prepare and file into the public records a written "declaration" of immovability.

2. Incorporeal Immovables

a. Definition

LSA-C.C. Art. 470 defines incorporeal immovables as "[r]ights and actions that apply to immovables."

b. Illustrations

The second sentence of **Art. 470** provides several helpful examples of incorporeal immovables: "personal servitudes established on immovables, predial servitudes, and petitory or possessory actions." Comment (b) tells us that this list is illustrative (as opposed to exhaustive) and that "[a]ll rights and actions that have an immovable object are incorporeal immovables."

B. Movables

As we noted earlier, the category of "movable" includes anything which the law does not consider to be immovable. **LSA-C.C. Art. 475.** "Movable," then, is the "default" category.

1. Corporeal Movables

a. Definition

LSA-C.C. Art. 471 defines corporeal movables as "things, whether animate or inanimate, that normally move or can be moved from one place to another."

b. Illustrations

Several illustrations of movables can be gleaned from the articles on movables. **LSA-C.C. Art. 472** indicates that building materials which have been assembled "on site" for the erection of a building or other immovable construction remain, until their incorporation therein, movables. **LSA-C.C. Art. 474** adds that unharvested crops or ungathered fruits "when they belong to a person other than the owner of the ground" are "movables by anticipation."

Looking back to the immovable articles, we can generate still other examples of movables. Reasoning *a contrario* from **LSA-C.C. Art. 462,** we discover that the following are movables: (i) other constructions that either (a) are not permanently attached to the ground or (b) owned separately from the ground; and (ii)(a) harvested crops and (b) gathered fruits. **LSA-C.C. Art. 468** adds to these several examples of de-immobilized component parts of an immovable, i.e., (a) those de-immobilized in fact "by detachment or removal" (¶3) and (b) those de-immobilized in effect (¶1): "damaged or deteriorated."

2. Incorporeal Movables

a. Definition

Incorporeal movables are defined in **LSA-C.C. Art. 473** as "[r]ights, obligations, and actions that apply to a movable thing."

b. Illustrations

Sentence two of **Art. 473** gives some examples of incorporeal movables: "bonds, annuities, and interests or shares in entities possessing juridical personality." Paragraph two of this article also informs us that "[i]nterests or shares in a juridical person that owns immovables are considered as movables as long as the entity exists." This list of examples, as was the list for incorporeal immovables, is illustrative.

III. Significance

A. Property Law

1. Modes of Acquiring Ownership

a. Accession

The classification of things into "immovable" and "movable" is important in the law of "accession." Whereas accession in relation to immovables follows one set of rules, i.e., those found in **LSA-C.C. Arts. 490–494**, accession in relation to movables follows another, i.e., those found in **LSA-C.C. Arts. 507–516.** Between these two sets of rules, there are, as we will see later on, numerous significant differences.

b. Acquisitive Prescription

The immovable-movable classification is also important for purposes of acquisitive prescription. Whereas acquisitive prescription in relation to immovables follows one set of rules, i.e., those found in **LSA-C.C. Arts. 3473–3488**, acquisitive prescription with relation to movables follows another, i.e., those found in **LSA-C.C. Arts. 3489–3491.** One difference between the two (there are others) is the time frame in which one can acquisitively prescribe one kind of thing as opposed to the other: for immovables, abridged acquisitive prescription takes place in 10 years while unabridged takes place in 30 years; for movables, abridged takes place in 3 years while unabridged takes place in 10 years.

2. Transfer of Ownership: Effectivity vis-à-vis *Third Persons*

Comparing **LSA-C.C. Art. 518** with **LSA-C.C. Arts. 517** and **2442**, one learns that the transfer of ownership of an immovable becomes effective against third persons at a time other than that at which the transfer of a movable becomes effective against third persons. In the case of an immovable, the pivotal moment is that at which the act of transfer if recorded in the appropriate public records (the conveyance records of the parish in which the immovable is located). By contrast, in the case of a movable, the pivotal moment is that at which the movable is delivered to the transferee.

3. Servitudes: Objects

Personal servitudes such as habitation (**LSA-C.C. Art. 630**) and right of use (**LSA-C.C. Art. 639**), as well as predial servitudes (**LSA-C.C. Art. 698**), can only be established on immovables. The personal servitude of usufruct, by contrast, can be established on either a movable or an immovable.

4. Accessory Real Rights: Mortgage and Pledge

Under current Louisiana law, it is possible for a creditor to obtain a security right in either immovable or movable property. But the means whereby the creditor may do so varies depending on whether the property on which the security right is created—the "collateral"—is immovable or movable.

Let us consider, first, security rights in immovable property. The creation, effects, and termination of such a right, known as "mortgage," are governed by **LSA-C.C. Arts. 3278–3337**.

Now, let us consider security rights in movable property. The creation, effects, and termination of such rights are governed, at least in most instances, by Louisiana's version of "Article 9" of the Uniform Commercial Code, which, of course, is of Anglo-American origin. In these instances, the creditor is said to have a "security interest" in the collateral. In a (very) few other instances, however, the traditional civil law of "pledge" still governs these matters. *See* **LSA-C.C. Arts. 3141–3175**.

B. Other: Obligations

1. Formalities

a. Sale

Under **LSA-C.C. Arts. 2440** and **1839**, a sale or other onerous transfer of an immovable must in principle be made in writing, be it by authentic act or by act under private signature. Exceptionally, even an "oral" sale of an immovable may be enforced, provided that the seller acknowledges the transfer under oath and the immovable has been delivered (that is, turned over) to the buyer. On the other hand, there are no formalities at all required for the sale or other onerous transfer of a movable.

b. Donation *Inter Vivos*

While **LSA-C.C. Art. 1541** informs us that a donation *inter vivos* must, as general rule, be made by authentic act (a general rule that includes donations *inter vivos* of immovables), **LSA-C.C. Art. 1543** explains that "[t]he donation *inter vivos* of a corporeal movable may also be made by delivery of the thing to the donee without any other formality."

2. Sales: Lesion

According to **LSA-C.C. Art. 2589**, if it turns out that the price paid for an immovable is less than one-half its fair market value, the seller may rescind the sale, subject to the duty to refund the purchase price. There is no equivalent rule for sales of movables.

SUB-CHAPTER C

Corporeal and Incorporeal Things

I. Definitions

A. Corporeals

"Corporeal" things, paragraph one of **LSA-C.C. Art. 461** tells us, are those that "have a body, whether animate or inanimate, and can be felt or touched." Examples are as legion as they are familiar: land, buildings, animals, vegetation, clothing, tools, appliances etc.

B. Incorporeals

"Incorporeal" things, according to paragraph two of the same article, are those that "have no body, but are comprehended by the understanding." The Civil Code, in no fewer than three articles, provides several examples of incorporeals. First, **Art. 461** itself gives these: "rights of inheritance, servitudes, obligations, and right of intellectual property." Second, **LSA-C.C. Art. 470**, which is addressed to those incorporeals that are also immovable, provides as follows:

> Rights and actions that apply to immovable things are incorporeal immovables. Immovables of this kind are such as personal servitudes established on immovables, predial servitudes, mineral rights, and petitory or possessory actions.

Finally, there is **LSA-C.C. Art. 473**, which pertains to incorporeals that are also movable:

> Rights, obligations, and actions that apply to a movable thing are incorporeal movables. Movables of this kind are such as bonds, annuities, and interests or shares in entities possessing juridical personality.

Among these varied examples of incorporeals, there is one common denominator: all are "rights" of one kind or another.

With one exception, the classification of things into corporeals and incorporeals rarely presents difficulties. That one exception concerns what might be called "documentary incorporeals." By "documentary collateral" we mean a right that is evidenced in some kind of document. Consider the first example given in **Art. 473**—a "bond." In common parlance, a "bond" is a document that evidences an obligation of one person, the issuer, to pay money on certain terms and conditions to another person, the payee (for example, a United States Treasury bond). Because this *document* "has a body... that can be felt or touched," one might be tempted to conclude that a bond is a "corporeal" thing. The law, however, views bonds quite differently. From the perspective of the law, it is not the *document* that is the "bond," but rather the *relationship* between the issuer, who has a duty to pay, and the payee, who has a right to collect payment. On this view, the document is not a "thing" in itself but rather is merely "evidence" of a "thing," that is, the right to payment. And this thing—the right—like all other rights, is an incorporeal.

The analysis is the same with the last example listed in **Art. 473**—"interests or shares in entities possessing juridical personality"—at least where those interests or shares are "certificated." The paradigmatic case is that of a corporate stock certificate. To be sure, the certificate itself has a body and can be felt and touched. But this certificate—this piece of paper—has no intrinsic value of its own and, by itself, is no-"thing" at all. Its sole function is to provide evidence of something that does have value, namely, the bundle of rights that the certificate holder has against the corporation that issued the certificate, such as voting rights and the right to share in corporate distributions (for example, dividends). And those rights, like all rights, are incorporeals.

II. Significance

We care whether something is a corporeal or an incorporeal because the law treats corporeals and incorporeals differently for a variety of purposes.

A. In Property Law

Within the domain of property law, two differences stand out above the others.

One has to do with the law of principal real rights, that is, a right that confers on the holder direct and immediate authority over a thing.

Whereas some real rights (namely, ownership and usufruct) can be established on either corporeals or incorporeals, others (namely, habitation, right of use, and predial servitude) can be established only on corporeals.

The other difference has to do with the law of possession. Whereas corporeals are susceptible of possession, paragraph one of **LSA-C.C. Art. 3421** tells us, most incorporeals are not. To be sure, some (though not all) incorporeals are susceptible of something called "quasi-possession," which the Code describes as "analogous" to possession in paragraph two of **Art. 3421.** As we will see, however, this analogy is sometimes a strained one.

B. Outside Property Law

The significance of the corporeal-incorporeal dichotomy does not, however, stop at the borders of property law. This distinction is also important, perhaps even more important, in several other legal domains.

First, the distinction is important in the law of donations *inter vivos*, to be specific, that which concerns donative formalities. Take a look at **LSA-C.C. Arts. 1541** and **1543.** The former article tells us that, as a general rule, a donation *inter vivos* must be made in "authentic act" form. **LSA-C.C. Art. 1833** explains that that means the donation must be evidenced by a writing that not only is signed by the parties (the donor and donee) but is also witnessed and then signed by a notary and two witnesses. The latter article carves out an exception to this general rule, one according to which certain corporeals—corporeal movables, to be precise—can be donated by means of the "delivery" of the thing to donee, without the need for "any other formality." Only corporeals fall within the scope of this exception.

Second, the corporeal-incorporeal distinction is important in the law of sales, to be specific, that which concerns the manner of delivery. Look, now, at **LSA-C.C. Arts. 2477** and **2481.** Both concern the point in time at which the "delivery" of an item that has been sold is deemed to take place, an issue that is important for determining who under **LSA-C.C. Art. 2467**, as between the buyer and the seller, bears the risk of the loss of the thing. **Art. 2477**, addressing the delivery of corporeal movables, lays down a rule of "real" delivery: delivery occurs when the seller physically hands the thing over to the buyer. By contrast, **Art. 2481**, addressing the delivery of incorporeal movables, lays down a rule of "fictitious" delivery: delivery is "deemed" to occur as of the moment at which the document that evidences the incorporeal (in the case of a documentary incorporeal) is "negotiated" (that is, simply handed over or endorsed and then handed over) or at which ownership of the incorporeal is transferred from the seller to the buyer (in the case of a non-documentary incorporeal).

Chapter Three

The "Lesser" Classifications

I. Consumables and Nonconsumables

A. Definitions

1. Consumables

LSA-C.C. Art. 536 provides that consumable things are "those that cannot be used without being expended or consumed, or without their substance being changed."

2. Nonconsumables

LSA-C.C. Art. 537 provides that nonconsumables are "those that may be enjoyed without alteration of their substance, although their substance may be diminished or deteriorated naturally by time or by the use to which they are applied."

B. Illustrations

1. Consumables

Art. 536 gives the following examples of consumables: "money, harvested agricultural products, stocks of merchandise, foodstuffs, and beverages."

2. Nonconsumables

Art. 537 gives the following examples of nonconsumables: "lands, houses, shares of stock, animals, furniture, and vehicles."

C. Nature of the Criterion for Distinction

Is the criterion for distinguishing consumable from nonconsumable things objective or subjective? In other words, in deciding whether a given thing is consumable or nonconsumable, does one take into account only the objective characteristics of the thing or does one, instead (or in addition), take into account the "destination" of the thing, that is, the use to which the owner of the thing has put it?

Take, for example, a collection of rare early U.S.-minted coins, which are displayed in a glass-covered display case. On the one hand, objectively speaking, it seems to be consumable: after all, it is just money, which we know is consumable. But, on the other hand, the person using the coins for display does not see it that way. In his mind, it was a nonconsumable: the coins were not to be used as legal tender, but as a collection or craft or work of art. From this point of view, the value of the coins lay not in what they could buy at the store, but in what they represented as a historical or artistic matter. And that value was dependent on the coins *not* being used as money. So, what is the collection: consumable, which is what an objective analysis would suggest, or nonconsumable, which is what a subjective analysis would suggest? The sad truth is that there is very little, if any, authority on this point. The legislation is silent, the jurisprudence is nonexistent, and the doctrine—what little there is—is in disarray.

D. Significance

1. In Property Law: Nature and Effects of Usufruct

In property law, the significance of this classificatory scheme is important in only one context: the law of **usufruct.** A usufruct whose object is a nonconsumable (traditionally known as a perfect usufruct) and a usufruct whose object is a consumable (traditionally known as an imperfect usufruct) are subject to quite different legal regimes under **LSA-**

C.C. **Arts. 538–539** and **LSA-C.C. Arts. 628–629. Arts. 538** and **539** give you just one example: a usufructuary's powers over a thing vary according to whether it is consumable or nonconsumable. Whereas the usufructuary of a nonconsumable cannot alienate the thing, the usufructuary of a consumable can.

2. Outside Property Law: Nominate Contracts

This classificatory scheme is also significant in the law of contracts. Look at **LSA-C.C. Arts. 2891, 2893**, and **2910.** These articles define two different, yet related, nominate contracts, namely *commodatum* (loan for use) and *mutuum* (loan for consumption). The difference is in the nature of the thing loaned. Whereas only consumable things may be the object of a *mutuum* (loan for consumption), only nonconsumable things may be the object of a *commodatum* (loan for use).

II. Fruits and (Mere) Products

Things that are produced from (generated by) another thing can, collectively, be referred to as "products." This category can be subdivided into "fruits" and "mere products."

A. Definitions

1. Fruits

Paragraph one of **LSA-C.C. Art. 551** explains that fruits are "things that are produced by or derived from another thing without diminution of its substance." The category of fruits can itself be subdivided into two subcategories: natural fruits and civil fruits. **Art. 551, ¶2.** Natural fruits are the "products of the earth or of animals." ***Id.*, ¶3.** Civil fruits are "revenues derived from a thing by operation of law or by reason of a juridical act." ***Id.*, ¶4.**

2. Mere Products

Mere products, according to **LSA-C.C. Art. 488**, are those things that are "derived from a thing as a result of diminution of its substance." Products are not subdivided into "natural" and "civil" in the Civil Code articles, but such a distinction may have some utility. A natural product would be a corporeal product while a civil product would entail something like revenues derived from the production of a natural product and, further, that represent payment for that product.

B. Illustrations

1. Fruits

a. Natural Fruits

Some examples of natural fruits are cow's milk, sheep's wool, the offspring of animals, crops, "fruits" in the common sense of the word (i.e., apples, oranges, grapes), and honey. In each case, the thing is produced from something else, but without diminishing the substance of that something else in the process.

b. Civil Fruits

Paragraph four of **Art. 551** gives us the following examples of civil fruits: rent on a lease, interest on a loan or a bank account, and cash dividends from corporate stock.

2. Products

Examples of products include dirt dug out of and minerals mined or pumped out of the ground, an organ removed from the body of an animal, and a radio removed from a car. In each case, the thing is produced from something else and, in the process, diminishes the substance of that something else.

C. Complications

Some products, unfortunately, are not all that easy to classify. The most important examples are minerals and timber.

1. Natural Fruits v. Natural Products

a. Minerals

Minerals produced from mines, wells, and quarries ordinarily constitute mere products. This is so because their extraction or removal alters or diminishes the substance of the underlying land.

The civil law tradition, however, has long recognized that minerals may, by way of exception, be treated as fruits under certain special circumstances. This exception, commonly known as the "open mine" doctrine, can be stated as follows: minerals produced from a mine, well, or quarry will be treated as "fruits" of the land if and only if the source from which they came was already "open" before the inception of the juridical situation that gives rise to the question of classification. Suppose, for example, that a certain person acquires a usufruct on some "oil and gas" land. To decide who, as between the usufructuary and the naked owner, is entitled to the oil and gas that may be produced from the land during the existence of this usufruct, it will be critical to determine whether the oil and gas constitute fruits or mere products: if they are fruits, then they belong to the usufructuary, but if they are mere products, then they belong to the naked owner. In such a case, the classification of the oil and gas will depend upon the applicability of the "open mine" doctrine. If the wells from which the oil and gas are produced were already open before the usufruct was established, then the oil and gas will be fruits and, as such, will belong to the usufructuary. But if those wells were not yet open before the usufruct was established—in other words, if the wells were opened during the existence of the usufruct—then the oil and gas will be mere products and, as such, will belong to the naked owner.

Insofar as it might be applied to the juridical situation of usufructuary and naked owner, the "open mine" doctrine, originally a doctrinal and jurisprudential creation, has been codified, with some modifications, in the Louisiana Mineral Code, specifically, **Arts. 190** and **191.** These articles shed light on two points of interest that were left somewhat obscure under the original doctrine. The first is what constitutes a "mine"; the second, what constitutes "open." Paragraph A of **Art. 191**, which addresses oil and gas, treats the mine as the entire "pool" of oil or gas penetrated by any well and treats it as "open" so long as, at the inception of the usufruct, there is in place a well that can be shown to be "capable of producing in paying quantities." Consider what this means for the usufructuary: as long as there is a single well in place that, even if it is not yet "working" (that is, not yet actually producing minerals), is at least "capable" of doing so, the usufructuary may thereafter treat as fruits—and therefore keep—whatsoever oil or gas he may produce from that well *or from any new well* that he might have occasion to drill *into the same pool.* Paragraph B of the same article, which addresses coal, treats the mine as "all seams proposed to be developed in the mining plan" and treats it as "open" so long as there is a "mining plan" in place, minerals have been discovered, and actual production has commenced on at least some of the land covered by the plan, even if the particular land on which it has commenced is not subject to the usufruct. If these requirements are met, then any coal the usufructuary may produce from the already-producing shaft *or from any new shaft* he may happen to dig *into the same "seams"* will be fruits of the land and, as such, will belong to him.

b. Timber

Timber is ordinarily considered to be a "mere product" of the land from which it is produced. Upon first hearing, this proposition may seem counterintuitive: after all, once the timber is removed, it may well "grow back," much as grapes picked from a vine—which are undoubtedly "fruits" of the vine—will "grow back." But in the case of timber, the "growing back" takes quite a long time, so long, in fact, that one would be justified in concluding that, at least for the time being, the removal of the timber has "diminished the substance" of the land.

Nevertheless, for timber as for minerals there has long been an exception, one that parallels the exception for minerals. This exception is known as the "tree farm" rule or, as the French call it, the rule of "regulated cuts." According to this rule, timber that is produced from a "tree farm" will be considered fruits (as opposed to mere products) of the land, provided that the tree farm was already in place at the inception of the juridical situation that gives rise to the question of classification. In order for the tree farm to be considered "in place," it is not necessary that timber operations have already begun, but only that a plan for such operations has been finalized.

As applied to the juridical situation of usufructuary and naked owner, this rule has been largely replaced by another, one that is even more favorable to the usufructuary. This other rule is found in **LSA-C.C. Art. 462**:

> When the usufruct includes timberlands, the usufructuary is bound to manage them as a prudent administrator. The proceeds of timber operations that are derived from proper management of timberlands belong to the usufructuary.

As it has been interpreted by our courts, this article entitles the usufructuary to the ownership of the timber that he produces from timberlands, *even if no tree farm was in place prior to the inception of the usufruct*, so long as his production of this timber qualifies as "prudent administration" or "proper management" of the timberlands. Though our courts have refused to qualify timber so produced as a fruit or a mere product, the *effect* of the rule on this classification is clear enough: it is that such timber is treated as if it were a *fruit*.

D. Significance

The distinction between fruits and products is important for several reasons.

1. In Property Law

a. Modes of Acquiring Ownership: Accession: Ownership of Unconsented-To Production

The classification of things into "fruits" and "mere products" is important, first of all, in the law of accession. **LSA-C.C. Art. 488** states that products are *always* owned by the owner of underlying the thing. According to **LSA-C.C. Art. 483**, fruits, too, belong to the owner of the underlying thing, *but only as a general rule*. To this general rule there are some important exceptions. One is found in **LSA-C.C. Art. 486**: "[a] possessor in good faith acquires the ownership of the fruits he has gathered." Thus, in sorting out who, as between the owner of a thing, on the one hand, and a good faith possessor of the thing, on the other, is entitled to the "products" of that thing, it is critical to know whether those products are "fruits" or "mere products."

b. Dismemberments of Ownership: Usufruct: Rights of Usufructuaries

According to **LSA-C.C. Art. 550**, which concerns usufructs of nonconsumables (perfect usufructs), "[t]he usufructuary is entitled to the fruits of the thing subject to usufruct." This right extends only to "fruits" properly so called. "Mere products," by contrast, belong to the "naked owner."

2. *Matrimonial Regimes Law: Community Property*

The fruit-mere product distinction may also be important in the context of "community property" law. **LSA-C.C. Art. 2339** provides that the "fruits" of the separate property of one spouse are community property, that is, belong to both spouses together, unless the spouse who owns that separate property makes a prior "reservation" of the fruits as his separate property. This same article goes on to lay down the same rule for "minerals" and certain mineral-related revenues of separate property, regardless whether they are fruits or mere products. But for other mere products, there is no comparable rule; as a result, other mere products remain the separate property of the spouse from whose separate property they are produced.

III. Single and Composite

A. Definitions and Illustrations

1. *Single (Simple) Things*

A single or simple thing is one that, from the standpoint of the law, constitutes a homogenous, undifferentiated unity. Its distinctive characteristic is that it cannot be subdivided into smaller or lesser components. Resorting to analogy from chemistry, one could say that it is like an "element" as opposed to a "compound." Simple examples include rocks, pieces of metal, wood, animals, plants, and a piece of money.

2. *Composite (Complex) Things*

It is possible, indeed not uncommon, for multiple single things to become associated with each other in one way or another or to one extent or another. If, from the standpoint of the law, this "association" does not produce a larger, greater unity, one of which the simple things so associated with each other create a "whole that is greater than the mere sum of its parts," then the result is nothing but a "collection" of single things. But if, from the standpoint of the law, this association does produce a larger, greater unity, a whole greater than the mere sum of its parts, a whole within which, though each single thing retains its separate physical existence to some extent, it nevertheless loses its separate identity to some extent, then the result is a composite or complex thing, one of which each of the associated single things constitutes a component part. Examples include a piece of furniture, a car, a ship, a diamond ring, and, perhaps most important, a tract of land together with certain of its "improvements."

B. Significance

1. Property and Obligations Law: Ownership, Sales and Mortgage: Transfer and Encumbrance of Immovables

Insofar as immovables are concerned, the distinction between single things (including collections of single things), on the one hand, and composite things, on the other, is important in the contexts of sales and mortgages. **LSA-C.C. Art. 469** provides that "[t]he transfer or encumbrance of an immovable includes its component parts." If a given immovable and the things in or on it remain "single" things vis-à-vis each other, if, in other words, the latter are not "component parts" of the former, then the sale or the mortgage of the former will not affect the latter. But if that immovable and the things in or on it together form a composite thing, then the sale or the mortgage of the former will affect the latter as well.

2. Property Law: Accession: Movables

In the law of accession with respect to movables, when two single things become united in such a way as to form a composite thing, the ownership of one or the other thing sometimes changes hands. Consider, first, the example of a piece of jewelry composed of a metal band and a relatively inexpensive jewel, in other words, a cheap "ring." If it should happen that the band belongs to one person and the jewel to another, then, when the two are united, the owner of the "principal" of these two things—the band—will become the owner of the whole. In the process, ownership of the jewel will have passed from the original owner of it to the owner of the band. Essential for this shift in ownership is that the two things become so closely associated that together they form a new united, composite whole. **LSA-C.C. Arts. 510** and **508.**

IV. Improvements v. INATs

A. Definitions/Illustrations

1. Improvements

The term "improvements" appears in the caption to **LSA-C.C. Art. 493**, which concerns "accession" with respect to things of this kind. As the contents of this article reveal, the category "improvements" comprises three subcategories: "buildings, other constructions permanently attached to the ground, and plantings made on the land." It will be noted that there is a connection between these classes of things and several of those that are addressed in **Art. 463**, which spells out the various component parts of tracts of land. In fact, the first two expressions—"buildings" and "other constructions permanently attached to the ground"—have precisely the same meanings in both articles. As for the third expression—"plantings"—it refers, at a minimum, to the various kinds of vegetation mentioned in **Art. 463**, that is, "standing timber," "unharvested crops," and "ungathered fruits." And it is possible that the term "plantings" covers still other forms of vegetation as well.

2. INATs

The category of things that is correlative to that of "improvements" forms the target of **LSA-C.C. Art. 493.1**, which, like **Art. 493**, concerns "accession." This article deals with things so "integrated" into an immovable as to constitute its component parts under **LSA-C.C. Art. 465** and things so "attached" to a building or other immovable construction as to constitute its component parts under **LSA-C.C. Art. 466**. It would have been nice if the drafters of the article had found or, at least, coined a term whereby one might conveniently refer to these things. But they did not. Still it would be helpful to have one. I propose that we call them INATs, an acronymic moniker composed of the first two letters of each of the two categories, that is, "*IN* tegral parts" (**Art. 465**) and "*AT* tachments" (**Art. 466**). The expression has the added, accidental advantage of sounding a lot like "in it" when it is spoken out loud and, therefore, will serve as a useful reminder of how this category of thing differs from the category of "improvements," which can profitably be thought of as "*on* its."

B. Nature of the Criterion of Distinction

The distinction between improvements and INATs is an objective one, based on the physical characteristics of the thing that is united with the underlying immovable and on the nature and degree of its integration with that immovable.

C. Subclassifications: Consented-To and Unconsented-To Improvements and INATs

The law that concerns improvements and INATs attaches significance for various purposes to whether or not the improvement or INAT in question was built or installed with the consent of the owner of the underlying immovable. "Consented to" improvements or INATs are those that are added to the underlying immovable *with* the consent of the owner of that immovable. "Unconsented to" improvements or INATs are those that are added to the underlying immovable *without* the consent of the owner of that immovable.

D. Significance: Property Law: Accession with Respect to Immovables

1. Ownership

Who owns a given thing that has been placed upon or into an immovable varies depending on at least one and possibly as many as two factors. The first is whether the thing in question is an improvement or an INAT. If it is the latter, then resolution of the ownership question could not be simpler. **Art. 493.1** provides that *all* INATs belong to the owner of the underlying immovable regardless whether they are consented to or unconsented to (and, for that matter, regardless of anything else). Thus, if it is an INAT, it belongs to the owner of the underlying immovable. But if the thing in question is an improvement, then the resolution of the ownership question requires the consideration of a second factor, namely, whether it was consented to or not. Paragraph one of **Art. 493** tells us that if it was consented to, then it belongs to the *maker*, but if it was not, then it belongs to the *owner of the underlying immovable.*

2. Remedies

The law of accession, in addition to determining who owns a thing that gets produced from or added to another underlying thing, also provides various "remedies" as between the "producer" or "adder" of the one thing, on the one hand, and the owner of the underlying thing, on the other. To take just one example, under certain circumstances the owner of the underlying thing may demand that the "adder" of the other thing remove it at his expense. Here is another example: where, according to the "ownership" rules of accession, ownership of the added thing revests from the "adder" to the owner of the underlying thing, the adder may, under some circumstances, demand that the owner reimburse him by some measure.

These varied remedial rights, it turns out, vary greatly depending on whether (i) the thing united to the immovable is an improvement or an INAT and/or (ii) the improvement or INAT is consented to or unconsented to.

a. Unconsented-To Improvements and/or INATs

To the extent that the law of accession itself provides any remedies at all for unconsented-to improvements or INATs (in some contexts there are no remedies), those remedies, which are the same *regardless whether the thing united with the immovable is an improvement or a constituent*, are set forth in **Arts. 496** and **497**. The former, which concerns unconsented-to improvements and INATs made by a "*good* faith possessor," withholds from the owner of the underlying thing the remedies of demanding removal at the possessor's expense and of collecting damages from the possessor and gives to the possessor the remedy of demanding any of several indemnities (e.g., the cost of the materials and workmanship that the possessor invested in the improvement or INAT). The latter, which concerns unconsented-to improvements and INATs made by a "*bad* faith possessor," is relatively more generous to the owner of the underlying immovable. The article gives him both the right to demand removal at the possessor's expense and the right to collect damages. As for the possessor, he receives the right to demand reimbursement in one measure or another, subject to the owner's decision to keep, rather than to demand removal, of the added thing.

b. Consented-To Improvements and/or INATs

1) Consented-To Improvements

Remedies with respect to consented-to *improvements* are established in paragraph two of **Art. 493.** Improvements of this kind, it will be recalled, belong to the "adder." The only remedy accorded to the adder is the right to return to the land to remove the thing; under no circumstances may he demand any sort of indemnity or reimbursement from the owner of the underlying immovable. As for the owner of the underlying thing, he is given, to start with, only one remedy—demanding removal. If the owner makes such a demand in proper form (writing) and if the adder does not comply within 90 days, then the owner receives an additional remedy: "appropriat[ing] ownership" of the improvement, which requires sending a second communiqué to the adder by certified mail. Under no circumstances, however, can the owner force the adder to remove the thing, remove the thing himself and then send the adder the bill therefor, or collect damages from the adder.

2) Consented-To INATs

Art. 495 establishes the remedies with respect to consented-to *INATs*. To start with, the adder is given the right to remove the thing. If the adder does not exercise this right, then the owner of the underlying thing may demand removal. If such a demand is made and if the adder does not comply, then the owner receives several additional, alternative remedies: he may (1) remove the INAT himself and then send the adder the bill therefor or (2) keep the INAT. But if the owner chooses the latter remedy, the adder, in turn, receives another remedy, namely, the right to demand any of various measures of indemnity from the owner.

PART II

Possession

Chapter Four

Possession in General

I. Introduction: Possession and Ownership

In the popular mind, possession and ownership are often confounded, treated as though they were two sides of the same coin. That is not surprising: in the typical case, the owner and possessor are one and the same.

In legal thinking, by contrast, possession and ownership are sharply distinguished. To be sure, these two relationships to things are intimately connected at several points. To take one example, possession can "ripen" into ownership. **LSA-C.C. Art. 3446** describes "acquisitive prescription" as "a mode of acquiring ownership or other real rights by possession for a period of time." What this means is that if one possesses a thing for a sufficient period of time, even something that originally belonged to someone else, one will become the owner of that thing. To take another example, possessors are treated as if they were owners for certain purposes and in certain situations. According to **LSA-C.C. Art. 531**, the one who possesses a thing is "presumed" to be its "owner." Nevertheless, for most purposes, possession and ownership are treated as radically different states. As we shall see, when possession and ownership become severed, the possessor and the owner enjoy various rights against each other. And—this is the truly surprising thing—in some cases the possessor comes out on top of the owner!

II. The Concept of Possession

A. Definitions

Many persons, including some who should know better, use the word "possession" to refer indiscriminately to several different things. Sometimes the term "possession" is used to refer a certain *right* that one can acquire if one possesses a thing for a certain period of time. But this right itself is not "possession"; it is, rather, an "effect"—consequence or result—of possession. For that reason, this right should be called something other than "possession." And, in fact, it is, at least when people are speaking properly: the term is "right to possess." At other times the term "possession" is used to refer to the act or state of exercising control over or having custody of a thing, without further qualification. The trouble with this use of the term is that it is overly broad, that is, it covers situations that it ought not to cover. Chief among these other situations are those in which one person—let us call him A—exercises control over a thing with the permission of and on behalf of another—let us call him B. In this situation, A is not in "possession" of the thing, in the proper sense of the word, and therefore some other term, aside from "possession," should be used to refer to it. And, in fact, that is so, at least when, once again, people are speaking properly: the term is "precarious possession."

What, then, is "possession" properly so called? First and foremost, it is not a "right" but a "fact." As **LSA-C.C. Art. 3422** puts it, it is a "matter of fact." To be still more precise, one could say that it is a certain kind of factual relationship between a person and a thing, not altogether different in kind from the factual relationship that presently exists between me and the laptop computer on which I am typing, a relationship of "use." Thus, to say that a certain person X is in possession of a certain thing A is more like saying X is "on" or "inside" A than it is like saying X "owns" A. Second, this factual relationship, as we will explain in greater depth shortly, entails two elements. The first, a material or physical element, consists of exercising control over or having custody of a thing. The second, a psychological or mental element, consists of thinking of oneself (as opposed to someone else) as the owner of the thing one possesses. It is for referring to this and *this alone* that the word "possession" (and all of its cognates, e.g., the verb "possess," the prepositional phrase "in possession") should be reserved.

III. Scope of Possession: Things Susceptible of Possession

A. Public and Private Things

To be susceptible of possession, by which we normally mean possession by *private* persons, the thing in question must be private. Public things are *per se* insusceptible of possession.

B. Corporeal and Incorporeal Things

a. Corporeals

That corporeals are susceptible of possession cannot be gainsaid. Indeed, as the term possession was originally defined in Roman law, it applied only to corporeals. Unlike some other civil law and mixed jurisdictions, Louisiana still retains this Roman law rule. **LSA-C.C. Art. 3421** defines possession as the "detention or enjoyment of a corporeal thing."

b. Incorporeals

Strictly speaking, incorporeals are insusceptible of possession. But some of them are, nevertheless, susceptible of something like it, namely, "*quasi*-possession." According to **LSA-C.C. Art. 3421, ¶2**, "[t]he exercise of a real right, such as a servitude, with the intent to have it as one's own is quasi-possession." This possibility, as this legislative text itself indicates, is restricted to "real rights," to the exclusion of "credit rights." Though the text does not say so, the possibility is subject to yet another limitation: it extends only to "principal," as opposed to "accessory," real rights. The essence of quasi-possession is the "exercise," that is, the use, of the right. For example, the holder of a "servitude of passage" quasi-possesses his servitude by simply "passing" (walking or driving a vehicle) over the designated passageway.

"The rules governing possession," **LSA-C.C. Art. 342, ¶2** tells us, "apply by analogy to the quasi-possession of incorporeals." As we will see, however, this analogy is less than perfect.

IV. Constitutive Elements of Possession

The constitutive elements of or, if you prefer, the requisites to possession are signaled in a number of Civil Code articles. Among them is **LSA-C.C. Art. 3424**, which provides that "[t]o acquire possession, one must intend to possess as owner and must take corporeal possession of the thing." There are, then, two elements of possession, one "material"—taking corporeal possession—and the other "mental"—intending to possess as owner. In the civilian literature, these elements are often referred to, respectively, as *corpus* and *animus domini*, terms coined by Savigny, the great German scholar of the Roman *ius civile*.

Let us see now if we cannot get a clearer picture of these two elements. We will begin with *corpus*, then move on to *animus*.

A. *Corpus*

Corpus (corporeal possession) is defined in **LSA-C.C. Art. 3425**: "the exercise of physical acts of use, detention, or enjoyment over a thing." For an act to count as *corpus*, it must, first of all, involve some *physical* interaction with the thing. Acts that do not put the would-be possessor into physical contact with the thing, for example, paying property taxes or merely leasing the thing to another person, are not sufficient. In addition, *corpus* requires an act of "use," "detention," or "enjoyment." "Use" has here its common meaning, that is, to exploit the advantages of a thing; "detention," a legal term of art, means to "hold" or to exercise "custody" of a thing; and "enjoyment," another legal term of art, means to "take the fruits" of a thing. Acts that do not involve the physical use, detention, or enjoyment of a thing do not establish corporeal possession.

Though the text of **Art. 3425** does not say so, it is nevertheless the case that "not just any" act of physical interaction with (use, detention, enjoyment of) the thing will be considered sufficient to satisfy the *corpus* requirement. According to our courts, the physical acts of the purported possessor, if they are to "rise" to the level of *corpus*, must be characterized by a certain intensity and a certain duration. But perhaps "certain" is not the best adjective to use here, for, as it turns out, "how much is enough" is anything but certain. Of course, it is not required that the possessor use, detain, or enjoy the thing in *all* or *even most* of the ways in which it might conceivably be used, detained, or enjoyed: a single mode of use, detention, or enjoyment may be "enough." But whatever acts the possessor performs, they must, at a minimum, be such that, if someone were to observe the purported possessor in action, they might cause the observer to say to himself, "It's possible that this guy thinks he's the owner of that thing."

What is necessary and sufficient to satisfy this "minimal" requirement varies depending on a number of factors. One factor is whether the supposed possessor has a "title" and is in "good faith." To establish *corpus*, a possessor who has title and is in good faith need not show "as much" in the way of physical acts of use, detention, or enjoyment as must a possessor who lacks title or who is in bad faith. Another factor is the nature or condition of the possessed thing. For undeveloped property, relatively minimal acts of use, detention, or enjoyment will suffice. More substantial acts or at least different acts may be required for developed property. Even among undeveloped properties, how much is "enough" may vary. For example, our courts have ruled that "more" is required to establish *corpus* of "farmland" than is required to establish *corpus* of "woodland."

Let us now consider some examples of acts that our courts have concluded may or may not be sufficient for *corpus*. All of the examples given here pertain to land. Under the heading "sufficient": growing crops, grazing cattle, regular cutting and removal of timber, burning of a marsh, building of a home, mowing grass (in some circumstances). Under the heading "insufficient": paying property taxes, granting leases, conducting surveys, occasional hunting or fishing, occasional gathering of fruit or wood, sporadic cutting and removal of timber, mowing grass (in other circumstances).

B. *Animus*

1. Substantive Matters

Animus domini, the second element of possession, is defined as "intent to possess *as owner*." **LSA-C.C. Art. 3424.** Of the two elements of possession, this one is the more elusive. And that is because the formula "intent to possess as owner" is easily susceptible of—indeed, tends to invite—misunderstanding.

Many students of Louisiana property law, when they first hear the phrase "intent to possess as owner," assume that it must mean "belief that one is the owner." **Nothing could be further from the truth!** Yes, "belief that one is the owner," like "intent to possess as owner," is a state of mind and, further, it is a state of mind that a possessor may have. But that state of mind—commonly referred to as "good faith"—is a *different* state of mind from that of *animus domini*. It is well-settled that one may be in "bad faith," that is, know full well that one is not the owner, and nevertheless still have *animus domini* and, as a result, still be a possessor. Thus, whatever *animus domini is*, it is not—and it cannot be—belief that one is the owner.

What, then, *is animus domini*? Some describe it as "thinking of oneself as the owner." But even this formulation may be misunderstood. What is critical is that the purported possessor develop a mindset with respect to the thing according to which he *intends to act like the owner*. For a possessor who *is* in good faith, this mindset will come naturally: if one believes that one is the owner, then one will, upon taking *corpus* of it, necessarily intend to "act like the owner" (at least in the absence of some psychosis!). For a possessor who is in bad faith, however, this mindset will arise only if and when he makes a decision to try to "hold" or "keep" the thing for himself or, to use an older formulation, to "stake a claim" to the thing. Such a decision, it bears noting, logically entails making a commitment to resist any and all efforts by the "true owner" to reclaim or reassert dominion or control over the thing.

From what has been said so far about the content of *animus domini*, it should be clear that a grant of "permission" to use the thing is the "kiss of death" for this state of mind. If X truly "intends to act like the owner" of a certain thing, then his response, should Y purport to give him permission to use that thing, would have to be "Excuse me, but I don't need your approval. This is *mine*!" If, instead, X were to accept X's grant of permission, then one would have no choice but to conclude that X lacks *animus domini*.

2. Procedural Matters: Presumptions and Burden of Proof

Because *animus domini* is a "state of mind," direct evidence of it is, of course, unavailable, which is to say that whatever evidence of it there may be will necessarily be "circumstantial." Circumstantial evidence, of course, is often inconclusive.

Recognizing this very practical problem of proof, the legislature has established an evidentiary presumption to assist the trier of fact. The presumption is set out in **LSA-C.C. Art. 3427**:

> One is presumed to intend to possess as owner unless he began to possess in the name of and for another.

What this provision means is that as long as the purported possessor can prove that he had *corpus* (and subject to the proviso explained in the next paragraph of the Précis), he will be deemed to have had the necessary *animus*. The effect of this presumption is to assign the "burden of proof" on the issue of *animus domini* to the opponent of the purported possessor: to win, the opponent must prove that the possessor did *not* intend to possess as owner.

As we just noted, this presumption—"if you've got *corpus*, you're presumed to have *animus domini*"—is subject to a "proviso," that is, a condition. The condition appears in the last clause of **Art. 3427**: "unless he began to possess in the name of and for another." This means that one who begins to possess "in the name of and for another" does not get the benefit of the presumption or, in other words, bears the burden of proving that he had *animus*, that is, intended to possess for himself. What we mean by one who "began to possess in the name of and for another" is one who detains property *by permission*, e.g., a lessee or licensee. We call such a person a detainer or a precarious possessor. The bottom line, then, is this: one who starts out as a precarious possessor cannot take advantage of the presumption of **Art. 3427**.

V. Extent of Possession

How much of the thing (in terms of spatial extent) will the possessor be considered to possess? In the case of movables, the answer is simple: it is either all or nothing. But in the case of immovables, especially land, the answer is more complex. The answer, it turns out, depends on whether or not the possessor has "title."

Before we get into the details of the applicable rules, let us make sure we know what we are talking about when we speak of a "title" in this context. According to comment (b) to **LSA-C.C. Art. 3426**, a title is "an act sufficient to transfer ownership," more commonly referred to as "an act *translative* of ownership." This is an act that, were it to be made by the true owner and to be free of defects, would be effective to transfer ownership. Examples of such acts include sale, donation (both *inter vivos* and *mortis causa*), exchange, and giving in payment (in French, *dation en paiement*). Such an act must include a description of the immovable that is the object of the sale, a description that "reasonably identifies" it (which normally requires some indication of the location and perhaps the size of the immovable).

A. With Title

1. Nature of Constructive Possession

If the possessor has title to the thing, how much of it does he possess? The answer is found in the first sentence of **Art. 3426.** This article tells us that so long as he corporeally possess at least "part" of the thing, he will be "deemed" to possess up to "the limits of his title." The article tells us that we call this kind of fictitious possession "constructive possession."

a. Requisites for Constructive Possession

As Art. 3426 makes clear, the possessor, to get the benefit of th efiction of constructive possession, must satisfy two requirements: he must have a title and he must corporeally possess at least part of the thing described in that title. To these two the jurisprudence and the doctrine add one other—that the possessor intend to possess (have *animus domini*) with respect to the whole of the thing.

Aside from these three there are no other requirements. It is not necessary, for example, that the title be free of defects. *See* **Art. 3426 cmt. (b)** ("One may have constructive possession by virtue of a defective title."). To the contrary, the title can be relatively null or even absolutely null. Indeed, it does not even have to be in writing. Nor is it necessary that the possessor be in "good faith," in other words, that he believe that the title is valid. *See* **Art. 3426 cmt. (b)** ("One may have constructive possession regardless of good or bad faith.").

B. Without Title

1. Substantive Matters: Definition of Actual Possession

If the possessor does *not* have title to the thing, then how much of it is he deemed to possess? The answer to that question is found in the *second* sentence of **Art. 3426**: "In the absence of title, one has possession only of the area he actually possesses."

2. Procedural Matters: Modes of Proving Actual Possession

But how does one prove "the area [one] actually possesses"? Comment (d) to **Art. 3426** gives this answer: "Adverse possession must be inch by inch possession (*pedis possessio*) or possession within enclosures."

The notion of "inch by inch possession" is really rather simple. To prove it, one would put on evidence (presumably testimonial) that indicates precisely which "square inches" one used, e.g., drove cattle over, hunted on, planted crops on.

The notion of "possession within enclosures" is a bit more complicated. To prove it, one must put on evidence showing that one possessed "generally" and "more or less all" of an area of land that is bounded on the pertinent sides by "enclosures." "Enclosure" is another word for "boundary." **Art. 3426 cmt. (d).** Boundaries come in two varieties: "natural" and "artificial." Examples of natural boundaries include a tree line (that is, the line at which the "pasture" ends and the "woods" begin) and water bodies such as a steam, a river, a lake, or a swamp; examples of artificial boundaries, a fence, a levee, a ditch, a highway, stakes planted along a boundary line, and, at least under some circumstances, a line painted on the ground. In any event, to qualify as an "enclosure," the thing in question must be sufficient to give definite notice to the public and all the world of the character and extent of the possession, to identify fully the property possessed, and to fix with certainty the boundaries or limits thereof.

VI. Acquisition, Conservation and Loss of Possession

A. Acquisition of Possession

One can acquire possession in either of two ways: (i) one can begin a brand new possession (original possession) or (ii) one can acquire and take over someone else's existing possession (derivative possession).

1. Original Possession

One acquires possession *originally* when one begins a new possession. To establish a new possession, as we have seen, two things are necessary: *corpus*, i.e., corporeal possession of the thing, and *animus domini*, i.e., intent to possess the thing as owner. The new possessor can, of course, do both of these things himself, i.e., he may personally take physical acts of use, enjoyment, etc. on the thing and he may personally intend to possess as owner. But that is not necessary.

a. Vicarious *Corpus*

According to **LSA-C.C. Art. 3428**, one may "acquire possession of a thing through another who takes it for him and in his name. The person taking possession must intend to do so for another." This is what is referred to as the principle of vicarious or imputed *corpus*. Note that the possessor can claim the acts of *corpus* of another for himself only if this other intends to possess for him and in his name. We have a name for this kind of person, that is, one who exercises corpus on a thing with the permission of and for another, namely, "precarious possessor." Thus, the principle involved here could be restated in either of the following ways: (1) the possessor exercises *corpus* "vicariously" through the acts of his precarious possessor or (2) the *corpus* of a precarious possessor is "imputed" to the person by whose permission and on whose behalf he acts.

b. Vicarious *Animus*

In the typical case, the possessor himself has the requisite *animus domini*, in other words, he personally intends to possess the thing as owner. Not only *does* he, but he *must*. In other words, *animus domini* ordinarily has to be personal rather than vicarious.

Nevertheless, under certain limited circumstances, the law allows for the possibility of vicarious *animus domini*. The common denominator of these circumstances is two-fold: (1) the would-be possessor is unable, as a matter of law, to enter into juridical acts on his own, in other words, he suffers from a legal incapacity and (2) either by law or by juridical act, someone else has been appointed to represent him, that is, to enter into juridical acts on his behalf. In such a case as this, the *animus* of the representative to the effect that the incapable he represents is the owner of the thing will be accounted to the incapable as *animus domini*. Let us consider some examples. Take, first, the case of a juridical person, say, a corporation, who, it is claimed, is "in possession" of something. The corporation, lacking a "mind of its own," not only does not, but cannot have an *animus domini* of its own. But that is not a problem. As long as some person authorized to represent him—perhaps an officer or a director—thinks of the corporation as the owner of the thing, the corporation will be deemed to have *animus domini.* Next, take the case of an individual who has been fully interdicted on account of its having been proven that, thanks to some mental illness, he is in incapable of consistently making reasoned decisions regarding his person and his property. To be sure, this person could, in fact, have or lack *animus domini*, for he, unlike the corporation, does have a mind, however "off" it might be. But by virtue of the order of interdiction, whatever animus he may have will not "count." What will count, instead, is the animus of his representative, known as a "curator." As long as his curator thinks of him as the owner of the thing, he will be deemed to have *animus domini.*

2. Derivative Possession

To acquire possession, one need not necessarily begin a brand new possession of one's own. Under certain circumstances and to some extent, one can, instead, acquire and then take over a possession that someone else has already begun. Possession of this kind is called derivative.

The legislative basis for derivative possession is found in **LSA-C.C. Arts. 3441** and **3442.** Respectively, they read as follows:

> Possession is transferable by universal title or by particular title.
>
> The possession of the transferor is tacked to that of the transferee if there has been no interruption of possession.

These articles, though not entirely without utility, are nevertheless misleading in several significant respects. Their most fundamental defect, that from which all the others flow, is that they fail to draw appropriate distinctions between transfers of possession by "universal title" (otherwise known as "universal successions"), on the one hand, and transfers of possession by "particular title" (otherwise known as "particular successions"), on the other. This is not the place for a detailed explication of universal and particular successions and of the differences that separate them. The place for *that* is under the heading "Junction of possessions," which appears below. Nevertheless, in this place we must, if we are to shed any light at all on the topic of derivative possession, at least "hit the highlights." Here goes. In a universal succession (e.g., the transfer of a thing by virtue of a "universal legacy" or an "intestate" succession), the transferee (e.g., a universal legatee or an heir) is understood to "continue" the possession of the transferor. **LSA-C.C. Art. 936, ¶1.** But in a particular succession (e.g., the transfer of a thing by virtue of a sale or a "particular legacy"), the transferee (e.g., a buyer or particular legatee) is understood to "start a new possession of his own." **LSA-C.C. Art. 936, ¶2.**

a. Derivative Possession Via a *Universal* Succession

Because a universal successor "continues" the possession of his ancestor-in-title, he, by definition, receives "everything" that his ancestor-in-title had. That means, to start with, that he is given credit for his ancestor-in-title's *corpus.* But it also means that he is given credit for his ancestor-in-title's *animus domini,* at least until such time as he is in a position to form an *animus* of his own.

An example may serve to drive the point home. Suppose that a certain person X has established possession (*corpus* and *animus domini*) of a certain forest. One day, while X is out doing *corpus* in his forest, he dies of a stroke. In his testament (yes, he had one), he left "all" of his property (this would be a universal legacy) to a certain person Y. At the moment of X's death, Y not only did not know that X had died, he did not even know that X had made a testament, much less had left anything to him in it. In fact, Y does not learn what has happened and how he stands until some three months after X's death. But now that he knows, he wants to claim that he, like X before him, "possesses" the forest. He seems to have two problems: (1) he has never exercised *corpus* himself and (2) though he has *animus domini* now, he did not have it—indeed, did not have any *animus* at all—for the past three months. Are these seeming problems real? The answer is an emphatic "no." As a universal successor of X, Y "continues" X's possession. Whatever else that may mean, it at least means this: he is credited with X's *corpus* and with X's *animus domini.*[1]

1. It should be noted that the result here would not be any different if X, prior to dying, had voluntarily quit his *corpus* of the forest and, thereupon, entered into mere "civil possession" of it. Even in this case, Y would be given credit for X's (past) acts of *corpus.*

b. Derivative Possession Via a *Particular* Succession

Because a particular successor, unlike a universal successor, starts a "new possession" of his own, rather than "continues" the possession of his ancestor-in-title, it might seem that "derivate possession" would be out of the question in the case of a particular succession. Insofar as *animus domini* is concerned, this turns out to be true. A particular successor cannot claim as his own the *animus* of anyone other than himself or, if he is incapable, of his representative.[2] But insofar as *corpus* is concerned, it is not true. A particular successor, no less so than a universal successor, gets credit for the *corpus* of his ancestor-in-title. Though difficult to square with theory, this result has significant practical advantages.

Let us, again, consider an illustration. Recall our friend X, the possessor of the forest. Suppose that, instead of dying and leaving everything, the forest included, to Y, he sells the forest to Y. Thereafter Y never sets foot in the forest. Some months later, Y has occasion to wish to claim that he, like X before him, "possesses" the forest. As to *animus domini*, he has no problem: he has got it on his own. But as to *corpus*, he does, indeed, seem to have a problem. But does he? The answer is "no." Thanks to the particular succession between X and him, Y is given credit for X's *corpus*.[3]

B. Conservation of Possession

It is one thing to *establish* possession and another, to *keep* it. We have considered the former. We shall now consider the latter. The question that must be asked and answered is this: once possession has been established, what is necessary in order to maintain (or conserve) it?

---

2. Of course, in all but the most bizarre circumstances (e.g., psychosis, radical error), the particular successor in such a case will almost certainly have his own *animus domini*. For that reason, the non-transferability of *animus domini* in particular successions is of little practical consequence.

3. It should be noted that the result here would not be any different if X, prior to selling the forest, had voluntarily quit his *corpus* of the forest and, thereupon, entered into mere "civil possession" of it. Even in this case, Y would be given credit for X's (past) acts of *corpus*.

1. *Substantive Matters*

a. *Animus Domini*

The retention of *animus domini* is indispensable to the conservation of possession. As we shall see when we study the *loss* of possession a little later on, the moment that *animus* dies, possession dies with it.

b. *Corpus*

LSA-C.C. Art. 3431 reads as follows: "Once acquired, possession is retained by the intent to possess as owner even if the possessor ceases to possess corporeally." Comment (b) adds this:

> [T]o retain an acquired possession, the intent to own suffices. Thus, even if the possessor no longer exercises physical acts over the thing, he nevertheless may be considered to be in possession.

We call possession of this kind, that is, an acquired possession that is deemed to endure solely by virtue of a continuing intent to possess as owner (*possessio solo animo*), civil possession.

It would, however, be a mistake to assume the civil possession arises *every time* there is a "loss of *corpus*." In this regard, there are two possible errors that must be avoided at all costs.

The first error has to do with "abandonment." Comment (c) to **Art. 3431** provides as follows:

> Civil possession is the retention of the possession of a thing merely by virtue of the intent to own it, as when a person, *without intending to abandon possession*, ceases to reside in a house or on the land which he previously occupied or when a person ceases to exercise physical control over a movable *without intending to abandon possession.*

This comment tells us that if the possessor abandons the thing completely, then he is not deemed to have civil possession of it. This is because abandonment means to relinquish corporeal possession with the intent of no longer possessing (or having any other interest in) the thing. Further confirmation of this conclusion is found in the first part of **LSA-C.C. Art. 3433**: "Possession is lost when the possessor manifests his intention to abandon it."

The second error has to do with "eviction." The second part of **Art. 3433** tells us that "Possession is lost ... when he [the possessor] is evicted by another by force or usurpation." As we will learn shortly when we study the "loss of possession," to be evicted is to be deprived of *corpus.* Thus, an evicted possessor, not less than a civil possessor, "has *animus domini*" yet "lacks *corpus.*" What makes the difference between the two is *how and why* each lost *corpus*: in the case of the evicted possessor, the loss is against his will, that is, involuntary; in the case of the civil possessor, the loss is of his own accord, that is, voluntary.

The lesson of these points about "abandonment" and "eviction," then, is this: for civil possession to arise out of corporeal possession, the possessor (i) must give up his *corpus voluntarily* and (ii) must not give up his *animus* at all.

2. Procedural Matters: Presumption and Burden of Proof

One who claims to be in civil possession of a thing gets the benefit of an evidentiary presumption. "The intent to retain possession is presumed unless there is clear proof of a contrary intention." **LSA-C.C. Art. 3432.** In other words, one who, after acquiring possession, voluntarily ends his *corpus* is presumed to retain his *animus.* This shifts the burden of proof to the *other* party, requiring him to prove that the possessor lost his *animus.*

C. Loss of Possession

How might a possessor lose possession? We have anticipated this question in our consideration of the conservation of possession.

The search for the answer to this question begins with an analysis of **Art. 3433**:

> Possession is lost when the possessor manifests his intention to abandon it or when he is evicted by another by force or usurpation.

According to this article, then, there are two ways to lose possession: (i) the possessor abandons it (and manifests his intention to do so) and (ii) the possessor is evicted. This answer to the question is good as far as it goes, but it does not go quite far enough. It turns out that there is yet another situation in which one might lose possession, namely, that in which one purports to transfer ownership of the thing, yet retains *corpus* of it pending delivery to the transferee.

French doctrine, recognizing *all* these possibilities, has developed a three-fold, systematic schematic of modes of losing possession. The possibilities, so schematized, are as follows: (i) the loss of *corpus* and *animus* together, (ii) the (involuntary) loss of *corpus* alone, and (iii) the loss of *animus* alone. Let us consider each of these in turn.

1. Loss of Both Corpus *and* Animus

The first mode of losing possession entails a simultaneous loss of *corpus* and *animus*. This mode of losing possession is commonly known as "abandonment."

2. Loss of Corpus *Alone*

Possession of a thing ceases when the possessor, though still desiring to possess that thing, loses his *corpus* over the thing against his will, i.e., involuntarily ceases to exercise corporeal possession over the thing. The unwilling loss of *corpus* can come about in several ways, among them, eviction, destruction, and escape.

a. Eviction (Usurpation)

Eviction or usurpation, according to the jurisprudence and the doctrine, requires two things. The first requirement is that there be some act by someone with an interest adverse to the possessor that effectively deprives the possessor of *corpus*, that is, makes it impossible for the possessor to exercise *corpus*. Though not necessarily required, in all but the rarest of circumstances this act will be sufficient to qualify as an act of *corpus* on the part of the adverse party. The second requirement is that this act be so significant and salient that, were the actual possessor to witness it, it would bring home to him at least the possibility that his dominion is being seriously challenged.

A survey of the pertinent jurisprudence yields numerous examples of acts that are (or are not) sufficient to pull off evictions. Examples of acts that do, or at least may do so, include the erection of a fence or other enclosure or boundary marker. Examples of acts that do not, or at least may not do so, include all of the examples that we gave earlier of acts that are insufficient to amount to *corpus* (everything from merely paying taxes to occasional cutting of wood).

b. Destruction

As a matter of logic one cannot retain *corpus* over what no longer exists. The destruction of the possessed thing, then, brings an end to possession.

c. Escape

If the thing possessed happens to be a wild animal, then there is yet another way in which possession may be lost. It is for the wild animal to return to its natural condition in the wild.

3. *Loss of* Animus *Alone*

Though somewhat unusual, it is possible for the possessor to end his *animus domini*, yet retain his *corpus.* Take, for example, the example of a seller who, despite the sale, retains custody of the thing sold for the convenience of the buyer. Whereas he formerly possessed the thing for himself, he now "possesses" it for someone else. Thus, though he still has *corpus*, he has lost his *animus.*

VII. Vices of Possession

To be effective, possession must have certain qualities. According to **LSA-C.C. Art. 3435**, "[p]ossession that is violent, clandestine, discontinuous, or equivocal has no legal effect." Turning this rule around, one can say that possession must be peaceable, open, continuous, and unequivocal. The opposite qualities, i.e., those enumerated in **Art. 3435**, are referred to as the "vices" of possession. Let us look at each of them in turn.

A. Violence

To say that a possession is "violent" means that it "[wa]s acquired or maintained by violent acts." **LSA-C.C. Art. 3436, ¶1.** The part of this definition that refers to "acquisition" presents no difficulties. The same is not true of the part of it that refers to "maintenance." Though the point may be disputed, my own conclusion, which finds support in French doctrine and the larger civil law tradition, is that the verb "maintain," properly understood, means "reacquire." The implications of this interpretation are as follows. If a possessor, after having lost possession due to eviction or usurpation, retakes possession by violence, then his possession becomes violent. But, if on the contrary, the possessor retains possession by violence, that is, while still in possession, uses violence to repel an attempted eviction or usurpation, his possession remains non-violent.

Violence is, at once, a "temporary" vice and a "relative" vice. The temporary quality of this vice is captured in the second sentence of the first paragraph of **Art. 3436**: "When the violence ceases, the possession ceases to be violent." The vice is relative in this sense: possession is considered to be violent only with respect to those who are exposed to that violence; with respect to others, the possession is not violent.

B. Clandestinity

To say that a possession as clandestine means that it is "not open or public." **Art. 3436, ¶2.** The vice of clandestinity, like the vice of violence, is temporary. As soon as the possessor begins to possess publicly, his possession is freed of that vice. In addition, clandestinity, like violence, is relative: possession is clandestine only with respect to those from whom the possessor conceals his possession; with respect to others, the possession is not clandestine.

C. Discontinuity

A possession becomes "discontinuous" when it "is not exercised at regular intervals." **Art. 3436, ¶2.** What constitutes a "regular interval" will, of course, vary from thing to thing. To "exercise" possession, for this purpose, apparently means to "do *corpus*," though there is some uncertainty on this point.

This notion that possession is vitiated when the possessor fails to "do *corpus*" at regular intervals, at least at first blush, seems to be in tension with another fundamental principle of the law of possession, i.e., civil possession. To say that one is civilly possessing is to say that one's possession, once acquired by simultaneous *corpus* and *animus*, can be retained by *animus* alone or, to speak more plainly, that a possessor who voluntarily ceases to possess the thing corporeally will be deemed to remain in possession of the thing so long as he continues to intend to possess the thing as owner. If that is true, if one can, in effect, stop exercising corporeal possession and still hang onto possession via the fiction of civil possession, then how can it be true that possession, to be and remain effective, must revert to being corporeal periodically?

Of the civilian commentators who have noted this problem, all have attempted to reconcile the two principles, i.e., to explain how the two principles, despite first appearances, are nevertheless compatible. Of these solutions, the most promising is this: to restrict the domain of *viable* civil possession to the periods *between* successive regular acts of corporeal possession.

D. Equivocation

A possession is "equivocal" when the possessor's *animus* is ambiguous, that is, when one cannot tell for sure, from looking at the circumstances, whether the person with *corpus* of the thing intends to possess it for himself (in other words, is a true possessor) or, rather, intends to "possess" it for another (in other words, is a precarious possessor). **Art. 3436, ¶2.** Here is an example. Suppose that one of two roommates moves out of the shared domicile, but, in so doing, leaves some of his things behind, things that the remaining roommate continues to use. If the remaining roommate has "possession" of these things at all (which may be questioned), this possession is equivocal.

VIII. Detention (Precarious Possession)

A. Definition

Precarious possession, according to **LSA-C.C. Art. 3437**, is "[t]he exercise of precarious possession with the permission of or on behalf of the owner or possessor." The other, more technical, term for precarious possession is "detention." Comment (b) to this article reminds us of what we have already learned regarding how precarious possession differs from true possession: "The precarious possessor... does *not* intend to own the thing he detains." Described in terms of the constitutive elements of possession, the difference, then, can be expressed this way: detention is *corpus* without *animus domini.*

B. Illustrations

1. Simple Precarious Possession

a. Lease

The contract of lease is that "by which one party, the lessor, binds himself to give to the other party, the lessee, the use and enjoyment of a thing for a term in exchange for a rent that the lessee bind himself to pay." **LSA-C.C. Art. 2668.** In such a contract, the lessee serves as a precarious possessor of the leased thing for the lessor, the true possessor.

b. Deposit

"Deposit" is "a contract in which a person, the depositor, delivers a movable thing to another person, the depositary, for safekeeping under the obligation of returning it to the depositor upon demand." **LSA-C.C. Art. 2926.** In such a contract, the depositary serves as the precarious possessor of the deposited thing for the depositor, the true possessor.

c. Pledge (Possessory Security Right)

The contract of "pledge," a so-called "accessory" contract, is one whereby one person, either the obligor himself or someone acting in his interest, turns something over to the obligee as "security" for the obligation, in other words, to guarantee performance of the obligation. **LSA-C.C. Art. 3133.** During the contract of pledge, the thing given in pledge remains in the custody and control of the obligee-pledgee. If the obligor performs the secured obligation, then the pledged thing is returned to its owner. But if the obligor defaults on the obligation, then the obligee-pledgee is entitled to cause the pledged thing to be sold and the proceeds of the sale to be applied to satisfy the secured obligation. In such a contract, the obligee-pledgee serves as the precarious possessor of the pledged thing for the pledgor, the true possessor.

d. Loan for Use (*Commodatum*)

"Loan for use" is "a contract by which a person, the lender, delivers a nonconsumable thing to another, the borrower, for him to use and return." **LSA-C.C. Art. 2891.** In such a contract, the borrower serves as the precarious possessor of the loaned thing for the lender, the true possessor.

2. Complex (Compound) Precarious Possession

a. Co-Ownership

Where one of several co-owners exercises *corpus* on the co-owned thing, a complex possessory situation arises. In such a situation, true possession and precarious possession take place "in parallel" or, if one prefers, "side by side." With respect to *his own share* of the co-owned thing, the co-owner with *corpus* thinks of himself as "the owner." As to that share, then, the co-owner acts as a *true* possessor. But with respect to the *shares of the other co-owners*, the co-owner with *corpus* recognizes that he is not the owner and, further, recognizes that he acts at the sufferance, that is, with the permission and on behalf, of the others. Consequently, as to *these shares*, the co-owner acts as a *precarious* possessor.

b. Servitude

Likewise complex is the possessory situation that arises when the holder of a servitude exercises his servitude rights. In this case, however, what happens "side by side" is not *possession* and precarious possession, but rather *quasi-possession* and precarious possession. Take, for example, a landowner who enjoys a predial servitude of passage over his neighbor's land. When the landowner, exercising his servitude rights, passes over his neighbor's land, the landowner, of course, quasi-possesses *his servitude right.* But he does more than just that. As to his neighbor's *land*, that is, the corporeal immovable on which his servitude lies, as opposed to his servitude right itself, the landowner acts as a precarious possessor *of that land* for his neighbor. Thus, the landowner's acts of use, at one and the same time, "count" as *quasi-corpus* for himself as *quasi*-possessor of the right and as vicarious *corpus* for his neighbor, who is the true possessor of the underlying corporeal immovable.

C. Procedural Matters: Presumptions

LSA-C.C. Art. 3427 tells us that "One is presumed to intend to possess as owner unless he began to possess in the name of and for another." Look at the last clause of the article: "unless he began to possess in the name of and for another." This means that one who begins to possess "in the name of and for another" does not get the benefit of the presumption. Not only can he not claim the benefit of the presumption set out in **Art. 3427**, but he must fight against the presumption set out in **Art. 3438**: "A precarious possessor... is presumed to possess for another although he may intend to possess for himself." The effect of these presumptions puts on the precarious possessor, should he ever want to claim that he ceased being merely a precarious possessor and became, instead, a true possessor, the burden of proving that he at some point started to intend to possess as owner. If you start out as a precarious possessor, the law will treat you as a precarious possessor unless and until you prove you have stopped being a precarious possessor, in other words, that you have begun to possess for yourself.

D. Termination

Precarious possession is a condition that can be escaped. That is to say, it is possible to change a precarious possession into a real possession (and, if proof of this change can be produced, to rebut the presumption that precarious possession continues). This change, according to French doctrine, is referred to as an "interversion of title."

The topic of interversion of title is addressed in **LSA-C.C. Art. 3439.** As even a cursory examination of the article reveals, the article establishes not one but two standards for interversion of title, one applicable to co-owners, the other applicable to all other precarious possessors.

1. Co-Owners

How a *co-owner* may intervert his title as against the other co-owners is addressed in **Art. 3439, ¶1**: "[a] co-owner... commences to possess for himself when he demonstrates this intent by overt and unambiguous acts sufficient to give notice to his co-owner." Doctrine and jurisprudence agree that "mere occupancy, use, and payment of taxes will *not* suffice" to provide such notice. Nevertheless, there are several things that a co-owner may do, short of providing "actual notice," that will suffice. One is to procure and record a judgment of possession that (fraudulently) recognizes him but him alone as the "sole" heir of the co-owners' ancestor-in-title. Another is to procure and record an instrument in which he appears as the sole transferee of the property (e.g., a sale to him alone as buyer). Acts of these kinds, our courts have concluded, "overtly" and "unambiguously" give notice to the other co-owners that the concerned co-owner now intends to possess for himself.

2. Other Detainers (Lessees, Depositaries, Pledgees, Borrowers, Servitude Holders)

The rule whereby any *other* kind of precarious possessor (other than a co-owner) may intervert his title is set out in **Art. 3439, ¶2**: "[a]ny other precarious possessor... commences to possess for himself when he gives actual notice of this intent to the person on whose behalf he is possessing." This standard must mean something different from the standard that is applicable to co-owners, but precisely how it is different is not immediately clear. If the word "actual" as used in the expression "actual notice" has its common and generally prevailing meaning, which one must suppose it does, then what is required is notice *in fact*. To give such notice, the precarious possessor would have to inform the true possessor, be it in writing or orally, that he now intends to possess for himself, using more or less those very words. If that is so, then many of the kinds of acts that would suffice as "overt and unambiguous acts" by a co-owner will not be sufficient here. Consider, for example, the procurement and recordation of a "sole heir" judgment of possession or a "sole buyer" title. Because an act of this kind does not in fact apprise the true possessor of the precarious possessor's change of *animus*, interversion of title will not take place.

IX. Junction of Possessions (Continuation of Possession; Tacking of Possessions)

When it is in his interest to do so,[4] the possessor may, under certain circumstances, be permitted to "count as his own" the time of possession that had been accumulated by this "ancestor-in-title" (or "author"), that is, the person from whom he purportedly acquired the thing. This phenomenon is referred to in **LSA-C.C. Art. 3442** as the "tacking" of possessions. For reasons that will be explained in due course, it would be better to speak of "junction" of possessions.

An essential prerequisite for the junction of possessions is that there be some sort of "juridical link" between the current possessor and the previous possessor. *See* **Art. 3442 cmt. (d)** ("Tacking of possession presupposes a juridical link."). The term "juridical link" is not defined here or elsewhere in the Civil Code nor in any of the comments. But one comment—comment (d) to **Art. 3442**—does at least tell us how a juridical link "arises": "This link may arise through universal succession or particular succession." These expressions—"universal succession" and "particular succession"—are defined in **LSA-C.C. Art. 3506(28)**, which reads in part as follows:

> Successor.—Successor is, generally speaking, the person who takes the place of another.
>
> There are in law two sorts of successors: [i] the universal successor, such as the heir, the universal legatee, and the general legatee; and [ii] the successor by particular title, such as the buyer, donee or legatee of particular things, the transferee.

The term "heir" is explained in **LSA-C.C. Art. 876**: "There are two kinds of successors corresponding to the two kinds of succession described in the preceding articles: .... Intestate successors, also called heirs." A "uni-

4. There are at least two situations in which it might be "in the interest" of the possessor to assert the junction of possessions. The first is when he does not, on his own, have enough time of possession to satisfy the delay requirement for the acquisition of the "right to possess," which, as we will see, is one year. The second is when he does not, on his own, have enough time of possession to satisfy the delay requirement for "acquisitive prescription," which, as we will see, may be three years, ten years, or thirty years, depending on the case.

versal legatee" is one who receives a "universal legacy." **LSA-C.C. Art. 1585** defines "universal legacy" as a legacy [in other words, a donation *mortis causa*] that involves the "disposition of all of the estate, or the balance of the estate that remains after particular legacies." A "general legatee" is one who receives a "general legacy." A "general legacy," according to **LSA-C.C. Art. 1586**, is

> ... a disposition by which the testator bequeaths a fraction or a certain proportion of the estate, or a fraction or certain proportion of the balance of the estate that remains after particular legacies... [or] all, or a fraction or a certain proportion of one of the following categories of property ...: separate or community property, movable or immovable property, or corporeal or incorporeal property.

A "buyer," of course, is the person who acquires a thing through a "sale," a concept so commonly known that no definition of it is needed here. The term "donee," as used in this context, refers to the recipient of a "donation *inter vivos*," more commonly known as a "gift." A "legatee of particular things" (more commonly called a "particular legatee") is one who receives a "particular legacy." **LSA-C.C. Art. 1587** defines a "particular legacy" as "[a] legacy that is neither general nor universal." What all of these various "successors"—heirs, universal legatees, general legatees, buyers, *inter vivos* donees, and particular legatees—have in common is that each is on the receiving end of some supposed "transfer" of ownership. A "juridical link," then, is nothing but an act or event of transfer. And to say that, for junction of possessions to be possible, there must be a "juridical link" between the current possessor and the previous possessor is to say nothing more than that the latter must have purported to transfer his interest in the thing to the former in one of these various ways.

Though a juridical link between current and prior possessors is necessary for junction of possessions, it is not sufficient. On top of the "juridical link" requirement, there is a second requirement: that both of the "possessions" be "effective," meaning, first, that both involve "true" (as opposed to "precarious" possession) and, second, that both be free of "vices."

To determine whether this second requirement is satisfied in any given case, one must, first, determine whether the "juridical link" (transfer) arises from a "universal" succession or from a "particular" succession. This is so because the mechanisms that must be used to determine the "effectiveness" of the "possessions" varies from one type of succession to another.

It will be of considerable help to us in understanding what these "mechanisms" are and how they differ from each other if we, to start with, deepen our understanding of the differences between universal and particular succession. Let us consider, first, precisely what right or rights each kind of successor (universal or particular) gets from his transferor and, second, how, as a matter of legal theory, the possession of each kind of successor (universal or particular) is thought to be related to that of his transferor.

The question of what rights successors receive from their ancestors is addressed "later on" in the very same article that defines "successors," that is, **Art. 3506(28).** Paragraph three to that article tells us about universal successors (that is, intestate heirs, universal legatees, and general legatees): "The *universal* successor represents the person of the deceased, and succeeds to all his rights and charges." Particular successors (that is, buyers, *inter vivos* donees, particular legatees) are addressed in paragraph four: "The *particular* successor succeeds only to the rights appertaining to the thing which is sold, ceded or bequeathed to him." How, then, should we describe the difference between universal and particular successors in terms of what they get from their transferors? Whereas the universal successor gets *all* of his transferor's rights in everything without restriction, the particular successor gets *only those* of his ancestor's rights that appertain to the one particular thing that is the object of the transfer.

The question of how, as a matter of legal theory, the possession of a successor is thought to be related to the possession of his transferor is addressed in **LSA-C.C. Art. 936.** Paragraph two deals with universal successors: "A universal successor continues the possession of the decedent with all its advantages and defects, and with no alteration in the nature of the possession." This rule is based on the theoretical fiction that a universal successor is the *alter ego* of his transferor; in the case of a universal succession, it is "as if" the succession never occurred and the transferor himself is still very much alive and in control. As between a universal successor and his ancestor, then, there are not two distinct possessions, but rather one and the same ongoing possession. Paragraph three deals with particular successors: "a particular successor… commence[s] a new possession." This rule rests on the notion that a particular successor, in sharp contrast to a universal successor, is not the *alter ego* of, but is rather a "stranger" to, his transferor. Instead of "continuing" his transferor's possession, he starts a new possession "of his own," one that is distinct from that of his transferor.

Let us now consider the implications of all of this "theory" for the "junction of possessions," more specifically, for the requirement that both of the "possessions" be "effective."

We start with universal succession. One can, to start with, question whether it really makes sense to talk about a "junction" of possessions in such a case. To speak of "junction" is to presuppose that there are separate things to be joined. Yet in the case of a universal succession, there is only one continuous possession, shared by the transferor and after him, his universal successor. This is not a case of "junction" in the true sense of the word so much as one of "continuation." In addition, insofar as the "effectiveness" requirement is concerned, it is misleading to say that "both possessions" must be "effective," for there is, to repeat, only one possession. What is required, then, is that the ongoing, single possession be "effective." Further, whether this single possession is effective will depend on the attributes that it had *when the transferor was still in possession.* This implication follows ineluctably from the notion that the successor has no independent existence of his own, in other words, that he is nothing but the *alter ego* of his transferor.[5]

And now for particular succession. As to this kind of succession, we face a serious theoretical difficulty right off the bat. If the possession of the particular successor is separate and independent from that of his transferor, in other words, that when he begins to possess, he starts a new possession of his own, then "junction of possessions" would seem to be impossible for him. Why? Because, as an independent possessor, he should, in principle, be required to "do everything" by his lonesome, without the help of his transferor, including satisfying whatever "time of possession" requirement he may want or need to satisfy. This is all true. Nevertheless, on precisely this point, the doctrine and the jurisprudence,

5. It is, of course, possible that the universal successor, like his ancestor-in-title, might be able to change the attributes of the ongoing, continuous possession. But he could do so only on the same terms and subject to the same limitations as those that would have been applicable to his ancestor-in-title.

in a nod to practicality, have set aside theory to some extent. According to this doctrinal and jurisprudential authority, a particular successor, despite his independence from his transferor, may nevertheless "tack" his transferor's time of possession to his own, provided that both his possession and that of his transferor have "the same qualities," which means, in context, that both possessions be "effective."

Some concrete illustrations may help to drive home the points of all this theoretical musing. We will look at, first, an illustration that involves universal succession, then one that involves particular succession.

Imagine a certain person X who, desiring to farm a certain tract of land, leases it from its owner, a certain Y, for a term of one year. Once X starts to farm, he, of course, will be a precarious possessor of the land for Y, the true possessor. Seven months pass, after which X dies. Because he had no testament, his estate devolves through intestacy. He has only one heir, his daughter, Z. Now it turns out that, before X died, he had told Z about the land he farmed, but in so doing had been guilty of a little "lie": he told Z that he, X, "owned" the land. Z believed the lie. And so it was that when, following X's death, Z went out to the land to continue X's farming operations, Z did so thinking that she, like X before her, was the owner of the land. Six more months pass. At this point, Y, noting that the term of the lease is up, heads out to the land to reclaim it. There he finds Z, whom he asks to leave. Z refuses, insisting that, even if she is not the owner of the land as she had thought, she has, nevertheless, acquired the right to possess it. In support of this contention, she invokes the "junction of possessions," that is, claims that she is entitled to add to her own time of possession the time of X's possession for the purpose of satisfying the one-year delay requirement for the acquisition of the right to possess. Will this claim stand? No. As a universal successor of X, she "inherits" and then continues *his* possession with, as **Art. 936, ¶2**, puts it, "all its advantages and *defects*." X's possession suffered from a huge defect: it was precarious. True, taken *by herself as herself*, she has *animus domini* and, therefore, could claim that she has had possession from the time at which she assumed *corpus* of the land (though, in the end, this contention would not help her, for she still would not have sufficient time). But that does not matter. As a universal successor—alter ego of the transferor—she is not entitled to be treated "as herself by herself." She *is* her transferor. As such, she is what he was—a precarious possessor.

Now, let us change the illustration just a bit. Let us suppose that Z, instead of inheriting the land from X through intestacy, *buys* the land from him. After that, everything unfolds as it did before. Under these changed circumstances, will Z be able to invoke the rule of "junction of possessions" in order to satisfy the one-year delay requirement of the acquisition of the right to possess? The answer, again, is "no," but the reason for the answer is now different. In this illustration, Z is X's *particular* successor. That means, among other things, that he begins a new possession of his own, one whose attributes are dependent solely on what Z does and thinks, and that, conversely, she does not in any sense "continue" the possession of X. Because Z has both *corpus* and *animus domini*, she is now in possession of the land, and this possession is fully effective. But she still cannot "tack" X's time of possession onto her own to get over the "one year" hump. And that is because she cannot satisfy the requirement for such tacking. That requirement, it will be recalled, is that both her possession and that of her ancestor must have "the same qualities," specifically, be effective. There is the rub: though Z's possession is effective, X's was not. Tacking is therefore barred.

X. Effects of Possession

A. Procedural Rights: Presumption of Ownership

The possessor is presumed to be the owner. As **LSA-C.C. Art. 3423** puts it, "[a] possessor is considered provisionally as owner of the thing he possesses until the right of the true owner is established." *See also* **LSA-C.C. Art. 530, ¶1** ("The possessor of a corporeal movable is presumed to be the owner." There are at least two contexts in which this presumption is important.

The presumption can benefit possessors in tort suits to recover damages for loss of or injury to property. By virtue of the presumption of ownership, a mere possessor of a thing can recover damages for the tortious destruction of or injury to that thing, at least where the tortfeasor cannot prove that someone else is the owner.

The presumption can also benefit possessors in suits for the vindication of ownership interests, i.e., petitory actions (for immovables) and revendicatory actions (for movables). When such an action is instituted against the possessor, the burden of proof rests on the plaintiff, i.e., the putative owner, who must show that he rather than the possessor is the true owner. We will have occasion to see just how the presumption operates in this context when we cover petitory and revendicatory actions later on.

B. Substantive Rights

1. The "Right to Possess"

a. Acquisition

Possession, provided it lasts long enough, will have yet another effect: it will give rise to a legally protectable interest in the thing, namely, the right to possess it. According to the second clause of **LSA-C.C. Art. 3422**, "one who has possessed a thing for over a year acquires the right to possess it." Unlike possession *per se*, which is merely a "fact," the right to possess is a true right—just as much a right as the real right of ownership or the credit right of a lessor to collect rent from a lessee—and, as such, can be protected through judicial process.

b. Loss

Like possession itself, the right to possess can be lost. **LSA-C.C. Art. 3434.** The possible causes are two: abandonment and eviction. In the case of abandonment, the loss of the right to possess is instantaneous. *See* ***id.*****, sent. 1** ("lost *upon* abandonment"). In the case of eviction, by contrast, the loss does not take place until the passage of a year and then only if, within that year, the evicted possessor "does not recover possession." *See* ***id.*****, sent. 2.** This "recovery" of possession may be accomplished in either of two ways: (1) reestablish possession by re-evicting or re-usurping the evictor; or (2) bring a successful possessory action against the evictor.

2. Accession

That one is a possessor has important consequences in the field of the law of accession. Accession is the process whereby the owner of a certain thing acquires the ownership of the things that that thing produces or of things that are added to that thing. *See* **LSA-C.C. Art. 482.**

a. Rights with Respect to Fruits and Products

A possessor has certain rights *vis-à-vis* the owner with respect to the fruits and products of the thing. Depending on whether the possessor is in good faith or bad faith, he will be entitled to keep the fruits or at least to the reimbursement of the expenses he incurred in producing those fruits. And though he has no claim to the products of the thing, he may, if he is in good faith, demand reimbursement of the expenses he incurred in producing those products. *See* **LSA-C.C. Arts. 486 & 488.**

b. Rights with Respect to Enhancements (Improvements and INATs)

A possessor has certain rights *vis-à-vis* the owner with respect to the enhancements that the possessor makes to the thing, specifically, improvements or INATs that he adds to the thing. Depending on whether the possessor is in good faith or bad faith as well as a few other factors, he will be entitled to remove and keep the enhancements or to reimbursement of some kind, e.g., the cost of the materials and workmanship or the enhanced value of the thing. *See* **LSA-C.C. Arts. 496 & 497.**

3. Others

There are several other substantive legal effects of possession, effects that, in terms of their importance, dwarf those that we have already considered. These include (1) the judicial protection of the "right to possess" and (2) the acquisition of ownership and other real rights based on possession through "occupancy," "quasi-occupancy," and "acquisitive prescription." These consequences are so important, in fact, that they deserve extended treatment in a separate place. In the next chapter, we will consider the judicial protection of the right to possess; in the chapter after that, the acquisition of ownership and other real rights based on possession through "occupancy" and "quasi-occupancy"; and in the chapter after that, the acquisition of ownership and other real rights based on possession through "acquisitive prescription."

Chapter Five

Judicial Protection of Possession

I. Introduction

Under certain circumstances, the possessor of a thing may be entitled to receive "judicial protection" of his possession, specifically, official judicial recognition of his possession, injunctive relief to halt future interference with that possession, and/or damages for past interference with that possession. **LSA-C.C. Art. 3444.** The mechanisms whereby possessors may obtain such protection vary depending on the nature of the object of possession, specifically, whether it is "immovable" or "movable." For immovables, the legislature has long provided a detailed and complex procedure, one known as the "possessory action." But for movables the legislature has made no similar provision. Stepping in to fill this gap, our courts have permitted the possessor of a movable, at least under some circumstances, to use the "revendicatory action"—the action for the vindication of ownership rights in movables—for this purpose.

For the moment, we will confine our attention to the "possessory action." This is for two reasons. The first is practical: in the real world of the law, few people ever bother to bring revendicatory actions to try possessory rights. The second is pedagogical: because the assertion of possessory rights in movables is so intimately connected with the assertion of ownership rights in movables, it is better to put off covering the former until the latter is covered.

II. The Possessory Action

A. Scope

According to **LSA-C.C.P. Art. 3655**, the possessory action provides a means of vindicating possessory rights in "immovable property" and in certain "real rights" in such immovable property. As to these real rights, of course, it would be better to say "protect *quasi*-possession." This observation sheds some light on just which "real rights" in immovables might be contemplated: as a matter of logic, they could include only those real rights that are susceptible of quasi-possession, that is, (i) personal servitudes, i.e., usufruct, right of use, habitation, and (ii) predial servitudes. We might, then, describe the scope of the "things" covered by the possessory action as every kind of immovable that is susceptible of possession or *quasi*-possession.

III. The Possessory Action

A. Prerequisites to the Possessory Action

The prerequisites to a possessory action are set out in **LSA-C.C.P. Art. 3658.** This article provides as follows:

To maintain the possessory action the possessor must allege and prove that:

> (1) He had possession of the immovable property or real right therein at the time the disturbance occurred;
> **(2) He and his ancestors in title had such possession quietly and without interruption for more than a year immediately prior to the disturbance, unless evicted by force or fraud;**
> **(3) The disturbance was one in fact or in law, as defined in Art. 3659; and**
> (4) The possessory action was instituted within a year of the disturbance.

Let us now consider each of these prerequisites in turn. For convenience of presentation, I begin with the third prerequisite, then turn to the others in the order in which they appear in the article.

1. *Disturbance in Fact or in Law*

a. Necessity

A possessor cannot bring a possessory action unless and until he has first been "disturbed" by the person against whom he wishes to bring suit.

b. Definition and Varieties

The Code of Civil Procedure does not provide us with a definition of disturbance in general. It divides the category of "disturbance" into two classes, disturbances in fact and disturbances in law, then defines each of those terms. Let us look at those definitions.

1) Disturbance in Fact

According to **LSA-C.C.P. Art 3659, ¶2**, a disturbance in fact is "an eviction or any other physical act which prevents the possessor of immovable property or a real right therein from enjoying his possession quietly, or which throws any obstacle in the way of that enjoyment." This definition tells us two things. First, it identifies the common denominator of all disturbances in fact: physical acts that prevent the possessor from enjoying his possession or that throw an obstacle in the way of that enjoyment. Second, it suggests that the class of disturbances in fact can itself be subdivided into "evictions," on the one hand, and what we might call "mere disturbances," on the other.

a) Eviction

"Eviction" here means the same thing that it means in **LSA-C.C. Art. 3433**, entitled "Loss of possession." Eviction is the involuntary loss of *corpus* over a thing as a result of the acts of another or, to put it another way, the possessor is evicted when someone else establishes corporeal possession over the thing.

b) Mere Disturbance

A mere disturbance is some act that, though insufficient to strip the possessor of his *corpus* over the thing or to establish *corpus* over the thing in favor of another, nevertheless interferes with or puts an obstacle in the way of the possessor's enjoyment of the thing. Examples might include a momentary trespass by the disturber.

2) Disturbance in Law

The legislation that defines disturbances in law—**LSA-C.C.P. 3659(C)**—as recently revised. The revision represents a significant improvement over the original, which suffered from numerous infelicities and ambiguities. Here's how the revised legislation reads:

> C. A disturbance in law is the occurrence or existence of any of the following adversely to the possessor of immovable property or a real right therein:
>
> (1) The execution, recordation, or registry, after the possessor or his ancestors in title acquired the right to possess, of any instrument that asserts or implies a right of ownership or right to the possession of the immovable property or a real right therein.
>
> (2) The continuing existence of record of any instrument that asserts or implies a right of ownership or right to the possession of the immovable property or a real right therein, unless the instrument was recorded before the possessor and his ancestors in title commenced possession.
>
> (3) Any other claim or pretension of ownership or right to the possession of the immovable property or a real right therein, whether written or oral, except when asserted in an action or proceeding.

Let's now examine each of these subparagraphs more closely.

Paragraph C(1). – (1) The use of the disjunctive conjunction "or" in the opening line ("the execution, recordation, recordation, *or* registry") makes it clear that each one of the enumerated events, standing on its own, constitutes a distinct disturbance. It follows that, if a certain "instrument" of the kind required (that is, one that "asserts" or "implies" a right or possession that is "adverse" to the possessor) were to be "executed" (that is, drawn up and signed), then "recorded" (in the public records), and then "registered" (in the public records), then the possessor would have suffered not one, not two, but three distinct disturbances. This distinction may be important for purposes of prescription (see below) in the event that the instrument in question is recorded or registered on a date later than that on which it was executed. (2) This subparagraph imposes a temporal requirement, namely, that the "execution", "recordation", or "registry" of the offending instrument must occur "after" the possessor or his ancestor-in-title "acquired the right to possess", that is, after he or has ancestor has already been in possession for a year. Thus, the possessory plaintiff cannot obtain relief on the basis of an instrument that was recorded prior to that time, that is, one recorded before his or his ancestor's possession began or even one recorded during his or his ancestor's first year of possession. **LSA-C.C.P. Art. 3659 cmt. (b).**

Paragraph C(2). – (1) Not only the "execution", "recordation", or "registry" of an adverse instrument, but also the very "continuing existence of record" of such an instrument (in other words, its continuing presence in the public records), amounts to a disturbance in law. It is important to recognize that this kind of disturbance in law, which is distinct from and in addition to those enumerated in subparagraph C(1), is ongoing and continuous, in contrast to those enumerated in subparagraph C(1), which are temporally punctiliar. That this is so is important for purposes of prescription (see below). As **cmt. (d)** to Article 3659 notes, "[b]ecause the continuing existence of record is a continuing disturbance, the one-year prescriptive period under Article 3658(4) for bringing a possessory action complaining of this disturbance in law effectively does not commence to run under these circumstances." (2) This subparagraph, like the first, imposes a temporal requirement, though one that differs from that imposed by the first, namely, that the instrument of whose "continuing existence of record" the plaintiff complains must have been filed *after* he or his ancestor-in-title "commenced possession" (as opposed to "acquired the right to possess"). Thus, the possessory plaintiff cannot obtain relief on the basis of an instrument that was recorded prior to that time, that is, one recorded before his or his ancestor's possession began. **LSA-C.C.P. Art. 3659 cmt. (c).**

Paragraph C(3). – This paragraph, as revised, answers an important question that the original legislation left obscure: whether a disturbance in law must be in writing. The revision answers this question with a firm "no." Thus, even an *oral* "claim or pretension" can constitute a disturbance in law.

All three subparagraphs speak of the "assertion", "implication", "claim", or "pretension" or the like of a "right of ownership" or other "real right" or of a "right to . . . possession." What does this mean? That what must be asserted, implied, etc. is that the asserter, implier, etc. has some real right—ownership, a servitude, etc.—or a right to possess or even merely a fact of possession that is in some way "adverse" to the possessor. The classic example involves an act of sale of the immovable between parties (buyer and seller) neither of whom is the possessor. Through this act, the seller by implication asserts that he has the ownership of the thing and the buyer, that he is receiving the ownership of the thing. And this assertion of ownership is as adverse to the possessor as adverse can be.

2. Possession at the Time of the Disturbance

To prevail in a possessory action, the plaintiff must show that he had possession of the thing at the time of the disturbance. Contemplated here is possession as a matter of fact, not the right to possess. Corporeal possession is a possibility, of course, but civil possession and even constructive possession are likewise sufficient. As long as the party bringing the action has some form of possession at the time of the disturbance, this requirement is met.

3. Uninterrupted Possession for One Year Prior to the Disturbance

a. Elements of the Requirement

As the wording of the second paragraph of **LSA-C.C.P. Art. 3658**—"possession... for more than a year immediately prior to the disturbance"—suggests, the requirement established therein has to do with the "right to possess" (as opposed to the fact of possession). The right to possess, it will be recalled, is a substantive right that the possessor acquires after he has been in possession for "more than a year." As the courts have interpreted this part of **Art. 3658**, two things are required of the possessor. First, he must show that he *acquired* the right to possess at some time prior to the disturbance. Second, he must show that he *did not lose* that right prior to the disturbance or, to put it another way, that he conserved (maintained) that right up until the disturbance.

b. Exception to the Requirement

In two extraordinary situations, the possessor is dispensed from this requirement for the possessory action, that is, he need not show that he acquired and thereafter maintained the right to possess.

1) Eviction by "Force"

The first exception is for the case in which the possessor has been "evicted by force." **LSA-C.C.P. Art. 3658(2).** The word "force" as used in this context means "violence."

2) Eviction by "Fraud"

The law also makes an exception for the case in which the possessor has been "evicted by... fraud." **LSA-C.C.P. Art. 3658(2).** "Eviction by fraud" occurs when the disturber, after tricking the possessor into leaving the thing (in other words, giving up his *corpus*), swoops in and usurps the possessor's possession.

4. Action Within One Year of the Disturbance

The final prerequisite to a possessory action is one of "prescription": the action must be brought within one year of the disturbance. If the plaintiff fails to initiate suit by that deadline, then his ability to obtain possessory relief with respect to that disturbance will come to an end.

Insofar as the requirement of prescription is concerned, one particular disturbance is singled out from all the rest for distinctive treatment. It is the disturbance in law known as the "continuing presence of record of an instrument." Prescription of a possessory action based on *this* kind of disturbance does not begin to run until the disturbance *ends*, and such a disturbance is deemed to continue as long as the instrument remains in the public records or until the interest described in the instrument terminates, whichever comes first.

In most cases, the prescription of the possessor's possessory action is really "no big deal" for the possessor. All that he ordinarily loses is what we might call his "procedural" possessory rights, that is, the "right to complain" and the "right to get relief." But he ordinarily does *not* lose any of his "substantive" possessory rights: despite his failure to sue by the deadline, he still remains in possession and he still retains the right to possess.

There is one case, however, in which that is not true, in other words, in which his failure to bring suit within the prescriptive period will have not only procedural, but also substantive law consequences. And that is when the "disturbance" in question is an *eviction*. Recall that an eviction causes an instantaneous "loss of possession." There is no rule that accords to a mere disturbance in fact or a disturbance in law the same effect. Recall further that if the possessor, following an eviction, fails to "recover possession" within a year, then he also loses his right to possess. Once again, there is no rule that accords any other kind of disturbance that effect. It should be clear, then, that a possessor who has been disturbed by an eviction is under considerable pressure to act and to act within the year.

B. Proper Parties Plaintiff

1. True Possessors

The true possessor (as opposed to a precarious possessor) is always a proper party plaintiff in a possessory action. That is true even when a precarious possessor has the *corpus* of the immovable at the time of the disturbance: the true possessor is entitled to sue the one who disturbed his precarious possessor.

2. Precarious Possessors

From the days of Ulpian and Paul until 1982, it was rock solid civil law that a precarious possessor could not bring a possessory action to protect his precarious possession. But in that year, the legislature, in the course of revising the Civil Code articles on possession, broke with the tradition. The new law is set forth in **LSA-C.C. Art. 3440**: "Where there is a disturbance of possession, the possessory action is available to a precarious possessor, such as a lessee or a depositary, against anyone except the person for whom he possesses." Thanks to this provision, the possessory action is available to the precarious possessor against anyone who disturbs his possession. The only exception is that a precarious possessor cannot bring a possessory action against the true possessor, that is, the one for whom he possesses.

Chapter Six

Occupancy

I. "Occupancy" Properly So Called

A. Definition

"Occupancy," according to **LSA-C.C. Art. 3412**, "is the taking of possession of a corporeal movable that does not belong to anyone." To this definition comment (b) to the article adds an important element, namely, that it is "a mode of acquiring ownership." In the case of occupancy, the vesting of ownership takes place instantaneously. As the second sentence of **Art. 3412** puts it, "[t]he occupant acquires ownership the moment he takes possession."

B. Constitutive Elements

As our definition of "occupancy" suggests, there are three constitutive elements of or, if you prefer, three prerequisites to occupancy. They are (i) taking possession of (ii) a corporeal movable (iii) that has no owner. Let us examine each of these.

1. Possession

To acquire ownership of a thing through occupancy, one must, first of all, possess it. In this context, "possession" refers specifically to "corporeal possession" that is, *corpus* plus *animus domini.*

2. *Corporeal Movable*

The domain of occupancy, according to **Art. 3412**, is limited to things that are, at once, corporeal and movable. Thus, one cannot acquire ownership of an incorporeal thing or an immovable thing via occupancy.

3. *Thing that has no Owner* (Res Nullius)

The third prerequisite to occupancy is that the thing in question "not belong to anyone," in other words, that it have no owner. The Roman law term for such a thing is *res nullius* (literally, "thing of no one"). For purposes of analysis, the kinds of things which fit this description can be divided into two categories: (i) things that have never been owned and (ii) things that, though once owned, have ceased to be owned.

a. Things that Have Never Been Owned

Let us consider a few possibilities of things that have never been owned.

1) Constituents of Certain Common Things

The constituent elements of common things, e.g., gases in the air or water in the high seas, having never been owned, can be occupied.

2) Certain Wild Animals

Wild animals that have never been deprived of their natural liberty have never been owned. As a general rule, then, such wild animals are susceptible of occupancy. There is an exception to this general rule, one that is alluded to in **LSA-C.C. Art. 3413, ¶1**, comment (b) to **Art. 3413**, and comment (d) to **Art. 3412.** Through special legislation, the state has asserted ownership over certain kinds of wild animals. With respect to those wild animals, occupancy is impossible because they belong to someone, i.e., the state. This exception, though, arises not from the civil law of property but from Louisiana's autochthonic natural resources and environmental law, so it is of no concern to us.

To deepen our understanding of the general principle, we need to look more closely at its two constituent elements: (i) "wild animal" and (ii) "never deprived of natural liberty."

a) Wild Animal

1] DEFINITION BY EXPOSITION

"Wild animal" is described in **LSA-C.C. Art. 3417**, cmt. (d), ¶1:

> Wild animals comprehend those wild by nature, which, because of habit, mode of life, or natural instinct, are incapable of being completely domesticated and which require the exercise of art, force, or skill to keep them in subjection.

In principle, the category "animal," as used in the expression "wild animal," encompasses *every* life form that a modern biologist would situate in the "animal kingdom" (as opposed to the "plant kingdom," the "fungus kingdom," and so on). Thus, the category includes more than just "mammals" (e.g., bears, deer, squirrels, rabbits, nutria, muskrat, raccoons). It includes as well, first, animals in the lower "vertebrate" classes—fowl (e.g., ducks, doves, quail), reptiles (e.g., snakes, turtles), amphibians (e.g., frogs), and fish (e.g., catfish, trout, bass)—and, beyond that, all manner of invertebrates, among others shellfish (e.g., shrimp, crawfish, oysters) and insects (e.g., bees). This principle—that "animal" means, well, "animal"—is, it is sad to say, not consistently followed in the legislation. Thus, some of the articles use such expressions as "wild animals or birds" or "wild animals... or fish." Though technically imprecise, these expressions rarely cause confusion.

2] DEFINITION BY CONTRAST

The antonym of "wild animal" is domestic animal. That term is defined in **Art. 3417**, cmt. (d), ¶1:

> Domestic animals include those which are tame by nature, or from time immemorial have been accustomed to the association of man, or by his industry have been subjected to his will, and have no disposition to escape his dominion.

Dogs and cats are prime examples of domestic animals. Also included are the various so-called "farm animals," such as horses, mules, cattle, sheep, and goats.

b) Never Deprived of Natural Liberty

The animals with which we are now concerned not only must be wild but also must never have been deprived of their "natural liberty." Positively defined, this means something like "the animal is still at loose in the great outdoors." But that definition is not terribly informative. We can get a clearer understanding of this term if we define it negatively, i.e., if we enumerate the instances in which wild animals have been deprived of their "natural liberty."

1] WILD ANIMALS THAT HAVE BEEN CAPTURED

When a wild animal has been captured, it has been deprived of its "natural liberty."

2] ENCLOSED WILD ANIMALS

LSA-C.C. Art. 3415, ¶1 provides that "[w]ild animals or birds within enclosures, and fish or shellfish in an aquarium or other private waters, are privately owned." The theory behind this rule is that an enclosed animal, even if it enters the enclosure voluntarily, is subject to the dominion of him who has created the enclosure and, therefore, is no longer at liberty. Thus, if someone removes crawfish from another's pond, he takes possession of something that belongs to another, i.e., the one who owns the pond. Such things are *not* subject to occupancy.

3] WILD ANIMALS THAT HAVE BEEN TAMED

A tamed wild animal, one in the habit of returning, is no longer "in a state of natural liberty."

3) Certain Domestic Animals

According to **LSA-C.C. Art. 3417**, "[d]omestic animals that are privately owned are not subject to occupancy." Properly interpreted, this article does *not* foreclose occupancy of all domestic animals. Rather, it forecloses occupancy only of those domestic animals *that happen to be private owned.* It is possible, of course, for there to be a domestic animal that has never been owned, for example, a feral cat. Such a thing is surely susceptible of occupancy.

b. Things That, Though Once Owned, Have Ceased to be Owned

1) Abandoned Things

LSA-C.C. Art. 3418 provides that "[o]ne who takes possession of an abandoned thing with the intent to own it acquires ownership by occupancy." A thing is considered to be abandoned, the same article informs us, "when its owner relinquishes possession with the intent to give up ownership."

Any corporeal movable might possibly fall into the category of "abandoned thing." One possibility that deserves special mention is "domestic animal." When the owner of a privately owned domestic animal gives up his possession of that animal with the intent to give up his ownership, the animal becomes susceptible of occupancy.

2) Certain Wild Animals

As we saw earlier, captured, enclosed, and tamed wild animals are the kinds of wild animals that are deemed to have lost their natural liberty and, therefore, are not susceptible of occupancy. But they can once again become susceptible of occupancy, provided two things happen. First, the animal must recover its natural liberty. For a captured animal this means that the animal must escape; for an enclosed animal, that it must leave the enclosure (and not wander into another one); for a tamed animal, that it must lose the habit of returning to its owner. Second, the owner must fail to pursue or cease pursuing the animal. So long as the owner actively continues to try to recover the animal, the owner preserves his ownership right in the animal and the animal, therefore, remains insusceptible of occupancy.

II. "Quasi"-Occupancy

A. Definition

LSA-C.C. Arts. 3419 and **3420** establish, respectively, two "special" modes of acquiring ownership of certain kinds of corporeal movables. These articles are situated alongside the articles that we have just examined—the articles on "occupancy"—within the chapter of the Civil Code that is entitled "Occupancy," creating the impression (*pro subjecta materia*) that they have something to do with the institution of occupancy. But between these two modes of acquiring ownership and that institution, there is less than a perfect "fit."

Let us look, first, at **Art. 3419.** This article describes the (or at least a) mechanism whereby one who has "found" a corporeal movable that is "lost" can become the owner of it. This mechanism requires, first, that the finder make a diligent effort to locate the owner and to return the thing to him and, second, that the finder possess the thing for three years.

Whatever this mode of acquiring ownership may be, it cannot be occupancy. Consider, first, the status of a "lost" thing. A lost thing, by definition, if one that belongs to someone, a someone who has inadvertently mislaid it or otherwise lost track of it. Thus, if a thing is lost, as opposed to being abandoned, it is still owned. But according to **Art. 3412**, occupancy is a mode of acquiring ownership of something that "does not belong to anyone." Consider, next, how long one must possess a lost thing to acquire ownership of it under **Art. 3419**: three years. But according to **Art. 3412**, the acquisition of ownership through occupancy is instantaneous.

The mode of acquiring ownership established in **Art. 3419**, then, is not a brand of occupancy. What, then, is it? The great French civil law scholar Planiol thought that it was a form of acquisitive prescription. This characterization, however, is open to objection. The acquisitive prescription of movables is addressed in **LSA-C.C. Arts. 3489–3491.** The mode of acquiring ownership described in **Art. 3419** does not correspond to any of those described in **Arts. 3489–3491.** The truth, then, is that this mode of acquiring ownership is *sui generis*, neither occupancy nor acquisitive prescription. Still, it would be helpful to have some term whereby to refer to it. Because it is at least "like" occupancy in certain respects, I propose that we call it "quasi-occupancy."

Next, let us look at **Art. 3420.** This article describes the (or at least a) means whereby one can acquire ownership of "treasure." Treasure is defined as a "movable thing hidden in another thing... for such a long time that its owner cannot be determined." This means that treasure, properly so called, either has no owner, or that, though it has an owner, we cannot figure out who it is. In the latter case, the treasure is *ex hypothese* an "owned thing." *See* **Art. 3420 cmt. (c)** ("A treasure is not a lost thing, an abandoned thing, *or a thing that has no owner.*"). Yet occupancy, as we have seen, presupposes a thing that is owned by no one. *See* **Art. 3412.** It follows, then, that the mode of acquiring ownership established in **Art. 3420** is not a brand of occupancy.

What, then, is this mode of acquiring ownership? Acquisitive prescription is out: a comparison of **Art. 3420** with **Arts. 3489–3491**, the articles on acquisitive prescription of movables, reveals that the former has nothing to do with the latter. And so, once again, we find ourselves in the face of a mode of acquiring ownership that is neither occupancy nor acquisitive prescription but is, instead, *sui generis.* For the same reasons I gave in connection with **Art. 3419**, I propose that we lump the mode of acquiring ownership established in **Art. 3420** together with that established in **Art. 3419** into the category "quasi-occupancy."

B. Varieties

1. Quasi-Occupancy of Lost Things

a. Definition

1) By Exposition

Following foreign doctrine, we can define a "lost" thing as one that has "gone astray" from the owner or of which the owner has been involuntarily "dispossessed." It matters little what may have caused the owner to become "separated" from his thing. The cause could, of course, be the negligence of someone, be it the owner (as when the owner forgets where he left the thing) or a third person (as when a shipper of the thing ships it to the wrong address). But it could just was well be a *force majeure*, such as a flood that carries the thing off.

Lost things must be distinguished from both abandoned things and stolen things. Consider, first, abandoned things. For a thing to be considered abandoned, the owner must want to relinquish his ownership of it. This is not so with a lost thing. For a thing to be considered lost, the owner must want to retain his ownership of it. Further, whereas an abandoned thing belongs to no one, a lost thing remains the property of him who has lost it. Next, consider lost things. For a thing to be considered lost, it must escape the owner's control "fortuitously," i.e., the escape must not result from a deliberate effort to deprive the owner of his ownership or possessory interest. For a thing to be considered stolen, however, someone else must deliberately remove the thing from the other's control with a view to depriving him of his ownership or possessory interest.

b. Requirements

1) Diligent Effort

To acquire ownership of a lost thing via quasi-occupancy, one must "make a diligent effort to locate its owner or possessor and to return the thing to him." What may be entailed in this "diligent effort" is addressed in **Art. 3419 cmt. (d)**: "A diligent effort... may involve publishing or advertising in newspapers, posting notes, or notifying public authorities."

2) Three Years' Possession

To acquire ownership of a lost thing via quasi-occupancy, one must also possess it for three years, reckoning from the date on which one first made diligent efforts to locate the owner.

2. Quasi-Occupancy of Treasure

a. Definition

According to **Art. 3420** "[t]reasure" is a "movable hidden in another thing, movable or immovable, for such a long time that its owner cannot be determined." How long is "long enough" varies with the circumstances.

b. Requirements

For the acquisition of the ownership of treasure, there seems to be only one requirement: that the treasure be "found." Strictly speaking, "possession" is *not* required. Though in most instances "finding" would necessarily entail taking "possession," it is possible to imagine circumstances in which that would not be so, for example, where a marine treasure hunter, while in his ship on the surface of the sea, finds a cache of gold coins inside a sunken ship by means of an underwater remote-controlled camera.

c. Rules of Allocation

LSA-C.C. Art. 3420 establishes some bright-line rules for the distribution of treasure. If the finder finds it in or on his own thing, then he gets it all; if he finds it in or on the thing of another, then he and this other split it 50–50.

Chapter Seven

Acquisitive Prescription

Having finished our examination of occupancy and quasi-occupancy, we come to the third and undoubtedly the most important of the modes of acquiring real rights through possession: acquisitive prescription.

SUB-CHAPTER A

Acquisitive Prescription in General

I. Definition

A. By Exposition

LSA-C.C. Art. 3446 describes "acquisitive prescription" as "a mode of acquiring ownership or other real rights by possession for a period of time." It is important to note that not only ownership but also certain rights less than full ownership can be acquired in this way. But in the case of these "lesser" real rights, what is required, strictly speaking, is not possession but rather "quasi-possession" for the requisite period of time.

B. By Contrast

1. The Varieties of Prescription

Acquisitive prescription is not the only kind of prescription. According to **LSA-C.C. Art. 3445**, "[t]here are three kinds of prescription: acquisitive prescription, liberative prescription, and prescription of nonuse." The concept of acquisitive prescription can be clarified by contrasting this form of prescription with the others.

Liberative prescription and prescription of nonuse are described, respectively, in **LSA-C.C. Arts. 3447** and **3448.** According to the former, "[l]iberative prescription" is a "mode of barring of actions as a result of inaction for a period of time." It is the principle whereby certain claims, specifically, those for the protection of credit rights, are deemed to be barred if they are not asserted in a timely fashion. "Prescription of nonuse," according to **LSA-C.C. Art. 3448,** "is a mode of extinction of a real right other than ownership as a result of failure to exercise the right for a period of time." This prescription takes aim at "lesser" real rights ("less" than ownership) that the holder thereof fails to use.

2. Comparison

a. Differences

1) Necessity of Possession

Whereas acquisitive prescription rests on and, indeed, requires possession, liberative prescription and prescription of nonuse do not. In fact, in the case of the prescription of nonuse, someone *not* possessing (to be more precise, *quasi*-possessing) something is required.

2) Domain

The domains of acquisitive prescription, liberative prescription, and prescription of nonuse are different. Narrowest in scope is the prescription of nonuse, which, according to **LSA-C.C. Art. 3447 cmt. (b), ¶4,** affects only certain dismemberments of ownership—the servitudes—and the possessory action. Slightly broader in scope is acquisitive prescription, which affects not only certain dismemberments of ownership—the servitudes—but also ownership itself. Neither prescription of nonuse nor acquisitive prescription has any connection with credit rights. Liberative prescription, by contrast, affects only credit rights.

b. Similarities

If one were to ask the typical Louisiana lawyer what distinguishes acquisitive prescription, on the one hand, from liberative prescription and the prescription of nonuse, on the other, he would probably say something like this: whereas acquisitive prescription is a mode of *creat-*

ing new rights, liberative prescription and the prescription of nonuse are modes of *destroying* existing rights. This response implies, among other things, that acquisitive prescription is not destructive of anything.

This implication, though, is not sound. Every time that acquisitive prescription produces a new right, it simultaneously destroys something else. Consider, for example, the case in which a person becomes the owner of a thing through acquisitive prescription. At the very moment at which this person's new ownership right is created, the old ownership right of the person who had been the owner up until then is extinguished. Or, consider the case in which a person becomes a usufructuary of a thing through acquisitive prescription. At the very moment at which this person's right of usufruct is created, the old ownership right of the person who had been the owner up until then is "cut back" to the lesser real right of "naked ownership."

II. Basic Principles

A good part of the "law of acquisitive prescription" is found in a part of the Civil Code that addresses all forms of prescription in common and indiscriminately. That part of the Civil Code addresses four aspects of prescription, acquisitive prescription included, namely, (i) the calculation of the required lapse of time, (ii) interruption, (iii) suspension, and (iv) renunciation. What we want to do now is to look at these "common" rules.

A. Calculation of the Lapse of Time

1. Commencement

"In computing a prescriptive period," **LSA-C.C. Art. 3454** tells us, "the day that marks the commencement of prescription is not counted." That means, then, that the first day that *is* counted is the day *after* "the day that marks the commencement of prescription."

2. Accrual

The rules on the accrual of prescription are spread out over two articles, **LSA-C.C. Arts. 3454** and **3456.** The first provides that "[p]rescription accrues upon the expiration of the last day of the prescriptive period." The latter provides that "[i]f a prescriptive period consists of one or more years, prescription accrues upon the expiration of the day of the last year that corresponds with the date of the commencement of prescription." As applied to prescriptive periods measured in years, these two articles lead by different routes to the same end. The latter, however, is markedly easier to apply. First, one identifies the date that "marks the commencement of prescription." In the case of acquisitive prescription, that date, the second sentence of **LSA-C.C. Art. 3454** implies, is the date on which the prescriber first takes possession, that is, on which he first achieves *corpus* and *animus domini*. Second, one adds to the year of that date a number of years equal to the relevant prescriptive period, e.g., three years or ten years. Consequently, if one were to start to possess a tract of land on say, June 5, 2012, then abridged acquisition prescription would accrue at the end of the day June 5, 2022.

LSA-C.C. Art. 3454, second sentence, last clause, recognizes the possibility that the prescriptive period might not accrue until a still later date. That happens when the last day of the prescriptive period, as measured by the general rule, falls on a "legal holiday." In that case, prescription does not accrue until "the expiration of the next day that is not a legal holiday." Legal holidays are listed in **LSA-R.S. 1:55.** They include not only "holidays" in the common sense of that word, such as Christmas, Easter, New Year's Day, Thanksgiving Day, Independence Day, Memorial Day, Labor Day, and *Mardi Gras*, but also every Saturday and Sunday.

B. Interruption of Prescription

1. Definition

Prescription can be "interrupted." Interruption stops the progress of prescription in its tracks and, what is more, wipes out the time of prescription that has been accumulated up to that point.

2. Varieties

The doctrine recognizes two varieties of interruption: natural interruption and civil interruption. Whereas natural interruption stems from some physical act on, to, or with the thing, civil interruption stems from a juridical act or a judicial act regarding the thing. Let us now consider each of these types of interruption in turn.

a. Natural Interruption

Natural interruption is addressed in **LSA-C.C. Art. 3465**, which provides that "[a]cquisitive prescription is interrupted when possession is lost." As we learned earlier in our study of the law of possession, possession can be lost in any of three ways. The two most important are "eviction" and "abandonment." These constitute the causes of natural interruption of prescription.

1) Eviction

Eviction in the context of the interruption of acquisitive prescription means precisely the same thing as eviction in the context of possession. In that latter context, it will be recalled, eviction refers to some act that cuts off the possessor's *corpus* of the thing against his will and, further, is of such magnitude that it would be sufficient to bring home to the possessor, were he to witness the act, that his dominion over the thing is being seriously challenged.

When eviction in this sense occurs, acquisitive prescription is interrupted—instantly. **LSA-C.C. 3465, ¶1.** But look at paragraph two of **Art. 3465**, which takes away some of the punch of this rule: "The interruption is considered never to have occurred if the possessor recovers possession within one year." As we learned earlier in our study of the law of possession, possession may be "recovered" in either of two ways: by (1) reestablishing corporeal possession, be it by evicting or usurping the evictor, or (2) filing (and eventually winning) a timely possessory action. Thus, even though interruption occurs upon eviction, it will be deemed never to have occurred if the prescriber recovers possession within a year.

2) Abandonment

Like eviction, abandonment has the same meaning in the context of acquisitive prescription as in the context of possession. As was noted earlier, abandonment is the juridical act whereby the possessor simultaneously relinquishes his *corpus* and *animus domini* with respect to the thing.

Possession is interrupted immediately upon the possessor's abandonment of the thing. That this is so is confirmed by comment (b) to **LSA-C.C. Art. 3465**: "there should be no doubt that acquisitive prescription is... interrupted when the possessor abandons his possession."

Can interruption of prescription due to abandonment be retroactively "wiped out," as can interruption of prescription due to eviction? Look, again, at **Art. 3465, ¶2**: "The interruption is considered never to have occurred if the possessor recovers possession within one year." This legislation draws no distinction between causes of the loss of possession, in particular, between eviction and abandonment. Taken literally and standing on its own, then, this legislative text suggests that what is true of eviction is also true of abandonment (loss of the right to possess).

b. Civil Interruption

There are two causes of civil interruption: (1) suit by the owner against the possessor for the recognition and protection of his ownership right and (2) acknowledgment of the owner's ownership right by the possessor.

1) By the Owner (Suit)

The first mode of civil interruption of prescription—that accomplished by means of a legal action brought by the owner against the possessor—is addressed in **LSA-C.C. Arts. 3462–3463.** To produce a civil interruption, the suit in question must, in one sense or another, seek to "try title" to the land, that is, request a judgment to the effect that the plaintiff is the "owner" of the land. Legal actions of this type include, in the case of immovables, the petitory action and the boundary action and, in the case of movables, the revendicatory action. As a general rule, such a suit, if it is to have interruptive effect, must be brought in a court of proper jurisdiction and venue.[1] But by way of exception, even if the plaintiff gets the jurisdiction or the venue wrong, all hope is not necessarily lost. **LSA-C.C. Art. 3462, sent. 2**, states: "If action is commenced in an incompetent court, or in an improper venue, prescription is interrupted only as to a defendant served by process within the prescriptive period."

The interruption accomplished by the filing of a suit, like at least some other forms of interruption, may be retroactively undone. Consider **LSA-C.C. Art. 3463:**

> An interruption of prescription resulting from the filing of a suit... continues as long as the suit is pending. Interruption is

1. What constitutes a court of proper jurisdiction and venue is determined by the Code of Civil Procedure.

> considered never to have occurred if the plaintiff abandons, voluntarily dismisses, or fails to prosecute the suit at trial.

The meanings of "voluntarily dismiss" and "fails to prosecute" are clear enough. But to identify what we mean by the "abandonment" of a suit, we must have resort, once again, to the Code of Civil Procedure. **LSA-C.C.P. Art. 561** provides: "An action is abandoned when the parties fail to take any step in its prosecution or defense in the trial court for a period of five years. This provision shall be operative without formal order." Thus, if the plaintiff does not do anything to "move the ball forward" in the litigation, e.g., does not file any motions, does not request any discovery, does not ask the court to schedule any hearings or status conferences, then his suit will be considered "abandoned." And when that happens, any interruptive effect the suit may have had will come to an end and, beyond that, will be deemed never to have occurred at all.

2) By the Possessor (Acknowledgement)

LSA-C.C. Art. 3464 provides that "[p]rescription is interrupted when one acknowledges the right of the person against whom he had commenced to prescribe." To much the same effect is comment (b) to that article: "Acquisitive prescription is interrupted when the possessor acknowledges the right of the owner."

Regarding the form that such an acknowledgment may take, the rule is "anything goes." **LSA-C.C. Art. 3463 cmt. (e).** First of all, an acknowledgment need not be express; it may be, instead, merely implied, even tacit. One classic example of tacit acknowledgment is this: where the prescriber, after possessing the thing for a time and knowing full well that it belongs to someone else, takes out a lease of the thing from this "someone else." Second, an acknowledgement need not be in writing; it may be, instead, merely oral or designated by some other sign.

3. Effect of Interruption

The effect of the interruption of acquisitive prescription is specified in **LSA-C.C. Art. 3466:**

> If prescription is interrupted, the time that has run is not counted. Prescription commences to run anew from the last day of interruption.

So, when prescription is interrupted, the time that has already accumulated is wiped out. In other words, the prescriber does not get to pick up where he left off. Thus, when the interruption ends, it is as though the "clock" of the prescriber's time starts "ticking" again from "zero."

C. Suspension of Prescription

1. *Definition*

Prescription can be "suspended." Unlike interruption, which stops the running of prescription altogether, suspension merely "paralyzes" or "retards" the running of prescription for a time.

2. *Causes for Suspension*

a. General Rule

The general rule regarding the suspension of prescription is found in **LSA-C.C. Art. 3467**: "Prescription runs against all persons unless exception is established by legislation." Suspension of prescription, then, is something extraordinary.

b. Exceptions

The exceptions to the general rule are few and limited in number. Let us look at some of them now.

1) Familial Relationships

By the terms of **LSA-C.C. Art. 3469**, prescription is suspended between "spouses during marriage." This suspension is temporary, that is, prescription is suspended for so long as the marriage lasts. Suspension ends when the marriage ends, i.e., at death, at divorce, or at annulment. Unlike divorce or annulment, legal separation does not end the suspension of prescription. There is another familial relationship besides marriage that provides cause for the suspension of acquisitive prescription: that between parent and child. The suspensive effect of this relationship is also temporary as prescription is suspended only "during minority."

2) Certain "Fiduciary" Relationships

According to **Art. 3469**, "[p]rescription is suspended as between... curators and interdicts during interdiction, tutors and minors during tutorship, and caretakers and minors during minority." What these situations have in common is that they entail relationships of trust, what in the common law tradition is called "fiduciary" relationships.

3) Registered Immovables of Municipalities

Municipalities benefit from yet another cause of suspension of prescription, but it is one that requires them to be proactive. The municipality must file into the conveyance records a document that "contains a description of the property and a declaration that it is public property belonging to the municipality." **LSA-R.S. 9:5804.** The recordation of such a document has the effect of suspending the running of prescription: "[T]he recording shall suspend the running of prescription during the time the ownership of the property shall remain vested in the name of the municipality." ***Id.***

4) **Contra Non Valentem, Etc.**

Relying on the traditional civil law maxim *contra non valentem agere nulla currit præscriptio* (prescription does not run against him who is incapable of acting), our jurisprudence has recognized a number of other situations, aside from those that are provided for by legislation, in which prescription is suspended. Those situations are as follows: (1) where there was some legal cause which prevented the courts or their officers from taking cognizance of or acting on the plaintiff's action; (2) where there was some condition coupled with the contract or connected with the proceedings which prevented the creditor from suing or acting; (3) where the debtor himself has done some act effectually to prevent the creditor from availing himself of his cause of action; and (4) where the cause of action is not known or reasonably knowable by the plaintiff, even though his ignorance is not induced by the defendant, provided that it is not attributable to the plaintiff's own willfulness or neglect.

To date, the Louisiana courts have had occasion to apply the maxim only in cases that involved *liberative* prescription. When the courts are finally invited to apply it to cases that involve *acquisitive* prescription, should they accept the invitation? A survey of foreign civil law doctrine and jurisprudence, including that of France, supports an affirmative answer.

3. *Effect of Suspension*

The effect of the suspension of prescription is spelled out in **LSA-C.C. Art.** 3472:

> The period of suspension is not counted toward accrual of prescription. Prescription commences to run again upon the termination of the period of suspension.

So, when prescription is suspended, the prescriber gets credit for the time that accumulated before the cause of the suspension arose. And the prescriber picks up where he left off when and if the cause of the suspension is removed, adding to the time that he accumulated before the cause of the suspension arose. Thus, when the suspension ends, it is as though the "clock" of the prescriber's time *resumes* "ticking," picking up exactly from where it left off.

D. Renunciation of Prescription

1. *Definition*

Prescription can be "renounced." Comment (c) to **LSA-C.C. Art. 3449** tells us that "[r]enunciation of prescription is a technical term designating the abandonment of rights derived from an accrual of prescription." The concept is analogous to that of "waiver."

2. *Attributes*

To be effective, renunciation of prescription must be "clear," "unequivocal," and "absolute." In other words, the intention to renounce must be manifested so clearly that there can be no doubt but that the alleged renouncer desired to give up his rights.

According to foreign doctrine, for renunciation of prescription to be effective, it must also be made "knowingly" (in French, *en connaissance de cause*), that is, with full knowledge of the facts and the law. In other words, one cannot renounce a right that one has acquired through prescription unless one knows one has that right. There is, then, no such thing as an "unwitting" renunciation.

3. *Form*

Whether a renunciation of prescription is subject to any requirements of form depends on the classification of the thing in which the putative prescriber has supposedly acquired an interest as movable or immovable.

a. Immovables

According to **LSA-C.C. Art. 3450**, "with respect to immovables, renunciation of acquisitive prescription must be express and in writing."

b. Movables

The renunciation of acquisitive prescription in *movables*, however, is not subject to any special requirements of form. That this is so finds confirmation in **Art. 3450, ¶1, sent. 1**, which tells us that, as a general rule, "[r]enunciation may be express or tacit."

Though the meaning of an express renunciation of acquisitive prescription is immediately clear, that of a tacit renunciation of acquisitive prescription is not. What the Civil Code means by tacit renunciation is found in **Art. 3450, ¶1, sent. 2**: "Tacit renunciation results from circumstances that give rise to a presumption that the advantages of prescription have been abandoned." To put it another way: tacit renunciation results from any act that, if performed before the running of prescription, would have constituted an "acknowledgment" of prescription, provided that the act is made knowingly. Here are some examples. First, the possessor, knowing full well that he has acquired an interest in the thing via prescription, leases the subject property from someone else. Second, the possessor, knowing full well that he has acquired an interest in the thing via prescription, files suit to partition the thing between himself and someone else. Third, the possessor, knowing full well that he has acquired an interest in the thing via prescription, complies with someone else's demand to surrender the thing.

3. *Time of Renunciation*

According to **Art. 3449**, one may renounce prescription "only after it has accrued." To attempt to renounce prescription before it has accrued, then, is to act prematurely. But this does not mean that a premature renunciation has no effect at all; it does, but the effect is that of an acknowledgment.

4. *Effect of Renunciation*

When a possessor renounces prescription, the effects of his prescription are retroactively wiped out. That means, first, that he is considered never to have been the owner and, second, that the prior owner is considered to have always remained the owner.

III. Effects of Acquisitive Prescription

The principal effect of acquisitive prescription, that from which all of the others flow, is that the prescriber acquires ownership or whatever other real right he has exercised. This effect, of course, arises at the end of the prescriptive period.

Though prescription does not produce its effects until the end of the prescriptive period, these effects, according to the doctrine, are felt "retroactively." In other words, the effects of prescription, once reproduced, are deemed to "relate back" to the moment at which prescription began.

The retroactivity of acquisitive prescription has several important consequences. First, any real rights that the original owner may have created on the property during the prescriptive period, e.g., a predial servitude in favor of a neighboring estate or a mortgage in favor of a bank, are retroactively invalidated. Second, any real rights that the prescriber may have created on the property during the prescriptive period are retroactively validated. Third, the prescriber, even one who possessed in bad faith, is entitled to keep the fruits and the products that he took from the property during the prescriptive period.

SUB-CHAPTER B

Constitutive Elements of Acquisitive Prescription: Elements Common to All Modes of Acquisitive Prescription

I. Thing Susceptible of Acquisition by Prescription

Among the requirements that are common to *all* forms of acquisitive prescription we must, to start with, number the requirement that the thing in question be "susceptible of acquisition by prescription." It must be acknowledged that this proposition, though in some sense seemingly self-evident, does not immediately "jump out" at one who reads the pertinent Civil Code articles. That is because the only express reference to such a requirement to be found in those articles appears in **LSA-C.C. Art. 3475**, which, by its terms, pertains only to *abridged* acquisitive prescription of *immovables*: "The requisites for the acquisitive prescription of ten years are: possession of ten years, good faith, just title, and *a thing susceptible of acquisition by prescription.*" There is no counterpart to such a rule among the articles on unabridged acquisitive prescription of immovables or for either species of acquisitive prescription of movables. But look at **LSA-C.C. Art. 3488**: "The rules governing acquisitive prescription of ten years apply to the prescription of thirty years to the extent that their application is compatible with the prescription of thirty years." The rule regarding a thing's susceptibility to acquisitive prescription falls into that category. For this reason, we can consider the species of unabridged acquisitive prescription of immovables to be "covered" under the rule that "acquisitive prescription presupposes a thing that is susceptible of prescription." But that still leaves acquisitive prescription of movables, whether abridged or unabridged, "uncovered." As to these modes of acquisitive prescription, there is a regrettable *lacuna* in the legislation. The good news is that there is really no doubt regarding how this *lacuna* should be "filled." It is clear from general legal principles (not to mention the logical principle of "non-contradiction"!), and is well settled in both the doctrine and the jurisprudence, that one cannot prescribe a movable that is not susceptible of acquisitive prescription. We can, then, confidently conclude that the requirement "susceptibility of prescription" applies to *all* forms of acquisitive prescription.

The task that remains is to determine which things satisfy the requirement, i.e., which things are and are not susceptible of acquisitive prescription. The answer to that question depends in large part on the classification of the thing, to be more precise, on whether the thing is a common thing, a public thing, or a private thing.

A. Common Things

Common things are not susceptible of acquisitive prescription. Comment (b) to **LSA-C.C. Art. 3485** tells us that "*[c]ommon things* and public things are insusceptible of acquisitive prescription." **LSA-C.C. Art. 449** further tells us that "common things may not be owned by anyone." If that is true, then they cannot possibly be prescribed against.

B. Public Things

Public things are also not susceptible of acquisitive prescription. Look back at comment (b) to **Art. 3485**: "Common things and *public things* are insusceptible of acquisitive prescription." Comment (b) to **LSA-C.C. Art. 450** also tells us that public things are "out of commerce." That which is out of commerce is, by definition, insusceptible of acquisitive prescription.

C. Private Things

1. General Rule

As a general rule, private things are susceptible of acquisitive prescription. Look at **Art. 3485**: "All private things are susceptible of prescription unless prescription is excluded by legislation."

2. Exception

This general rule, **Art. 3485** tells us, admits of exceptions, exceptions carved out by other provisions of law. One such exception is that set out in LA. CONST. ART. 12, § 13 (1974), which provides that "[p]rescription shall not run against the state in any civil matter, unless otherwise provided in this constitution or expressly by law." This constitutional provision refers not only to liberative prescription and prescription of nonuse, but also acquisitive prescription. *See* **LSA-C.C. Art. 453 cmt. (c)** ("Private property of the state is exempt from prescription.").

Applying these rules seldom presents any great difficulties. To this generalization, there is one important exception: where the thing in question belongs to a political subdivision of the state. In such a case, the challenge is to determine whether the thing is public or private. (The distinction between public and private things of political subdivisions was addressed earlier in this Précis.) Making this determination is critical: if the thing is public, then it cannot be prescribed against; but if it is private, then it can be.

II. Possession

"Possession" is also among the essential requisites for *all* forms of acquisitive prescription. We find authority for this proposition in **LSA-C.C. Art. 3446**, which purports to define acquisitive prescription: "Acquisitive prescription is a mode of acquiring ownership or other real rights *by possession* for a period of time." **LSA-C.C. Art. 3476, ¶1** further tells us that "[t]he possessor must have corporeal possession, or civil possession preceded by corporeal possession, to acquire a thing by prescription."

"Possession" in the context of the law of acquisitive prescription has the same meaning as it does in the context of the law of possession. It is, in short, a factual relationship between a person and a thing characterized by that person's having *corpus* of the thing (be it presently or formerly and be it in reality or constructively) and *animus domini* toward the thing.

LSA-C.C. Art. 3476, ¶1 addresses the question of what kind or *kinds* of possession can provide the predicate for a claim of acquisitive prescription. It says: "The possessor must have corporeal possession, or civil possession preceded by corporeal possession, to acquire a thing by prescription." So, corporeal possession, not surprisingly, is sufficient, but it is not necessary, because civil possession will do. Constructive possession, however, is not mentioned by name. Nevertheless, this seems to be simply because the drafters of the article thought it so obvious that it need not be mentioned. In any event, comment (f) to **LSA-C.C. Art. 3476** and comment (b) to **LSA-C.C. Art. 3488** make it clear that constructive possession, too, is sufficient. In the end, then, any of the three forms of possession suffices.

For purposes of acquisitive prescription as for other purposes, possession must possess certain virtues or, to put the point negatively, must avoid certain vices. **Art. 3476, ¶2** tells us that "[t]he possession must be continuous, uninterrupted, *peaceable*, public, and unequivocal." The lesson, then, of **Art. 3476, ¶2** is that possession, to form a basis for a claim of acquisitive prescription, must be free of the "vices of possession" about which we learned earlier in our study of the law of possession.

III. Delay

A. General Principles

In order to acquire a real right in a thing via acquisitive prescription, one not only must possess a thing, but also must possess it for a specified period of time. The length of time varies according to the nature of the thing—immovable or movable—and according to the nature of the prescription—abridged or unabridged.

B. Continuation of Possession and Tacking of Possessions

1. In General

If it were necessary that the possessor *himself* possess the thing for the entire duration of the specified period, then acquisitive prescription, in particular, ordinary acquisitive prescription of immovables, would seldom be accomplished. To avoid that result, the law permits the possessor, under certain circumstances, to add the time of his ancestor-in-title's possession (if any) to his own.

That this is so should hardly come as a surprise. As we saw in our study of the law of possession, in particular, the part of it entitled the "junction of possessions," the possessor, under certain circumstances, is permitted to add his ancestor-in-title's time of possession to his own for various purposes, including satisfaction of the delay requirement for acquiring the "right to possess." What we are considering now is but a particular application of general principles on junction of possessions.

Let us recall the most basic of those general principles. Though the junction of possession can take place as much in a particular succession as in a general succession, the mechanism whereby this occurs varies from one case to the other. Reflecting this difference in mechanism is a difference in terminology. In the case of a universal succession, the successor, who is considered to be the alter ego of the ancestor, is understood to "continue" the possession of the ancestor. In such a case, the time of possession amassed by the ancestor is considered to belong as much to the successor as it did to the ancestor. Hence, one speaks of the "continuation" of possession when the junction of possessions is entailed in such a succession. By contrast, in the case of a particular succession, the successor, who is considered to be a stranger to the ancestor, "starts a new possession" of his own. In such a case, the time of possession amassed by the ancestor, though it is his and his alone and not that of the successor, can nevertheless be added, "tacked on," to that of the successor, provided certain requirements are met. Hence, one speaks of the "tacking" of possessions when the junction of possessions is entailed in such a succession.

2. Special Problem: Spatial Extent of Joined Possession

In the context of the law of acquisitive prescription, we encounter a complication with respect to the junction of possessions that we did not encounter in the context of the law of possession. That complication can perhaps best be expressed with the help of a question: "Granted that a universal successor, by 'continuing' his ancestor's possession, or a particular successor, by 'tacking' to his ancestor's possession, may be able to count his ancestor's time of possession as his own, with respect to *how much* of the possessed thing does this take place?" Though it is theoretically possible that this question might arise in connection with any number of things, provided they be large enough, in practice it arises only in connection with immovables, to be still more specific, land. In any event, it turns out that the answer to the question varies dramatically depending on the nature of the succession, that is, whether it is universal or particular.

a. Universal Successors: Spatially Unrestricted Tacking

A universal successor, as the alter ego of his ancestor-in-title, continues whatever possession the ancestor-in-title had, no more and no less. Consequently, the spatial extent of the universal successor's possession is identical to that of his ancestor-in-title.

Consider this example. A certain X, with title to a certain tract of land A, takes corporeal possession not only of A but also of the adjacent tract of land B. In time, X voluntarily quits his *corpus* of both tracts, at which point his possession of them becomes "civil." Later, X dies intestate, survived by his sole heir Y. After X's death, Y takes corporeal possession of both tract A and tract B. In this case, Y continues the possession of X as to both tract A and tract B.

b. Particular Successors

1) General Rule: No Tacking Beyond Title

A particular successor, as a stranger to his ancestor, begins a new, different possession of his own. In the words of **LSA-C.C. Art. 3506(28)**, "only… the rights appertaining to the thing which is sold, ceded or bequeathed to him" get transferred to a particular possessor. But rights appertaining to *other* things that the ancestor may have had do *not* get transferred to a particular successor. The upshot of these principles is that a particular successor "can't tack beyond his title," in other words, cannot count as his own his ancestor's time of possession with respect to any land other than that described in the title that the particular successor got from his ancestor.

Consider this example. A certain X, with title to a certain tract of land A, takes corporeal possession not only of A but also of the adjacent tract of land B. In time, X voluntarily quits his *corpus* of both tracts, at which point his possession of them becomes "civil." Later, X sells tract A (but only tract A) to Y. After the sale, Y takes corporeal possession of both tract A and tract B. In this case, though Y can tack X's possession of tract A to his own, he cannot tack X's possession of tract B to his own.

In a case such as this one, the application of the principle "a particular successor can't tack beyond his title" seems almost self-evident. After all, no successor, be he universal or particular, can claim the benefit of "more than he got." And in the case of a particular succession, all that the successor "gets" is the ancestor's right in the particular thing that is the object of the transfer.

But now consider the following hypothetical, a slight variation of the original. Imagine, now, that when X first took possession of tract B—the one to which he did not have title—he did so by mistake, believing that tract B was within his title. Imagine further that, immediately before the sale of tract A by X to Y, X took Y out to show him "his land"; that this land, as it was shown to Y, included not only tract A but also tract B; that X, in fact, intended to sell and Y intended to buy not only tract A but also tract B; but that, when X and Y thereafter drew up the act of sale, X, still not realizing that tract B lay outside of tract A, simply copied the description of tract A out of the act of sale that he, X, had received from his own ancestor-in-title. Understand, then, the situation: though the parties intended to make Y a particular successor not only of tract A but also of tract B, the act of sale—the "title" that Y receives—by its terms, refers only to tract A. As unfair and counterintuitive as it may seem, the principle that a particular successor may not tack beyond his title comes into play no less in this hypothetical than in the original! Later on down the road, if Y should have to resort to acquisitive prescription to defend his right to tract B, he will not be able to tack X's time of possession of that tract on to his own. The terms of Y's title prevent it. Or so it would seem!

2) Exception: "Boundary Tacking" (Tacking Beyond Title Up to Visible Boundaries on Adjacent Land)

The rule that a particular successor cannot tack beyond his title is subject to an exception. The foundation for this exception, commonly known as "boundary tacking," is found in **LSA-C.C. Art. 794**: "If a party and his ancestors in title possessed for thirty years without interruption, within visible bounds, more land than their title called for, the boundary shall be fixed along these bounds."

Using this article as a springboard, the jurisprudence and the doctrine have identified a number of prerequisites for boundary tacking. First, the land to which the successor has title must be adjacent to (contiguous with) the land as to which he wishes to claim the benefit of boundary tacking. This is the so-called "juridical link" requirement. Second, the land with respect to which the successor wishes to claim the benefit of boundary tacking must be bounded by "visible bounds," that is, a natural or physical boundary. When we say the boundary must be visible, we mean that a party cannot simply extend his possession beyond his title to the middle of a field. Absent some real boundary up to which possession might take place, e.g., a fence, tree line, or ditch, boundary tacking is not available. Third, not only the successor, but also his ancestor before him, must have possessed the land as to which the successor wishes to claim the benefit of boundary tacking. Fourth, the sum of the time of possession of the successor and the time of possession of the ancestor must equal, if not exceed, 30 years.

Let us return, now, to the earlier hypothetical in which Y, under general tacking principles, would be precluded from tacking X's possession of tract B onto his own. Is it possible that, by invoking boundary tacking, Y might be able to extricate himself from this predicament? The answer is "maybe." Everything depends on whether Y can show that the prerequisites for boundary tacking were satisfied. Clearly some of them are, for example, that the land to which Y has title—tract A—is adjacent to that as to which he wants to invoke boundary tacking and that Y and his ancestor, X, both possessed the land as to which he wants to invoke boundary tacking. What we do not know, however, is whether tract B was bounded by visible bounds and whether the sum of the times of X's and Y's respective possession of that tract at least equals 30 years. If the answers to both of these questions turn out to be "yes," then Y will, after all, be able to "tack" with respect not only to tract A, for which he has title, but also tract B, for which he does not.

It is important to note that boundary tacking is available only in connection with unabridged (that is, 30 years) acquisitive prescription of immovables. That this is so is indicated by the very text of **LSA-C.C. Art. 794**, which speaks of "possess[ion] for thirty years." This is as it must be. As we will learn later when we study the abridged acquisitive prescription of immovables, one of the requirements therefor is "just title" to the land with respect to which acquisitive prescription is claimed. Now, in any case in which boundary tacking might be an issue, it is a given that the successor does not have a just title to the land in question. That is so because, by definition, he will not have any title to it at all. If he did have such a title, then he would not be in the position of having to rely on the exception of boundary tacking; to the contrary, he would be able to rely on the general rule, that according to which he is allowed to tack within his title.

SUB-CHAPTER C

Constitutive Elements of Acquisitive Prescription: Elements Common to All Modes of Acquisitive Prescription

Having examined the elements that are common to all modes of acquisitive prescription, we now need to examine the elements that are peculiar to each of those modes. To do so, we must distinguish, first of all, between acquisitive prescription of immovables, on the one hand, and acquisitive prescription of movables, on the other. Within each of those categories, we must draw yet another distinction, namely, that between unabridged and abridged acquisitive prescription.

I. Immovables

A. Unabridged Acquisitive Prescription

Unabridged acquisitive prescription of immovables has only one unique requirement, namely, the length of the required delay. According to **LSA-C.C. Art. 3486**, that length is 30 years.

B. Abridged Acquisitive Prescription

Abridged acquisitive prescription of immovables has several distinctive requirements. Most of these are patent on the face of the applicable Civil Code articles (**LSA-C.C. Arts. 3473** and **3475**): (i) just title, (ii) good faith, and (iii) a delay of 10 years. But there is yet another respect in which abridged prescription differs from ordinary prescription, a difference that is not clearly reflected in the Civil Code. This difference pertains to the "junction" of possessions ("continuation" of possession or "tacking" of possessions). As we shall see, the junction of possessions for purposes of abridged prescription is subject to a host of restrictions that do not affect the junction of possessions for purposes of unabridged prescription.

1. Just Title

The requirement of just title is addressed in **LSA-C.C. Art. 3483.** Many of the elements of just title are specifically enumerated in this article. But there are still several others, not mentioned in the article, that derive from general principles. We will examine each of these sets of elements in turn.

a. Elements Enumerated in Article 3483

1) Juridical Act

LSA-C.C. Art. 3483 tells us that a "just title" is, first and foremost, a "juridical act." This term is not defined in **Art. 3483** or, for that matter, anywhere else in the Civil Code. Its meaning, however, is clear. Consider, first, comment (b) to **Art. 3483**, which informs us that "a *juridical act*… is… a licit act intended to have legal consequences." Further information about juridical acts can be gleaned from **comment (b)** to **LSA-C.C. Art. 395**. A juridical act, then, is a voluntary act, that is, an act of will, done by the actor for the very purpose of attempting to produce the legal effects that he knows will be produced by that kind of act. Examples of juridical acts are legion: contracts, testaments, acknowledgments, renunciations, etc.

2) A Translative Act

a) Definition

To qualify as a "just title," the juridical act in question must be, to use the words of **Art. 3483**, "sufficient to transfer ownership or another real right." In more technical terms, the requirement is that the juridical act be "*translative* of ownership or of another real right." **Art. 3483 cmt. (b).** Comment (b) further tells us that "the law merely requires an act which, if it had been executed by the true owner, would have conveyed ownership or established another real right." The article itself provides several examples: "such as a sale, donation, or exchange." To these could be added one other: "giving in payment" or as many in Louisiana, following French usage, still call it, *dation en paiement*.

b) Distinctions

1] DECLARATIVE ACTS

An act which is merely declarative, rather than translative, of rights cannot be a just title. The classic example is the so-called "judgment of possession," the rather ill-chosen name for the judgment whereby the court recognizes who the successors of a deceased person are and to what property of his they are entitled. This judgment is not *translative*, that is, it does not, of itself, convey or transfer anything from the deceased to his successors. Rather, it merely *declares*, that is, recognizes or acknowledges, what the successors have already received from the deceased, be it by virtue of some legacy that he left to them or by virtue of the law of intestacy. It is the legacy or the intestate succession that does the transferring from deceased to successors, not the judgment of possession. Therefore, a judgment of possession does not provide a "just title."

Does this mean that successors who obtain a judgment of possession have no just title? Not at all. If the successor in question was left a legacy, then this legacy—another term for "donation mortis causa"—is the successor's title. Provided it meets all the requirements of a just title, *this* title may well be just. If the successor in question was not left a legacy—if, in other words, he was an intestate successor—then he is a "universal successor" and, as such, inherits whatever title, if any, the deceased may have had. If *that* title was just, then the successor can now claim it as his own. The point is simply this: the *judgment of possession itself* adds *nothing* to whatever title (if any) the successor may have received through the succession.

2] ACTS GENERATIVE OF MERELY PERSONAL (CREDIT) RIGHTS

A juridical act that creates or transfers mere credit (as opposed to real) rights cannot constitute a just title. Perhaps the most common example of such an act is a lease. A lease does not convey or transfer to the lessee an ownership right or any other kind of real right in the leased property; it merely grants the lessee the right—and a purely personal right at that—to use the leased property for a certain term. Acts that convey nothing but credits rights are not "translative," in the sense in which that term is used here, and, for that reason, will not do for just title.

3) A Written Title

To be just, the title must be "written." **LSA-C.C. Art. 3483.** Thus, an oral title, and *a fortiori* one that is "tacit," will not suffice.

4) In Proper Form

To be just, the writing that constitutes the title must be "valid in form." **LSA-C.C. Art. 3483**. Precisely what form is required depends on whether the juridical act is gratuitous (a donation) or onerous (a sale, exchange, or *dation en paiement*). If it is gratuitous, then the writing must be in "authentic form."[2] **LSA-C.C. Art. 1541.** If it is onerous, then authentic form *may* be used for the writing, but it is *not required.* A mere "act under private signature"[3] will suffice. **LSA-C.C. Art. 2440.**

5) A Recorded Title

"The act must be... filed for registry" if it is to provide a just title. To be filed properly, the act must be placed in the "conveyance records" (as opposed to the "mortgage records") of "the parish in which the immovable is situated." **LSA-C.C. Art. 3483.**

b. Elements Derived from General Principles

1) Not Absolutely Null

An absolutely null act, inasmuch as it has no legal effects, cannot supply a just title. This self-evident principle finds support in comment (c), paragraph three, to **LSA-C.C. Art. 3483**, which reads as follows: "According to French doctrine and jurisprudence, an *absolutely null* juridical act does not constitute a just title. This view has been followed by Louisiana courts." The term "absolutely null" is defined in **LSA-C.C. Art. 2030**: "A contract is absolutely null when it violates a rule of public order, as when the object of a contract is illicit or immoral." Some examples of this are contracts for meretricious services and gambling contracts.

It matters, for purposes of the law of just title, whether the juridical act in question is relatively as opposed to absolutely null. In other words, the rule is not that nullity of *any kind* precludes just title, but that only *absolute* nullity precludes just title. "A contract is relatively null," **LSA-C.C. Art. 2031** tells us, "when it violates a rule intended for the protection of private parties, as when a party lacked capacity or did not give free consent at the time the contract was made." Thus, whereas an abso-

2. **LSA-C.C. Art. 1833(A)** defines "authentic form" as a writing executed before a notary public or other officer authorized to perform that function, in the presence of two witnesses, and signed by each party who executed it, by each witness, and by each notary public before whom it was executed."

3. As **LSA-C.C. Art. 1837** and **cmt. (b)** thereto indicate, an "act under private signature" is defined as a writing that is signed by both parties. But note the exception mentioned in the comment.

lutely null contract violates a rule of public order, a relatively null contract does not. There is yet another difference between the two types of nullity, one that is of greater relevance to the matter at hand: unlike an absolutely null act, which is null *ab initio*, in other words, produces no legal effects from the get go, a relatively null act, unless and until it is declared null, is fully productive of legal effects. Thus, whereas an absolute nullity renders a title unjust, relative nullity does not.

2) Not Subject to a Still-Pending Suspensive Condition

Imagine an act translative of ownership, such as a sale or a donation *inter vivos*, that is subject to a suspensive condition. Such an act does not convey ownership or any other real right unless and until the condition is fulfilled. That is so because, by virtue of well-established principles of the law of obligations in general, the obligations of which such an act is generative, above all, the obligation "to give" ownership or some other real right, does not yet fully exist. Thus, until the condition is fulfilled, such an act is not "translative" of title and, as a result, does not provide a just title.

The same is *not* true of an act that is subject to a *resolutory* condition. An act of this type conveys ownership or whatever other real right is its object *presently*, i.e., at the moment the act is entered into. To be sure, that ownership interest or other real right can and will be wiped out if and when the condition is later fulfilled, but unless and until that happens, the transferor is deemed to have translated his real right to the transferee.

3) Not Putative (But Real)

To be just, a title must be real as opposed to putative. A putative title (from the Latin verb *putare*, meaning "to think") is one that "is believed to exist but which in reality does not exist," as comment (e) to **LSA-C.C. Art. 3483** puts it. One of the most common cases in which the problem of putative title arises is that of a botched sale, specifically, one in which, through a mistake of the parties, the description of the land that is included in the act of sale refers to less land than the parties had intended to convey. With respect to the "extra" land, that is, the land that lies outside that which is described in the act of sale, the buyer's title is merely "putative."

2. Good Faith

a. Substantive Matters

1) Definition

Paraphrasing **LSA-C.C. Art. 3480**, one could define "good faith" for purposes of acquisitive prescription this way: it is a reasonable belief, in the light of objective considerations, that one is the owner of the thing one possesses.

But what, precisely, must one believe in order to believe that one is "the owner of the thing one possesses"? In other words, exactly what *other* things must one believe in order to have *this* belief? That is the important and, it turns out, somewhat difficult question. This much is certain: belief that one owns what one possesses presupposes the belief that one's author-in-title was the true owner. But must the possessor, in addition to *this*, also believe that there are no "defects" (that is, causes of absolute or relative nullity) in his own title, that is, the title he received from his ancestor-in-title?

In France the answer is now, and apparently always has been, "no, one does not have to believe that one's own title, too, is free of defects." According to the great French civil law scholar Planiol, "[i]t is not necessary that the possessor be ignorant of the other defects [i.e., other than that his transferor was not really the owner] that may exist in his title of acquisition. The alienator was, for example, incapable." So, in France, belief that one's own title, as opposed to one's author's title, is defective on account of lack of capacity, lack of free consent, or some other cause of relative nullity is *immaterial* to good faith. The only thing that matters is one's belief about the integrity of one's author's title.

But Louisiana is—or at least was—different. The Civil Code of 1870, unlike the French Civil Code, set forth a definition of the antonym of "good faith," i.e., "bad faith": "The possessor in bad faith is he who possesses as master, but who assumes this quality, when he well knows that he has no title to the thing, *or that his title is vicious and defective.*" Under that article, then, good faith was precluded not only by knowledge that one's author's title was defective, but also by knowledge that one's own title was defective. Though this article was not reproduced in the revision, it is at least possible that the redactors of the revised articles did not intend to abandon the principle of that article in its entirety. Indeed, to the extent that the 1870 Code article took aim at *absolutely* null "defects" (in contrast to *relatively* null "defects"), the principle of that article is perfectly compatible with the definition of "good faith" found in current **Art. 3480.** A person who is on the receiving end of a purportedly translative act that he *knows* is absolutely null cannot "reasonably believe" that he "is the owner" of the object of that act.

2) Nature

The "good faith" required for acquisitive prescription is, at once, both "subjective" and "objective." "Subjective" good faith is good faith in fact. A person is in subjective good faith if his actual state of mind is such that he believes he is the owner, no matter how unreasonable, unrealistic, or downright stupid that belief may be. "Objective" good faith is *constructive* or *fictitious* good faith. For a possessor to be in objective good faith, it must be the case that a reasonable person under the same circumstances would believe that he is the owner. In short, then, a possessor is in good faith if and only if (1) he truly believes, in his "heart of hearts," that he is the owner (subjective good faith) and (2) this belief is "reasonable" (objective good faith).

3) Timing

LSA-C.C. Art. 3482 says that "[i]t is sufficient that possession has commenced in good faith; subsequent bad faith does not prevent the accrual of prescription of ten years." This is the modern expression of the ancient Roman law maxim *mala fida superveniens usucapionem non impedit* (bad faith that comes later does not impede acquisitive prescription). So, the only point in time at which good faith is required is the time at which possession commences.

b. Procedural Matters

1) The Presumption of Good Faith

To figure out who bears the burden of proof on the issue of good faith, i.e., the person who claims abridged acquisitive prescription or the person who opposes that claim, we look to **LSA-C.C. Art. 3481**, which provides that "[g]ood faith is presumed." In the words of comment (b) to that article, the effect of this presumption is that "one who alleges that the possessor is not in good faith has the burden of proving his allegation."

2) *Evidence of Bad Faith*

To see how the opponent of the putative possessor carries that burden or, in other words, rebuts the presumption, one must look at the rest of **LSA-C.C. Art. 3481**: "This presumption is rebutted on proof that the possessor knows, or should know, that he is not owner of the thing he possesses." In other words, the opponent must put on proof of "bad faith," more specifically, proof of either "subjective" bad faith ("proof that the possessor knows") or "objective" bad faith ("proof that the possessor... should know").

It bears noting that the opponent, to meet his burden of proof, need only show that the possessor "suspected" or, at the very least, "should have suspected" that he did not own the thing. In short, "suspicion" kills "good faith.[4]

a) Errors of Fact

1] IN GENERAL

LSA-C.C. Art. 3481 says that "[n]either *error of fact* nor error of law defeats this presumption." Comment (c) to **Art. 348** is to much the same effect: "[i]t has long been held that an error of fact does not defeat good faith." Error of fact, of course, refers to some mistake with respect to the pertinent facts, in this case, the facts regarding ownership.

The proposition "error of fact does not defeat good faith," though true in some sense and to some extent, is nevertheless overly broad and, to that extent, misleading. That one is even faced with the question "was X in good or bad faith" necessarily presupposes that X, at the very least, made a mistake of some kind. Thus, the real question is not "did X make an error?"—that is, in context, a given—but rather was the error "reasonable." If the error was reasonable, then, yes, the presumption of good faith stands; but if it was not, then the presumption of good faith falls.

4. Does this mean that a prospective transferee of property, if he has "suspicions" about his prospective transferor's title, is, at it were, forever "stuck" with bad faith? Not at all. But it does mean that if he ever wants to get from bad faith to good faith, he will have to investigate, that is, he must conduct an inquiry, and a reasonable one at that, to determine whether his suspicions have any foundation in fact. If he conducts the inquiry and the inquiry reveals that his suspicions were unfounded, then he will, at that point, find himself in good faith. But if he does not conduct the inquiry and if, had he done so, what he would have discovered would have confirmed his suspicions, then he will be charged with knowledge of everything he should have discovered.

The proposition, then, should be re-written as follows: "Proof of an error of fact, *standing alone*, does not defeat the presumption of good faith. But if that error of fact was unreasonable, then the presumption is defeated."

2] SPECIAL PROBLEMS

a] Quitclaim Deeds

LSA-C.C. Art. 2475 provides that the seller of a thing "warrants title" to it, that is, guarantees that he owns the thing that he is selling. But this is just a suppletive (default) rule, one out of which the seller and the buyer are free to contract. In such a case, the buyer is said to "waive" the warranty of title. **LSA-C.C. Art. 2503, ¶1.**

Under current Louisiana law, such a "sale without warranty of title" can come in either of two varieties. The first, which has long been known to the civil law, might be called a "simple" or a "mere" nonwarranty sale. *See* **Art. 2503**. In this kind of sale, the seller, while purporting to transfer to the buyer the very thing that the buyer wishes to acquire (e.g., "Seller does hereby sell, transfer, grant... to Buyer the hereinafter described property...."), nevertheless specifically and expressly refuses to warrant that he has title to that thing (e.g., "This sale is made without warranty of title"). The second, which was imported into Louisiana law from the common law tradition, is known as a "quitclaim deed." *See* **LSA-C.C. Art. 2502 & cmt. (b)**. In this kind of sale the seller, instead of purporting to transfer to the buyer the thing itself that the buyer wishes to acquire, rather purports to transfer to him "whatsoever right, title, or interest" in the thing that the seller "may" happen to have (if any). This kind of sale, with this kind of "granting" clause, excludes the warranty of title by implication, an implication that, for obvious reasons, is considered to be crystal clear. Of these two kinds of nonwarranty sales, the quitclaim, interestingly enough, is the more radical in terms of its consequences for the buyer. In the case of a simple nonwarranty sale, if it turns out that the seller was not, in fact, the owner, then ordinarily the buyer can, at least, get his money back. **Art. 2503, ¶1**. But in the case of a quitclaim deed, if it turns out the seller was not, in fact, the owner, then the buyer has no remedy at all, that is to say, he is "out" both the thing and the price. **Art. 2502, ¶1**.

Given that the seller of a thing who resorts to a nonwarranty sale—above all, one who uses a quitclaim deed—seems to say to the buyer "I do not promise you that I really own the thing," one might suppose that a buyer who takes title by way of such a sale is *per se* in bad faith. But that is not the case. It is well settled, in both the jurisprudence and the doctrine, that the mere fact that the purchaser has taken title to the thing via a quitclaim deed is not sufficient, by itself, to rebut the presumption of good faith. The explanation for this seeming anomaly is "practical." As we will learn later on when we study the "protection" of ownership, more specifically, the "petitory action," the standard of proof that the purported owner of immovable property must meet in order to carry his burden of proof is often exceptionally high (called "perfect title"), so high, in fact, that many a purported owner cannot possibly meet it. Recognizing this abstract risk and wishing to avoid it, many sellers of immovable property as a matter of course adopt a policy of writing nothing but quitclaim deeds. This they do even though, in fact, they do not doubt and, further, have no reason to doubt their titles. Because that is so, our courts have refused to view the seller's use of a quitclaim deed as a tacit admission that he believes his title may be defective. *See* **Art. 2502, ¶2.**

Nevertheless, the buyer's receipt of a quitclaim deed, though not *conclusive* evidence of bad faith, is still *some* evidence of bad faith. Thus, that fact, when combined with other facts that demonstrate reason for doubting the seller's ownership, may be sufficient to prove bad faith. Examples of such other evidence would include (1) that the sales price was suspiciously low and that the buyer knows, or at least *ought* to know, this or (2) that there is a "gap" in the seller's title (e.g., the surname of the seller differs from the surname of the person who, to judge from the conveyance records, was the last person to buy it) and the buyer knows, or at least *ought* to know, this.

Bad faith due to an error of fact is not necessarily a permanent condition. To be sure, when the buyer learns facts sufficient to put a reasonable person on notice that the seller's title is suspect, he is, at that moment, in bad faith. But he can end his bad faith or, if you prefer, reestablish his good faith, if he conducts a reasonable inquiry into the suspected problem and, as a result of that inquiry, reasonably concludes that his suspicions were unfounded.

b] Clouds on Title Reflected in the Public Records

In some cases, there can be a "cloud" on the seller's title that could and, perhaps, should have been discovered through a competent title search. But it is important to note, first of all, that they buyer's failure to conduct such a search, without more, will not land him in bad faith. But what if the buyer conducts such a search, and his title examiner "misses" the cloud on the seller's title? Does that mean that the buyer is in "objective" bad faith, on the theory that he "should have known" of the problem? Not necessarily. That one's title examiner overlooked defects in one's author's title is just one of several factors that enter into the larger "good faith" calculus. To perform that calculus, one must consider, in addition to factors that have nothing to do with the title search (e.g., whether the transfer is with warranty or the seriousness of the consideration), factors such as the condition of the public records, the thoroughness of the particular title search, the competence and reputation of the title examiner, the type of defect involved, likelihood that the defect would be missed, and the gravity of the error made by the title examiner.

b) Errors of Law

As we saw earlier, **LSA-C.C. Art. 3481** provides that "error of law," just like "error of fact," does *not* rebut the presumption of good faith. Like the proposition "error of fact does establish bad faith," the proposition "error of law does establish bad faith" must be understood with care. It would be better to make the point this way: error of law, *by itself*, does not establish bad faith; what is important is whether the error is reasonable or unreasonable; if the error is reasonable, then the presumption of good faith stands; but if the error is unreasonable, then it falls.

The notion of a "reasonable" error of law may at first blush strike some as peculiar, perhaps even oxymoronic. After all, isn't it the case that "[n]o one may avail himself of ignorance of the law," to quote **LSA-C.C. Art. 5**? And does that not mean that everyone, as a matter of law, is charged with a full knowledge of the law? And does that not mean that no error of law can be considered "reasonable"? Though the answer to the first of these three questions is "yes," the answer to each of the latter two questions is "no." Whatever the principle in **Art. 5** means—a difficult topic for another book—it is definitely *not* that everyone is deemed to know all of the law for all purposes in all situations. In fact, in the private law, there are many contexts in which "perfect" legal knowledge not only is not required but also is not even expected. One such context is that of the "vices of consent" to conventional obligations, where one is permitted to annul a contract on the ground that one entered into it on the basis of an "error of law." Another such context is that in which we now find ourselves, that is, that of "good faith" for purposes of acquisitive prescription. *See **id.*** **cmt. (c).**

The question still remains of what separates a "reasonable" from an "unreasonable" error of law. Suffice it to say this. The more complex, the more arcane, and the more obscure the rule of law in question, the more likely it is that ignorance of it will be regarded as "reasonable." But the more straightforward, the more familiar, and the more obvious the rule of law in question, the more likely it is that ignorance of it will be regarded as "unreasonable."

3. *Delay*

a. Length

The length of the required delay for abridged acquisitive prescription is distinctive. Per **LSA-C.C. Arts. 3473** and **3475**, it is 10 years.

b. Junction of Possessions

Likewise unique to abridged acquisitive prescription are several special "junction of possession" rules. These rules do not apply to junction of possessions for purposes of *un*abridged acquisitive prescription.

Within the law of junction of possessions, as we have seen, the distinction between universal successions, which allow for "continuation of possession," and particular successions, which allow for "tacking of possessions," is paramount. The distinction affects the junction of possession for purposes of satisfying the delay requirement for acquisition of the right to possess. It also affects junction of possessions for purposes of satisfying the delay requirement for unabridged acquisitive prescription when the "spatial extent" of the continuity or tacking of possession is at issue. This we already know. What we have yet to learn is that the distinction also affects junction of possessions for purposes of satisfying the delay requirement for abridged acquisitive prescription.

Since a universal successor merely continues his author's possession, one that is indistinguishable from that of his author, he need not, in order to acquire a real right by abridged acquisitive prescription, satisfy the requirements of that prescription all by himself. It is not necessary, for example, that he begin his own possession in good faith or that he have a just title of his own. In fact, whether he himself is in good faith or whether he himself has a just title of his own are matters of indifference. All he needs to do is to show (i) that his author satisfied the requirements, i.e., possessed the thing, was in good faith, and had just title and (ii) that he, the successor, has not lost his author's possession. If he does that, "junction of possessions" for purposes of abridged acquisitive prescription follows as a matter of course.

For a particular possessor, by contrast, things are not so simple. Since a particular possessor begins a new possession, one that is distinct from that of his author, he must, in order to acquire a real right in the thing by abridged acquisitive prescription, satisfy *all* of the requirements for that prescription *by himself*, at least in principle. Among the consequences of this principle are that a particular successor, in order to acquire a real right in the thing by abridged acquisitive prescription, (i) must be in good faith and (ii) must have just title when he assumes possession.

This principle, if followed rigorously, would have other consequences, among them that a particular successor, in order to acquire a real right in the thing by abridged acquisitive prescription, must satisfy the applicable delay requirement—10 years of possession—all by himself, without tacking on the time of his author's possession. But with respect to this one element of abridged acquisitive prescription, the law grants him a conditional dispensation: it permits him to tack on the time of his author's possession as long as his author, too, satisfied all of the requisites for abridged acquisitive prescription, i.e., good faith and just title, save for possession for the required period. It follows, then, that a particular possessor who is in bad faith or lacks a just title cannot tack his own possession to that of his author so as to claim abridged acquisitive prescription. That is true even if his author was in good faith and had just title.

II. Movables

A. Unabridged Acquisitive Prescription

Unabridged acquisitive prescription of movables has only one unique element: the length of the required delay. According to **LSA-C.C. Art. 3491** that length is 10 years.

B. Abridged Acquisitive Prescription

As a general rule, abridged acquisitive prescription of movables differs from unabridged acquisitive prescription of movables in the same respects as abridged acquisitive prescription of immovables differs from unabridged acquisitive prescription of immovables. Thus, abridged acquisitive prescription of movables has four distinctive features: (i) a special kind of title, (ii) good faith, (iii) an abridged delay, and (iv) special tacking rules. Let us go through these one at a time.

1. Special Kind of Title: Act Translative of Ownership

It is commonly thought that, in order to become the owner of a movable thing through abridged acquisitive prescription, the possessor must have a "just title" to that thing. The Civil Code, however, does not bear out that contention. According to **LSA-C.C. Art. 3490**, what is required is not a just title *per se* but rather merely "*an act sufficient to transfer ownership.*" So, when it comes to abridged acquisitive prescription of movables, the requirement of "just title" is replaced by a requirement of "act translative of ownership." These two concepts, of course, are not unrelated. To the contrary, "act translative of ownership" is one of the elements, arguably the most important element, of "just title." But just title, it will be recalled, entails still many more elements. To substitute "act translative of ownership" for "just title" is, then, to strip away these other elements. Which elements are those? Two immediately come to mind. One is that the title be written; the other, that it be recorded. The bottom line, then, is this: to take advantage of abridged acquisitive prescription of movables, one must have an act translative of ownership, but that act may be oral and, even if it is in writing, it need not be recorded.

2. Good Faith

The Civil Code does bear out the contention that abridged acquisitive prescription of movables, like abridged acquisitive prescription of immovables, requires "good faith." **Art. 3490** tells us that "[o]ne who has possessed a movable, as owner, *in good faith*… acquires ownership by prescription." This good faith is the same as that required for the abridged acquisitive prescription of *im*movables.

3. *Delay*

a. Length

Under **Art. 3490**, the length of the delay required for abridged acquisitive prescription of movables is three years.

b. Junction of Possessions

The possibility of "joining possessions" can arise with respect to the abridged acquisitive prescription of movables. **LSA-C.C. Arts. 3441** and **3442**, the fount of the law on junction of possessions, do not distinguish between immovables and movables.

Junction of possessions for purposes of this prescription is subject to the same peculiar rules that affect abridged acquisitive prescription of immovables. Those rules again were: (i) for a universal successor to count his ancestor's time of possession as his own, he need only show that his *ancestor* was in good faith and had a translative title and (ii) for a particular successor to count his ancestor's time of possession as his own, he must show that both he *and* his ancestor were in good faith and had a translative title.

PART III

Principal Real Rights

Chapter Eight

Ownership

SUB-CHAPTER A

General Principles

I. Definition

"Ownership," according to the first sentence of **LSA-C.C. Art.** 477, is the "right that confers on a person direct, immediate, and exclusive authority over a thing." To much the same effect is the definition developed by Planiol, which is reproduced in comment (b) to the article: "the right by virtue of which a thing is subjected perpetually and exclusively to the acts and will of a person."

II. Constitutive Elements

The elements of the right of ownership are identified in the second sentence of **Art.** 477: "The owner of a thing may use, enjoy, and dispose of it" within certain limits. This article is rooted in the property law of ancient Rome, which defined ownership as the union of three distinct rights over a thing: *usus*, *fructus*, and *abusus*. Let us examine each of these rights in turn.

A. *Usus*

The owner is free, first of all, to "use" the thing as he sees fit, that is, to avail himself of its attributes for whatever purposes he desires. For example, in the case of land, the owner can live on it or exploit it economically, that is, cultivate it, conduct a business on it, hunt on it.

B. *Fructus*

The term "enjoy" as used in **Art. 477** has a narrower connotation than does the same term as used in standard English. Here, it refers to the right to the "fruits" of the thing, a term that was explained at length earlier in this Précis. That ownership entails this right is confirmed by **LSA-C.C. Art. 483**, which provides that "the owner of a thing acquires the ownership of its natural and civil fruits."

C. *Abusus*

The owner can also "abuse," that is, dispose of, the thing. This power of disposition has two aspects: physical and juridical.

1. Physical Disposition

The owner can dispose of the thing in a *physical* sense. This means that he can, if he chooses, diminish its substance (that is, take products out of it), transform it into something else, or even destroy it.

2. Juridical Disposition

The owner can dispose of the thing in a *juridical* sense. This means that he can rid himself of his legal interest in the thing, that is, terminate his ownership of it. There are, at bottom, two different ways in which this termination of ownership might be accomplished. The first is by "transfer." We have already seen some of the possible mechanisms for transferring one's ownership, namely, the different juridical acts that are called "acts translative of ownership": sale, exchange, and donation. The second is "abandonment." Under **LSA-C.C. Art. 3418**, the owner can "abandon" the thing by "relinquish[ing] possession with the intent to give up ownership."

C. Characteristics

The right of full ownership, traditional civilian doctrine teaches, has three distinctive characteristics. It is "absolute," "exclusive," and "perpetual." Let us look at each of these characteristics a bit more closely.

1. Absolute

The right of full ownership is "absolute" in two senses. First, it is not contingent or relative. Second, it has no *inherent*, as opposed to external, limits. A full owner can, in principle, do whatever he wants with the thing. The same is not true of the holder of a usufruct or a predial servitude, whose right is, by its very nature, subject to multiple limitations.

2. Exclusive

The right of full ownership is "exclusive." This means, above all else, that the owner has a "monopoly" on the thing, that is, that he *alone* can use it, take its fruits, and dispose of it. This "monopoly" right implies another: the right to exclude others from the thing.

3. Perpetual

The right of ownership is "perpetual," that is, once it is established, it remains in existence indefinitely. Suppose that the owner of a thing does not "exercise" his right at all, that is, does not use, enjoy, or dispose of the thing, not even partly. What happens to his ownership right as a result of this inactivity? The answer is "nothing." As the second paragraph of **LSA-C.C. Art. 481** puts it, "[o]wnership exists independently of any exercise of it and may not be lost by nonuse." Next, suppose that the owner of a thing dies. What happens to his ownership right as a result? Again, the answer is "nothing." His ownership right, far from being "extinguished" or "terminated," simply passes to his successors.

SUB-CHAPTER B

Extent of Ownership: Accession

I. Explication

A. Definition

The institution of "accession" is introduced in **LSA-C.C. Art. 482**: "The ownership of a thing includes by accession the ownership of everything that it produces or is united with it, either naturally or artificially, in accordance with the following provisions."

The question "What is the nature of accession?" has given rise to a sometimes lively debate. According to some, accession is a "consequence"—to use the more technical term, *effect*—of ownership. Others contend that accession, as one of the modes of acquiring ownership, constitutes a *cause* of ownership. Both positions, in my view, have merit, that is, accession can properly be seen as both an effect of ownership and a cause of ownership at the same time. Which it appears to be depends on one's perspective, more precisely, on the thing that is the focus of one's attention. In any case of accession, two things are necessarily involved: the thing that was there to begin with, i.e., the "original" thing, and the thing that it produces or that is added to it, i.e., the "new" thing. Viewed from the standpoint of the original thing, accession is an effect of ownership: because one owns *that* thing, one also owns the new thing. But viewed from the standpoint of the new thing, it is a cause of ownership: one becomes the owner of the *new* thing as a result of one's ownership of the original.

B. Varieties

Civilian scholars are wont to distinguish between what they perceive to be two different kinds of accession: natural and artificial. This distinction is adverted to in **Art. 482** of our Civil Code by the use of the phrase "either naturally or artificially." According to VOCABULARIE JURIDIQUE, natural accession is "[a]ccession due to the act of nature alone," e.g., accession with respect to naturally-occurring plants and their fruits, the offspring of animals, alluvian, and abandoned river beds, whereas artificial accession is "[a]ccession proceeding from the industry of man applied to a thing," e.g., accession with respect to constructions and plants planted by man and their fruits.

C. Prerequisites

In order for an accession problem to arise, several requirements must be satisfied. The first two are fairly obvious. And the first of these we have already mentioned: there must be at least two distinct things. Second, one of these things must be produced from or united with the other by either an act of nature (natural accession) or an act of man (artificial accession). For convenience, we may call the thing that is produced from or united with the other thing the "new thing" and the thing that produces the new thing or to which the new thing is united the "original thing."

Less obvious are the third and fourth. The third is that at least two persons must be involved in the events that give rise to the supposed accession problem. The fourth is that these two persons must play distinctive roles in those events. One person must supply the original thing. The other must either supply the new thing or supply the materials or the labor (or both) necessary for the production of the new thing or for the new thing's becoming united with the original thing.

For ease of reference, it will be helpful if we can give short, distinctive names to these two persons. The one who supplies the original thing we will call, simply, the "owner"; the one who supplies the new thing or the materials or labor for it, we will call the "contributor."

D. Types of Rules

Within the law of accession, one encounters two very different kinds of rules. It is essential that you not confuse them. First, there are "rules of ownership," that is, those that determine who, as between the owner and the contributor, owns the new thing. Second, there are "remedial rules," that is, those that determine whether and, if so, on what conditions the contributor can (or must) remove the new thing or, if he cannot do that, if he is at least entitled to some sort of indemnity for his efforts.

II. Regimes of Accession

Our Civil Code sets up three different regimes of accession. They are "accession of fruits and products," "accession with respect to immovables," and "accession with respect to movables." We will look at each of these in turn, beginning with accession with respect to immovables and ending with accession of fruits and products.

A. Accession with Respect to Immovables

1. Preliminary Matters

a. Distinctive Prerequisites

There is one (and only one) distinctive prerequisite to accession with respect to immovables. It is that the original thing be an immovable.

b. Nature of Rules

The ownership and reimbursement rules are suppletive as opposed to mandatory; in other words, they are rules of "private" order as opposed to "public" order. Comment (c) to **LSA-C.C. Art. 493** states that "[t]his article applies in the absence of other provisions of law *or juridical act.*" Thus, the two persons who are involved in the events that give rise to the accession problem may, if they so choose, "contract out" of the rules on accession and impose on themselves a regime of accession of their own devising.

2. The Rules

a. Artificial Accession

Within the field of artificial accession with respect to immovables, we must, at the outset of our analysis, distinguish between two rather different situations. The first is that in which *the contributor* causes the new thing to be united with the immovable using things that belong to him or to someone else other than the owner. In such a case, the contributor's role consists not only of supplying the new thing itself or the materials from which it is to be created, but also the labor needed to unite it to the immovable. The second is that in which *the owner* causes the new thing to be united with the immovable using things that belong to someone else. In this case, the contributor's role is limited to supplying the new thing itself or the materials from which it is to be created; as for the labor needed to unite the new thing to the immovable, it is supplied by the owner.

1) Union Accomplished by the Contributor Using Things That Did Not Belong to the Owner of the Original Immovable

a) Ownership Rules

For those situations in which the contributor, using things that do not belong to the owner, unites the new thing to the immovable, there are two distinct sets of ownership rules, one for each of two distinctive kinds of new thing. These two kinds of things, which we studied earlier in this Précis, are "improvements," on the one hand, and INATs on the other hand. It will be recalled that "improvements" include such things as "buildings," "other constructions permanently attached to the ground," and "plantings" and that "INATs" refers to "integral parts" of an immovable under **LSA-C.C. Art. 465** (hence the "IN-") and to "attachments" under **LSA-C.C. Art. 466** (hence the "-AT").

1] ACCESSION OF IMPROVEMENTS

The question who, as between the owner and the contributor, owns an improvement is governed by the first paragraph of **Art. 493**, which reads as follows:

> Buildings, other constructions permanently attached to the ground, and plantings made on the land of another with his consent belong to him who made them. They belong to the owner of the ground when they are made without his consent.

This paragraph makes it clear that the critical factor in determining who owns an improvement is whether the owner consented to the contributor's uniting it to his land. If the owner consented, then the contributor owns it; if the owner did *not* consent, then the owner owns it.

With respect to the issue whether the owner consented to the improvement, the contributor bears the burden of proof. That this is so is made clear by **LSA-C.C. Art. 491**, which provides that "[b]uildings, other constructions permanently attached to the ground, standing timber, and unharvested crops or ungathered fruits of trees," in a word, "improvements," "are presumed to belong to the owner of the ground." This is known as the presumption of "unity of ownership."

Art. 491 tells us still something more about the **Art. 493** ownership rights of the contributor that may be of great importance. It is that the contributor may assert these rights against third persons—everyone other than the owner—if and only if the "public records" contain some sort of evidence of the existence of these rights. As **Art. 491** puts it, improvements are deemed to belong to the owner "unless separate ownership is evidenced by an instrument filed for registry in the conveyance records of the parish in which the immovable is located." Comment (c) provides an even clearer statement of the principle:

> Separate ownership of buildings, of other constructions permanently attached to the ground, of standing timber, and of unharvested crops or ungathered fruits of trees may be asserted toward third persons only if it is evidenced by an instrument filed for registry in the conveyance records of the parish in which the immovable is located. In the absence of such an instrument, third persons are entitled to assume that these things are component parts of the ground.

What this means is that, even if, as between the owner and the contributor, the improvement belongs to the contributor (because the owner consented to it), nevertheless from the standpoint of third persons, the improvement will be deemed to belong to the owner unless there is something in the public records to alert them to the possibility that things might be otherwise. This situation is sometimes referred to as "relativity of ownership": as between the parties, one person owns the thing, but as to third parties, someone else does.

An illustration will serve to explain both why ownership of the improvement as to third persons might be an issue and, when it is, how the contributor might protect himself. Suppose that the contributor is a lessee of the tract of land on which he places the improvement and the owner, the lessor. The act of lease, which is in writing, expressly authorizes the contributor-lessee to build the improvement. But the lease is never recorded in the public records. The contributor-lessee then moves onto the leased land and builds the improvement. After the improvement is built, the owner-lessor sells the land to another person. Then the lease ends. As he leaves, the contributor-lessee tries to take "his" improvement with him. The new landowner objects, claiming that the improvement belongs to *him* rather than to the contributor-lessee. The new landowner's theory is as follows: (1) because neither the lease nor any other evidence of the contributor-lessee's separate ownership was filed into the public records, from my point of view, as a third person, the improvement belongs to the owner-lessor; (2) under **LSA-C.C. Art. 463**, an improvement is a component part of the land when it belongs to the owner of the land; (3) inasmuch as the improvement was, from my point of view, owned by the owner-lessor, it was a component part of the land; (4) under **LSA-C.C. Art. 469**, the sale of land entails its component parts; (5) therefore, when the owner-lessor sold his land to me, ownership of the improvement, as a component part thereof, passed with it. This theory is sound. Could the contributor-lessee have done anything to have avoided this result? Yes. All that was required was that he record the act of lease in the public records. Had he done so, the ownership rights he enjoyed under **Art. 493** would have been effective not only against the owner-lessor, but against third persons, including the buyer of the land.

2] ACCESSION OF INATS

The question who, as between the owner and the contributor, owns an INAT is governed by **LSA-C.C. Art. 493.1**, which provides that "[t]hings incorporated in or attached to an immovable so as to become its component parts under Article 465 and 466 belong to the owner of the immovable." It is important to note that this article, in contrast to that which governs the ownership of improvements, says nothing about "consent." What that means is that though consent is *determinative* of the question who owns an improvement, it is *irrelevant* to the question who owns a component part. The ownership rule for INATS, then, is simple: *every* INAT *always* belongs to the owner, *regardless* whether the contributor had the owner's consent to unite it to the underlying immovable.

It goes almost without saying that in the case of an INAT one never faces the kind of "relativity of ownership" problem that can arise in the case of an improvement. Relativity of ownership is a problem *only where the new thing can be owned separately from the original immovable.* As we have seen, in the case of land and its improvements, separate ownership is possible. It can happen that a building, other construction, or planting (e.g., standing timber, unharvested crops, ungathered fruit) will belong to someone other than the owner of the ground. But the same is not true of a component part under **LSA-C.C. Arts. 465** or **466** because such a thing cannot be owned separately from the land, building, or other construction into which it is integrated or to which it is attached. With respect to component parts under **Arts. 465** or **466**, unity of ownership is the only possibility.

Unlike the other rules on accession with respect to immovable, this rule—that separate ownership of INATs is impossible—is mandatory as opposed to suppletive. The owner and the contributor cannot enter into a contract whereby the latter shall remain the owner of his INAT.

To sum up, for INATs, the rule fixing ownership as between the parties (the owner and the contributor) and the rule fixing ownership as to third persons is the same. The INAT belongs to the owner no matter from whose standpoint the question of ownership may be asked.

b) Remedial Rules

As we noted earlier in the Précis during our examination of the classification of things into improvements and INATs, the part of the Civil Code that pertains to accession with respect to immovables establishes one set of remedial rules for improvements and INATs that are joined to the underlying immovable with the consent of the owner and another set of remedial rules for those that are joined without such consent. For ease of reference, we may call improvements and INATs of the first kind "consented-to" and those of the second kind "unconsented-to."

1] WHERE THE OWNER OF THE ORIGINAL IMMOVABLE CONSENTED TO THE PRODUCTION OR UNION OF THE NEW THING

a] Consented-To Improvements

Paragraph two of **LSA-C.C. Art. 493** provides in part as follows: "When the owner of buildings, other constructions permanently attached to the ground, or plantings no longer has the right to keep them on the land of another, he may remove them subject to his obligation to restore the property to its former condition." Thus, the contributor's remedy—and, as it turns out, his *only* remedy in this situation—is that he has the right to remove the improvement, subject to a duty of restoration.

If the contributor does not exercise this right, then the "ball," in terms of remedies, moves to the owner's "court." According to sentence two of the second paragraph of **Art. 493**, "if he [the contributor] does not remove them [the improvements] within 90 days after written demand, the owner of the land may, after the ninetieth day from the date of mailing the written demand, appropriate ownership of the improvements." Thus, the "first" remedy given to the owner is the right to demand that the contributor remove the improvement. If the demand is not met, then the owner acquires a second remedy, namely, the right to "appropriate ownership," in other words, to have the improvements as his own. In order to avail himself of this second remedy, the owner must first "jump" through a few procedural "hoops." First, he must wait at least 90 days from the date on which he sent the written demand. Second, he must send the contributor a second notice, this one by certified mail, of his intention to appropriate ownership. Once the owner obtains the receipt indicating that the contributor has received this notice, ownership of the improvement automatically vests in him. To appropriate ownership of the improvement, the owner need do nothing further, in particular, need not pay the contributor any sort of indemnity.

The remedy that the contributor enjoys in this situation, just like his ownership right itself, is "relative," that is, though it is effective against the owner, it may or may not be effective against third persons. Whether it is effective against third persons is governed by **LSA-C.C. Art. 498**, which reads as follows:

> One who has lost the ownership of a thing to the owner of an immovable may assert against third persons his rights under Articles 493, 493.1, 494, 495, 496, or 497 when they are evidenced for registry in the appropriate conveyance or mortgage records of the parish in which the immovable is located.

Thus, the contributor of a consented-to improvement may assert his accession-based remedial rights against persons other than the original owner only if the public records contain evidence of the existence of those rights.

b] Consented-to INATs

Remedial rights with respect to consented-to INATs are addressed in **LSA-C.C. Art. 495.** The first paragraph, which concerns the contributor, provides as follows:

> One who incorporates in, or attaches to, the immovable of another, with his consent, things that become component

> parts of the immovable under article 465 and 466, may, in the absence of other provisions of law or juridical acts, remove them subject to his obligation of restoring the property to its former condition.

This remedy, it will be noted, is identical to the remedy provided to the contributor for consented-to improvements by **Art. 493.**

If the contributor fails to avail himself of this remedy, then certain remedies become available to the owner, remedies that, once exercised, may in turn give rise to still further remedies in favor of the contributor. The possibilities are spelled out in the second paragraph of **Art. 495**:

> If he [the contributor] does not remove them [the INATs] after demand, the owner of the immovable may have them removed at the expense of the person who made them [the contributor] and pay, at his option, the current value of the materials and of the workmanship or the enhanced value of the immovable.

Thus, as is true in the case of an improvement, the "first" remedial right accorded to the owner is that of demanding that the INAT be removed. There is, however, at least one difference between these two "demand removal" remedies: unlike the demand required in the case of an improvement, which must be in writing, the demand required in the case of an INAT apparently need not be in any particular form. In any event, if the demand is not met, then the owner acquires some additional, alternative remedies. Before availing himself of these alternatives, the owner apparently is not required to wait any specific length of time, as he must do in the case of improvements. One alternative is for the owner to cause the INAT to be "removed at the expense" of the contributor. What this means is that the owner may hire a third person to remove the INAT and then "send the bill" for the work to the contributor, who must then pay it. The other alternative is for the owner to "keep" the thing. To do that, however, the owner must pay the contributor some sort of indemnity (which is as much as to say that the contributor has the right to such an indemnity). There are two alternative measures of indemnity, from which the owner is free to choose: the *current* value of the labor and materials that the contributor put into the new thing or the increase in the value of the underlying immovable due to the new thing's having been joined to it.

The remedies accorded by **Art. 495** to contributors of INATs, no less than those accorded by **Art. 493** to contributors of improvements, are relative. **LSA-C.C. Art. 498**, which we quoted in full earlier, includes "Article 495" in the list of those the remedial rights created by which can be "assert[ed] against third persons" only if "they are evidenced for registry." Thus, the contributor of a consented-to INAT may assert his accession-based remedial rights against persons other than the original owner only if the public records contain evidence of the existence of those rights.

2] WHERE THE OWNER OF THE ORIGINAL IMMOVABLE DID NOT CONSENT TO THE PRODUCTION OR UNION OF THE NEW THING

Having completed our examination of the remedial rules that apply where the owner of the original immovable consented to the production or union of the new thing, we must now examine the remedial rules that apply where the owner of the original immovable did not consent to the production or union of the new thing. We will consider, first, the domain or scope of these rules and, second, their content.

a] Domain

The remedial rules for unconsented-to improvements and INATs that are contained in the part of the Civil Code that pertains to accession with respect to immovables, unlike those for consented-to improvements and INATs, are not comprehensive, that is, they do not cover every imaginable case in which the owner or the contributor might hope to enjoy some remedy. Indeed, as we shall see, these remedial rules cover only a few of those cases.

Among the articles found in the part of the Civil Code that pertains to accession with respect to immovable, only two deal with unconsented-to improvements and INATs: **LSA-C.C. Arts. 496** and **497.** The former concerns good faith possessors and the latter, bad faith possessors. The common ground between the two articles, then, is "possessors." It follows that if the contributor in question is not a possessor, then these rules tell us nothing at all.

Does this mean that for non-possessors, including "precarious possessors" (such as lessees or usufructuaries), there are *no* remedies with respect to unconsented-to improvements and INATs? Not at all. What it means—all it means—is that no such remedies are provided for in *this part* of the Civil Code. It remains possible, however, that some such remedies might be provided for in other parts of the Civil Code. And, in fact, they often are. Consider, for example, the case of a lessee of land who joins an improvement to it without the landowner's consent or a lessee of a building who joins an INAT to it without the building owner's consent. **LSA-C.C. Art. 2687**, which appears in the part of the Civil Code that pertains to the contract of "lease," establishes a complex set of interlocking remedies for the contributor and the owner. Or, again, consider the case of a usufructuary who contributes to an improvement or an INAT without the consent of the owner. Remedies for the two are provided for in **LSA-C.C. Art. 601**, which is situated in the part of the Civil Code that pertains to the personal servitude of "usufruct."

b] Content

1} PRELIMINARY MATTER: GOOD FAITH V. BAD FAITH

As we have already noted, of the two articles in the part of the Civil Code that address the problem of remedies for unconsented-to improvements, one (**Art. 486**) concerns "good faith" possessors and the other (**Art. 487**), "bad faith" possessors. What determines which of the two articles governs a given case, then, is the "state of mind" of the possessor. Because that is so, it is essential to understand the meanings of "good faith" and "bad faith" in this context.

These terms are defined—"good faith," directly, and "bad faith," by implication—in **LSA-C.C. Art. 487.** According to that article, "[f]or purposes of accession, a possessor is in good faith when he possesses by virtue of an act translative of ownership and does not know of any defects in his ownership."

It is important to note that "good faith" in this context, i.e., the law of accession, does not have quite the same meaning as it does in the context of acquisitive prescription. Comments (b) and (c) to **Art. 487** as well as comment (b) to **LSA-C.C. Art. 3480**, which concerns acquisitive prescription, note several of these differences.

One difference, the most obvious, concerns the relationship between "good faith," on the one hand, and "just title," on the other. As is noted in comment (b) to **Art. 3480**, "for purposes of acquisitive prescription, good faith and just title are separate ideas, whereas for purposes of accession, the two ideas are blended." Comment (c) to **Art. 487** puts it this way: "In matters of accession, good faith is dependent upon the existence of a just title; in matters of prescription good faith and just title are distinct requirements." Thus, in the context of accession, "just title" is understood to be an *element* of "good faith." The very text of **Art. 487** indicates as much. To be in good faith for purposes of accession, that article tells us, one not only must "not know of any defects in his ownership" (which corresponds to the acquisitive prescription "good faith" requirement), but also must possess the thing under "an act translative of ownership" (which corresponds to the acquisitive prescription "just title" requirement).

This difference is undeniable. Nevertheless, in the end it proves to be less a distinction of substance than one of terminology and systematization. In one case as in the other both "good faith" and "just title" are required. It is just that, in one case, we treat these two requirements as if they were separate and, in the other, we treat them as if one were an element of another.

More important are the differences, some of them subtle, regarding what one must believe, on the one hand, and what kind of title one must have, on the other, as between the two contexts. Consider, first, what one must believe. To be in good faith for purposes of acquisitive prescription, not only must one *subjectively* believe that one is the owner, but that belief must be *objectively* reasonable. It is not at all clear whether the same is true for purposes of accession. **Art. 487** says simply that one must not "know" of any defects in one's title. The word "know," when used by itself and without modifiers such as "reasonably" or auxiliaries such as "should" or "ought," ordinarily refers to *subjective* belief alone. It is at least possible, then, that the belief required for "good faith" in the context of accession need not be reasonable. Consider, next, what kind of title one must have. In the context of acquisitive prescription, what is required is "just title," properly so called. In the context of accession, however, all that is required is an "act translative of ownership." The two are not identical. In fact, "act translative of ownership" is merely one element of "just title"; in other words, for one's title to be "just," it must be more than merely an "act translative of ownership," that is, it must be this *plus something more.* The "something more," as **Art. 3483** and the comments thereto indicate, is as follows: (1) written, (2) valid in form, (3) filed into the appropriate public records, (4) not absolutely null, and (5) not putative. In the context of accession, this "something more" is not required. And so it is that "a possessor may be in good faith even though his title is null or annullable on account of defects of substance or form... or merely 'putative.'" **Art. 487 cmt. (d)**.

2} THE RULES

Art. 496 addresses the case of the *good faith* possessor. The article begins by declaring that the owner "may not demand the[ ] demolition and removal" of the improvement or INAT, but "is bound to keep them." This declaration is apt to be misunderstood. It does not mean that the owner cannot demolish and remove the improvement, that he must, as it were, just "put up with" it perpetually. All it means is that, if he wishes to demolish and remove it, he must pay for the demolition and removal himself, in other words, that he cannot "send the bill" for it to the contributor. The article goes on to declare that the owner is "bound... to pay" some sort of indemnity to the contributor. There are three indemnity alternatives, from which the owner alone is free to pick and choose: (1) the original "cost of the materials and of the workmanship; (2) the "current value" of those materials and that workmanship, or (3) the "enhanced value" of the underlying immovable attributable to the new thing's having been joined to it.

Though **Art. 496** does not say so in so many terms, it appears that the owner cannot recover any sort of "damages" from the contributor. As we will shortly see, **Art. 497** expressly grants the owner this remedy as against a bad faith possessor. The absence of similar language in **Art. 496** implies, *a contrario*, that there is no such remedy as against a good faith possessor.

Art. 497 addresses the case of the *bad faith* possessor. This article, in sharp contrast to the last, begins by according the owner an option: he can either (1) demand the "demolition and removal" of the improvement or INAT "at the expense of the possessor (something that, it will be recalled, is not permitted under **Art. 496**) or (2) "keep them." He may choose the latter, however, only on the condition that pay the contributor some sort of indemnity. Regarding the measure of this indemnity he has only two choices (as opposed to the three provided by **Art. 496**): (1) the "current value of the materials and the workmanship" or (2) the "enhanced value of the immovable attributable to the new thing's having been joined to it. "In addition," the article continues, the owner may in any case may "demand... damages for the injury that he may have sustained."

The remedies provided by **Arts. 496** and **497**, like so many of the other remedies established in the law of accession with respect to immovable, are "relative." **Art. 498** lists these two articles among those the remedial rights established by which cannot be asserted against third parties absent evidence of the existence thereof in the public records.

Excursus on Reimbursement of Expenses

Suppose that a possessor, instead of joining a "new thing" to the original thing, simply modifies it in some way, for example, digs a ditch on a tract of land. Things of this kind are sometimes referred to as "inseparable improvements," *see, e.g.*, **Art. 497**, inasmuch as they are "permanently merged with the soil" and have no "identity as separate works." **Art. 497 cmt. (c)**. Strictly speaking, however, such things are not "improvements" at all, and they do not give rise to "accession" problems properly so called. Recall that accession with respect to immovables requires that a "new thing" be produced from or united with the original immovable. In the case of an "inseparable improvement," the possessor neither produced nor added a "new thing"; rather, all he did was to *modify existing things.*

It should be clear, then, that whatever rights and remedies may arise with respect to "inseparable improvements," they must be provided for and governed by some body of law other than that of "accession." This other body of law is that which pertains to "reimbursement of expenses" for possessors. *See* **Art. 497 cmt. (c)**. It is found in **LSA-C.C. Arts. 527–529.**

There are two factors which determine what, if any, expenses the possessor can recover: (i) whether the possessor is in good faith or bad faith and (ii) whether the expenses are necessary or useful. It is not entirely clear whether we are to use for this purpose the definition of "good faith" set forth in the articles on acquisitive prescription or that set forth in the articles on accession. But inasmuch as recovery for expenses is closely related to reimbursement for improvements—a problem of accession—but has no close relation to anything connected with acquisitive prescription, it would appear that the definition in the law of accession is the better choice.

The distinction between "necessary expenses" and "useful expenses" is described in the comments to **Arts. 527** and **528.** Comment (b) to **Art. 527** explains that a necessary expense is one "incurred for the preservation of the property" as opposed to one "for ordinary maintenance and repairs." Examples of necessary expenses include "property taxes" and "assessments." According to comment (b) to **Art. 528,** "[u]seful expenses are those that, though not needed for the preservation of the property, result in enhancement of its value."

The rules regarding the recovery of necessary and useful expenses by possessors are set out in **Arts. 527** and **528.** Boiled down to their essentials, the rules amount to this: whereas a good faith possessor can recover both kinds of expenses, a bad faith possessor can recover only necessary expenses.

2) *Union Accomplished* by the Owner *Using Things That Belonged to Another*

a) Ownership Rules

LSA-C.C. Art. 494 provides that when the owner of an immovable "makes on it constructions, plantings or works" using the "materials of another," he is entitled to "retain them." Though the article does not say so, what it does say—the owner enjoys this "right of retention"—implies that the owner, rather than the contributor, owns them. This inference is confirmed by the placement of the article within the series of articles on accession with respect to immovable. The immediately preceding article—**LSA-C.C. Art. 493.2**—provides that "[o]ne who has lost the ownership of a thing [i.e., a contributor] to the owner of an immovable may have a claim against him [the owner]... in accordance with the following provisions." **Art, 494** is one of these "following provisions."

Because this rule of ownership, like that for INATs established in **Art. 493.1**, grants the owner ownership *in all cases*, one need not worry about the problem of "relativity of ownership" here. Relativity of ownership, it will be recalled, presupposes the possibility of separate ownership.

b) Reimbursement Rules

Art. 494 establishes only a few remedial rights, both of which benefit the contributor. The first is the right to receive an indemnity for the materials used by the owner. For this particular indemnity, only one measure is recognized: the "current value" of the materials. The second is the right to recover damages. These rights are cumulative. As the article states, the owner of the immovable can retain the constructions only upon "reimbursing the owner of the materials their current value *and repairing the injury that he may have caused to him.*"

The remedies accorded to the contributor under **Art. 494** are relative. According to **Art. 498**, the remedial rights granted by "Article 494" cannot be asserted against third persons if there is no evidence of these rights in the public records.

b. Natural Accession

Natural accession with respect to immovables takes place under a number of circumstances, all of them having to do with water bodies. The principal cases are (1) "alluvion" and "dereliction" that forms along the bank or shore of a waterbody (**LSA-C.C. Arts. 499–500**); (2) "avulsion" along a river or stream (**LSA-C.C. Art. 502**); (3) the formation of an island when a river or stream opens a new channel (**LSA-C.C. Art. 503**); (4) the abandonment by a river or stream of its bed (**LSA-C.C. Art. 504**); and (5) the formation of an island on the bed of a navigable river or stream (**LSA-C.C. Art. 505**).

1) Alluvion and Dereliction

To understand the rules regarding accession with respect to alluvion and dereliction, one must, of course, have some idea of what these terms mean. "Alluvion" is accretion, that is, build-up of deposited sediment, formed *successively and imperceptibly* on the bank of a river, stream, or other waterbody. "Dereliction" is land that was originally part of the bed of the waterbody but that is "left dry" (i.e., ends up above the ordinary low water mark) as a result of the water having *imperceptibly and permanently* receded from the bank of a river or stream.

a) Along a River or Stream

Alluvion and dereliction formed along the bank of a river or stream, whether navigable or not, belongs to the "riparian owner," that is, the owner of the bank. **Art. 499.** According to **Art. 501**, when alluvion forms along land owned by more than one riparian owner, the alluvion is divided so that each owner receives a fair proportion of the area of alluvion and the frontage on the river, without respect to the timing or the sequence of formation, according to the relative values of the frontage and the area.

b) Along a Lake or the Seashore

According to **Art. 500**, "[t]here is no right to alluvion or derelication on the shore of the sea or of lakes." This article must be interpreted with care, for it is easily misunderstood. All that it means is that the right of *private individuals* to alluvion and dereliction formed along rivers and streams that is granted by ***Art. 499*** does *not* extend to alluvion and dereliction formed along lakes and the sea. It does not mean that *no one* has the right to such alluvion and dereliction. Indeed, just a moment's reflection reveals that some one may own it, for it is not counted among "common things." If private individuals do not own it, then there is no one left who might do so other than the "government." And so it is. According to doctrine and jurisprudence, alluvion and dereliction along the seashore belong to the state, but in its *private capacity.*

2) Avulsion

Avulsion is the "sudden action of the waters of a river or stream" that "carries away an identifiable piece of ground and unites it with other lands on the same or opposite bank," detaches an identifiable part of riparian land and attaches it to other lands on the same or opposite bank." **LSA-C.C. Art. 502.** According to **Art. 502**, avulsion does not affect the ownership of the land involved, at least not immediately. The original owner of the land that was carried off "may claim it within a year, or even later, if the owner of the bank with which it is united has not take possession." ***Id.*** But if he does not do so, then the owner of the bank can acquire ownership of it by taking possession.

3) Islands From New Channels

The transformation of riparian land into an island as a result of the opening of a new channel by a river or stream, whether navigable or not, does not affect the ownership of that land. **Art. 503.** The island continues to belong to the original owner.

4) Abandoned Bed

If a navigable river or stream abandons its bed, then the old bed belongs to the owners of the lands on which the new bed lies. These owners divide the old bed in proportion to the quantities of land that they lost. **Art. 504.**

Left unstated in **Art. 504**, presumably because it was thought to be obvious, is what happens to the ownership of the land that forms the new bed of such a navigable river or stream. The answer is found in **Art. 450, ¶ 2**: "Public things that belong to the state are such as ... the bottoms of natural navigable water bodies." Thus, the new bed belongs to the state in its *public* capacity.

5) Islands on Beds

Art. 505 states that islands and sandbars that form on the beds of navigable rivers and streams, provided they are not attached to the banks, belong to the state. Though the article is mute on this point, the doctrine and jurisprudence have concluded that the state owns such land in its *private* capacity.

B. Accession with Respect to Movables

Most, if not all, cases of accession with respect to movables can be collected under three headings, all of them drawn from traditional civil law doctrine. They are "adjunction," "transformation," and "mélange."

1. Adjunction

a. Definition

"Adjunction" is the physical union of two movables in such a way that each retains its separate identity, in other words, that each is still recognizable as a distinct physical thing. Adjunction is addressed in **LSA-C.C. Arts. 508–510.**

b. Prerequisites

Adjunction, without more, does not result in accession. As sentence one of **Art. 510** states, "[w]hen two corporeal movables are united *to form a whole, and one of them is an accessory of the other*" (italics added), adjunction occurs. For adjunction to have that effect, the following requirements must be satisfied.

1) Principal and Accessory

As **Art. 510** points out, the relationship between the two movables must be that of *principal* and *accessory.* In determining which of the two is the principal and which is the accessory (if, indeed, they have that relationship at all), one must ask and answer the following questions. Asking these questions *in this order* is of critical importance because the secondary question (which, as we will see, involves comparative value) arises *if and only if* the primary question has no clear answer and the tertiary question (which, as we will see, involves comparative bulk) arises *if and only if* the secondary question has no clear answer.

a) Function

As **Art. 508** explains, "[f]or the purposes of accession as between movables, an accessory is a corporeal movable that serves the use, ornament, or complement of the principal thing." So the first question to be asked is "does one thing provide some sort of service to the other, e.g., serve as an ornament to or complement of the other or facilitate its use?" If the answer is "yes," then the inquiry is at an end: the movable that serves this purpose is the accessory and the movable that is served, the principal. If the answer is "no" or "I can't tell," then one must proceed to the next stage of the test.

b) Value

Art. 509 provides "[i]n the case of doubt... the most valuable [of the two or more things]... shall be deemed the principal." Thus, if there is no definitive answer to the first question, the second question that must be asked is "is one of the movables more valuable than the other?" If the answer is "yes," then the inquiry is complete: the less valuable movable is the accessory and the more valuable movable, the principal. If the answer is "no" or "I can't tell," then one must proceed to the next stage of the test.

c) Bulk

Art. 509 provides that if the values of the things are nearly equal, then the more bulky is deemed to be the principal. Thus, if the second question yields no definitive answer, then the final question that must be asked is "is one of the movables bulkier than the other?" If the answer is "yes," then one need not inquire further: the less bulky movable is the accessory and the more bulky movable, the principal. But if the answer is "no" or "I can't tell," then what one does next is anyone's guess.

2) Whole

Art. 510 provides that in order for adjunction to lead to accession, the two movables must become so "united" as "to form a whole." According to well-settled doctrine and jurisprudence, two movables are joined in this fashion *if and only if* they are "permanently attached." Permanent attachment, in this context, is a function not only of the nature and degree of the physical integration of the two movables (in other words, by what means and to what degree they are physically "stuck" together) but also of "societal expectations" regarding the "closeness" and likely duration of that integration. Our jurisprudence provides numerous examples. It has been held, for instance, that accession takes place when automobile tires (accessory) are attached to an automobile (principal). That is true even though the degree of integration, as a physical matter, is rather slight. The critical factor in this instance, one must suppose, is "societal expectations."

c. Effects

1) Ownership

According to **Art. 510**, once the prerequisites for adjunction are met, "the whole [including the accessory] belongs to the owner of the principal thing."

2) Remedies

a) Owner of Principal

Under **LSA-C.C. Art. 515**, if the principal was used without the knowledge of its owner, he may demand, "in lieu of the ownership of the new thing," that "materials of the same species, quantity, weight, measure, and quality or their value be delivered to him" by the person who used it. In addition, the owner of the principal, in such a situation, is entitled to "damages" from the person who used his thing. **LSA-C.C. Art. 516.**

b) Owner of Accessory

1] SEPARATION AND RETURN

If the accessory is "more valuable" than the principal and if the accessory was used without the knowledge of its owner, then the owner may, extraordinarily, demand that the two things be separated and that the accessory be returned to him. **Art. 510, sent. 3.** This remedy is available to him even if the separation would cause injury to the principal. ***Id.***

2] REIMBURSEMENT

If the separation remedy is not available or if, though it is available, the owner of the accessory chooses to forgo it, then he may demand that the owner of the principal reimburse him for the "value" of the accessory. **Art. 510, sent. 2.** Whether the "value" contemplated here is "current" or "original" is unknown.

3] DAMAGES

Under **Art. 516**, if the accessory was used without the knowledge of its owner, he is entitled to "damages" from the person who used it.

2. Transformation

a. Definition

A "transformation" occurs when one uses materials that belong to another to create a new thing.

b. Varieties

1) "Labor Plus Capital" Transformation

a) Definition

Sometimes the "transformer," in addition to using materials that belong to another, also uses materials of his own to make the new thing. Transformation of this kind may be called "labor plus capital" transformation, for the transformer contributes not only his labor—the effort needed to transform the original materials into a new thing—but also his property. This kind of transformation is addressed in **LSA-C.C. Art. 513.**

b) Prerequisites

For labor-plus-capital transformation to result in accession, it must be impossible to "conveniently separate" the part of the new thing that is traceable to the original thing from the part that is traceable to the new capital. *See* **Art. 513.** Where these two parts of the new thing can be so separated, they will be, and each part will be returned to its respective original owner.

c) Effects

1] OWNERSHIP

According to **Art. 513**, if the materials cannot be conveniently separated, the two persons involved share the ownership of the new thing as co-owners in indivision. The second sentence of **Art. 513** provides that the shares of the two persons are determined in relation to the values of their respective contributions to the new thing, i.e., that of the transformer, in relation to the value of his labor and materials, and that of the other person, in relation to the value of his materials.

2] REMEDIES

a] Reimbursement

Inasmuch as the two persons involved own the new thing as co-owners in indivision, there is no place for the remedy of reimbursement in connection with this kind of transformation.

b] Replacement and Damages

Under **LSA-C.C. Art. 515**, if the transformer used the materials of the other person without the other person's knowledge, the other person may demand, "in lieu of the ownership of the new thing," that "materials of the same species, quantity, weight, measure, and quality or their value be delivered to him" by the transformer. In addition, the other person may be entitled to "damages" from the transformer. **LSA-C.C. Art. 516.**

2) "Labor Only" Transformation

a) Definition

Sometimes the "transformer," in making the new thing, uses nothing but materials that belong to another. Transformation of this kind may be called "labor only" transformation, for the transformer's only contribution to the creation of the new thing is his labor. This kind of transformation is addressed in **LSA-C.C. Art. 511.**

b) Prerequisites

Labor-only transformation in itself and without more results in accession.

c) Effects

1] OWNERSHIP

Art. 511 provides that the new thing produced by labor-only transformation belongs to the person from whose materials it was produced, "regardless of whether they [the materials] may be given their earlier form." This, however, is only a general rule. The second paragraph of that article states that the new thing belongs to the transformer if the value of his labor "substantially exceeds" the value of the other person's materials.

The exception itself admits of an exception. Even if the value of the transformer's labor substantially exceeds the value of the other person's materials, **LSA-C.C. Art. 512** allows the court to award ownership of the new thing to the other person if the transformer acted in "bad faith." For purposes of this rule, the transformer is in "bad faith" if he knows (actual knowledge) or should know (constructive knowledge) that the other person's materials do not belong to him. ***Id.***

2] REMEDIES

a] Reimbursement

The remedies in a case of labor-only transformation vary depending on which of the three "ownership rules" applies. Where the general rule of ownership applies, i.e., the person other than the transformer acquires ownership of the new thing, **Art. 511** states that the transformer can demand that the other person reimburse him for the value of his labor. Where the exception to the exception applies, i.e., the transformer acquires ownership, the final sentence of **Art. 511** provides that the other person can demand that the transformer reimburse him for the value of his materials. Where the exception to the general rule of ownership applies, the transformer, having acted in bad faith, has no reimbursement right.

b] Replacement and Damages

If, under the applicable ownership rule, the person other than the transformer is entitled to claim the ownership of the new thing and if the other person's materials were used without his knowledge, the other person may demand the remedies of "replacement" and "damages" that are established in **Arts. 515** and **516**, respectively, remedies that, as we have seen, are made available to similarly-situated persons in other cases of accession with respect to movables.

3. *Mélange*

a. Definition

Mélange is the mixture of two or more mixable movables, none of which could be considered as principal or accessory, that belong to different owners. There is no requirement that the person who creates the mélange be one of these owners. Thus, it is possible for mélange to occur under circumstances in which the provider of the labor himself makes no capital contribution. The person who creates the mélange may be called the *mixer*; each of the movables that he mixes, a *mixant.* A movable qualifies as a "mixant" if (i) it exists as an ensemble or collection of minute and roughly homogeneous or interchangeable units and (ii) these units are readily susceptible of being intermingled with the minute units of one or more other mixants. Examples of mixants include (i) gases, (ii) liquids, and (iii) collections of small solids such as dirt, rocks, nails, and coins. Mélange is addressed in **LSA-C.C. Art. 514.**

b. Prerequisites

Mélange, without more, does not result in accession. It does so in only two situations. The first is that in which separation cannot be "conveniently made." **Art. 514, ¶2.** The second is that in which, though separation could be conveniently made, neither person is entitled to demand it or, if any of them is so entitled, he declines to do so. ***Id.* at ¶1.** One may not demand separation if one "consented to the mixture." ***Id.***

c. Effects

1) Ownership

Paragraph two of **Art. 514** provides that the owners of the mixants share the ownership of the new thing as co-owners in indivision. The article goes on to state that the share of each is determined in relation to the value of his contribution to the new thing, i.e., the value of his mixant. In the context of mélange, the value of the mixer's labor is not of importance in determining the ownership of the mixture.

This rule of proportionate ownership in indivision is only a general rule, one that admits of an exception. Paragraph three of **Art. 514** provides that if the value of one of the mixants is "far superior" to that of the other (or others), the owner of the more (or most) valuable mixant may (but need not) claim the full ownership of the entire mélange.

2) Remedies

a) Reimbursement

If the owner of the most valuable mixant claims ownership under **Art. 514**, that article allows the owner of the less valuable mixant to demand that the owner of the more valuable mixant reimburse him for the value of his mixant.

b) Replacement and Damages

Any mixant owner who, under the applicable ownership rule, is entitled to claim all or part of the ownership of the mélange and whose mixant was used without his consent may demand, in lieu of that ownership, that the mixer deliver to him a mixant of the same species, quantity, weight, measure, and quality under **Art. 515.** Such a mixant owner may also demand damages from the mixer under **Art. 516.**

C. Accession of Fruits and (Mere) Products

1. Fruits

LSA-C.C. Art. 483 states that "[i]n the absence of rights of other persons, the owner of a thing acquires the ownership of its natural and civil fruits." As a general rule, then, the owner of a thing owns its fruits.

The "other persons" who may have "rights" in the fruits, such that the general rule would be pushed aside, include, to begin with, certain kinds of "precarious possessors." One possibility is a "usufructuary" of the thing from which the fruits are produced. **Art. 483 cmt. (c).** As we will learn later on, a usufructuary, by definition, is entitled to the ownership of the fruits of the thing that is subjected to his usufruct. *See* **LSA-C.C. Art. 550.** Another possibility is a so-called "farm lessee." The whole point of a lease of the surface of a tract of land for the purpose of farming is so that the lessee may raise crops that will, at least for the most part if not in their entirety, belong to him.

Likewise included in the category "other persons" who may have "rights" in fruits are certain possessors. On this point, a sharp distinction must be drawn between possessors in "good faith" and posssessors in "bad faith."

Under **LSA-C.C. Art. 486, ¶1, sent. 1**, a good faith possessor "acquires the ownership of fruits he has gathered." As for fruits that the possessor has worked to produce but that he is unable to gather, they fall within the scope of the general rule, that is, they belong to the owner. But according to sentence two of **Art. 486, ¶1**, the owner must reimburse the good faith possessor for the "expenses" he incurred in producing those ungathered fruits.

A bad faith possessor, by contrast, is *not* entitled to *any* of the fruits, not even those that he has already gathered. As between him and the owner of the underlying thing, all fruits belong to the latter. Consequently, any fruits that he has gathered must be restored to the owner. **Art. 486, ¶2.** Nevertheless, the bad faith possessor is entitled to reimbursement from the owner for the expenses he has incurred in producing the fruits, both those that he has gathered and those that he leaves behind ungathered.

2. Mere Products

Mere products, in contrast to fruits, *always* belong to the owner of the thing from which they are produced. **LSA-C.C. Art. 488, sent. 1.** Nevertheless, under the second sentence of the same article, if the products are produced by a "good faith" possessor, then the owner must reimburse him for his production expenses. A bad faith possessor, by contrast, has no such reimbursement right. ***Id.* at ¶2.**

Chapter Nine

Modified Ownership: Ownership in Indivision

I. Definition

"Ownership in indivision" or, as it is more commonly called, "co-ownership," is "[o]wnership of the same thing by two or more persons." **LSA-C.C. Art. 797.** Thus, there are three elements of co-ownership: (i) ownership, (ii) the same thing, and (iii) two or more persons.

A. Ownership

One would suppose that the significance of defining "ownership in indivision" as a form of "ownership" is, among other things, that it is composed of the same constitutive elements—the rights of *usus*, *fructus*, and *abusus*—and the same characteristics—absoluteness, exclusivity, and perpetuity—as is ownership. And that is true in some sense and for some purposes, but only for some. With respect to the co-owned thing itself, the co-owners—as a group and acting together—have full *usus*, *fructus*, and *abusus* and these rights are absolute, exclusive (of persons other than the co-owners), and perpetual. But that is obviously true and, in the end, not very interesting. Much more interesting is what of the *usus*, *fructus*, and *abusus* of the co-owned thing each of the co-owners, by himself and in isolation from the others, has and to what extent what each has may be considered absolute, exclusive, and perpetual. A complete answer to this question will have to wait for later. Suffice it to say for now that each co-owner, on his own, has a "part" of the *usus*, a "part" of the *fructus*, and a "part" of the *abusus* (though the meaning of "part" varies as applied to these different rights) and that the right that each of them has to his respective "slice" of these three rights is absolute, exclusive (in some sense, even as to the other co-owners), and perpetual.

B. The Same Thing

Co-owners own the "same thing" together. The interest that each co-owner has in the thing is not to any distinctive particular physical part of the thing, but to a mathematical share or fraction of the whole thing. Thus, if two persons co-own an acre of land, it would be wrong to think that one co-owner owns, say, the "back" half and the other, the "front" half. Here is how Planiol explained it:

> The right of each owner bears upon the whole (and not a given part) of the thing held in common. The share of each is therefore not a tangible share but a portion expressed by a fraction: a third, a fourth, a tenth. It is the right of ownership that is divided among them. The thing is not. It is held in indivision. The right of each co-owner must be pictured as striking every molecule of the thing.[1]

Another way to make the same point is this: the interest of each co-owner, instead of being "localized" on some discrete part of the thing, is "dispersed" over the entirety of it.

C. Two or More Persons

The third and final element of the definition—"two or more persons"—unlike the others, is neither misleading nor elusive. There are, however, two points that, though obvious, are still worth noting: (i) the persons may be natural or juridical and (ii) the number of persons is, in principle, unlimited.

1. Marcel Planiol, Traité Elémentaire de Droit Civil § 2497.

II. Domain

Any "thing," as that term has been heretofore defined in this Précis, can be co-owned. This thing may be corporeal, but it may just as well be incorporeal. **LSA-C.C. Art. 818** alludes to at least part of this possibility: "The provisions governing co-ownership apply to other rights held in indivision to the extent compatible with the nature of those rights." These "other rights," as the comment to the article notes, include "other real rights," that is, real rights other than ownership. But the category "other rights" includes still more, namely, "credit rights," for example, the right to collect damages for a delict or quasi-delict or to collect money owed under a contract.

That is not all. The comment to **Art. 818** alludes to the fact that the rules on co-ownership may be applied even to "possession," notwithstanding that possession, as we have seen, if neither a right (in other words, an incorporeal thing) nor, for that matter, any other kind of "thing" in any sense of that word.

III. Creation

Co-ownership can arise in any number of ways. For convenience, the possibilities can be collected under two broad headings: (1) by operation of law and (2) by juridical act.

A. By Operation of Law

In some instances, co-ownership arises by operation of law, regardless of the wishes of the co-owners. There are several possibilities.

1. Intestate Succession

An "intestate" succession—the kind of succession that takes place when the deceased person did not leave a "testament" (will)—that takes place in favor of two or more heirs gives rise to co-ownership as among those co-heirs. To take a simple example, imagine that a single woman dies intestate, survived by her three children. Under **LSA-C.C. Art. 888**, the ownership of the estate of this woman—the whole of it—will fall to her three children, in indivision, with the result that each of them will own an undivided one-third share of the estate.

2. Commingling or Mixture of Materials

LSA-C.C. Art. 513, which concerns accession with respect to movables, provides that "[w]hen one uses partly his own materials and partly the materials of another to make a new thing, unless the materials can be conveniently separated, the thing belongs to the owners of the materials in indivision." Thus, the "commingling" of materials of two or more persons in such a way as to produce a new movable thing may give rise to ownership of that thing in indivision. The same thing can happen where "mixable" materials that belong to two or more persons are mixed together. **LSA-C.C. Art. 514.**

3. Termination of Community: Divorce and Separation

Paragraph one of **LSA-C.C. Art. 2369.1** tells us that "[a]fter termination of the community property regime, the provisions governing co-ownership apply to former community property, unless otherwise provided by law or by juridical act." This "termination" may come about as a result of any number of causes, for example, the death of one of the spouses, a divorce judgment, a judgment of separation from bed and board (in the case of a "covenant marriage"), a judgment of "separation of property," or the striking of a separation-of-property agreement. In all of these cases, save for death, the consequence of the termination is that the spouses (or former spouses) become co-owners in indivision of their former community property. In the case of death, the consequence varies depending on whether the deceased spouse disposed of his interest in the community property by testament and, if he did not, whether he was survived by descendants. If the deceased spouse did so, then the surviving spouse and the legatee of the deceased spouse become co-owners of the former community property. If he did not do so and if he was not survived by descendants, then his surviving spouse becomes the sole owner of all of the former community property. *See* **LSA-C.C. Art. 889.** If he did not do so and if he was survived by descendants, then his surviving spouse and his descendants become co-owners of the former community property, the surviving spouse of what had been her half and the descendants of what had been his half, and the surviving spouse receives a usufruct over the descendants' half (which means that, in reality, the descendants receive shares of the "naked ownership" of what had been the deceased's half). *See* **LSA-C.C. Art. 888 & 890.**

4. Acquisitive Prescription by Co-Possessors

Co-ownership can arise through acquisitive prescription. As we noted earlier, "possession" is susceptible of co-ownership, which is another way of saying that multiple persons may "co-possess" undivided shares of a thing. If these co-possessors satisfy the requisites for acquisitive prescription, then they will, at the end of the delay, become co-owners of the thing. Take this example. Two children, having acquired through intestate succession a certain tract of land X that, until her death, had belonged to their mother, go out and take possession of another tract of land Y, mistaking it for tract of land X. If their co-possession of tract of land Y continues for 30 years, they will, through acquisitive prescription, become the co-owners of that tract.

5. Quasi-Occupancy of a Treasure

When a treasure is found, it is possible for co-ownership of the treasure to arise. That would be the case if the finder were to find it in or on a thing that belongs to another. In such a case, as we saw earlier, the finder of the treasure and the owner of the thing in which the treasure is found become 50/50 co-owners of the treasure.

6. Occupancy and Quasi-Occupancy by Co-Possessors

Though rare, it is possible for two or more persons, acting together, to take co-possession of a *res nullius* or of a lost thing or of a treasure. In the case of a *res nullius*, the co-possessors, through occupancy, immediately become co-owners of it. In the case of a lost thing, the co-possessors, provided they have made the requisite "diligent effort" to locate the owner, become co-owners, through quasi-occupancy, after the passage of three years. In the case of a treasure, the resulting co-ownership situation would vary depending on where the treasure is found. If the co-possessors find it in or on something that belongs to them, then they will become co-owners of it in equal shares. But if they find it in or on a thing that belongs to another, then they will become co-owners of the "finder's share," that is, one-half, so that each of them has a one-quarter interest in the whole, and the person in or on whose thing it is found will have the other one-half undivided share.

B. By Act of Will

1. Bilateral Acts: Sales, Exchanges, Donations Inter Vivos, Dations En Paiement

When two persons together acquire a thing through an *inter vivos* transfer, they become the co-owners of it. Suppose, for example, that two persons pool their funds in order to purchase a thing. As "co-purchasers," they will become co-owners of the thing. The same result would follow were a donor to donate one and the same thing to two donees.

2. Unilateral Acts: Donations Mortis Causa

A donation *mortis causa* (in other words, a legacy) made in favor of multiple donees makes all of them co-owners of that thing. That is true whether the thing so donated (the "object" of the "legacy") is a universality of things, as in the case of a "universal legacy" (a donation of all of the donor's property), or a single thing, as in the case of a "particular legacy."

IV. Division of Shares

A. General (Default) Rule

The "size" of each co-owner's share, in other words, how his share of the thing compares, mathematically speaking, with those of the others, may vary. The general (default) rule is found in the second sentence of **LSA-C.C. Art. 797**: "the shares of all co-owners are presumed to be equal." In other words, the allocation is by "heads." Thus, if there are two co-owners, each is presumed to hold a one-half share; if there are three, each is presumed to hold a one-third share; and so on.

B. Exceptions

To this general rule, there are two exceptions.

1. Division Mandated by Law

In some instances, the law (meaning, in this case, some legislative provision) itself provides that the allocation of shares between co-owners shall be otherwise than by heads. One example is provided by **LSA-C.C. Art. 513**, which, as we have seen before, concerns the species of "accession with respect to movables" known as commingling. If one person uses both his materials and the materials of another to create a new movable thing and if these two sets of materials cannot be conveniently separated, then the one who made the thing and the owner of the other materials co-own the thing in indivision. But they do not necessarily co-own it in equal shares. To the contrary, their respective shares are determined in proportion to the value of the "input(s)" of each into the production of the new thing. Another example is provided by paragraph two of **LSA-C.C. Art. 514**, which lays down a similar rule for cases of accession with respect to movables that involve "mixture."

2. Division Mandated by Juridical Act

In a case of co-ownership created by juridical act, the judicial act itself may mandate a deviation from the usual "all shares are equal" rule. To take just one example, imagine that a donor (*inter vivos* or *mortis causa*) makes a donation to two persons, but in so doing specifies that the first shall have a one-fourth share and the latter, a three-fourths share. This stipulation by the donor will be controlling.

V. Rights of Co-Owners

A. Rights in *the Co-Owned Thing Itself*

1. Fruits

LSA-C.C. Art. 798 governs the co-owners' respective rights to fruits of the co-owned thing. It provides that:

> Co-owners share the fruits and products of the thing held in indivision in proportion to their ownership.
>
> When fruits or products are produced by a co-owner, other co-owners are entitled to their shares of the fruits or products after deduction of the costs of production.

These two paragraphs differ in scope. Whereas the first paragraph lays down a general rule that covers fruits or products regardless of how they may be produced, specifically, regardless whether they are produced naturally or artificially and, in the latter case, regardless who—a co-owner or someone else (e.g., a possessor)—produces them, the second lays down a special rule for fruits and products that are produced artificially by the acts of a co-owner.[2] If the fruits or products are produced without the effort of any of the co-owners, then the division is simple: it is made in proportion to the co-owners' respective shares of the underlying thing. But if that is not so—if the production involves the effort of any of the co-owners—then that co-owner must first be given an allowance, out of what has been produced, in the amount of the value of his cost of production. After that part has been deducted, the remainder is divided among the co-owners in proportion to their shares, in accordance with the general rule.

2. Use

a. General Rule: Equal Use

The co-owners' respective rights to use the co-owned thing are addressed in **LSA-C.C. Art. 802.** It provides that "a co-owner is entitled to use the thing held in indivision according to its destination, but he cannot prevent another co-owner from making such use of it." What the first part of this article means is that each co-owner has just as much right as any other to "use" the co-owned thing and to use *all* of it, provided that the use to which he puts it is consistent with its "destination." The destination of the co-owned thing, in the words of our jurisprudence, is "the use to which the common property is best suited or is

---

2. As used here, the terms "fruit" and "products" have the same meanings that we assigned to them earlier when we examined the classification of things into "fruits and (mere) products."

reasonably being put." The right to equal use, it should be noted, belongs to each co-owner no matter how large or small may be his share of the co-owned thing; even a 1% co-owner is, in principle, entitled to equal and full use. In addition to the "destination" limitation on use, there is another, one that arises in the nature of things. Found in the second part of **Art. 802**, it is this: the use to which one co-owner puts the co-owned thing cannot be such as to interfere with the other co-owners' use of it. When only one of the co-owners wishes to use the thing or when, though more than one wishes to do so, their uses are fully compatible with each other, this limitation presents no complications. It is otherwise when more than one of the co-owners wishes to use the thing and the proposed uses are incompatible.

b. Exception: Use Defined by Agreement

The rule of **Art. 802** is subject to an "exception," one found in **LSA-C.C. Art. 801**. The exception is this: "[t]he use and management of the thing held in indivision is determined by agreement of all the co-owners." This article permit the co-owners to derogate from the rule of equal use by agreement, specifically, a management-and-use agreement. The co-owners can strike any such agreement they may wish. They may confide the use of the thing to a third person, even to the exclusion of themselves. They may even go as far to authorize only *one* of them to use the thing, to the exclusion of the others.

3. Conservatory Acts

LSA-C.C. Art. 800 provides that "[a] co-owner may without the concurrence of any other co-owner take necessary steps for the preservation of the thing that is held in indivision." We have encountered the phrase, or one very much like it—"necessary expenses incurred for the preservation of the thing"—in the law governing the rights of possessors, in particular, a possessor's right to recover his expenses from the owner of the thing. *See* **LSA-C.C. Arts. 527–529.** As we learned in our study of that law, an expense is "necessary to preserve the thing" when it is incurred to protect the thing from a threat, usually imminent, of decay, destruction, or loss. Excluded from the scope of "necessary expenses" are those that are merely for "ordinary maintenance and repair."

4. *Ordinary Maintenance and Repair*

Speaking of expenses for "ordinary maintenance and repair," a co-owner's right to incur them is addressed, albeit obliquely, in **LSA-C.C. Art. 806.** According to that article, "[a] co-owner who on account of the thing held in indivision has incurred necessary expenses, *expenses for ordinary maintenance and repairs*, [etc.]... is entitled to reimbursement." A co-owner, then, can recover expenses for ordinary maintenance and repair as well as necessary expenses. To say that he may recover such expenses is to presuppose that he has the right to incur them. It would seem, then, that **Art. 800** is incomplete. To the list therein of expenses that a co-owner may incur on his own, one must add expenses for ordinary maintenance and repair.

5. *Improvements and Alterations*

LSA-C.C. Art. 804, which pertains to "improvements and alterations" to the co-owned thing, provides that "[s]ubstantial alterations or substantial improvements to the thing held in indivision may be undertaken only with the consent of all the co-owners." Two aspects of this article are deserving of comment: what it says expressly and what it implies.

First, let us consider what it says expressly. If what is contemplated is a "substantial" improvement or alteration, a single co-owner, acting by himself, cannot make it. To the contrary, concurrence of all of the co-owners is required. Note that *tacit or implied* consent is sufficient: paragraph two of **Art. 804** refers to "the express or implied consent of his co-owners."

Now, let us consider the implication. To say that a co-owner cannot make "substantial" improvements or alterations by himself is to imply that he *may* make *less than substantial*, in other words, "insubstantial," improvements or alterations by himself. Presumably he can make such improvements or alterations even over his co-owners' objection.

What is the difference between a substantial and an insubstantial improvement or alteration? This much is certain: the line separating the two is not "bright." Whether a given improvement or alteration qualifies as "substantial" is a "question of fact," that is, it is the kind of question the resolution of which, in the event of a dispute, will be confided to the discretion of the trier of fact.

One other question that must be raised in connection with **Art. 804** is how the concepts "improvement" and "alteration" as used therein line up with the concepts "improvement" and "INATs" as used in the law of accession in general. It is to be regretted that there is no clear answer to this question. This much, however, seems to be certain: the concept of "INATs" either (1) is entailed in the **Art. 804** concept of "improvement," in which case "improvement" for purposes of this article is broader than "improvement" for purposes of **Art. 493**, or (2) is entailed in the **Art. 804** concept of "alteration." Either way, INATs are "covered."

B. In the Co-Owner's Share of the Co-Owned Thing

1. Disposition

a. Alienation

Under sentence one of **LSA-C.C. Art. 805**, each co-owner is free to alienate—that is, to transfer—all of his share or parts of his share. He may do so without the concurrence, or, indeed, even the knowledge, of his co-owners.

b. Creation of Real Rights

The first sentence of **Art. 805** provides that a co-owner, in addition to alienating his share of the co-owned thing, may "encumber" it. To "encumber" something is to create on it a real right less than ownership.

1) Accessory Real Rights (Security Rights)

This "lesser" real right that the co-owner may create on his share may be some kind of "accessory" real right. For example, if the co-owned thing is an immovable, the co-owner may create a mortgage on his share of it or, if that thing is a movable, a **UCC-Art. 9** security interest on his share of it.

2) Principal Real Rights Less Than Ownership: Servitudes

The power to "encumber" ordinarily includes as well the power to create lesser "principal" real rights, that is, servitudes. As applied to at least one servitude, namely, the personal servitude of *usufruct*, the notion that a co-owner's power of encumbrance extends to servitudes presents no problem: a co-owner may grant someone a usufruct over his share. But as applied to the other servitudes, specifically, predial servitudes and the personal servitudes of right of use and habitation, there is a considerable problem: these servitudes can be created only on corporeals but each co-owner's share of the co-owned thing is an incorporeal. For this reason, it would seem that a co-owner cannot create a servitude of this kind on his share.

But appearances can be deceiving. The legislature has made a special provision for cases in which a co-owner attempts to create such a servitude on his share, a provision that gives to his attempt at least a *contingent* effect. Look, first, at **LSA-C.C. Art. 716**:

> When a co-owner has consented to the establishment of a predial servitude on his undivided part only, the consent of the other co-owners is not required, but the exercise of the servitude is suspended until his divided part is determined at the termination of the state of indivision.

This principle is extended to other servitudes by **LSA-C.C. Art. 813**:

> When a thing is partitioned in kind, a real right that burdens the share of a co-owner attaches to the part of the thing allotted to him.

Thus, a co-owner can grant this kind of servitude on his share of an immovable, but the servitude will be "suspended"—will not take effect—unless and until the immovable is partitioned and only if, in that partition, part of the immovable is awarded to the co-owner who granted it.

c. Creation of Personal Rights: Lease

Art. 805 gives each co-owner still one more power with respect to his share: that of "leasing" it. This notion may seem puzzling at first, for when one thinks of leased things, one ordinarily imagines corporeals. The truth is, however, that incorporeals no less so than corporeals can be leased. *See* **LSA-C.C. Art. 2673.** In the case of a lease of a co-owner's share, what the lessee receives, in effect, is, subject to the limitations on use imposed by the lease itself, the same *usus* rights of the underlying co-owned thing as are available to the co-owner himself.

VI. Improvements and Alterations: Accession

We have already seen that a co-owner has the right to make improvements or alterations to the co-owned thing under certain circumstances. If the co-owners concur, he can make substantial improvements or alterations. Even if they do not concur, he can make insubstantial improvements or alterations. What we want to consider now is the question of accession or, to be more precise, (i) who owns any such improvement or alteration once it is made and (ii) what remedies the co-owner who makes it, on the one hand, and those who do not, on the other, have *vis-à-vis* each other.

A. Ownership

Imagine that one of the co-owners makes an improvement or alteration to the co-owned thing. Searching for the answer to the question "who owns it," one might suppose that one should start with **Art. 804**, which, as we have already seen, concerns the power of co-owners to make improvements. A close reading of the article, however, reveals that it does not contain any "ownership" rules of its own. Further, though the article does contain cross-references to two of the articles that are found in the part of the Civil Code that pertains to accession with respect to immovables, namely, **LSA-C.C. Arts. 496** and **497**, those articles, as we learned earlier, concern not the *ownership* of improvements, etc., but rather *remedies* with respect to such things as between the contributor and the owner. Properly interpreted, then, **Art. 804** says *absolutely* nothing about which of the co-owners owns improvements that one of them may make to the co-owned thing. It would seem, then, that this question—the "ownership question"—must be resolved on the basis of "general principles," specifically, those found in the part of the Civil Code that pertains to accession in general.

This conclusion, however, simply leads to more trouble. The source of the trouble is this: how the general principles of accession should be applied to situations of co-ownership is anything but clear. Consider the case of a building that one of several co-owners of a tract of land has built upon that land. Of the articles on accession in general, **Art. 493** controls here, for, as we have seen, that article determines the ownership of "improvements" made to land. According to that article, who owns the improvement turns on whether the "landowner" consented to its being joined to the original immovable. But who is the "landowner" in a case of co-ownership? In principle, each of the co-owners is an "owner" in some sense and all of the co-owners, considered as a group, are "the owner." So, precisely whose consent determines ownership here? Is it the consent of all of the co-owners, including the one who built the building? Or, is it only the consent of the other co-owners? In any event, what if the co-owners whose consent is relevant (whether they include or exclude the co-owner who built the thing) disagree? Is the rule one of "the majority prevails"? Or should one, instead, proceed co-owner by co-owner, concluding that as to the consenting co-owner(s), the building belongs to the co-owner who built it, but as to those who did not, it belongs to them? There is, as yet, no jurisprudence on point. The few scholars who have addressed the question seem to prefer the second alternative, that is, the co-owner by co-owner approach, but they offer little justification for their opinion.

B. Remedies

Now, let us consider to what remedies the respective parties—the co-owner who makes the improvement or alteration and those who do not—are entitled as against each other. **Art. 804** answers this question, but it does so in part only. First, to the extent that **Art. 804** provides any remedies at all, it is remedies as to "substantial" improvements and alterations only. Left unaddressed are the remedies available with respect to "insubstantial" improvements and alterations. Second, though **Art. 804** contains a cross-reference to two of the accession articles that establish remedies, namely, **Arts. 496** and **497**, those articles, it will be recalled, are rather narrow in scope. First, they apply only in the case of accession with respect to *immovables.* Second, they apply only to the kind of situation in which the landowners have *not consented* to the improvements. It follows, then, that if the question of remedies arises in the context of co-ownership, **Art. 804** offers no guidance at all regarding how to resolve that question if it involves (1) insubstantial improvements or alterations, (2) improvements or alterations to movables, or (3) improvements or alterations made "*with the consent* of the owner," whatever that might mean where there is more than one "owner." In these three situations, then, we have no choice but to resort to the remedial rules of the general law of accession.

The trouble does not stop there. Even in the cases to which **Art. 804** *does* apply, there is considerable uncertainty. The pertinent part of that article reads as follows:

> When a co-owner makes substantial alterations or substantial improvements consistent with the use of the property, though without the express or implied consent of his co-owners, the rights of the parties shall be determined by Article 496. When a co-owner makes substantial alterations or improvements inconsistent with the use of the property or in spite of the objections of his co-owners, the rights of the parties shall be determined by Article 497.

The term "use," as used in this article, presumably means "destination."

This provision, boiled down to its essence, establishes two rules. First, if the co-owner makes an improvement or alteration (which, recall, must be "substantial" if this part of **Art. 804** is to apply at all) (i) that is inconsistent with the "use" of the thing or (ii) to which his co-owners objected, then he is treated as a "bad faith" possessor for purposes of remedial rights. Second, in all other cases (of substantial improvements or alternations), he is treated as a "good faith" possessor for purposes of remedial rights. Let us now consider how these rules might play out concretely.

In a case that falls under the second rule (good faith), the "owner," according to **Art. 496**, must first of all "keep" the thing, which, in the context of co-ownership, presumably means that the co-owner(s) who opposes the improvement or alteration cannot compel the co-owner who made it to remove it at his own expense. So far so good. In addition to "keeping" it, however, the "owner," according to **Art. 496**, must pay him who made it, at the option of the "owner," an indemnity in the amount of the current value of the materials and workmanship or the enhanced value of the immovable. But how is the choice between these alternative remedies to be made when the "owner" is multiple? Is the choice confided to the co-owner(s) who did not make the improvement or alteration, to the exclusion of the one who did? Regardless of the answer to this question, what is to be done if the co-owners who are permitted to participate in the decision don't agree? Is it a case of "the majority rules"? If not, how is the disagreement to be resolved?

In a case that falls under the first rule (bad faith), this uncertainty is, in effect, "doubled" or, better yet, "tripled." In such a case, the "owner," according to **Art. 497**, has the option of (1) compelling the one who made the thing to remove it at his expense or (2) keeping it but paying him one of three alternative measures of indemnity, among which the "owner" is free to choose. In addition, the "owner" may recover "damages" caused by the making of the improvement or alternation. As to each of these three choices, we encounter the same, recurring problem: does the co-owner who made the thing get to participate in the decision and, regardless of that, how is disagreement among those who get to participate to be resolved.

VII. Termination of Co-Ownership

Co-ownership can come to end in any number of ways. We will consider the most important of them below.

A. Loss of the Thing

The loss (which means, in this context, the destruction of the thing), by definition, puts an end to any and all real rights to which it may theretofore have been subjected. The same is true of co-ownership.

B. Juridical Act of Transfer by the Co-Owners

The co-owners themselves may put an end to their co-ownership through an appropriate juridical act of transfer. By "act of transfer" is meant "act translative of ownership," in other words, a sale, donation, exchange, or *dation en paiement*. The co-owners might—each of them—transfer their interests to a single person through acts of this kind. Or, they might, instead, "consolidate" ownership in a single one among themselves through a transfer to him by the others of their respective shares of ownership. In either case, the transferee acquires unitary, full ownership.

C. Partition

The most common cause of the termination of co-ownership is the partition of the co-owned thing.

1. Availability

a. General Rule

One of the most basic principles of the law of co-ownership is that "[n]o one may be compelled to hold a thing in indivision with another unless the contrary has been provided by law of juridical act." **LSA-C.C. Art. 807, ¶1.** To give effect to this principle, the law of co-ownership accords to each co-owner the right, at least as a general rule, to demand partition of the co-owned thing whenever he wishes. ***Id.* at ¶2, sent. 1.**

b. Exceptions

There are, however, some significant exceptions to this general rule.

1) Contrary Provision in a Juridical Act

As we have seen, the first paragraph of **Art. 807** provides that a co-owner, by way of exception, may be compelled to remain a co-owner and may be denied the right of partition "*by... juridical act.*" There are several possibilities here.

a) Act Creating Indivision

One is that, in a case of indivision created by juridical act, that juridical act itself may preclude partition, at least for a time. This possibility is addressed in **LSA-C.C. Art. 1300, ¶1**, which provides that "a donor or testator can order that the effects given or bequeathed by him [to multiple donees], be not divided for a certain time." This power, however, is not unlimited. As a general matter, the donor cannot stipulate a period of non-partition in excess of five years; if he tries to do so, any co-owner may, notwithstanding the stipulation, still demand partition at the end of five years. **LSA-C.C. Art. 1300, ¶2.** By way of exception, if the donor is an ascendant of the donees and if the donees are minors, the donor may stipulate that the thing not be partitioned until the eldest becomes a major, even if that period exceeds five years. **LSA-C.C. Art. 1301.**

b) Convention Among Co-Owners

The co-owners themselves can agree not to partition the co-owned thing. *See* **Art. 807, ¶2, sent. 2.** Nevertheless, this power, too, is not unlimited. The maximum permissible term for such a nonpartition agreement is 15 years. *See* ***id.*** ("Partition may be excluded by agreement for up to fifteen years.") If the co-owners should stipulate a longer term, their agreement will still be effective, but any of them will be free to demand a partition at the end of the 15th year.

2) Contrary Provision of Law

One instance of a situation in which partition is precluded "by law" can be found in **LSA-C.C. Art. 808.** According to that article, "[p]artition of a thing held in indivision is excluded when its use is indispensable for the enjoyment of another thing owned by one or more of the co-owners." The classic example is that of a co-owned alleyway that provides one of the co-owners with his sole means of access to a tract of land he owns by himself.

2. Juridical Nature

a. Conventional

If the co-owners can agree, then the partition can be effected in any manner they may desire. *See* **LSA-C.C. Art. 809** ("The mode of partition may be determined by agreement of all the co-owners."). The co-owners may even choose to resort to means and methods that would be precluded in a "judicial" partition, such as the "marshaling of assets," when the co-owned "thing" is, in reality, a collectivity of things, or a "private" sale of the co-owned thing.

b. Legal (Judicial)

But if the co-owners cannot agree, either on whether partition should occur or on the means of partition, then they must seek the assistance of the court. The second sentence of **Art. 809** provides: "In the absence of such an agreement, a co-owner may demand a judicial partition."

3. Modes

There are two ways in which a judicial partition may be effected: "in kind" and "by sale."

a. In Kind

Partition in kind is the distribution of parts of the co-owned thing to the individual co-owners. This method is preferred to the alternative, partition by licitation. In other words, if partition in kind *can* be done, then it *must* be done. But there are several prerequisites to partition in kind, and if any of them should be unmet, then the court will have no choice but to resort to partition by licitation.

The prerequisites for partition in kind are set forth in **LSA-C.C. Art. 810**, which provides that

> [t]he court shall decree partition in kind when the thing held in indivision is susceptible to division into as many lots of nearly equal value as there are shares and the aggregate value of all lots is not significantly lower than the value of the property in the state of indivision.

There are, then, two requirements. The first, physical divisibility, is that the thing itself must be susceptible of being divided into as many parts as their co-owners. The second, value equivalency, has two aspects. One is that the value of each proposed "part" must be "nearly equal" to that of every other; the other, that the sum of the values of these parts must not be "significantly lower" than the value of the co-owned thing as a whole. What constitutes "nearly equal" and "significantly lower" are "questions of fact."

b. By Sale

Partition by sale involves the sale of the co-owned thing, followed by the distribution of the proceeds of the sale among the individual co-owners in proportion to their shares of ownership in the co-owned thing. Regarding the mode of sale, there are two possibilities: "private sale" and "licitation."

A private sale is a typical, ordinary sale. One common instance is that in which the co-owners personally and directly sell the co-owned thing to a buyer whom they have found out in the market, normally through the aid of some sort of advertising (for example, listing the co-owned thing with an agent), and with whom they have set the terms of the deal, including the setting of the price, through mutual negotiation. An important variation is that in which one co-owner "buys out" the others, that is, the others sell their respective shares of the thing to him, making him the sole owner, but, again, through mutual negotiation of all the terms, including the price.

Licitation is a sale conducted by "auction." The auction may be conducted by some governmental authority (in the typical case, a sheriff) or, more extraordinarily, by a non-governmental auctioneer appointed by the court. In either case, the buyer is the "highest bidder."

Until recently, the law of partition evidenced a preference for licitation over private sale. In fact, the court was permitted to order a private sale only upon the agreement of all of the co-owners. This preference, however, oftentimes resulted in inequity. Imagine a case in which a tract of land is owned by two co-owners, one of them cash-rich and the other cash-poor, and does not meet the requirements for a partition in kind. In such a case, the cash-rich co-owner could, by unilaterally refusing to agree to a private sale, force a licitation, one at which he then not only could out-bid the cash-poor co-owner but also buy the land for pennies on the dollar, resulting in a significant wealth transfer from the latter to the former.

Through a series of recent amendments to the controlling legislation, the legislature has taken action to address this inequity. The most pertinent parts of the new legislation read as follows:

LSA-C.C. Art. 811

> A. When the thing held in indivision is not susceptible to partition in kind, the court shall decree a partition by licitation or, as provided in Paragraph B of this Article, by private sale and the proceeds shall be distributed to the co-owners in proportion to their shares.
>
> B. In the event that one or more of the co-owners are absentees or have not consented to a partition by private sale, the court shall order a partition by private sale and shall give first priority to the private sale between the existing co-owners, over the sale by partition by licitation or private sale to third parties. The court shall order the partition by private sale between the existing co-owners as identified in the conveyance records as of the date of filing for the petition for partition by private sale. The petition for partition by private sale shall be granted first priority, and the sale shall be executed under Title IX of Book VII of the Code of Civil Procedure.

LSA-C.C.P. Art. 4607

> When a partition is to be made by licitation, the sale shall be conducted at public auction and after the advertisements required for judicial sales under execution. When a partition is to be made at private sale without the consent of all co-owners, the sale shall be for not less than the appraised value of the property, and documents required pursuant to a court order shall be executed on behalf of the absentee or non-consenting co-owner by a court-appointed representative, who may be a co-owner, after the advertisements required for judicial sales under execution are made. All counsel of record, including curators appointed to represent absentee defendants, and persons appearing in proper person shall be given notice of the sale date. At any time prior to the sale, the parties may agree upon a nonjudicial partition.

It would be an understatement to say that this new legislation represents a significant change in the law. First and foremost, the new legislation reverses the order of preference as between private sale and licitation, elevating the former over the latter. Under this legislation, as long as *one* co-owner desires a private sale, the court is obligated to explore the possibility of it and, if the prerequisites for it are satisfied, is obligated to order it, even if all the other co-owners dissent. Further, the legislation creates an order of preference *within* the category of private sales, specifically, elevating sales to a co-owner ("buy out" sales) over private sales to third parties. In either case, the legislation imposes rather stringent requirements on private sales, the chief of which is that the proposed private buyer, be he a co-owner or a third party, must be willing to pay a price in the amount of 100% of the appraised value of the co-owned thing.

Though the new legislation is salutary from the standpoint of good policy, it nevertheless leaves a bit to be desired. First, it employs a number of terms that have no fixed meaning in Louisiana law, such as "absentee" and "first priority." Second, it leaves a number of questions unanswered. One is "what happens if more than one co-owner is willing to buy out the others by paying them their respective shares of 100% of the appraised value?" Here's another: "what happens if, though (only) one of the co-owners is willing to buy out the others by paying them their respective shares of 100% of the appraised value, there's a third party in the picture who's willing to buy the thing for more than the appraised value?" It is to be hoped that the legislature will take quick action to eliminate these infelicities and address these questions.

4. Effects

a. Interests of Co-Owners

1) In Kind: Localization

According to **Art. 810**, in the case of a partition in kind, each co-owner gets a proportionate physical share of the formerly co-owned thing. In the process, his interest, which, as we learned earlier, had once been "dispersed" over the whole co-owned thing, comes to be "localized" as to the discrete part of the co-owned thing that is allocated to him. As to that part, he is now the sole, unitary owner.

2) By Licitation

According to **Art. 811**, in the case of a partition by licitation, each co-owner gets a proportionate share of the proceeds of the sale. Ownership of the co-owned thing itself passes in full to whomever buys it at the auction.

b. Interests of Third Parties

1) Third Parties Who had Real Rights in the Formerly Co-Owned Thing

A partition of the co-owned thing, be it in kind or by licitation, has no effect whatsoever on real rights that burden *the co-owned thing itself* (as opposed to one of the co-owner's shares of the co-owned thing). *See* **LSA-C.C. Art. 812.** This means that the real right continues to burden all of the divided parts of the formerly co-owned thing, if it was partitioned in kind, or continues to burden the whole thing, if it was partitioned by licitation. In the former case, each co-owner takes his part subject to the real right; in the latter, the buyer takes the whole thing subject to that right.

2) Third Parties Who Had Real Rights in a Former Co-Owner's Share

Real rights that burden this or that co-owner's *share* of the co-owned thing (as opposed to the co-owned thing itself), by contrast, *are* affected by a partition of that thing. What effect it is will depend on the type of partition. If the thing is partitioned in kind, then, under **LSA-C.C. Art. 813**, the right will "attach[] to the part of the thing allotted to" the co-owner whose share had been burdened by it. But if the thing is partitioned by licitation, **LSA-C.C. Art. 815** tells us, then the right will "attach[] to his share of the proceeds of the sale."

Chapter Ten

Dismemberments of Ownership: Servitudes and Building Restrictions

SUB-CHAPTER A

Predial Servitudes

I. Definitions

The definition of "predial servitude" is found in **LSA-C.C. Art. 646**: "A predial servitude is a charge on a servient estate for the benefit of a dominant estate.... The two estates must belong to different owners." Let us see if we can break this definition down.

A. Estate

"Estate," the word chosen by the translators of the French versions of the Louisiana Digest of 1808 and Civil Code of 1825 to represent the French term *heritage*, means as "a distinct corporeal immovable." *See* **Art. 646 cmt. (b)**. As this comment goes on to explain, the category "distinct corporeal immovable" includes "tracts of land," "buildings," "timber estates," and even "individual apartments," but excludes "[c]onstructions other than buildings, though classified as immovables by nature... and incorporeal immovables."

A predial servitude presupposes not just one but two of these "estates." Each of them bears a distinctive name, one that reflects the distinctive role it plays in the servitude relationship.

1. Servient

The "*servient* estate," it is commonly said, is that which bears the "charge" (i.e., the "burden") of the predial servitude. Traditional though it may be (the tradition goes back to the Romans), to speak in this way is to indulge in unscientific anthropomorphosis. A predial servitude is, at bottom, a juridical relation, one that, like every other juridical relation, entails a right and a correlative duty. Now, as Planiol explained

> [a] relation of a juridical order cannot exist between a person and a thing: that would be nonsensical. By definition, every right is a relation between persons. This is the elementary truism on which the entire science of the law is founded.[1]

Yiannopolous makes the same point, focusing specifically on juridical relations that entail "real rights" (such as predial servitude):

> According to a broadly accepted definition, a real right is the judicially recognized authority to draw from a thing directly all or part of its economic advantages. The thing appears subjected to the authority of a person—one speaks of a right in the thing—and figures as an essential feature in the legal relationship. This, however, is a metaphor, because, by definition, things cannot participate in a legal relationship.[2]

The point of all this is that the "charge" of the predial servitude does not, because it cannot, fall on an estate, which is a "thing," but must fall on a "person." To suggest otherwise, is, as Planiol, Yiannopoulos, and other scholars have correctly stated, to abandon prose for poetry.

---

1. Marcel Planiol & Georges Ripert, Traité Pratique de Droit Civil Français § 37, at 42 (Maurice Picard ed., 2d ed. 1952).

2. 1 A.N. Yiannopoulos, Property § 204, at 373, *in* Louisiana Civil Law Treatise (3d ed. 1991).

What, then, should one say about the bearer of the "charge" entailed in a predial servitude relationship? It is simply this: that the charge is born by *whosoever may happen to own the servient estate.* If the "charge" in question is part of a predial servitude, then when the current owner of the servient estate A sells the estate to B, then the charge shifts from the shoulders of A to those of B. And if, thereafter, B sells the estate to C, then the charge shifts from the shoulders of B to those of C. And so on it will go. This is the "literal" meaning of the metaphor, "the servient estate is that which bears the 'charge' of the predial servitude."

2. Dominant Estate

The "dominant estate," tradition tells us, is that which "benefits" from the predial servitude. This notion is no less anthropomorphic than the traditional notion of "servient estate." Estates do not benefit from real rights; people do. As comment (c) to **Art. 646** tells us,

> This apparent personification of the dominant estate has its roots in Roman sources. According to modern analysis, however, things cannot have rights; rights belong to persons only. Therefore, legislative declarations... that predial servitudes are due to an estate must be taken as metaphors; they merely mean that predial servitudes are not attached to a particular person but that they are due to anyone who happens to be owner of the dominant estate.

Thus, the "dominant estate" metaphor has a literal meaning that is correlative to that of the "servient estate" metaphor.

B. Charge (on a Servient Estate)

The key to understanding the term "charge," as an element of "predial servitude," lies in what we just finished doing, that is, demystifying the metaphorical notion of "servient estate." The charge of a predial servitude, we just concluded, lies not on a thing but on the person who owns that thing. The scientific term used to denote a charge on a person is "duty" (or, sometimes, "obligation"). Thus, to figure out what "charge" means in the context of predial servitudes, we must determine just what duty the owner of the servient estate, *as owner of that estate*, owes.

This question is addressed in **LSA-C.C. Art. 651.** It provides:

> The owner of the servient estate is not required to do anything. His obligation is to *abstain from doing something on his estate* or to *permit something to be done on it.*

The "charge" of a predial servitude, then, is the duty of the owner of the servient estate either (i) to abstain from doing something there or (ii) to permit something to be done there. Both are examples of duties "not to do." *Cf.* **LSA-C.C. Art. 1756, sent. 2.**

It is crucial to note that both of the kinds of duties to which **Art. 651** refers are "passive." As the first sentence of **Art. 651** puts it, "[t]he owner of the servient estate is not required to do anything."

Does this mean that a duty "to do" something—an "affirmative" duty—cannot form part of the "charge" of a predial servitude? If the rule laid down in the first two sentences of **Art. 651** were "absolute," then the answer would be no. But that rule is not absolute; to the contrary, it is merely a general rule, one that admits of at least one important exception. The locus of this exception is the third sentence of **Art. 651**: "He [the owner of the servient estate] may be required by convention… to keep his estate in suitable condition for the exercise of the servitude due to the dominant estate." Considered by itself, this provision does not clearly answer our question. That is so because, by its literal terms, the provision does not indicate whether, if the servient estate owner were to undertake such a "duty to keep his estate in suitable condition" by "convention," this duty would form part of the predial servitude charge and, for this reason, be "real" or whether it would be independent of and stand alongside that charge and, further, be merely "personal." This uncertainty is resolved in the latter part of comment (b) to **Art. 651**, which reads as follows:

> Parties also may stipulate that the owner of the servient estate shall maintain in good state of repair certain works necessary of the use and preservation of the servitude.… All these incidental affirmative duties of the owner of the servient estate qualify *as land charges or real obligations.*

The answer to our question, then, is that a duty "to do" can indeed form part of the charge of a predial servitude, provided that it is "incidental" to (facilitative of the fulfillment of) some duty "not to do" that forms the foundation or core of the charge.

C. Benefit (of a Dominant Estate)

To understand "benefit" as used in **Art. 646**, we must engage in an exercise not unlike that in which we just engaged in relation to "charge," that is, we must be guided by the literal, rather than the metaphorical, meaning of the "estate" to which it is related, in this case, the "dominant estate." The benefit of a servitude, as we have seen, belongs not to a thing, but to the person who owns that thing. The scientific term used to denote a "benefit" to a person is "right." Thus, to figure out what "benefit" means in the context of predial servitudes, we must determine just what right the owner of the dominant estate, *as owner of that estate*, has.

We can get at least some help in answering this question by looking, once again, at an article that we have already examined, namely, **Art. 651**, even though this article, by its terms, concerns only the meaning of "charge." Let us not forget that "charge" means "duty," that "benefit" means "right," and that "predial servitude," as a juridical relation, entails a "correlative" right and duty. It follows from this that the charge and the benefit in a predial servitude relationship are "correlative" to each other. Now, as we have already learned, the charge, at least at its core, must consist either of (1) the servient estate owner's not doing something on the servient estate that he otherwise would be entitled to do or (2) the servient estate owner's allowing the dominant estate owner to go onto the servient estate to do something there. Because the benefit is correlative to the charge, it follows that the benefit, at its core, must consist either of (1) the dominant estate owner's right to insist that the servient estate owner not do on his estate something that he otherwise would be entitled to do or (2) the dominant estate owner's right to go onto the servient estate to do something there.

This, then, is what the benefit of a predial servitude *may* be. But if we are to understand "benefit" in its fullness, we must also determine what it may *not* be. As it turns out, there are at least two limitations on the kinds of rights that may form part of this benefit.

One of these limitations—the less stringent and, in the end, less significant—is set out in comment (b) to **LSA-C.C. Art. 647**, the pertinent part of which provides as follows:

> The principle of utility... sets the outer limits of party autonomy in the field of predial servitudes. The law will allow... freedom to the extent that a servitude may serve a useful pur-

> pose; unreasonable whims of parties, serving no socially useful purpose, may not give rise to predial servitudes.

Thus, the "benefit" must be useful, not only for the person who seeks to acquire it, but also for society as a whole.

The second and more important limitation is established in **Art. 647** itself. According to that article, "[t]here must be a benefit to the dominant estate.... There is no predial servitude if the charge imposed cannot be reasonably expected to benefit the dominant estate." Upon reading this article, one might be tempted to think that, far from imposing any sort of restriction on the range of possible predial servitude benefits, it mere reiterates, somewhat redundantly, the part of the definition of "predial servitude" found in **Art. 646** that pertains to "benefit." But to read this article in that way is to misunderstand it completely. The article presupposes something that may not be immediately apparent, namely, that of the possible rights that one might imagine trying to put into a predial servitude, some are such that they benefit *an estate* and others are such that they benefit *a person.* And the point of the article is this: to make it clear that the benefit of a predial servitude may consist *only* of a right of the first kind, that is, one that benefits an estate.

The dichotomy between "benefits to estates" and "benefits to persons," as so formulated, is open to objection. As we have already noted repeatedly, "benefits" belong to "persons," not to "estates," and so, to speak of "benefit to an estate" is to speak metaphorically. As we have also noted before, the literal meaning of this metaphor—"benefit to an estate"—is "benefit to whosoever may happen to own the state." Thus, the proposed dichotomy, scientifically reconstructed, is this: "benefit to whosoever happens to own the estate" *versus* "benefit to a person."

This formulation may be more scientific, but it is no less opaque. What, really, is the essence of the distinction at which the legislation is driving? It seems to be this. There are, on the one hand, some conceivable benefits that the owner of an estate, *as the owner of the estate* (or, if you prefer, in his capacity as owner of the estate), will or at least might desire to get. This is what we mean, metaphorically speaking, by "benefit to an estate." Then there are, on the other hand, other conceivable benefits that the owner of an estate, *as just the "human being that he is"* (or, if you prefer, in his capacity as an "individual"), will or at least might desire to get. This is what we mean by "benefit to a person."

This, I think, helps, but it still leaves one wondering, "How do I tell what one might want as an owner and what one might want as an individual?" To this question, the doctrine and the jurisprudence have begun to develop an answer. It requires, first, positing a hypothetical "reasonable" owner of the estate in question and then considering what kinds of benefits he might like to have in the light of "certain relevant characteristics" of the estate. The rub here is in the "characteristics." Everyone agrees that these characteristics include those that pertain to the "nature" or to the "objective situation" of the estate. More controversial is whether they should include, as well, the "destination" of the estate. Why this should be controversial is beyond me. It seems to me that even a moment's reflection, provided it entails clear thinking, will be sufficient to reveal that this question was "asked and answered" long ago and, further, that it was answered in the affirmative. Look at the list of "classic" servitudes in **Art. 699.** What does one see? At the beginning of the list, there are numerous examples of rights that, it must be admitted, might be thought of as being related in one way or another to the "nature" or "objective situation" of the estate. For example, an elevated, upgradient estate, by nature, "needs" (if you will forgive my lapse back into anthropomorphic metaphor) a servitude of "drain." To take another example, an estate that is landlocked or has limited access to public thoroughfares, by its objective situation, "needs" a right of passage. But, now, read to the end of the list. Can one really say, with a straight face, that a servitude of "watering animals" and a servitude of "pasturage" cater to some natural or objective "need" of the dominant estate, which, *ex hypothese*, we must assume is being used to raise animals? Is there such a thing as "raising animal" land by nature? Is the use of land to raise animals part of its *objective* situation? The answer to each of these questions is clearly "no." If a tract of land happens to be being used to raise animals, it is not because of its "nature" or its "objective situation," but because of its "destination." And so, in the long-recognized, "classic" servitudes of watering animals and providing pasturage, we have undeniable examples of "benefits" related to destination.

It is now time to sum up. For the reasons given above, I propose that we define "benefit to an estate" as follows: a benefit (i.e., right) that any reasonable owner of the supposed dominant estate, in the light of the nature, objective situation, or destination of that estate, would or at least might want to get. As long as the benefit in question fits this description, it is "fair game" for a predial servitude.

Before wrapping up this discussion, I should make one final point, just to make sure there is no misunderstanding. The mere fact that a certain benefit qualifies as a "benefit to an estate" does not mean that it *has* to be or *can only* be established in the form of a predial servitude. No, the parties remain free to establish it in whatever form they desire. There are at least two alternatives to establishing it in the form of a servitude: (1) set it up as a "right of use," a kind of "personal servitude" that is precisely like a predial servitude, except that it, by definition, benefits a person rather than an estate or (2) put it into a "credit right" (or "personal right"), that is, a non-real right that, by definition, benefits only a person. The choice, which is up to the parties, will be guided by what effects they wish the right to have. If they wish for it to benefit whosoever may happen to come to own the dominant estate and to burden whosoever may happen to come to own the servient estate (in other words, if they want it to "run with the land," as the common lawyers would say), then they will choose "predial servitude." If they wish for it to benefit only a specific, individual person, regardless whether he owns this or that estate, but they want it to burden whosoever may happen to come to own the servient estate, then they will choose "right of use." And if they wish for it to benefit only a specific, named individual and to burden only another specific, named individual and if they do not want it to "run" with either piece of land, then they will choose "credit right." All that classifying the benefit as one "for an estate" does for the parties is to give them the option, should they so choose, to make the benefit predial.

D. Separate Ownership of Estates

The second paragraph of **Art. 646** tells us that, for a predial servitude to exist, the supposed dominant and servient estates must be "separately owned." This rule represents an application of the maxim *nemini res sua servit* (no one has a servitude on his own thing). ***Id.* cmt. (f).**

As comment (f) to **Art. 646** explains, the rule of **Art. 646, ¶2** is directed against the situation "in which two estates belong in their *entirety* to the same owner." It follows, then, that there is no obstacle to the creation of a servitude simply because one of the two estates may be owned by one of several co-owners of the other estate. As comment (f) goes on to note, "the co-owner of an estate owned in indivision may have a right of servitude on an estate of which he is the sole owner" and *vice-versa.*

II. Nature

Within the framework of categories of "things" set up in Book II, a predial servitude qualifies as an "incorporeal immovable." **LSA-C.C. Art. 649.** This classification should not come as a surprise: as we have seen, a predial servitude is, by definition, a "real right" on a "corporeal immovable."

III. Characteristics

A. Inseparability

1. From the Servient Estate

The second paragraph of **LSA-C.C. Art. 650** states that "[t]he predial servitude continues as a charge on the servient estate when ownership changes." In other words, once the predial servitude is established, the charge falls and will continue to fall on whosoever may happen to own (or, for that matter, even use) the servient estate. As the comment explains,

> [t]he person who happens to be the owner of the servient estate is bound to suffer the exercise of the right of servitude by the person who happens to be owner of the dominant estate. This follows from the nature of predial servitudes as real rights which give rise to real obligations.

In this regard, the charge of the predial servitude is radically different from the "personal obligations" (if any) that this or that servient estate owner might undertake toward this or that dominant estate owner. As comment (c) to **Art. 651** explains, "The owner of the servient estate may bind himself by a *personal* obligation to perform certain affirmative duties in connection with a predial servitude. These obligations... are not transferred to successors by particular title [in other words, to transferees of the servient estate] without express stipulation to that effect."

2. *From the Dominant Estate*

Just as a predial servitude is inseparable from the servient estate, so also "[a] predial servitude is inseparable from the dominant estate and passes with it." **Art. 650.A.** Two consequences follow from this notion of the inseparability of the benefit of a predial servitude from the dominant estate. The first is that the benefit is available to and will continue to be available to whosoever may happen to own (or, for that matter, even use) the dominant estate. The second, in the words of the last sentence of **Art. 650.A.**, is that "the right of using the servitude cannot be alienated, leased, or encumbered separately from the dominant estate." In other words, for the servitude to go, the dominant estate, or at least a part of it, must go, too.

B. Indivisibility

According to the first sentence of **LSA-C.C. Art. 652**, "[a] predial servitude is indivisible." That means, as the article goes on to explain, that "[a]n estate cannot have upon another estate part of a right of way... or any other servitude, nor can an estate be charged with a part of the servitude."

This principle of "indivisibility" has significant implications for the establishment of predial servitudes in situations that involve co-owned estates. As comment (b) to **Art. 652** notes, "no predial servitude may be established on, or in favor of, an undivided part of an estate." For that reason, "[t]he creation of a predial servitude on an estate owned in indivision by several co-owners requires the consent of all." ***Id.***

Perhaps even more significant are the implications of the principle for the continuation of predial servitudes in situations in which the dominant estate or the servient estate ends up being subdivided. Stated in abstract terms, the issue here is two-fold: (i) if and when the dominant estate is divided up, does the predial servitude continue to benefit all of its parts and (ii) if and when the servient estate is divided up, does the predial servitude continue to burden all of its parts? The answer to both questions turns out to be "yes." With regards to the dominant estate, the last sentence of **Art. 652** states: "A servitude is due to the whole of the dominant estate and to all parts of it; if this estate is divided, every acquirer of a part has the right of using the servitude in its entirety."[3] With

3. Though this is true, it is nevertheless also true that "the division of the estate may not result in the placing of an additional burden on the servient estate." **Art. 652 cmt. (b).**

regards to the servient estate, **Art. 652** is strangely silent. Nevertheless, as comment (c) to **Art. 652** explains, "on principle as well as in the light of a proper interpretation of pertinent provisions in [the] code[], it is clear that the division of the servient estate does not affect adversely the interest of the owner of the dominant estate." In other words, when the servient estate is subdivided, every acquirer of a part, at least in principle, must suffer the exercise of the predial servitude by the dominant estate owner.[4]

IV. Limitations

Paragraph two of **Art. 652** provides: "The use of a servitude may be limited to certain days or hours; when limited, it is still an entire right." As comment (c) to **LSA-C.C. Art. 653** explains, limitations of this kind are not considered to violate the principle of "indivisibility" of predial servitudes.

V. Classifications

According to **LSA-C.C. Art. 654**, there are three different kinds of predial servitudes: natural, legal, and conventional. This classification, though traditional, is not all that scientific. The rights that fall under the headings "natural" and "legal" servitudes, as numerous civil law scholars have noted and as several modern civil codes now recognize, are not predial servitudes at all, but rather really just "limitations on the content of ownership" or, as the Greek Civil Code puts is, "restrictions of ownership." ***Id.* cmt. (d)**. Viewed from this modern perspective, predial servitudes, properly understood, are inherently conventional. Be that as it may, Louisiana, for better or for worse, has chosen to reject the modern perspective and, instead, to "defer[] to the tradition." ***Id.***

4. The qualifier "at least in principle" is important here. If the predial servitude is the kind the use of which can be "localized" on a discrete part of the servient estate (e.g., a servitude of passage), if this localization has occurred, and if, in the subdivision of the servient estate, the part of it on which the servitude has been localized is allotted to a single owner, then that single owner, and he alone, will have to suffer the exercise of the servitude. The other owners—those to whom the other parts of the estate are allotted—will not be subject to it.

A. Natural Servitudes

LSA-C.C. Art. 654 explains that natural servitudes are those that arise from the natural (physical) situation of the estates.

1. Right of Drain

a. Definition

According to **LSA-C.C. Art. 655**, when there are two estates, one lower than the other, the lower estate is obligated to receive the waters that flow naturally from the higher estate. As **Art. 655** points out, the right of drain does not occur when an act of man has created the flow. Thus, the servitude encompasses natural drainage, not chemically altered effluent.

b. Rights and Duties

LSA-C.C. Art. 656 provides that the owner of the servient estate may not prevent or inhibit the flow of water, and the owner of the dominant estate may not do anything which would make the servitude more burdensome. Even the state, as owner of the servient estate, must comply with this duty not to interfere with the natural flow of water. In one celebrated case, the court ordered the state to remove a state highway the construction of which so interfered with the natural servitude of drain that it caused flooding of the dominant estate.

2. Right to Use Running Water

Under **LSA-C.C. Arts. 657–658**, the owner of an estate bordering on running water may use it as it runs, and the owner of an estate through which water runs may make use of it while it runs over his land provided he returns it to its ordinary channel where it leaves his estate.

B. Legal Servitudes

1. Legal "Public" Servitudes

Many of the servitudes that fall under the heading "legal" are "[s]ervitudes imposed for the public or common utility." **LSA-C.C. Art. 665.** These servitudes are all "relate[d] to the space which is to be left for the public use by the adjacent proprietors [riparian landowners] on the shores of naviagable rivers" or "left... for the making and reparing of levees, roads, and other public or common works."

Special legislation provides that property necessary for levee and levee drainage purposes may be taken by the state or levee board with compensation at fair market value *under certain circumstances*. This special legislation, though, applies only to rivers, not to lakes or the sea. Under this legislation, riparian property (that is, land situated along a river or stream) may be "appropriated" provided three criteria are met: (1) the land must be riparian when separated from the public domain; (2) the levee must be necessary for the control of flood waters from the river under ordinary conditions (but not, for example, when the flooding has been caused by hurricane winds); and (3) the extent of the property appropriated must be within the range of reasonable necessities of the situation, as produced by the forces of nature unaided by artificial causes. If the criteria are met, the appropriation of the property establishes a servitude in favor of the state.

Under **Art. 6, § 42** of the **1974 Constitution**, "batture" may be taken by the sate or one of its political subdivisions without compensation. For this purpose batture is defined as the natural bank of a river or stream, i.e., the area between ordinary high and low water marks.

2. Obligations of Neighborhood

The so-called "obligations of neighborhood," which constitute yet another kind of "legal servitude," are established in **LSA-C.C. Arts. 667–669**. According to **Art. 667**, though an owner may do what he wants with his own estate, he cannot do anything "which may deprive his neighbor of the liberty of enjoying his own [estate], or which may be the cause of damage to him." If, however, the owner has made works which have caused damage to his neighbor or deprived his neighbor of enjoyment, the owner may be liable for damages to his neighbor only if one of two things is true. First, it is shown "that he knew or... should have known that his works would cause damage, that the damage could have been prevented by the exercise of reasonable care, and that he failed to exercise such reasonable care." Second, it is shown that the activity that caused the damages was ultrahazardous activity."

It seems that much of what **Art. 667** giveth **Art. 668** taketh away. The latter article provides that an owner can do whatever he wants on his property, even if it may "occasion some inconvenience to his neighbor."

Art. 668, purporting to offer an example, notes that an act such as raising one's house, even though it may darken his neighbor's house, is allowed because "this act occasions only an inconvenience, but not a real damage."

Critical to a proper understanding of the interplay of **Arts. 667** and **668** is a proper understanding of the distinction between a mere "inconvenience" to a neighbor, which is allowed, and "damage" to a neighbor's property or "depravation" of a neighbor's enjoyment, which is not. The articles themselves shed little, if any, light on the distinction. The doctrine and the jurisprudence, stepping into the gap, have concluded that whether the effect on one neighbor of a certain act or omission of another constitutes "inconvenience" or "damage" depends on whether, under the circumstances, the neighbor who acted or failed to act was guilty of an "abuse of right." Whether such an abuse has occurred depends, at least in part, on the legitimacy of the *motivation* behind that act or omission. Among the few motivations that have been identified as illegitimate is this: performing the act or omission for no other reason than to "spite" one's neighbor. Also relevant to the abuse-of-rights question is a consideration of the comparative costs and benefits of the act or omission: if the act or omission causes great harm to the neighbor but no real advantage to the actor, then the actor may be found guilty of "damage" rather than "inconvenience."

Art. 669 governs the regulation of an inconvenience caused by works or materials for any "manufactory" or other similar operation. If such an inconvenience is caused "by diffusing smoke or nauseous smell," and no conventional servitude regulates the inconvenience, then "their sufferance must be determined by the rules of the police, or the customs of the place." In other words, if there is any remedy for this inconvenience at all, it lies not under these articles, but under public land use law (such as zoning ordinances).

3. *Encroaching Buildings*

Yet another important legal servitude, though one of relatively recent vintage, is that for "encroaching buildings." **LSA-C.C. Art. 670** provides that when a landowner in *good faith* constructs a building that encroaches on an adjacent estate and the owner of the adjacent estate does not complain within a reasonable time after he knew or should have known of the encroachment or, in any event, does not complain until after the construction has been substantially completed, the court may allow the building to remain and grant the builder a predial servitude over the part of his neighbor's land onto which his building encroaches. In order to acquire this servitude, however, the builder must pay his neighbor compensation for the value of the servitude and indemnify his neighbor for damages that the encroachment may have occasioned.

4. Common Enclosures

A number of legal servitudes pertain to the right of a landowner to "enclose" his estate by means of walls, fences, ditches, and the like and to protect the boundaries of his estate from encroachments by his neighbor's plants. These legal servitudes are addressed in **LSA-C.C. Arts. 673–688.**

a. "Common Walls"

The most heavily regulated of the "common enclosure" legal servitudes is that which concerns "common walls." In this context, "common wall" has a special, technical meaning. It is, first of all, a wall made of "solid masonry," i.e., mortar or bricks and mortar. Second, it is located on top of the boundary line, partly on the estate of one neighbor and partly on the estate of another. Third, it is co-owned by both of the neighbors.

Of two neighboring landowners, the one who "builds first" has the right to build a solid masonry wall to "partition" his estate from the other and, in so doing, to rest half of the wall on the other estate, provided that he "uses solid masonry at least as high as the first story and the width of the wall does not exceed eighteen inches, not including the plastering which may not be more than three inches in thickness." **Art. 673.** If the builder meets these requirements, then he acquires a servitude on his neighbor's estate to keep the wall there.

A wall built in accordance with **Art. 673**, without more, is not "common." That is because, unless and until the neighbor onto whose estate the wall encroaches pays for "his fair share" of the wall, it remains the sole property of the builder. If, however, the encroachee *does* pay his fair share, which is one half of the cost of the wall, then the wall becomes "common." **Art. 674.** The encroachee may exercise this right to make the wall common at any time, even after he has previously refused to exercise it. ***Id.***

A wall that separates adjoining buildings and that is located partly on one estate and partly on another is presumed to be "common," but only up to the highest part of the lower of the two buildings. **Art. 675.** This presumption, of course, may be rebutted by "proof to the contrary." ***Id.***

Once the wall is made common, the co-owners of it acquire certain reciprocal rights and duties. "Necessary repairs . . . , including partial rebuilding, are to be made at the expense of those who own it in proportion to their interests." **Art. 678.** A co-owner may avoid this duty by abandoning his part of the wall. **Art. 679.** Each co-owner is entitled to use the common wall "as he sees fit," so long as he does not interfere with the other co-owner's rights or compromise the structural integrity of the wall. **Art. 680.** A co-owner may make an opening in the common wall, but only after obtaining the consent of his co-owner. **Art. 681.** Finally, any co-owner may, at his own expense, raise the common wall higher, so long as the existing wall can bear the "additional weight." **Art. 683.**

b. Common Fences

A fence located on a boundary may be "common," that is, co-owned by the neighboring landowners, or separate, that is, owned by only one of them. It is, however, presumed to be common. **Art. 685, ¶1.**

When "the adjoining estates" (that is, those next to the estates as to which construction of fences is in question) are all "enclosed" (by fences), the owner of one of the estates may compel the owner of the other to "contribute to the expense of making and repairing common fences to separate the two estates." ***Id.* at ¶2.** But if the adjoining estates are not enclosed, then neither owner has this right unless it is "prescribed by local ordinance." ***Id.* at ¶3.**

c. Common Ditches

A ditch located on a boundary is presumed to be common. **Art. 686.** If it is, in fact, common, then the adjoining landowners are together responsible for its maintenance. **Art. 687.**

d. Removal of Plants

Trees, bushes, and plants on the boundary are presumed to be common. **Art. 687.** The owner of either of the estates has the right to "demand removal" of any such "common" trees, bushes, or plants that "interfere with the enjoyment" of it. ***Id.*** But he must bear the expense of removal. ***Id.***

In addition, if the branches or roots of one neighbor's *separately-owned* trees, bushes, or plants "extend over or into" the other neighbor's estate, the latter neighbor can demand that they be trimmed at the expense of the former (i.e., the one who owns the plants), **Art. 688, ¶1,** provided that the encroaching branches or roots actually "interfere with the enjoyment of his property," ***id.*** **at ¶2.**

5. Enclosed Estates (C.C. Arts. 689–696)

a. Entitlement to a Right of Passage[5]

1) General Rule

LSA-C.C. **Art. 689** provides that "[t]he owner of an estate that has no access to a public road... may claim a right of passage over neighboring property to the nearest public road." Planiol, interpreting **Art. 682** of the Code Napoleon, the source of our **Art. 689**, writes that an estate is deemed to be enclosed "not only when it has no issue upon the public road, but if it has merely an insufficient issue." This means that if an estate, otherwise landlocked, borders on a public road, but one to which, by law, the estate owner has no right of direct access, his estate should nevertheless be classified as "enclosed" and, as a result, he should be able to claim a right of passage by law.

5. In 2017, the legislature amended the Civil Code articles that establish the legal right of passage so as to expand that right to include "passages" for "utilities," defined as "a service such as electricity, water, sewer, gas, telephone, cable television, and other commonly used power and communication networks required for the operation of an ordinary household or business." **LSA-C.C. Art. 696.1.** ***Cf.*** **LSA-C.C. Art. 655** (redefining "servitude of passage" as "[t]he right for the benefit of the dominant estate whereby persons, animals, utilities, or vehicles are permitted to pass through the servient estate." As many Louisiana civil law scholars have noted, the amendments through which this expansion was accomplished suffer from numerous technical problems. There can be no doubt that, as a technical matter, this new legal servitude should have been set on its own legislative footing, preferably in the Revised Statutes, rather than grafted into the Civil Code articles on the traditional servitude of passage. However that may be, the principles applicable to the traditional legal servitude of passage, as discussed in this Précis, are applicable *mutatis mutandis* to the new servitude of passage for utilities.

2) Exception

If the estate comes to be enclosed as the result of "a voluntary act or omission of its owner," the owner has no right to demand a legal servitude of passage. **LSA-C.C. Art. 693.** Consider this example. An owner of a large tract of land, which borders on a public road, decides to divide his property into two tracts for sale: one tract in the front of the property, retaining a border on the public road, and the other tract in the back of the property, without a border on the public road. If the owner of the land then sells the front tract and keeps the back tract, he is said to enclose his estate through a "voluntary act" and, for that reason, cannot demand a right of passage under **Art. 689.**

One might think that the result would be the same where the landlocked situation of the estate arises as a result of the owner's having allowed a conventional predial servitude of passage that he had theretofore enjoyed to be extinguished by the prescription of nonuse. After all, the owner would seem to be guilty of a "voluntary... omission" in such a case. Not so. According to the jurisprudence, **Art. 693** contemplates a deliberate or negligent act of a landowner as opposed to simple nonuse. Thus, in such a case, the owner of the landlocked estate would be entitled to demand a right of passage under **Art. 689.**

The disability imposed on the self-enclosing landowner by **Art. 693**, it is important to note, does *not* get "passed on" to subsequent owners of the land. Our courts have found that the "voluntary act or omission" mentioned in **Art. 693** contemplates instances where the owner of the estate creates the enclosure *himself* by selling a portion of his property without reserving a right of passage. Thus, when someone merely *purchases* an estate, knowing it to be already enclosed, the article does not apply, and the purchaser is entitled to demand a right of passage under **Art. 689.**

b. Indemnity

1) General Rule

In order to receive the right of passage provided by **Art. 689**, the owner of the enclosed estate must "indemnify his neighbor [i.e., the landowners over whose estate the right of passage is granted] for the damage he [i.e., the owner of the enclosed estate] may occasion." This, however, is merely a general rule.

2) Exception

LSA-C.C. Art. 694 provides that "[w]hen, in the case of a partition, or a voluntary alienation of an estate or a part thereof, property alienated or partitioned becomes enclosed," "the owner of the estate on which the passage was previously exercised" must provide the owner of the enclosed estate with a right of passage over that route, even if it is not the shortest route to the public road, and—here is the kicker—must do so *gratuitously*!

Consider this example. In his testament, a man divides his property between his two children in such a way that one child's lot becomes enclosed. It turns out, however, that the testator had previously used a certain passageway over the other child's lot to get to and from the now enclosed lot. Under these circumstances, the child who received the enclosed lot can demand a right of passage over that same passageway and the child who received the other lot must grant it free of charge. This is a case of enclosure due to "partition" for purposes of **Art. 694.**

Here is another example. Recall the landowner who, after subdividing his property into two estates, one enclosed and the other not, sold the non-enclosed estate to someone else and kept the enclosed estate for himself. Suppose that, now, he does precisely the opposite, that is, sells the enclosed estate and retains the non-enclosed one. Suppose, further, that prior to the sale, he had used a certain passageway over the non-enclosed lot to get to and from the now enclosed lot. This is a case of "voluntary alienation" for purposes of **Art. 694.** For that reason, the buyer of the enclosed estate will be able to demand a right of passage over the seller's passageway and the seller will not receive any sort of indemnity.

c. Location of the Passage

1) General Rule

LSA-C.C. Art. 692 addresses the question of where the legal right of passage should be located. The general rule is that the right of passage should be located "along the shortest route from the enclosed estate to the public road at the location least injurious to the intervening lands." The first consideration, then, is what is the shortest route between the enclosed estate and the nearest public road. Beyond that, however, one must consider the injury that the selection of this route would cause to the would-be servient estate owner. If the shortest route would pass directly through a house on that estate, then, because the potential injury would be so great, another, less injurious route would have to be chosen.

Once the right of passage is fixed, the *owner of the servient estate*, that is, the estate burdened by the right of passage, may be able to have the servitude relocated. **LSA-C.C. Art. 695** provides that "[t]he owner of the servient estate has the right to demand relocation of the servitude to a more convenient place at his own expense, provided that it affords the same facility to the owner of the enclosed estate." That same article provides, however, that "[t]he owner of the *enclosed estate* has *no* right to the relocation of this servitude after it is fixed."

2) Exceptions

a) Where the Enclosure Results from a Partition or a Voluntary Alienation

As we learned earlier, if the enclosure results from a partition or voluntary alienation under **Art. 694**, the passage must be located where it formerly was (before the partition or alienation), even if that is not the shortest route to the nearest public road. The owner of the enclosed estate cannot demand a right of passage through some estate other than the one on which the old route lies.

b) Other

Our jurisprudence has established yet another exception to the "shortest route" general rule. If use of the shortest route would require the construction of costly works, such a bridge or elevated roadway, then the court, in its discretion, may locate the right of passage elsewhere than along the shortest route to a public road.

d. Loss of the Right

The right to demand a legal servitude of passage effectively terminates if and when the enclosed estate ceases to be enclosed, as would happen if the owner of the enclosed estate were to acquire adjacent land that has access to a public road. When such an event takes place, the question whether the owner of the (formerly) enclosed estate would have been entitled to a right of passage under **Art. 689** from the owner of the adjacent estate becomes moot, for there is no longer any need for the right.

C. Conventional Servitudes

1. Subclassification

Predial servitudes—what the Civil Code calls *conventional* predial servitudes—come in several varieties.

a. Classification Based on Nature of Charge on Servient Estate: Affirmative v. Negative

Conventional predial servitudes may be either "affirmative" or "negative." An affirmative servitude is one that "give[s] the right to the owner of the dominant estate to do a certain thing on the servient estate." **LSA-C.C. Art. 706, ¶2.** This kind of servitude entails the second of the two possible kinds of correlative "charge" and "benefit" that we identified earlier. Examples include servitudes of passage, support, drip, drain, drawing water, aqueduct, watering animals, and pasturage. A negative servitude is one that "impose[s] on the owner of the servient estate the duty to abstain from doing something on his estate." **LSA-C.C. Art. 706, ¶3.** This kind of servitude entails the first of the two possible kinds of correlative "charge" and "benefit" that we identified earlier. Examples include servitudes of view, light, preventing the raising of buildings or walls, and preventing commercial or industrial activities.

b. Classification Based on Evidence of Charge on Servient Estate: Apparent v. Nonapparent

Conventional predial servitudes may also be either "apparent" or "nonapparent." An apparent servitude is one that is "perceivable by exterior signs, works, or constructions." **LSA-C.C. Art. 707, ¶1.** A nonapparent servitude is one that gives "no exterior sign of [its] existence." **LSA-C.C. Art. 707, ¶1.**

What is meant by "sign" here is *not* a sign in the sense of a *message*, written in English or some other language or in symbols of some kind, that has been posted for public view. To the contrary, "sign" refers to some physical configuration of the servient estate that is suggestive of the possibility that some servitude might exist. For example, the presence on one estate of a paved roadway leading from a public street, on one side of that estate, to a carport located on an adjacent estate, at the other side of the first estate is a "sign" indicative of a possible predial servitude of passage over the first estate (servient) for the benefit of the second estate (dominant).

For obvious reasons, it turns out that most affirmative servitudes are apparent and most negative servitudes are nonapparent. But there are exceptions to these generalizations. Here is one: a servitude of foot-passage across an open, completely undeveloped prairie, though affirmative, would nevertheless be nonapparent (unless, perhaps, the owner of the dominant estate, having used the right so often and over the same path, had worn down a "rut" there). Here is another: a servitude of view or light through a window in a "common wall" (*see* **LSA-C.C. Art. 673** ***et seq.***), though negative, is nevertheless apparent.

2. Acquisition

Altogether there are three ways in which conventional predial servitudes may be acquired: (i) by title, (ii) by acquisitive prescription, and (iii) by destination. **LSA-C.C. Arts. 739–740.** Let us now look at each of these in turn.

a. By Title

1) Domain

Any and every imaginable kind of predial servitude can be acquired by title. This follows from **LSA-C.C. Arts. 739** and **740**, which provide, respectively, that nonapparent servitudes and apparent servitudes may be acquired in this fashion.

2) Requirements

a) Substantive Requirements

1] RE *THE ACT*

LSA-C.C. Art. 708 provides that "[t]he establishment of a predial servitude by title is an alienation of a part of the property to which the laws governing alienation of immovables apply." The creation of a predial servitude by title, then, involves an "alienation," that is, a *transfer*, of part of the grantor's "property" ("ownership" might be a better term). This alienation or transfer, **LSA-C.C. Art. 722** tells us, can be accomplished by means of "all acts by which immovables may be transferred," in other words, by any act "translative of ownership" of immovables. These acts include the "usual" ones: that is sale, donation, exchange, even *dation en paiement*. But they may also include, in this context, "partition." As comment (b) to **Art. 722** notes, "[p]redial servitudes may also be established by voluntary or by judicial partition." This would be the case, for example, where the court, in ordering a judicial partition of a tract of land in kind and, in so doing, dividing the tract into two lots, one of which borders on a road and the other of which does not, establishes over the former lot a predial servitude of passage for the benefit of the latter lot, so that the latter will not be "landlocked."

2] RE *THE GRANTOR*

a] Who Can Grant

1} OWNER OF THE SERVIENT ESTATE

In principle, the only person who is supposed to be able to subject an estate to a predial servitude—in other words, to establish a *servient* estate—is the owner of that estate. As **LSA-C.C. Art. 697** puts it, "[p]redial servitudes may be established by an owner of his estate." To the same effect is comment (b) to **LSA-C.C. Art. 708**, which states that "[t]he right of imposing a servitude permanently on an estate belongs to the owner alone."

2} CO-OWNER OF A SERVIENT ESTATE

"A predial servitude on an estate owned in indivision," according to the first paragraph of **LSA-C.C. Art. 714**, "may be established only with the consent of all the co-owners." Nevertheless, if one co-owner, acting on his own, attempts to grant such a servitude, it is "not null," but "its execution is suspended until the consent of all co-owners is obtained." ***Id.* at ¶2.** Thus, the purported servitude is, as it were, conditional. There is, however, yet another way in which the purported servitude might "come to life," a way identified in the second paragraph of **LSA-C.C. Art. 715**: "If he [the co-owner who created the servitude] becomes owner of the whole estate by any means which terminates the indivision [e.g., partition by licitation], the predial servitude to which he has consented burdens his property."

These rules take care of the case in which a co-owner purports to grant a predial servitude on the co-owned thing itself. But what happens when a co-owner instead attempts to grant a predial servitude over *just his share*? That would seem to be impossible, given that (1) a predial servitude requires a servient estate, (2) this "estate" must be a *corporeal* immovable, and (3) an undivided share of a corporeal immovable is, itself, an *incorporeal* immovable. The legislation, however, does not answer our question with an unqualified "no." Instead, **LSA-C.C. Art. 716** says this:

> When a co-owner has consented to the establishment of a predial servitude on his undivided part only, the consent of the other co-owners is not required, but the exercise of the servitude is suspended until his divided part is determined at the termination of the state of indivision.

What happens next depends on what kind of partition takes place. If it is "in kind," then **LSA-C.C. Art. 717** tells us that the servitude "burdens only the part allotted to him," that is, the granting co-owner. But if the partition is "by licitation," then what happens depends on who buys the formerly co-owned thing at the sale. **LSA-C.C. Art. 718** provides that if the granting co-owner buys it, then the servitude burdens "the entire estate," but that if someone else buys it, then the servitude is "extinguished."

3} POSSESSOR — PRESCRIBER OF THE SERVIENT ESTATE (SERVITUDE ON AFTER-ACQUIRED IMMOVABLE)

Suppose that a person who is in possession of an immovable and who is on his way to becoming the owner of it through acquisitive prescription purports to grant a predial servitude on it to another person. At that time, the predial servitude is null, for the possessor-prescriber is not the owner, at least not yet. But if and when acquisitive prescription accrues in favor of the possessor-prescriber, he not only will become the owner but, thanks to the "retroactive" effects of the accrual of prescription, will be deemed to have been the owner from the time at which his possession began. As a result, the defect in the predial servitude that the possessor-prescriber granted will, as it were, be "cured" and the predial servitude will be deemed to be valid and, not only that, but valid as of the time at which the possessor-prescriber granted it.

4} USUFRUCTUARY OF THE SERVIENT ESTATE

LSA-C.C. Art. 711 provides that "[t]he usufructuary may not establish on the estate of which he has the usufruct any charges in the nature of predial servitudes." This hardly comes as a surprise. Because an estate is, by definition, nonconsumable, the usufructuary of an estate is, by definition, a usufructuary of a nonconsumable. Furthermore, a usufructuary of this kind, by definition, has only the right to use (*usus*) and the right to the fruits (*fructus*) of the thing on which his usufruct lies, to the exclusion of the right to dispose of or to alienate the property (*abusus*). Finally, as we learned above, the creation of a predial servitude is an act of alienation (*abusus*) of the servient estate. It follows that a usufructuary of an estate who purports to grant a predial servitude on it attempts to give away something that is simply not his to give.

b] Capacity to Grant

To be in a position to grant a predial servitude, the owner, of course, must have "capacity" to do so. This problem is addressed in comment (c) to **LSA-C.C. Art. 708**: "Since the establishment of a predial servitude by title involves the execution of a juridical act, the grantor must be competent. Incompetents, such as minors and interdicts, may establish predial servitudes on their estates according to the rules prescribed for the alienation of their property."

c] Power to Grant

Not only must the grantor have the capacity to grant a servitude, but he must also have the power to do so. Ordinarily, as long as one "owns" the estate and has "capacity" to alienate it, one has the power to grant a servitude. But there are some exceptional cases in which this power may be limited, if not altogether excluded.

Let us consider, first of all, the situation of an owner of an estate who has placed a mortgage upon it. Is he now "free" to grant a predial servitude on his estate? Paragraph one, sentence one, of **LSA-C.C. Art. 721** appears to answer the question in the affirmative: "[a] predial servitude may be established on mortgaged property." As one reads on through the rest of **Art. 721**, however, one comes across some rather important qualifications to this answer. First, the second sentence of the same paragraph provides that "[i]f the servitude diminishes the value of the estate to the substantial detriment of the mortgagee, he [the mortgagee] may demand immediate payment of the debt." One has to imagine that this possibility will, in many instances, act as significant check on the power of the owner to establish predial servitudes. Second, the second paragraph provides "[i]f there is a sale for the enforcement of the mortgage, the property is sold free of all servitudes established after the mortgage."

In such a case, then, the owner's supposed power to create predial servitudes comes to naught.

Next, let us consider the situation of an owner of an estate who has already granted one or more other predial servitudes on it. In principle, that the owner has done so presents no obstacle to his granting still more. According to **LSA-C.C. Art. 720**, "[t]he owner of the servient estate may establish thereon additional servitudes." Nevertheless, this power is subject to an important restriction: it may be exercised, **Art. 720** tells us, only if and to the extent that the additional servitudes "do not affect adversely the rights of the owner of the dominant estate." In other words, "no servitude may be validly created to the prejudice of a pre-existing servitude." ***Id.* cmt. (b).**

3] RE *THE GRANTEE*

a] Who Can Receive

LSA-C.C. Art. 735 provides that not only the "owner" of the dominant estate, but also "any person acting in his name or in his behalf," can receive a predial servitude. Regarding precisely *who* falls into the category of persons who act "in the name of or on behalf of" the owner, comment (a) to the article says this: "a possessor in good or bad faith, an authorized or unauthorized mandatary, a manager of affairs [*negotiorum gestor*], a person making a *stipulation pour autrui*, a co-owner, a usufructuary, and a tutor or a curator." As strange as this may seem, the reference to "possessor" here includes *true*, that is, *adverse* possessors!

That the range of possible grantees of a predial servitude is so broad, extending even to persons with whom the owner of the dominant estate has no relationship, poses a risk to that owner, namely, that he might end up "stuck" with a servitude that he does not want. The rule of **LSA-C.C. Art. 737** is designed to give him at least some measure of protection against this risk. By its terms, the dominant estate owner "may renounce the contract by which a predial servitude was acquired for the benefit of his estate, if he finds the contract onerous, and if the contract was made without his authority or while he was incompetent." Note that there are two limitations on the owner's power to renounce: (i) he must not have authorized the grantee to receive the servitude and (ii) the contract creating the servitude must be "onerous." "Onerous" means that it requires the owner to do, not to do, or to give something, e.g., pay a price, in exchange for receiving the servitude. *Cf.* **LSA-C.C. Art. 1909.**

b] Capacity

The grantee of the predial servitude does not have to have any particular capacity in order to receive a predial servitude. **LSA-C.C. Art. 736** provides that "[a]n incompetent may acquire a predial servitude for the benefit of his estate without the assistance of the administrator of his patrimony or of his tutor or curator." This rule is clearly quite different from that regarding the capacity of the grant*or* of a predial servitude.

b) Formal Requirements

1] GENERAL RULE

As we have seen, a sale, donation, exchange, *dation en paiement*, or other juridical act purporting to establish a predial servitude is considered to be an alienation of immovable property. As such, it is subject to the same form requirements as would be any other transfer of immovable property. Paragraph one, sentence one, of **LSA-C.C. Art. 1839** states that "[a] transfer of immovable property must be made by authentic act or by act under private signature." Where the grant of the predial servitude is onerous, e.g., involves a sale, exchange, or *dation en paiement*, either of these alternatives—authentic act or act under private signature—will suffice. *See* **LSA C.C. Arts. 2440** (sale), **2667** (exchange) & **2659** (*dation en paiement*). But where the grant of the predial servitude is gratuitous, things are more complicated. If the grant involves a donation *inter vivos*, then, because the object of the transfer is an incorporeal immovable, it can be accomplished only by authentic act, to the exclusion of an act under private signature. *See* **LSA-C.C. Arts. 1541 & 1543.** If the grant involves a donation *mortis causa* (in other words, a legacy), then, despite the terms of ***Art. 1839***, not even authentic form will do; instead, one of the two forms for "testaments" must be used—either "olographic" form or "notarial" form. *See* **LSA-C.C. Arts. 1570 & 1574–1576.**

2] EXCEPTION

The form rule of **Art. 1839, ¶1, sent. 1** is just a generalization, one to which there is an exception. The exception appears in the next sentence of the article: "Nevertheless, an oral transfer is valid between the parties when the property has been actually delivered and the transferor recognizes the transfer when interrogated on oath." Interpreted *in pari materia* with other Civil Code articles pertaining to form, specifically, those that have to do with donations, this part of **Art. 1839** applies *only* to grants of predial servitudes that are *onerous*, to the exclusion of those that are gratuitous.

b. By Acquisitive Prescription

1) Domain

Some, but not all, predial servitudes can be created by acquisitive prescription. The "some" that can be are those that are apparent. **LSA-C.C. Art.** 740 ("Apparent servitudes may be acquired... by acquisitive prescription."). Nonapparent servitudes, by contrast, cannot be acquired in this fashion. **LSA-C.C. Art. 739** ("Nonapparent servitudes may be acquired by title only.").

2) Modes

An apparent predial servitude can be acquired through either unabridged (30-year) acquisitive prescription or abridged (10-year) acquisitive prescription. *See* **LSA-C.C. Art. 742, sent. 2.** To such a prescription "[t]he laws governing acquisitive prescription of immovable property apply." ***Id.*, sent. 1.**

3) Requirements

Having already studied the institution of acquisitive prescription in depth elsewhere in this Précis, we will not study it again here. What we will do, however, is to consider what, if anything, is peculiar or distinctive about the operation of that institution insofar as it concerns predial servitudes.

a) Possession

1] QUASI-POSSESSION

The most fundamental requirement for acquisitive prescription is "possession." Possession, properly so called, requires as its object a "corporeal" thing. Predial servitudes, however, are incorporeal. It might seem, then, acquisitive prescription of predial servitudes is impossible. But to think this way is to forget two important points that we made in our study of possession. The first is that alongside "possession" there stands "quasi-possession," which, it will be recalled, is defined as "[t]he exercise of a real right, such as a servitude, with the intent to have it as one's own." **LSA-C.C. Art. 3421, ¶2.** The second is that "[t]he rules governing possession apply by analogy to the quasi-possession of incorporeals." ***Id.*** Thus, in the case of acquisitive prescription of predial servitudes, the fundamental requirement, by analogy, is quasi-possession.

2] CONSTITUTIVE ELEMENTS

a] Corpus

What does it mean to have *corpus* of a predial servitude? The definition of "corpus" found in the **LSA-C.C. Art. 3425** says: "Corporeal possession is the exercise of physical acts of use, detention, or enjoyment over a thing." Now, this definition, though broadly worded, is aimed exclusively at corporeals. Even so, the definition of *corpus* for corporeals found in **Art. 3425** may be extended by analogy to create a definition of *quasi-corpus* for incorporeals, in particular, predial servitudes. Based on the notion of quasi-possession found in **Art. 3421, ¶2**, that definition might go something like this: "*Quasi-corpus* of a predial servitude is the exercise of acts of use or enjoyment of the rights afforded by that servitude."

b] Animus Domini

What kind of *animus* is required for quasi-possession of a servitude? The answer to this question is contained within the definition of quasi-possession itself: "The exercise of a real right, such as a servitude, *with the intent to have it as one's own* is quasi-possession." **Art. 3421, ¶2.** Thus, to have *quasi-animus* of a predial servitude, one must intend to have the right or rights afforded by that servitude as one's own, which is as much to say as that one must believe that one has those rights or, at the very least, must have decided to act as though one has them.

It will be recalled that, in the context of possession proper, the "kiss of death" for *animus* is a grant of "permission" from the owner to detain the thing. If one detains the thing under such a grant of permission, one is not a (true) possessor at all, but rather a *precarious* possessor.

In the context of quasi-possession, however, things are not nearly so black and white. In fact, quasi-possession, far from being incompatible with such a grant of permission, *presupposes* it! Take, for example, the case in which one of two neighboring landowners grants to the other a predial servitude of passage across his estate. This "grant" of a servitude, by definition, entails a giving of permission, specifically, a giving of permission to enter upon and to cross the land. To be sure, with respect to the underlying thing—the corporeal immovable called the "servient estate"—the grantee of this servitude is but a "precarious possessor."

Nevertheless, with respect to the servitude right itself, he is still a (true) quasi-possessor.[6]

b) Just Title

For purposes of abridged acquisitive prescription of predial servitudes, a "just title" is one that "would have established the servitude if it had been granted by the true owner." **Art. 742 cmt. (c).** With just one exception, there is nothing at all peculiar about "just title" in this context. The sole exception has to do with "partitions." Insofar as acquisitive prescription of corporeal immovables is concerned, neither an agreement nor a judgment of partition can serve as a "just title," and this for the simple reason that such an agreement or judgment is understood to be merely "declarative," as opposed to "translative," of ownership. But as we noted earlier in our study of the acquisition of predial servitudes by title, "title," in this context, can include an agreement or judgment of partition. Thus, when such an agreement or judgment purports to create a predial servitude and the grantee thereof begins to quasi-possess the supposed servitude right, it can be said that he does so under a "just title," provided that the other requirements for just title are also satisfied.

c) Good Faith

To be in "good faith" for purposes of the law of acquisitive prescription in general, one must reasonably believe that one is the "owner" of the thing that one possesses. *See* **LSA-C.C. Art. 3480.** That definition, though fine as applied to the "possession" of a "corporeal immovable" and to a person who, as possessor of such a thing, might possibly think that he "owns" *that thing*, hardly fits when it is a question of "quasi-possession" of an "incorporeal immovable" and a person who, as precarious possessor of the underlying corporeal immovable thing, would never think that he "owns" *that thing*. Thus, for the definition to "work" in this other context, it must be adjusted "by analogy." Making this adjustment, one can say this: for a quasi-possessor of a predial servitude to be in "good faith," "he must honestly believe that he is entitled to the right he exercises as a servitude." **Art. 742 cmt. (d).**

---

6. In our study of possession, we referred to this phenomenon, where the servitude holder, through one and the same acts, simultaneously quasi-possesses the servitude for himself and precariously possesses the underlying corporeal immovable for his grantor, as "compound" possession.

c. By Destination

1) Definition

Conventional predial servitudes may be created in yet another manner: "destination of the owner." **LSA-C.C. Art. 741** explains this mode of creating predial servitudes in the following terms: "Destination of the owner is a relationship established between two estates owned by the same owner that would be a predial servitude if the estates belonged to two different owners." There is a lot of information packed into this one sentence. It will be helpful if we can break it down.

For a predial servitude to arise by destination of the owner, several prerequisites must be satisfied. The first is that, at some point in time "back then," one and the same person must have owned "two estates." The notion of "two estates" requires some explanation, for it is apt to be (and has in fact often been) misunderstood, but this explanation will have to wait. Second, this "one and the same" owner must by himself or through another who acts with his knowledge and consent create a "relationship of service" that must be of a kind that "would be a predial servitude if the estates belonged to different owners." Determining whether this prerequisite is satisfied requires one to take up the position of a third-party observer, one who watches how the owner treats his two estates, what he does on one in relation to the other, and above all what he does on the purported servient estate-to-be. If his behavior "looks like" the kind of behavior one might expect to see from someone who has a predial servitude over that "estate," then the prerequisite is satisfied; if his behavior does not, then it is not. It might have been more accurate, then, for the redactors of the legislation to have used "*could* be" rather than "*would* be."

Now, let us consider the troublesome "two estates" requirement. It is not necessary, in order for this requirement to be satisfied, that the owner, prior to his establishing the required "relationship of service," own two tracts of land that are distinct from each other in the sense that he has "separate titles" for them, that is, that one was acquired by him through one juridical act (or other acquisitive juridical event) and the other was acquired by him through another, separate juridical act (or other acquisitive juridical event). To be sure, when that is the case, the "two estates" requirement is satisfied. But it may be satisfied otherwise. It is no less satisfied where the owner, to begin with, has only one "estate," thereafter creates the required "relationship of service" between two discrete parts of that estate, and then transfers at least one of these parts to someone else. In such a case, the "two estates" admittedly do not come into existence until after he has established the required relationship of service and after he has made the required transfer. But that, in fact, is all that is required. In short, whether the two estates exist as such *ante hoc* or *post hoc* is of no moment, so long as they exist as such at some time.

2) Manner of Creation

The manner in which a predial servitude may be created by destination varies depending on whether the servitude is apparent or nonapparent.

a) Apparent Servitudes

According to the second paragraph of **Art. 741**, an apparent servitude "comes into existence of right" as soon as the two estates cease to belong to the same owner, "unless there is express provision to the contrary" in the agreement between the parties. To say that the servitude comes into existence "of right" is to say that it does so "automatically" and without any further ado.

b) Nonapparent Servitudes

The rule for nonapparent servitudes is quite different. For a servitude of this kind to be created by destination, the owner of the two estates must do something more than merely transfer ownership of one of them to someone else and, further, must do this "something else" *before* he makes this transfer. This "something else" is that the owner must "file[] for registry in the conveyance records of the parish in which the immovable is located a formal declaration establishing the destination." In practice, this is rarely done.

3. Effects: Rights and Duties of the Owners of the Servient and Dominant Estates

a. The Owner of the Dominant Estate

Under the heading of the "rights" of the dominant estate owner, one must include, to start with, his *predial servitude right* itself. Depending on whether the servitude is affirmative or negative, this right consists either of going onto the servient estate to do something there or prohibiting the servient estate owner from doing something there.

In addition to his basic servitude right, the owner of the dominant estate has several others. One is the right to "make at his expense all the works that are necessary for the use and preservation of the servitude." **LSA-C.C. Art. 744.** Another is the right "to enter with his workmen and equipment into the part of the servient estate that is needed for the construction or repair of works required for the use and preservation of the servitude." **LSA-C.C. Art. 745.** In the exercise of this latter right, the dominant estate owner may "deposit materials for the works" on the servient estate. ***Id.***

The dominant estate owner is also subject to a few duties. The first is obvious: he may not, in his use of the servitude, go beyond the "extent and manner of use" to which he and the servient estate owner agreed (or that was fixed by acquisitive prescription or destination). Second, in the exercise of his right to go onto the servient estate to construct or repair works necessary for the use or preservation of the servitude, he is bound, first, to "caus[e] the least possible damage" to the servient estate and, second, to get his workmen, equipment, and materials off that estate "as soon as possible." **Art. 745.**

b. The Owner of the Servient Estate

The primary duty of the servient estate owner is established by the first paragraph of **LSA-C.C. Art. 748.** According to that article, "[t]he owner of the servient estate may do nothing tending to diminish or make more inconvenient the use of the servitude." In interpreting this article, the courts of Louisiana have taken the language within it seriously, above all the participial "tending." Under this interpretation, even the *slightest* inconvenience or diminishment of the use of the servitude falls under the ban. Consider this example. After granting the dominant estate owner a predial servitude of automobile passage that is 20 feet wide, the servient estate owner constructs a building that encroaches into the servitude area by two feet for part of the length of the passageway. Though the remaining 18-foot swatch of the original 20-foot wide passageway is more than adequate to enable the dominant estate owner to pass (his largest automobile is only five feet wide), nevertheless the servient estate owner is in breach of his **Art. 748, ¶1** duty.

Alongside this duty, the servient estate owner enjoys a few (though only a few) rights. The first is the right to continue to use the burdened part of his estate to the extent that his doing so does not run afoul of **Art.**

748. Thus, if the sevient estate owner were to grant his neighbor a predial servitude right of laying and operating an underground sewerage pipeline through his estate, nothing would prevent the servient estate owner, once the pipeline has been installed and buried, from planting crops on the surface above the pipeline. Of course, if it should prove necessary to the dominant estate owner to enter the servient estate to repair the pipeline and if, in so doing, he should destroy the servient estate owner's crops, the servient estate owner would, in principle, have no recourse. Second, where the dominant estate owner, in exercising his right to enter the servient estate under **Art. 745** to construct or repair works needed for the use or preservation of the servitude, breaches his duty to minimize damage to the servient estate or to complete his work as soon as possible, the servient estate owner is entitled to damages. Third, "[i]f the original location [of the servitude] has become more burdensome for the owner of the servient estate, or if it prevents him from making useful improvements on his estate, he may provide another equally convenient location for the exercise of the servitude which the owner of the dominant estate is bound to accept." **LSA-C.C. Art. 748, ¶2.** Even so, "[a]ll expenses of relocation are borne by the owner of the servient estate." ***Id.***

4. Extinction

a. Destruction

LSA-C.C. Art. 751 provides that "[a] predial servitude is extinguished by the permanent and total destruction of the dominant estate or of the part of the servient estate burdened with the servitude." It is important to note that, for the destruction of the servient estate to have this effect, it must meet two requirements: "total" and "permanent." As comment (c) to this article explains, "[i]f the destruction is partial, the servitude continues to exist for the benefit of the remaining part by virtue of the principle of indivisibility." If the destruction is merely "temporary," then, though the "exercise" of the servitude is for the moment suspended, the servitude is nevertheless not extinguished, and the exercise of it may resume once the previous state of affairs is reestablished. **Art. 752 cmt. (b).** This, in fact, is the point of **LSA-C.C. Art. 752**, which provides as follows:

> If the exercise of the servitude becomes impossible because the things necessary for its exercise have undergone such a change that the servitude can no longer be used, the servitude

is not extinguished; it resumes its effects when the things are reestablished so that they may again be used, unless prescription has accrued.

For example, if the area over which a predial servitude of passage is to be exercised is flooded after heavy rains or the overflow of a nearby river, the servient estate (passageway) is not "destroyed" and, therefore, the servitude is not extinguished. When the waters recede and the original state of affairs is reestablished, exercise of the servitude may resume. In similar fashion, if the water table beneath a well on which a servitude of drawing water has been granted recedes to the point at which the well no longer produces water, the servient estate (well) is not necessarily "destroyed" and, therefore, the servitude is not extinquished. If the well should be dug deeper so that water production resumes, then the exercise of the servitude, too, may resume.

b. Nonuse

LSA-C.C. Art. 753 provides that "[a] predial servitude is extinguished by nonuse for ten years." In this regard, predial servitudes are like all other dismemberments of ownership.

1) Substantive Elements

a) What Is "Use"

Inasmuch as the prescription of nonuse begins to run only when "use" ceases, it is critical to understand what does and, just as importantly, what does not suffice as "use."

Responding to the first question—what does suffice—**LSA-C.C. Art. 759** provides that "[a] partial use of the servitude constitutes use of the whole." Imagine that a dominant estate owner, though he enjoys a right of passage that is 20 feet wide, never uses but 10 feet's worth of the passageway. The servitude will not prescribe as to the unused 10 feet's worth, for use of part is tantamount to use of the whole.

LSA-C.C. Art. 761 provides part of the answer to the second question—"what does not suffice." According to that article, "[t]he use of a right that is only accessory to the servitude is not the use of the servitude." For example, "if one who has the servitude of drawing water from the well of his neighbor passes over the servient estate and goes to the well without drawing any water," then he "will lose the servitude because the passage is merely accessory to the right of drawing water." ***Id.* cmt. (b)**.

Our jurisprudence has also established that a use which is not "serious," in other words, constitutes a "mere gesture," is not sufficient "use" to interrupt prescription. Suppose that an owner of a dominant estate that enjoys a servitude of passage, finding that he no longer needs the servitude, stops using it. But then, on the eve of the running of prescription, he drives his car across the passageway from his estate to the public road and back, not to "go somewhere," but simply to "keep the servitude alive." Because this "use" is merely "gestural," his effort will fail.

b) Who Can Use

LSA-C.C. Art. 757 provides that "[a] predial servitude is preserved by the use made of it by anyone, even a stranger, if it is used as appertaining to the dominant estate." This, of course, includes use by a co-owner, provision for which is made in **LSA-C.C. Art. 762.** But even use by someone who has no interest in or relation to the estate or the dominant estate owner will suffice, provided that the use in some way "appertain[s] to the estate." Thus, the use by a postman of a passageway over which a right of passage has been established to go between a public road and the dominant estate to pick up and to deliver mail would be sufficient to stave off the prescription of nonuse.

c) Delay

As stated in **Art.** 753, the delay for prescription of nonuse of predial servitudes is 10 years. This is the standard delay for the prescription of nonuse.

1] COMMENCEMENT OF THE DELAY

The first paragraph of **LSA-C.C. Art. 754** provides that "[p]rescription... begins to run for affirmative servitudes from the date of their last use, and for negative servitudes from the date of the occurrence of an event contrary to the servitude." The second paragraph of **Art. 754** goes on to give examples of events contrary to the servitude: "destruction of works necessary for its exercise or the construction of works that prevent its exercise."

2] INTERRUPTION AND SUSPENSION

Prescription of nonuse can be interrupted or suspended. If prescription is interrupted, for example, by the proper use of it by the dominant estate owner, then, once the cause of interruption comes to an end, the

10-year period begins to run anew, starting back at "zero." By contrast, if prescription is merely suspended, then, once the cause of suspension comes to an end, the 10-year period, instead of starting over from scratch, "picks up where it left off."

LSA-C.C. Art. 755 identifies a cause of suspension of prescription of nonuse that is unique to predial servitudes: "If the owner of the dominant estate is prevented from using the servitude by an obstacle that he can neither prevent nor remove, the prescription of nonuse is suspended on that account for a period of up to ten years." The category "obstacle" includes, but is not limited to, what we earlier referred to as a "temporary" destruction of the servient estate under **Art. 751** and what, in the terms of **Art. 752**, is referred to as a "change" in the "things necessary" for the exercise of the servitude such that it can "no longer be used." As long as the obstacle is in place, prescription may be suspended for up to 10 years. If the obstacle remains in place longer than that, then prescription will begin to run again at the 10-year mark.

When the obstacle results from the destruction of a building or other constructions, **LSA-C.C. Art. 756** controls. The article draws a sharp distinction between constructions that belong to the dominant estate owner and those that belong to the servient estate owner. "If the servitude cannot be exercised on account of the destruction of a building or other construction that belongs to the owner of the dominant estate, prescription is not suspended." ***Id.*, sent. 1.** By contrast, "[i]f the building or other construction belongs to the owner of the servient estate, the preceding article [**Art. 755**] applies." ***Id.*, sent. 2.** Under **Art. 755**, of course, prescription would be suspended for up to 10 years.

3] ALTERATION OF THE DELAY BY CONTRACT

LSA-C.C. Art. 697 allows the parties to a conventional predial servitude to stipulate the "use and extent" of the servitude as they may desire, even if that means derogating from the ordinary rules of the law of predial servitudes, provided that the parties do not exceed the contractual freedom allowed in **LSA-C.C. Art. 1971**. Among the ordinary rules of the law of predial servitudes which the parties may desire to alter are those that pertain to the prescription of nonuse. Within certain limits, they are free to do so. For example, parties can reduce the time in which prescription will accrue. For instance, the parties to a predial servitude may stipulate that the servitude will prescribe for nonuse of five years as opposed to ten. The parties, however, may not contract to extend prescription beyond ten years, as that would be against the public policy of the state to keep property in commerce. *See also* **LSA-C.C. Art. 3471.**

2) Procedural Incidents: Burden of Proof

Who bears the burden of proof in regards to issues related to "nonuse" is governed by **LSA-C.C. Art. 764**: "When the prescription of nonuse is pleaded, the owner of the dominant estate has the burden of proving that he or some other person has made use of the servitude as appertaining to his estate during the period of time required for the accrual of the prescription." The burden, then, is on the beneficiary of the servitude.

c. Confusion

LSA-C.C. Art. 765 provides that "[a] predial servitude is extinguished when the dominant and the servient estates are acquired in their entirety by the same person." The cause of this extinction is "confusion," that is, the "unit[ing] in the same person" of "the qualities of obligee and obligor." **LSA-C.C. Art. 1903.** That a predial servitude cannot survive under such circumstances represents yet another application of the maxim *nemini res sua servit.*

Once a servitude has been extinguished by confusion, a "reversal" or "undoing" of the confusion—that is, the re-transfer of one or the other estate to some other person—will not reverse or undo the extinction, at least not of right (automatically). As **LSA-C.C. Art. 769** puts it, "[a] servitude that has been extinguished by confusion may be reestablished only in the manner by which a servitude may be created."

d. Abandonment

LSA-C.C. Art. 770 informs us that "[a] predial servitude is extinguished by the abandonment of the servient estate, or of the part on which the servitude is exercised," provided that the abandonment is "evidenced by a written act." Such an abandonment is understood to be made in favor of the owner of the dominant estate rather than to no one in particular. The owner of the dominant estate is "bound" (obligated) to "accept" the abandoned thing, be it the entire servient estate or only the part of it that is burdened, thereby becoming the owner of it. ***Id.*** Once that happens, of course, "confusion takes place." ***Id.***

e. Renunciation

One last cause of extinction of predial servitudes that deserves special mention is "renunciation." The dominant estate owner is free to renounce his right, provided he does it expressly and in writing. **LSA-C.C. Art. 771.**

SUB-CHAPTER B

Personal Servitudes

I. Usufruct

A. Definitions

The first sentence of **LSA-C.C. Art. 535** defines "usufruct" as a "real right of limited duration on the property of another." This definition leaves room for improvement. The trouble with it is that it is overly broad, that is, its scope extends to rights other than usufruct (e.g., the personal servitude of "habitation" and a predial servitude subject to a term both qualify as "real right[s] of limited duration on the property of another"). In fairness to those who drafted this definition, one must acknowledge that the task they set for themselves was not easy. The reason that is so is that the category "usufruct" entails two quite different kinds of rights, namely, the "perfect" or "true" usufruct, now known as the "usufruct of nonconsumables," and the "imperfect" or *quasi*-usufruct, now known as the "usufruct of consumables." As we will soon see, these rights are so different that it is difficult, if not impossible, to devise a simple definition that, at once, is broad enough to capture both of them yet not so broad that it captures other rights.

Though less than ideal, the definition of usufruct found in **Art. 535** nevertheless provides us with useful information. First, the definition tells us that usufruct is a real right. As we noted earlier in this Précis, a real right is one that confers on its holder "direct and immediate authority over a thing" as opposed to one that confers authority, direct and immediate or othwerwise, over a person (i.e., a personal or credit right). Second, the definition tells us that usufruct is of "limited duration." This feature of usufruct is inherent in it; in other words, usufruct, by its very nature, is temporally limited. Just how its duration is limited is spelled out in **LSA-C.C. Arts. 607** and **608.** Where the usufructuary is a natural person, the usufruct ends at his death; where the usufructuary is a juridical person, the usufruct ends upon the dissolution of the juridical person or the lapse of 30 years, whichever is earlier. In this respect, a usufruct is different from full ownership and from predial servitudes, which are, in principle, perpetual.

As a "dismemberment" of ownership, a usufruct, of course, represents only part of the larger ensemble of rights that together constitute ownership. When one subtracts usufruct from ownership, one is, then, left with a residuum of rights. That residuum is called "naked ownership."

B. Varieties

As mentioned above, there are two different kinds of usufruct: usufruct of nonconsumables (perfect or true usufruct) and usufruct of consumables (imperfect or quasi-usufruct). Into which of these two classes a given usufruct falls depends on the nature of the thing that is subjected to it, specifically, whether that thing is consumable or nonconsumable. We explored this classification of things in depth earlier in this Précis. There we learned that a thing is consumable if it would be "useless" to the usufructuary unless it could be consumed, expended, or changed, e.g., money, food, and beverages, but nonconsumable if it can be used without "altering" its "substance," e.g., land, buildings, animals, and shares of stock.

In terms of effects, the principal differences between the two types of usufruct are two-fold. First, there is a difference in terms of the powers conferred on the usufructuary while the usufruct lasts. The usufructuary of a nonconsumable, at least in principle, has only the powers of *usus* and *fructus*, to the exclusion of the power of *abusus*. **LSA-C.C. Art. 539.** The usufructuary of a consumable, by contrast, has not only the powers of *usus* and *fructus*, but also the power of *abusus*. **LSC-C.C. Art. 538.** Such a usufructuary is, as **Art. 538** rightly puts it, the "owner" of the thing, at least for the time being. Second, there is a difference in terms of the duties that the usufructuary (or his successors) owes when the usufruct ends. Whereas the usufructuary of a nonconsumable must restore the thing itself (or things themselves) to the naked owner, **Art. 539**, the usufructuary of a consumable need only either (1) pay the naked owner the original value of the thing(s) or (2) deliver to him a thing of like quality (or things of the same quantity and quality), **Art. 538.** We will have occasion to say more about these differences below.

C. Acquisition

The various means whereby a usufruct may be acquired or otherwise established are identified in **LSA-C.C. Art. 544**: "Usufruct may be established by a juridical act, either inter vivos or mortis causa, or by operation of law." This list, however, is not complete. As comment (c) to **Art. 544** tells us, there is yet one more way: acquisitive prescription. Let us go through these modes of acquisition one at a time.

1. By Juridical Act

a. General Exposition

A usufruct may be created by means of any juridical act that is "translative of ownership." Examples of such juridical acts, as we have noted before, include acts of sale, donation (*inter vivos* or *mortis causa*), and exchange. In practice, one rarely, if ever, comes across usufructs created by means of sale, exchange, or even donation *inter vivos*; usufructs established by donation *mortis causa* (in other words, testamentary legacy), by contrast, are quite common.

1) Particular Questions and Problems

a) Contractual and Testamentary Freedom

The extent to which a person who wishes to create a usufruct by juridical act may create one that deviates from the "usual" rules of usufruct is addressed in **LSA-C.C. Art. 545.** It provides that "[u]sufruct may be established for a term or under a condition, and subject to any modification consistent with the nature of the usufruct." What it means to subject a usufruct to a "term" or a "condition" is clear enough. But what does it mean to subject a usufruct to a "modification" that is "consistent" with the "nature" (in the ontological sense of "essence") of the usufruct? Before one can answer that question, one must first have a clear understanding of what is "essential" to usufruct and what is not. As it turns out, because "usufruct" is today so flexible and malleable a concept, few of the features that one typically associates with usufruct turn out, in the end, to be essential.

Consider, for example, the notion, which we examined earlier, that a usufruct of nonconsumables confers on the usufructuary only the powers of *usus* and *fructus*, to the exclusion of the power of *abusus*. From this notion one might be tempted to infer that it is impermissible for a person to establish a usufruct of nonconsumables that confers on the usufructuary the power of *abusus* in addition to the powers of *usus* and *fructus*. That, however, is not correct. Take a look at **LSA-C.C. Art. 568**, which provides that "[t]he usufructuary does not have the right to dispose of nonconsumable things *unless the right has been expressly granted to him.*" Next, look at comment (a) thereto, which notes that "the grantor may expressly grant to the usufructuary the right to dispose of nonconsumable things subject to the usufruct."[7]

Or consider the notion, also examined earlier, that, at the end of a usufruct of consumables, the usufructuary (or his successor) must turn over to the naked owner either the value of the consumables or consumables of the same quantity and quality. From this notion one might be tempted to infer that it is impermissible for a person to establish a usufruct of consumables that dispenses the usufructuary from this duty of "accounting." Again, however, that is not correct. Look at comment (b) to **Art. 545**, the second to last sentence: "The grantor may... relieve the usufructuary of consumable things of the obligation to account for their value to the naked owner."

In the end, the only typical feature of usufruct that proves to be sacrosanct under **Art. 545**, in other words, that the grantor of the usufruct simply cannot get around, is that of "lifetime duration." "[U]sufruct...

7. As this same comment goes on to explain, when the grantor of such a usufruct confers this extraordinary power of disposition on the usufructuary, we sometimes say that the usufructuary has been given the power of "converting" the usufruct from one of nonconsumables into one of consumables. The idea is that if the usufructuary should dispose of the thing by selling it, then the usufruct attaches to the proceeds of the sale—money—at which point, inasmuch as money is a consumable, the usufruct becomes a usufruct on consumables.

may not be created for a period exceeding the lifetime of an individual usufructuary, *i.e.*, as a heritable right." **Art. 545 cmt. (b).** Thus, though someone can grant a usufruct on his property through testament, he cannot set it up in such a way that, upon the usufructuary's death, the usufruct will fall to the usufructuary's successors.

Even on this point, however, the law is not as inflexible as it may at first seem. Though one cannot create a heritable right of usufruct, one can, nevertheless, do what, at least in some circumstances, may be the "next best thing." And that is to grant "successive usufructs," first, to the first person whom one wishes be usufructuary, and, after her death, to the next and so on. *See* **LSA-C.C. Art. 546** ("Usufruct may be established in favor of successive usufructuaries."). In such a case, the usufruct of each successive usufructuary is understood to be separate from and independent of those that came before and those that will come after it. Further, each of the successive usufructs in the series after the first is understood to arise only when the one that came before it ends, in other words, the second is subject to the "suspensive term" that the first have ended and so on down the line.

Alongside the limitations on contractual and testamentary freedom imposed by **Art. 545**, there is another imposed by **Art. 548.** This one concerns capacity to receive the usufruct:

> When the usufruct is established by an act *inter vivos*, the usufructuary must exist or be conceived at the time of the execution of the instrument. When the usufruct is established by an act *mortis causa*, the usufructuary must exist *or be conceived* at the time of the death of the testator.

In short, the rule is this: the usufructuary must be in existence (*in esse*) at the moment at which the grant of the usufruct is to become effective.

b) Contractual and Testamentary Interpretation

Determining whether the right created in a given juridical act is a usufruct or some other similar, yet different, real or personal right can be frustrating, for grantors often—"seldom" might be more accurate—take care to designate properly the types of rights that they intend to create. A few examples will serve to illustrate the problem.

In one case the grantor gave the grantee the right "to use, without cost, the surface of the south 1000 feet" of a certain tract of land. To determine what kind of right the grantee received, one must, first of all, determine the possibilities. There are at least two: a simple *precarium* (that is, a personal right to use the thing, free of charge, for an indefinite period of time) and a usufruct. The problem with calling this right a usufruct, of course, is that the juridical act which creates it says nothing about "fruits." Nevertheless, the court to which this issue was presented classified it as a usufruct.

In another case, the grantor gave the grantee the right to "receive all the rents, benefits, and emoluments of all of the property that I own at the time of my death." For obvious reasons, a bequest of this kind is commonly referred to as a "legacy of revenues." Classifying a legacy of revenues as the grant of a usufruct is problematic, for the legacy does not entail the right of *usus*. Nevertheless, our courts will, under some circumstances, treat such legacies as usufructs "of a sort," as is explained in comment (c) to **LSA-C.C. Art. 609.** If the legacy pertains to *all* of the testator's property, then the right is a personal right, i.e., one that the heirs or universal legatees are bound to discharge periodically; but if the legacy attaches to a *particular piece* of property, then the right is a usufruct. Thus, in the case referred to at the beginning of this paragraph, the court concluded that the legacy of revenues conferred on the legatee a merely personal right.

In a number of cases, the grantor gave to one grantee a "life estate" and to the other a "remainder" of the same property. The references are to rights known in the common law tradition, but not in the civil law tradition, rights that in some ways parallel those of usufruct and naked ownership, respectively. According to traditional common law theory, the holder of the "life estate" has full ownership of the thing until his death, at which time full ownership vests in the "remainderman." Such a double grant of full ownership, first to one person and then, upon his death, to another is, as we have seen, "prohibited" by our law (specifically, it is a "prohibited substitution," *see* **LSA-C.C. Art. 1520**). Our courts, however, have refused to interpret rights of this kind in that way, that is, in the way in which common law theory would suggest that they be interpreted. Desirous of giving grants of life estates and remainders at least some effect and recognizing that the practical consequences of such rights differ hardly at all from those of their civil law correlatives, the courts have, as a general rule, treated life estates as usufructs and remainders as naked ownership.

2. *By Operation of Law*

Under Louisiana law, legal usufructs, that is, those that are created by operation of law, can arise in just a few contexts. We are interested in two of them.

a. Spousal Usufruct

The most common legal usufruct, and the one of the most practical importance, is established by **LSA-C.C. Art. 890.** That article provides as follows:

> If the deceased spouse is survived by descendants, the surviving spouse shall have a usufruct over the decedent's share of the community property to the extent that the decedent has not disposed of it by testament.

Note the numerous requirements that must be satisfied if such a usufruct is to arise: (1) the decedent must die married; (2) between him and his surviving spouse there must have existed at least some community property; (3) the decedent must have been survived not only by his spouse but also by at least one descendant; and (4) the decedent must not have disposed of his half interest in the community property by testament.[8] When these requirements are satisfied, the decedent's surviving

8. As our courts have interpreted this fourth requirement, it means only this: that the decedent must not have disposed of his half interest in the community property by testament *in a manner that is "adverse" to the surviving spouse.* Imagine that the decedent-to-be draws up a testament in which he purports to leave all of his property, one half interest in community property included, to his surviving spouse. After his death, somehow, someway, some part of his property, including at least part of his half interest in the community property, ends up falling intestate. (One possibility: one of the decedent's descendants qualifies as a "forced heir" and, in an effort to get the "forced share" to which he is entitled, "reduces" the legacy that the decedent left to his surviving spouse.) In such a case, the surviving spouse would still enjoy a usufruct over whatever part of the decedent's half interest in the community property fell intestate, notwithstanding that the decedent had, in some sense, "disposed" of it "by testament." The reason? Because this disposition was not "adverse" to his surviving spouse.

spouse receives a usufruct over, and his descendents, the naked ownership of, the decedent's half interest in the community property. As for the surviving spouse's half interest in the community property, it remains unaffected, that is, it continues to belong to her "in full."

Like many other legal usufructs, the spousal usufruct is, by law, subject to a special "alternative" term—alternative, that is, to the usual term of the lifetime of the usufructuary. In the case of the spousal usufruct, this alternative is the date of the usufructuary's "remarriage." Thus, if the usufructuary remarries, then the usufruct will end then and there, but if she does not, then it will endure until her death or until it is otherwise extinguished.

b. Marital Portion Usufruct

In the rare case in which "a spouse dies rich in comparison with the surviving spouse," the surviving spouse "is entitled to claim the marital portion from the succession of the deceased spouse." **LSA-C.C. Art. 2432.** This "marital portion" ordinarily amounts to "one-fourth of the succession" of the deceased spouse, though there are exceptions. **LSA-C.C. Art. 2434.** Now, sometimes the surviving spouse gets the marital portion in "full ownership" and at other times, merely in usufruct. What makes the difference is whether the deceased spouse was survived by "children": if he was not, then the surviving spouse acquires ownership; if he was, then she acquires a usufruct. ***Id.***

3. By Acquisitive Prescription

Though rare, it is possible for a usufruct to be established through acquisitive prescription. Here is how. Suppose that one person, deliberately or mistakenly misrepresenting himself to be the owner of a certain tract of land, purports to grant a usufruct on that thing to another person. Thereafter the second person begins to avail himself of the purported usufruct, in other words, *quasi*-possesses that usufruct. Provided that this *quasi*-possession endure long enough, the second person will acquire the usufruct prescriptively. If the second person was in good faith and if the title given to him by the grantor was just, then only 10 years of *quasi*-possession will be required; otherwise, he will need 30 years of it.

D. Effects of Usufruct

1. Rights and Duties of the Usufructuary *During the Usufruct*

a. Rights

In examining the "rights" of the usufructuary, one must draw a sharp distinction, at the very beginning, between his rights over the underlying thing, on the one hand, and his rights over his usufruct, on the other. We begin our analysis with the former.

1) With Respect to the Thing Subject to the Usufruct

a) Disposition (*Abusus*)

1] USUFRUCT OF CONSUMABLES

The usufructuary of a consumable, as the "owner" of the thing, has over it an unrestricted power of *abusus.* He can destroy it (physical *abusus*), e.g., by consuming it, or transfer it (juridical *abusus*). In addition, he can abuse it only "in part," as, for example, by granting some real right less than full ownership over it, such as a **UCC-Art. 9** security interest.

2] USUFRUCT OF NONCONSUMABLES

In principle and as a general rule, the usufructuary of a nonconsumable has *no* power of *abusus* over it whatsoever. *See* **LSA-C.C. Art. 568** ("The usufructuary may not dispose of nonconsumable things."). To this general rule there are two exceptions. The first we have already seen. If the usufruct is created by juridical act and if the grantor expressly gives the usufructuary the right to dispose of the thing, then he may do so. ***Id.*** The second we have not yet seen. If the thing burdened with the usufruct is a "corporeal movable[]" of a kind that is "gradually and substantially impaired by use, wear, or decay," then he may dispose of it, "provided that he acts as a prudent administrator." ***Id.*** Examples of such corporeal movables include "equipment, appliances, and automobiles."

b) Fruits (*Fructus*)

LSA-C.C. Art. 550, reiterating what was stated in the articles that define "usufruct" (i.e., **Arts. 538** and **539**), tells us that "[t]he usufructuary is entitled to the fruits of the thing subject to usufruct."

1] DEFINITION

Earlier in this Précis, we studied the concept of "fruits" in depth. Nothing more need be said on this score here, save for these two reminders: (1) a fruit is something the production of which does not diminish the substance of the underlying thing from which it is produced and (2) fruits come in two kinds, first, natural, such as crops produced from land, and civil, such as rent produced from a lease.

2] ALLOCATION

It remains to consider how fruits, be they natural or civil, are divided as between the usufructuary, on the one hand, and the naked owner, on the other.

a] Natural Fruits

According to the first sentence of **LSA-C.C. Art. 555**, "[t]he usufructuary acquires the ownership of natural fruits severed during the existence of the usufruct." As for "[n]atural fruits not severed at the end of the usufruct," these, the same article further provides, "belong to the naked owner." Ownership of natural fruits, then, depends simply on *when* they are harvested, gathered, or otherwise collected.

b] Civil Fruits

The rule for the allocation of civil fruits is quite different. **LSA-C.C. Art. 556** informs us that "[t]he usufructuary acquires the ownership of civil fruits accruing during the existence of the usufruct"; that these "[c]ivil fruits accrue day by day"; and that the usufructuary is entitled to his fruits "regardless of when they are received." Fruits that accrue after the usufruct has ended, by contrast, belong to the naked owner.

An illustration will help to explain the operation of these rules. Suppose that the owner of thing, after leasing it to one person for a term of 30 days at a rent of $60 to be paid in a lump sum at the end of the lease term, immediately thereafter grants a usufruct on the same thing to another person and the naked ownership of it to yet another. Ten days into the lease, the usufructuary dies, bringing the usufruct to an end. For purposes of allocating the rent as between the usufructuary and the naked owner, the rent is deemed to accrue day by day, in this case, at a rate of $2/day ($60/30 days). For 10 of the 30 days, the usufruct was in effect. Consequently, $20 (10 days x $2/day) must be allocated to the usufructuary. For the remaining 20 of the 30 days, the usufruct was not in effect.

Consequently, the remaining $40 (20 days x $2/day) must be allocated to the naked owner.

c) Use (*Usus*)

1] IN GENERAL

The usufructuary, as the articles which define "usufruct" tell us (**Arts. 538** and **539**), has the right to "use" the thing that is burdened with the usufruct. But what does it mean to say that a usufructuary has the "use" of the thing? **LSA-C.C. Art. 539** gives us at least the start of an answer by stating that "the usufructuary has the right to possess them," i.e., the "things subject to the usufruct," and to "derive the utility... that they produce." This latter provision means, among other things, that the usufructuary can use the thing to satisfy his wants and needs, e.g., if it is a car, that he can drive it; if it is a tract of undeveloped land, that he can hunt and fish on it; if it is a house, that he can live in it.

2] LIMITATIONS ON USE

a] Usufruct of Consumables

In the case of a usufruct of a consumable, the usufructuary's right to "use" the thing is unlimited. This follows inescapably from the proposition that a usufructuary of this kind is the "owner," that is, has the *abusus*, of the thing. To say that one has the *abusus* of a thing is to say, among other things, that he is free to mis-"use" it, even to the point of destroying it, if he so chooses.

b] Usufruct of Nonconsumables

The situation of the usufructuary of nonconsumables is quite different. His right to use the thing is anything but unlimited.

1} DUTY TO ACT AS PRUDENT ADMINISTRATOR

First, the usufructuary of a nonconsumable, according to the second paragraph of **Art. 539**, is under a duty to use the thing as would a "prudent administrator." We will have more to say on this score shortly.

2} RESTRICTION ON IMPROVEMENTS AND OTHER PHYSICAL ALTERATIONS

Second, the usufructuary of a nonconsumable does not have a free hand when it comes to making improvements or alterations to the thing. Consider **LSA-C.C. Art. 558**, which provides as follows:

> The usufructuary may make improvements and alterations on the property subject to the usufruct at his cost and with the written consent of the naked owner. If the naked owner fails or refuses to give his consent, the usufructuary may, after notice to the naked owner and with the approval of the proper court, make at his cost those improvements and alterations that a prudent administrator would make.

It is possible, then, for the usufructuary to improve or alter the property. But he cannot do it *unilaterally*, i.e., without first consulting anyone else. The usufructuary must first try to get the approval of the naked owner. If he gets it, he may proceed. But if he does not, then, unless he is prepared to give up, he must seek court approval. In order for him to get this approval, the proposed improvement or alteration must be of the right kind, specifically, the kind that a "prudent administrator" would make. And what is "prudent"? Is any change that enhances the over-all value of the burdened thing necessarily "prudent"? Or what about any change that increases the income-earning potential of the burdened thing? Is prudence merely a matter of economics or must or may the court also factor into the "prudence" equation aesthetic, ethical, and emotional considerations? The answers to these questions are anything but clear.

3} RESTRICTION ON CHANGES IN DESTINATION

Prior to 1976, when the articles on usufruct were last comprehensively revised, Louisiana law, following French and Spanish law, forbade the usufructuary of a nonconsumable from changing its destination under any circumstances. It has been suggested by at least one noted Louisiana civil law scholar that the revision, specifically, the enactment of new (and current) **Art. 558**, effectively "suppressed" this prohibition. This suggestion seems to be based on the assumption, which appears to be correct, that "alterations," as used in this article, is broad enough to include not only "physical changes," but also "changes in destination" and, further, on comment (a) to this article, which indicates that this article was designed, at least in part, to "suppresse[] most of the detailed rules of **Arts. 568** and **569** of the Louisiana Civil Code 1870," the very articles that had supposedly provided the foundation for the "don't change the destination" rule. It seems to me, however, that the suggestion is overly broad. To be sure, the enactment of new (and current) **Art. 558** had an "effect" on, indeed, scaled back, the prohibition. But "scaled back" is one thing and "suppressed" another. As we have seen, **Art. 558** still requires the usufructuary, before making any "alterations"—which, for present purposes, we are assuming including changes of destination—to ask the naked owner for permission. Further, though **Art. 558** allows the usufructuary to "overrule" the naked owner's objection, the usufructuary can do so only if and to the extent that he can persuade a judge that the change in destination he wishes to make is "prudent." In short, the usufructuary is not "free" to change the destination of the thing as he might will; to make such a change, he must jump through the required procedural "hoops" and, if his plan is challenged, show that he is acting prudently.

2) With Respect to the Usufruct *Itself*

The usufruct, considered in isolation from the thing that is subject to it, is a "thing" in itself, to be precise, an incorporeal thing. Of this thing, the usufructuary is the "owner." For that reason, he has over that thing not only the powers of *usus* and *fructus*, but also the power of *abusus.* And because he has *that* power, he is entirely free to "lease, alienate, or encumber his right" as he might wish. **LSA-C.C. Art. 567, ¶1.** Of course, whatever rights he grants in this "thing" of his will "cease of right" when the usufruct ends, for *nemo dat quod non habet* (no one gives what he does have). For example, if he should sell his usufruct to someone else, the usufruct will still terminate when he (not the buyer) dies or some other event that is extinctive of the usufruct occurs. In any event, the usufructuary remains responsible to the naked owner for any damages that may be caused to the underlying thing by those to whom he has leased, alienated, or encumbered his usufruct. ***Id.* at ¶2.**

b. Duties

1) Inventory

Before entering into enjoyment of his usufruct, the usufructuary must "cause an inventory to be made of the property subject to the usufruct." **LSA-C.C. Art. 570, ¶1.** Under at least some circumstances, "[a] descriptive list may be used in lieu of inventory." ***Id.* cmt. (c).** The point of this requirement, of course, is to protect the naked owner, specifically, to generate a record, as it were "up front," of what property the usufructuary must restore or replace, for the naked owner's benefit, at the end of the usufruct.

2) Security

a) Duty to Post

1] GENERAL RULE

Upon assuming his place as usufructuary of a thing, the usufructuary must, at least as a general rule, provide "security." "Security for what?," one might well ask. The answer is straightforward: to guarantee that he will fulfill his duties to the naked owner, whatever those may be. In the case of a usufructuary of a nonconsumable, there is only one such duty—that of replacing the thing or paying its value at the end of the usufruct. But in the case of a usufructuary of a nonconsumable, there are many such duties. Many of these, e.g., the duty to use the thing as a prudent administrator and to restore the thing at the end of the usufruct, we have already seen. But there are still several others, as we will shortly learn. How the security "works" for the naked owner can be explained this way: the naked owner, should the usufructuary default on one or more of his duties and, in so doing, injure the naked owner, can enforce his security rights—in common parlance, "foreclose" upon the thing put up as security—and, in so doing, collect money that will serve him as compensation for that injury.

2] EXCEPTIONS

To the requirement that the usufructuary post security there are several exceptions, all of them laid out in **LSA-C.C. Art. 573.** First, legal usufructuaries, as a general rule (if one can speak of a "general" exception), are exempt. ***Id.*** **A, B & D.** To this exception there are several exceptions, that is, situations in which a legal usufructuary may be compelled to post security. Those that are of interest to us are these: (1) where the legal usufruct is an **Art. 890** spousal usufruct or an **Art. 2434** marital portion usufruct and the naked owner is not the child of the usufructuary, **Art. 573.B & D**; and (2) where the legal usufruct is an **Art. 890** spousal usufruct and the naked owner, though a child of the usufructuary, is also a forced heir, **Art. 573.B.** Second, one who acquired his usufruct by "reservation," that is, who transferred his thing under a reservation of usufruct (in essence, transferred only the naked ownership), is exempt. **Art. 573.D, sent. 2.**

b) Form of Security

Regarding the form of security that the usufructuary may or must provide, the law is rather flexible. According to comment (b) to **LSA-C.C. Art. 572**, the usufructuary may provide either a "surety," which, in most cases, would be in the form of a "bond" provided by a surety company, or a "special mortgage," that is, a mortgage on some piece or pieces of the usufructuary's other property.

c) Amount of Security

Regarding the amount of the security, we have first a general rule and then an exception. The former, which appears in the first paragraph of **Art. 572**, is that the usufructuary must provide security "in the amount of the total value of the property subject to the usufruct." The latter, established in the second paragraph of **Art. 572**, is broad and flexible: "The court may increase or reduce the amount of the security, on proper showing." "Proper showing," however, is left undefined.

3) Repairs

Under the first paragraph of **LSA-C.C. Art. 577**, the usufructuary is responsible for "ordinary maintenance and repairs for keeping the property subject to the usufruct in good order." For purposes of this rule, it is of no moment whether the need for the repairs arises "from accident, from the normal use of the thing, or from his [the usufructuary's] fault." *Id.* There is, however, one category of "ordinary maintenance and repairs" that is not at the usufructuary's charge, namely, those the need for which arose *before the usufruct began.* **LSA-C.C. Art. 578 cmt. (c).** For such ordinary maintenance and repairs, the naked owner is responsible. ***Id.***

In cases of ordinary maintenance and repairs for which the usufructuary is responsible, the naked owner may, during the existence of the usufruct, compel the usufructuary to make them. **LSA-C.C. Art. 579.** Of course, if the naked owner does not avail himself of this remedy, he may be able to collect damages for the usufructuary's default at the end of the usufruct.

In contrast to "ordinary maintenance and repairs," "extraordinary repairs" are generally at the charge of the naked owner rather than the usufructuary. **Art. 577, ¶2.** There is, however, an exception for extraordinary repairs that "have become necessary as a result of the usufructuary's fault or neglect." For such extraordinary repairs, the usufructuary is responsible.

If the naked owner does not make the extraordinary repairs for which he is responsible, the usufructuary may go ahead and make them himself at his own expense. **LSA-C.C. Art. 579.** But if the usufructuary does so, his sole remedy is to obtain "reimbursement by the naked owner *at the end of the usufruct.*" ***Id.***

The critically important difference between an "extraordinary" and an "ordinary" repair is explained in **LSA-C.C. Art. 578.** According to that article, "[e]xtraordinary repairs are those for the construction of the whole or of a substantial part of the property subject to the usufruct. All others are ordinary repairs."

4) Preservation

The usufructuary is responsible for "all expenses that became necessary for the preservation and use of the property." **LSA-C.C. Art. 581.** What is "necessary" is, of course, a question of fact, one to be "determined in the light of the obligation of the usufrudctuary 'for losses resulting from his fraud, default, or neglect.' Article 576." ***Id.* cmt. (c).**

5) Charges

The usufructuary is responsible for many of the "charges," that is, governmental assessments, that are imposed on the thing during his usufruct. **LSA-C.C. Art. 584** provides that "[t]he usufructuary is bound to pay the annual charges imposed during his enjoyment on the property subject to the usufruct, such as property taxes." **LSA-C.C. Art. 585** adds that "[t]he usufructuary is bound to pay the extraordinary charges that may be imposed, during the existence of the usufruct, on the property subject to it." One example of an "extraordinary charge," according to comment (b) to **Art. 585**, is a "paving assessment."

Whether the usufructuary is entitled to any sort of indemnity for these expenses at the end of the usufruct depends, first, on the nature of the charge. If it is "annual," then no; but if it is "extraordinary," then maybe. After that, sentence two of **Art. 585** states that it depends on whether the benefit of the charge is "of a nature to augment the value of the property subject to the usufruct." If it does, then the usufructary is entitled to reimbursement at the end of the usufruct "only for capital expended"; if not, then he is entitled to no reimbursement.

6) Prudent Administrator

A usufructuary of nonconsumables, we have seen, has the duty to use the thing as a "prudent administrator." Judging from the Civil Code articles that spell out the ramifications of this duty, one would have to conclude that the redactors conceived of it in largely negative terms, i.e., as a series of prohibitions on this or that form of imprudent or, if you prefer, "foolish" conduct. For example, if the usufructuary neglects to repair a construction to which the usufruct extends, thereby causing it to depreciate in value, he will be liable to the naked owner for damages under **LSA-C.C. Art. 576.** To take another example, if the usufructuary, through failure to use a servitude of passage that benefits the estate burdened by his usufruct, allows it to prescribe through nonuse, he will be liable to the naked owner for damages under **LSA-C.C. Art. 597**. Finally, if the usufructuary, despite knowing that an interloper has invaded part of the burdened estate, fails to inform the naked owner, with the result that, after the passage of a year, the interloper acquires the right to possess the estate or to *quasi*-possess a real right in the estate or, after the passage of 10 or 30 years, acquires ownership of part of the estate or a real right on it, then, again, he will owe the naked owner damages, this time under **LSA-C.C. Arts.** 597 and **598.**

2. *Rights and Duties of the* Naked Owner *During the Usufruct*

a. Usufruct of Consumables

During the usufruct, the naked owner of a thing subjected to a usufruct of consumables has no rights and, aside from the basic duty "not to interfere" with the usufructuary, no duties. That this is so follows inescapably from the fact that the usufructuary is, in effect, the "owner."

b. Usufruct of Nonconsumables

As the holder of the residual *abusus* of the thing that is subject to the usufruct, the naked owner, in principle, enjoys some power of disposition in regard to that thing. This power is addressed in **LSA-C.C. Art. 603**. According to the second sentence, the naked owner can "alienate or encumber property subject to the usufruct," provided that he does not "thereby affect the usufruct." But this manner of speaking is technically imprecise. *Nemo dat quod non habet* (no one gives what he does not have). For the naked owner, the "property subject to the usufruct," that is, the "underlying thing," is not his to give. It would be better, then, to say simply what the first sentence of the article says and to be content with that: "The naked owner may dispose of the naked ownership."

The naked owner, unlike the usufructuary, cannot make improvements or alterations to the burdened thing under any circumstances. **LSA-C.C. Art. 606.** He may, however, make "extraordinary repairs" to the thing (it will be recalled that these repairs are at his charge), provided he does so "in the manner least inconvenient and onerous for the usufructuary." ***Id.* cmt. (b).**

In principle, the naked owner, as the holder of the *abusus* of the thing, can grant real rights over it, such as predial servitudes. *See* **LSA-C.C. Arts. 604 & 710.** But this power is subject to an important limitation: the servitudes so granted must be such that "they may be exercised without injury to the usufructuary." **Art. 604.** In all but the rarest of cases, that will be impossible. Under the Mineral Code, the naked owner of a tract of land can grant a mineral servitude or mineral lease over the land, notwithstanding that it may infringe on the usufructuary's rights. **Min. C. Art. 196.** Nevertheless, if the grantee of such a right should injure the usufructuary, the grantee and the naked owner will be "liable in solido" for the usufructuary's damages. ***Id.***

3. "Other" Effect: Partition Powers

a. Relative: Partition of Usufruct or of Naked Ownership

1) Partition of Usufruct

"Usufruct is susceptible to division," that is, "may be conferred on several persons in divided or undivided shares." **LSA-C.C. Art. 541.** When it is conferred in undivided shares, these "several persons" become "co-owners" of the usufruct in indivision, commonly called co-usufructuaries. Like any other thing held in indivision, a "[u]sufruct... conferred on several persons... may be partitioned among the usufructuaries." ***Id.*** Comment (c) to that article adds that the usufruct may be partitioned either in kind or by licitation: "When a usufruct is conferred in undivided portions, the state of indivision may terminate at any time by partition in kind or by licitation." If the partition is in kind, then each of the former co-usufructuaries will be given an exclusive, singular usufruct on a discrete physical part of the underlying thing; if it is by licitation, then the usufruct as a whole (not the underlying thing) will be sold at auction to the highest bidder, who will then become the sole usufructuary of the underlying thing, and the proceeds of the sale will be distributed proportionately to the former co-usufructuaries.

2) Partition of Naked Ownership

Naked ownership, just like usufruct, can be conferred on more than one person. Comment (b) to **LSA-C.C. Art. 542** alludes to this possibility: "[w]hen the naked ownership of a thing is held by several persons in undivided shares...." Co-naked owners in indivision have the same ability to escape that condition of co-ownership as do co-usufructuaries: by partition. ***Id.*** Comment (b) to **Art. 542** explains the possible means of partition: "When the naked ownership of a thing is held by several persons in undivided shares ..., partition of the naked ownership in kind or by licitation may be demanded." In either case, the usufruct will remain unaffected. **LSA-C.C. Art. 542.**

b. Absolute: Partition of the Underlying Thing

As we have seen, any of multiple co-usufructuaries can demand the partition of the usufruct and any of multiple co-naked owners can demand the partition of the naked ownership. But when, if at all, can a co-usufructuary or a co-naked owner demand partition of the underlying thing, that is, the thing that is subject to the usufruct? This is the question that we want to consider now.

The answer to the question is provided in **LSA-C.C. Art. 543.** The general rule is that a partition of the underlying thing may be demanded only by one who has a "share in full ownership" of that thing. ***Id.* at ¶1.** For that reason, "[a] person having a share in naked ownership only or in usufruct only does not have this right," at least not ordinarily. ***Id.* at ¶2.** The law which confers the right to the partition of a "thing held in common" has no application to those who hold, respectively, the fragments of a dismembered title to the same property, for the reason that in such a case, the title being dismembered, each part is a distinct thing, held by a different owner, and there is no 'thing held in common.'" But there is an exception to this rule: if one of the co-naked owners and another of the co-naked owners join forces and demand partition together, then their "combined shares," following simple arithmetical logic, "shall be deemed to constitute a share in full ownership" and, on that basis, the partition will be ordered. ***Id.***

E. Termination

1. Causes of Termination

a. "Death" of the Usufructuary

At least as a general rule, a usufruct terminates—indeed, by definition *must* terminate, at the very latest—at the end of the usufructuary's "life." **LSA-C.C. Art. 607** provides that "[t]he right of usufruct expires upon the death of the usufructuary." As applied to natural persons, this rule "works" just fine. But as applied to juridical persons, it does not, at least not always. The problem, in short, is that because a juridical person has the potential to "live forever," limiting the duration of a usufruct to the "lifetime" of the usufructuary could, in the case of such a usufructuary, amount to no limitation at all. The legislature's answer to this problem is found in **LSA-C.C. Art. 608.** It provides that "a usufruct established in favor of a legal entity other than a natural person" (in other words, a juridical person) "terminates" under either of two sets of circumstances: (1) if the entity "ceases to exist" (in other words, if it "dies," juridically speaking), then upon its ceasing to exist; (2) if the entity does not cease to exist, then "upon the lapse of thirty years from the date of the commencement of the usufruct."

b. Destruction of the Underlying Thing

A second cause of termination of usufructs is the destruction of the thing that the usufruct burdens. This cause of termination is addressed in **LSA-C.C. Art. 613**: "The usufruct of nonconsumables terminates by the permanent and total loss, extinction, or destruction through accident or decay of the property subject to the usufruct." Note that there are three prerequisites to the termination of a usufruct in this fashion. First, the destruction of the underlying thing must be "permanent." A field that experiences a flood has been "destroyed" in some sense, but the destruction is not permanent. Second, it must be "total." This second requirement assumes particular importance where the usufruct is "universal" burdens (all or part of an entire patrimony) rather than "particular" burdens. In such a case, the usufruct continues to survive notwithstanding the destruction of some of the things that are subject to it; in fact, even with respect to the things that have been destroyed, the usufruct does not terminate. Were it otherwise, then the naked owner could compel the usufructuary to account every time that a thing subject to the usufruct was destroyed, opening the door to the possibility of multiple, "piecemeal" accountings. Third, the destruction must result from an "accident" or "decay," as opposed to the "fault" of some third person.

More must be said about the third of these requirements, for it is easily misunderstood. Taking the requirement at face value, one might be tempted to draw two inferences. The first is that if the thing subject to the usufruct is destroyed due to the fault of a third person, then the usufruct does not terminate at all. The second is that each and every time that the thing subject to the usufruct is destroyed due to accident or decay, the usufruct is terminated, period, end of story. Strictly speaking, however, neither of these inferences is entirely correct.

Let us start with the first inference, that is, that if the thing subject to the usufruct is destroyed due to the fault of a third person, then the usufruct does not terminate in any sense or to any extent. At first glance, **LSA-C.C. Art. 614** seems to confirm the inference. It provides that "[w]hen any loss, extinction, or destruction of property subject to usufruct is attributable to the fault of a third person, the usufruct does not terminate but attaches to any claim for damages and the proceeds therefrom." But the phrase "does not terminate," as used here, must be interpreted with great care. What it means—and all that it means—is that the usufruct does not terminate *absolutely*, in other words, the usufruct may continue to exist "for some purpose," "to some extent," "in some sense," or, still more to the point, "*as to* some things." That proposition is not inconsistent with the possibility that the usufruct may terminate *relatively*, that is, for some other purpose, to some other extent, etc. And that, in fact, is precisely what happens in such a case. *As to* the *original* object of the usufruct, the usufruct does, indeed, terminate. How could it be otherwise? As a matter of logic, one cannot possibly have a right on something that does not exist! Nevertheless, *as to* something else—specifically, the claim against the person whose fault caused the destruction—the usufruct does not terminate, but instead survives. Here, then, is the true meaning of **Art. 614.**

Next, let us consider the second inference, that is, that if the thing subject to the usufruct is destroyed due to accident or decay, then the usufruct is terminated, no matter what. That this inference is incorrect, at least in the sense of being overly broad, becomes clear once one reads **LSA-C.C. Art. 617**: "When proceeds of insurance are due on account of loss, extinction, or destruction of property subject to usufruct, the usufruct attaches to the proceeds." What happens in this case is not unlike what happened in the last case: the usufruct does terminate, but relatively rather than absolutely; the usufruct terminates *as to* the original thing that was subject to it, but it survives *as to* and now burdens something else. In the previous case, the "something else" was the claim against the faulty destroyer; in this case, it is the claim against the property insurer.

It is worth noting that, in both of these cases of "relative" termination of usufruct, one of the grand general principles of the civil law is at work—"real subrogation." Real subrogation is a fiction according to which one thing is deemed to take the place of—to be substituted for—another thing and, in so doing, to assume all of the juridical qualities and characteristics of that thing. These qualities and characteristics include subjection to real rights such as usufruct. Thus, what happens under **Art. 614** can be described as follows: the claim against the faulty destroyer having become subrogated to the destroyed thing, the usufruct that had burdened the latter now burdens the former. The same description *mutatis mutandis* can be given to the operation of **Art. 617.**

c. The Transformation of the Burdened Thing

The principle of real subrogation is likewise at work in several of the other possible causes of the termination of usufructs. These causes are identified in **LSA-C.C. Arts. 615** and **616.** What these causes share in common is the transformation or conversion of the burdened thing into something else, usually money.

Art. 615 deals with transformations (or conversions) of the burdened property that take place "without any act of the usufructuary." Two examples are specifically mentioned in the article itself: (1) the expropriation of an immovable for public use, resulting in the transformation of the immovable into "just compensation" paid by the expropriating entity, and (2) the liquidation of a corporation, resulting in the transformation of corporate stock into cash. There is a third possibility, one mentioned in comment (b) to the article: the redemption of corporate stock by the issuing corporation, resulting in the transformation of the stock into cash. In each of these cases, according to **Art. 615**, the usufruct "does not terminate" but rather "attaches to the money or other property." As we have seen, what language of this kind really means is that the usufruct terminates *as to* the original property—the immovable, the corporate stock, or whatever—but survives *as to* and now burdens that which is subrogated to the original property—the money or whatever else.

There is yet another case to which **Art. 615** may be applied, though it is not mentioned either in the article or in the comments to it. Suppose that, before the usufruct is established on the thing, the owner of it first grants some kind of security right on it, for example, a mortgage to secure performance of some obligation of his. Then, after the usufruct is established, the owner (or whoever may now owe that obligation, such as his successor) defaults on the obligation. At that point, the mortgagee enforces the mortgage, causing it to be seized and then sold at public auction. What, then, happens to the usufruct? The first paragraph of **LSA-C.C. Art. 620** provides that "[u]sufruct terminates by the enforcement of a mortgage placed upon the property prior to the creation of the usufruct." As we have already seen, in some instances in which the Civil Code provides that a usufruct "terminates," all that is meant is that it terminates *relatively* to the original thing; the possibility is left open that the usufruct might nevertheless survive *relatively* to another thing, specifically, to something that, under the principle of real subrogation, might replace it. This is another such an instance. Everything depends on whether, at the public auction, the price realized from the sale of the thing falls short of, equals, or exceeds the amount of the unsatisfied obligation that is owed to the mortgagee. If the price is less than or equal to that amount, then there is "nothing left" that might be subrogated to the original thing and, therefore, nothing as to which the usufruct might possibly survive. But if the price is greater than that amount, then after the mortgagee has been paid off, the remaining excess is subrogated to the original thing and as to it the usufruct survives. In such a case, then, the usufruct falls on this excess.

Art. 616 addresses certain cases of the "sale" of the burdened thing, specifically, (1) a sale to which the usufructuary and naked owner agree or (2) a sale made pursuant to a partition of the burdened thing. In each case, the usufruct terminates as to the original thing, but survives as to and falls on the proceeds of the sale.

d. Waste or Abuse

A usufruct of nonconsumables may be terminated if the usufructuary defaults seriously on his duty to preserve the substance of those nonconsumables. This possibility is addressed in **LSA-C.C. Art. 623**, which provides as follows:

> A usufruct may be terminated by the naked owner if the usufructuary commits waste, alienates things without authority, neglects to make ordinary repairs, or abuses his enjoyment in any other manner.

A usufructuary cannot be charged with "waste" of the thing simply because the thing, while on his "watch," becomes ruined as a result of "old age." This inference follows from **LSA-C.C. Art. 583**, "[n]either the usufructuary nor the naked owner is bound to restore property that has been totally destroyed through accident or because of age." "Waste," then, requires "active neglect" on the usufructuary's part.

It is important to note that if the usufructuary is guilty of waste or some other offence under **Art. 623**, the usufruct is not terminated *ipso facto*. Nor is the naked owner entitled *as of right* to an order terminating the usufruct. To the contrary, in the face of waste the naked owner acquires merely the right *to petition the court* for termination. **LSA-C.C. Art. 624, ¶1.** The court, upon receipt of such a petition, has several options. To be sure, the court may, in its discretion, terminate the usufruct. But the court may, instead, merely "decree that the property be delivered to the naked owner on the condition that he shall pay to the usufructuary a reasonable annuity until the end of the usufruct." ***Id.*** There is still a third possibility, but it requires the active cooperation—indeed, the initiative—of the usufructuary. According to the second paragraph of **Art. 624**, the usufructuary can "prevent" the termination of the usufruct or "delivery" of the thing to the naked owner by "giving security to insure that he will take appropriate corrective measures within a period fixed by the court."

e. Forced Sale of the Burdened Thing

LSA-C.C. Art. 620 states that "[u]sufruct terminates by the enforcement of a mortgage placed upon the property prior to the creation of the usufruct." When a thing burdened with a usufruct is sold to satisfy a superior mortgage, i.e., one placed on the thing before the usufruct was created, the usufruct is not terminated entirely. To be sure, the usufruct no longer burdens the mortgaged thing itself. But if the sale of the mortgaged thing should yield proceeds that include a surplus, that is, an excess over the sum owed to the mortgagee, then the usufruct will, through real subrogation, "jump" onto that surplus and burden it. This construction of **LSA-C.C. Art. 620** harmonizes it with **Art. 615.** It also harmonizes **LSA-C.C. Art. 616** with the other two articles. Under that article, if the naked owner and the usufructuary agree to sell the burdened property, the usufruct, in the absence of a stipulation to the contrary, attaches to the proceeds. **Art. 620** further provides that "the enforcement of a mortgage placed upon the property by the naked owner *after* the creation of the usufruct does not affect the right of the usufructuary."

f. Prescription of Nonuse

Like other principal real rights less than ownership, a usufruct can prescribe through nonuse. **LSA-C.C. Art. 621.** The prescriptive period, as usual, is 10 years. This prescription can be staved off not only by acts of the usufructuary himself, but also by acts of "any other person acting in his name," including even the naked owner.

2. Consequences of Termination

a. Usufruct of Nonconsumables

The first sentence of paragraph one of **LSA-C.C. Art. 628** informs us that upon the end of a usufruct of nonconsumables, the naked owners become the "full owners" of everything that was once subject to the usufruct, save those things, if any, that have been lost or destroyed. The second paragraph to **Art. 628** further explains that if there was such a loss and it was attributable to the usufructuary's fault, then the naked owners are entitled to an indemnity equal to "the value [that] th[at] property otherwise would have had at the termination of the usufruct."

The second sentence of the first paragraph of **Art. 628** also tells us that any fruits collected by the usufructuary or his successors after the usufruct ended and that were allocable, under the rules of allocation of fruits that we examined earlier, to the post-usufruct period must also be turned over to the naked owners.

b. Usufruct of Consumables

LSA-C.C. Art. 629 governs the termination of a usufruct of consumables. At the end of a usufruct of consumables, the usufructuary or his successors owe the naked owners either of two performances: (1) replacement of things of like quality and the same quantity or (2) the value the things had *at the commencement of the usufruct.* The usufructuary gets to choose, i.e., has the option of remedies.

II. Habitation

LSA-C.C. Art. 630 defines habitation as the "nontransferable real right of a natural person to dwell in the house of another." Habitation behaves, for the most part, just like usufruct. *See* **LSA-C.C. Arts. 631** (in general), **632** (regulation by title), **635** (standard of care: prudent administrator) & **636** (repairs and charges). It does, however, have a few distinctive features.

The first has to do with the kind of thing(s) on which a habitation may be established. **LSA-C.C. Art. 544** tells us that "[u]sufruct may be established on all kinds of things, movable or immovable, corporeal or incorporeal." The same is *not* true of habitation. Under **LSA-C.C. Art. 634**, habitation may be established only on a "house" or a "part" of a house, which, of course, is a distinctive kind of corporeal immovable (more precisely still, a distinctive kind of "building").

The second has to do with the possibility of transfer. **LSA-C.C. Art. 567** tells us that "[t]he usufructuary may lease, alienate, or encumber his right." The same is *not* true of habitation. According to **LSA-C.C. Art. 637**, [t]he right of habitation is neither transferable nor heritable. It may not be alienated, let, or encumbered." Notwithstanding this limitation, the habitator is, nevertheless, entitled to "share," as it were, the benefits of his right with various others, including his "family," **LSA-C.C. Art. 633**, and "friends, guests, and boarders," **LSA-C.C. Art. 634.**

III. Right of Use

LSA-C.C. Art. 639 defines "right of use" as a "personal servitude" that "confers in favor of a person a specified use of an estate less than full enjoyment." The reference here to "specified use... less than full enjoyment," comment (b) to the article explains, is intended to distinguish right of use from *usufruct*, which "confers advantages that exhaust the utility of the property." How right of use differs from *predial servitude* is signaled by the words "in favor of a person": whereas in the case of a predial servitude, the "specified use of an estate" is conferred on *another estate* (the dominant), in the case of a right of use, the "specified use of an estate" is conferred on *a person.*

Not just any kind of "use" can form the content of a right of use. According to **LSA-C.C. Art. 640**, a right of use can confer only the sorts of limited advantages that "may be established by a predial servitude." Examples include of such "advantages" include "rights of passage, aqueduct,... light of view" and even "fishing or hunting rights" and the right to "tak[e] certain fruits or products." ***Id.* cmt. (b).**

In the light of **Arts. 639** and **640**, it becomes clear that predial servitude, on the one hand, and right of use, on the other, are but variations on the same theme. Indeed, it may be profitable to think of right of use (though this is technically inaccurate) as a "predial servitude" that, instead of benefitting an estate (which, as we have seen, really means "whosoever happens to own the dominant estate"), benefits a particular individual, regardless whether he owns any estate or not.

Determining whether a certain right to limited use of an estate constitutes a predial servitude or a right of use can sometimes be dicey business. To be sure, in many cases the classification is obvious. The grant of a "right of way" to a railroad to lay a railway on one's land or the grant to a utility company or "cable TV" provider to lay wires under one's ground could only be a right of use, for there is no "estate" related to the right granted that might possibly receive the benefit: in such cases, the right is clearly for the benefit of a person, namely, the railroad company, utility company, etc. But in cases in which there is another estate "around" somewhere that might possibly be thought of as "related" to the right granted, careful interpretation is required. The rules for resolving questions of this kind are found in **LSA-C.C. Arts. 730–734**, which pertain to the "interpretation of servitudes."

SUB-CHAPTER C

Building Restrictions[9]

I. Definition

"Building restrictions," according to **LSA-C.C. Art.** 775, "are charges imposed by the owner of an immovable in pursuance of a general plan governing building standards, specified uses, and improvements." The term "charge" here has the same sense as it does in **Article 646**, which defines predial servitudes, that is, a "burden" imposed on an immovable or, to speak less anthropomorphically, a "duty" imposed on whoever may happen to own the immovable.

The wording of **LSA-C.C. Art. 775** imposes an important limitation on the range of permissible building restrictions, a limitation that is easy to miss. As this Article makes clear, building restrictions may govern "building standards," "specified uses," and "improvements," in other words, may determine how the immovable subjected to them may be constructed, used, or developed. ***Id.* cmt (a)**. Notably—and, as it turns out, deliberately—absent from this list of possibilities is "alienation." As comment (a) to the article observes, "[r]estraints on alienation, to the extent that they may be valid under Louisiana law, are not governed by this revision." ***Id.***

9. What follows is an exposition of the law of building restrictions as it appears *in the Civil Code*. The scope of cases to which that law applies was significantly curtailed in 1999 when the legislature enacted the "Louisiana Homeowners Association Act." *See* **LSA-R.S. 9:1141.1–1141.9**. This act creates rules governing the creation, effects, and termination of building restrictions within so-called "residential planned communities," rules that differ in important respects from those found in the Civil Code. Most residential subdivisions that have been created since this act went into effect qualify as residential planned communities. According to **LSA-C.C. Art. 783**, "[t]he provisions of... the Louisiana Homeowners Association Act shall supersede any and all provisions of this Title [the Civil Code title that pertains to building restrictions] in the event of a conflict."

II. Characterization

"Building restrictions are incorporeal immovables and real rights likened to predial servitudes." **LSA-C.C. Art. 777, sent. 1**. For that reason, these restrictions "are regulated by application of the rules governing predial servitudes to the extent that their application is compatible with the nature of building restrictions." ***Id.*, sent. 2.**

That "building restrictions" are merely "likened" to predial servitudes suggests there are some differences between them, as, indeed, there are. One of the most important, at least at the theoretical level, is that, in the case of building restrictions, there is no "servient estate" properly so called. As is noted in comment (c) to the article, "[r]estrictions imposed by subdivider prior to the creation of a subdivision do not qualify as predial servitudes because the requirement of two estates is not met." Other, more practical differences will be noted below.

III. Classification

A. By Type of Restricted Activity: Building Standards, Specified Uses, Improvements

As has already been noted, the Civil Code Article that defines building restrictions—**LSA-C.C. Art. 775**—provides that they may govern "building standards" for, "specified uses" of, or "improvements" to the immovable that is subjected to them. The overall range of possible building restrictions is, then, quite broad. To impress this point on the reader, I will provide a number of examples.

Building standards.—Requiring that buildings or other constructions should face a certain street or should be erected a number of feet from the street or the property line; be constructed in a certain architectural style; have a certain minimum or maximum square footage or height or width; that secondary buildings or constructions, such as storage sheds, be constructed of the same materials as the principal building.

Specified uses.—Prohibiting commercial activity (in other words, limiting use to residential purposes) or limiting the permissible types of commercial activities (e.g., no liquor stores); prohibiting short-term rentals of residential property; prohibiting the parking of cars or boats on the property or restricting the spaces in which they may be parked; prohibiting or restricting further subdivision of the property; requiring that the property be properly maintained (e.g., that the grass be regularly mowed or that the buildings be regularly repainted).

Improvements.—Prohibiting the construction of structures other than residences, such as storage sheds; prohibiting the installation of "temporary structures", such as mobile homes or trailers; requiring or limiting the planting of trees; prohibiting the erection of signs; requiring the construction of fences or limiting the types of fences that may be constructed; restricting the number, height, or intensity of floodlights.

B. By Nature of Duty: Negative vs. Affirmative

"Building restrictions may impose on owners of immovables affirmative duties that are reasonable and necessary for the maintenance of the general plan."[10] **LSA-C.C. Art. 778, sent. 1.** But there is an important limitation on this power to create affirmative duties: "Building restrictions may not impose upon the owner of an immovable or his successors the obligation to pay a fee or other charge on the occasion of an alienation, lease or encumbrance of the immovable." **LSA-C.C. Art. 778, sent. 2.**

IV. Creation

A. Means

Building restrictions may be established in one way and one way only: "by juridical act." **LSA-C.C. Art. 776, sent. 1.** The significance of this limitation is this: building restrictions, in sharp contrast to other princi-

10. We see here another important difference between predial servitudes, on the one hand, and building restrictions, on the other. As a general rule—one to which, it will be recalled, there is only one narrow exception—predial servitudes may *not* impose affirmative duties on the owner of the burdened (servient) estate. There is no such general rule for building restrictions.

pal real rights, cannot be created by acquisitive prescription, destination of the owner, accession, or otherwise by operation of law.

For this "juridical act" to be effective, it must be "executed by the owner of an immovable or by all the owners of the affected immovables." **LSA-C.C. Art. 776, sent. 2.** There are two distinct possibilities here.

Executed by "the owner."—The first possibility—"executed by the owner"—is far and away the more common in practice. As comment (b) to the article notes, "[b]uilding restrictions are ordinarily created by developers of land who intend to subdivide their property into individual lots destined to residential, commercial, or industrial uses." Thus, the "owner" to which the article refers is the unitary owner of the immovable in its as-yet undivided state.

This owner-developer may "execute" the required "juridical act" in either of two ways. The first is by means of stating the restrictions in a subdivision plat (a map of the subdivision). The second is by stating them in every one of the initial acts of sale of the lots in the subdivision. As long as the plat or the original acts of sale are properly registered (recorded in the conveyance records of the parish in which the subdivision is located), the restrictions stated therein will be binding, automatically as it were, on all persons who may thereafter acquire real rights in any of the subdivision lots. *See* **LSA-C.C. Art. 777 cmt. (c).**

Executed by "all the owners."—The second, and less common, possibility is that the juridical act may be "executed by all the owners." What is contemplated here, as comment (b) to the article explains, is that "[a]fter the establishment of a subdivision,... [the] landowners may occasionally enter into agreements designed to restrict the use of their property."

B. Special Requirement: General Plan of Development

The Civil Code Article that defines building restrictions—**LSA-C.C. Art. 775**—provides that they must and can only be created "in pursuance of a general plan." Comment (e) to the article explains the significance of this requirement:

> According to firmly established Louisiana jurisprudence, building restrictions constitute real rights only in the frame-

work of subdivision planning. They must be imposed, at least by implication, in favor of lots in a subdivision in accordance with a general development plan. If the restrictions are imposed on individual lots without regard to a general development plan, they may constitute veritable predial servitudes, provided, of course, that the requirements for the creation of predial servitudes are met.... If the requirements for the creation of predial servitudes are not met, the restrictions may only be personal obligations.

V. Interpretation

It will be recalled that "[d]oubt as to the existence, extent, or manner of exercise of a predial servitude shall be resolved in favor of the servient estate." **LSA-C.C. Art. 730**. Because building restrictions, as we have seen, are "real rights likened to predial servitudes" (**LSA-C.C. Art.** 777), it comes as no surprise that the rule is precisely the same for them: "Doubt as to the existence, validity, or extent of building restrictions is resolved in favor of the unrestricted use of the immovable." **LSA-C.C. Art. 783, sent. 1.**

VI. Enforcement

Building restrictions may be enforced in the same manner as may any other rights, be they real or personal, that is through an action for specific performance or an action for damages. The former possibility is addressed in **LSA-C.C. Art.** 779, which provides that "[b]uilding restrictions may be enforced by mandatory and prohibitory injunctions...." But the article goes on to add this important qualification: these injunctions may be issued "without regard to the limitations of Article 3601 of the Code of Civil Procedure." That means, among other things, that the plaintiff is not required to prove irreparable harm.

VII. Alteration

A. Amendment

1. Modes Established by the Juridical Act(s) that Create(s) the Restrictions

It is possible and, in practice, likely that the juridical act(s) through which the building restrictions are created may establish one or more mechanisms whereby they may be amended. In such a case, the "[b]uilding restrictions may be amended, whether such amendment lessens or increases a restriction, or may terminate or be terminated, as provided in the act that establishes them." **LSA-C.C. Art. 780, sent. 1.**

2. Modes Established by Suppletive Law

That the juridical act which establishes the building restrictions does not stipulate a mechanism for amending the restrictions does not mean that the restrictions can never be amended. To the contrary, the Civil Code supplies a default mechanism for amendments in such cases, a mechanism that requires the agreement of certain ones of the owners of the immovables that are subjected to the restrictions. Which owners and how many of them must agree varies depending on how long the restrictions have been in place at the time of the proposed amendment.

a. More Than Fifteen Years

If the restrictions "have been in effect for at least fifteen years," then they may be amended "for the whole or a part of the restricted area by agreement of owners representing more than one-half of the land area affected by the restrictions, excluding streets and street rights-of-way." **LSA-C.C. Art. 780, sent. 2.** Note that under this rule, what matters is not the *number of landowners* who agree, but rather the *size of the restricted area* that the landowners who agree represent.

b. More Than Ten Years

If the restrictions "have been in effect for more than ten years," then they may be amended "for the whole or a part of the restricted area ... by agreement of both owners representing two-thirds of the land area affected and two-thirds of the owners of the land affected by the restrictions, excluding streets and street rights-of-way." *Id.* Note that this rule differs from that which applies when the restrictions have been in effect for more than fifteen years in two respects. First, under this rule, the required fraction is different, namely, it is 2/3 instead of 1/2. Second, under this rule, there are two requirements, not just one. Not only must the owners who represent the required fraction of the *total land area* agree, as is the case with the "fifteen years plus" rule; in addition, a required fraction of the *total number of landowners* must agree. In other words, whereas the "fifteen years plus" rule imposes only a land-area requirement, the "ten years plus" rule imposes both a land-area requirement and a number-of-landowners requirement.

B. Termination

1. By Juridical Act

Building restrictions may be terminated by juridical act. **LSA-C.C. Art. 780**. In this regard, the rules are the same as they are for amendments to the restrictions. If the juridical act establishing the restrictions provides for a mechanism whereby they may be terminated, then this mechanism governs. If that juridical act makes no such provision, then the restrictions may be terminated by agreement of the landowners, subject to the "fifteen years plus" and "ten years plus" rules for amendments explained above.

2. By Prescription of Non-Use

Like many other principal real rights, such as predial servitudes and usufructs, building restrictions can be extinguished through the prescription of nonuse. According to **LSA-C.C. Art. 781**,

> No action for injunction or for damages on account of the violation of a building restriction may be brought after two years from the commencement of a noticeable violation. After the lapse of this period, the immovable on which the violation occurred is freed of the restriction that has been violated.

Though the first sentence of this article, insofar as it establishes a bar to litigation, appears to create a mere rule of liberative prescription, the second sentence, as comment (b) to the article notes, makes it clear that the rule here created "extinguishes the real right itself" and, as such, is a rule of prescription of nonuse. What distinguishes this prescription of nonuse from those applicable to other principal real rights is the term: here it is merely two years instead of the more common ten years. The consequences of the accrual of this prescription are limited to the particular restriction and the particular immovable in question. As comment (d) to the article notes, "[p]rescription of one type of restriction on a particular lot does not free that lot from other restrictions nor other lots from restrictions of the type that has been violated...."

3. *By Abandonment*

a. Of the Whole Plan

All the building restrictions to which the immovables are subject terminate together when the landowners "abandon[]" the "whole plan." **LSA-C.C. Art. 782.** For this to occur, there must be "a great number of violations of all or most restrictions." ***Id.* cmt. (b).** The effect of such an abandonment is that "the affected area is freed of all restrictions," **LSA-C.C. Art. 782**, and "the use of the property is free for all purposes." ***Id.* cmt. (b).**

b. Of a Particular Restriction

A particular restriction terminates upon a "general abandonment" of it. **LSA-C.C. Art. 782.** "Abandonment of a particular restriction is predicated on a sufficient number of violations of that restriction in relation to the number of lots affected by it." ***Id.* cmt. (b).** The effect of such an abandonment is that "the affected area is freed of that restriction only." **LSA-C.C. Art. 782.**

Chapter Eleven

Protection of Ownership

One who thinks that he owns something that is in someone else's possession or that, though in his possession, is treated by others as if it doesn't belong to him may enjoy one or more remedies. As **LSA-C.C. Art. 526** states, "[t]he owner of a thing is entitled to recover it from anyone who possesses or detains it without right and to obtain judgment recognizing his ownership and ordering delivery of the thing to him." Precisely which remedy is (or remedies are) available to such an owner depends on a host of factors. The most important is whether the thing in question is movable or immovable.

SUB-CHAPTER A

Immovables

I. The Petitory Action

One—and arguably the most important—procedural vehicle through which the owner of an immovable may be able to vindicate his ownership interest is the so-called "petitory action." This procedure, however, is not available in all circumstances. **LSA-C.C.P. Art. 3651**, which establishes the petitory action, provides that "[t]he petitory action is brought by a person who claims the ownership of, but who does not have the right to possess, immovable property...." To bring a petitory action, then, the owner must not have been in possession for a year.[1]

A. Burden of Proof

As one would expect, the plaintiff (that is, the party who alleges he is the owner) in a petitory action bears the burden of proof. This proposition is written between the lines of **LSA-C.C. Art. 531** and **LSA-C.C.P. Art. 3653**, which together make it clear that, no matter what the circumstances, the plaintiff must prove *something* in order to prevail.

But the plaintiff's burden of proof is not the same in all situations. What makes the difference is what might be called the "possessory situation" of the defendant. **LSA-C.C. Art. 531** provides as follows:

> One claiming the ownership of an immovable against another *who has been in possession of the immovable for one year after having commenced possession in good faith and with just title or who has been in possession of the immovable for ten years shall* prove that he has acquired ownership from a previous owner or by acquisitive prescription. In *all other cases*, he need only prove better title.[2]

The burden of proof established by the first sentence of the article, which is commonly referred to as "perfect title" or "title good against the world," applies only when the defendant's "possessory situation" satisfies one of two alternative requirements. The first requirement is that the defendant have been in possession for a year (in other words, that he have acquired the right to possess), in good faith, and with a just title. The expressions "good faith" and "just title," as used here, "are identical to the good faith and just title necessary to start the running of [short-term] acquisitive prescription" (*see* **LSA-C.C. Art. 531 cmt. (c)**), concepts that were explicated earlier in this Précis. The second requirement is that the defendant have been in possession for at least ten years. If the defendant's possessory situation satisfies neither of these requirements (for example, if the defendant has not yet acquired the right to possess or, though he

1. This does not necessarily mean that an owner of an immovable who *is* "in possession" of it is out of luck, stuck with no way to vindicate his ownership interest. In many such instances, the owner can bring a suit for a "declaratory judgment" that recognizes the interest and, further, provides appropriate monetary and/or injunctive relief.

2. **LSA-C.C.P. Art. 3653** is to the same effect.

has, he lacks good faith or just title and has been in possession less than ten years), then the less onerous burden of proof—"better title"—applies.

1. "Perfect Title" or "Title Good Against the World"

Where the defendant's possessory situation meets the requirements of the first sentence of Article 531, the plaintiff must prove "that he has acquired ownership from a previous owner or by acquisitive prescription." **LSA-C.C. Art. 531, sent. 1; LSA-C.C.P. Art. 3463(1).** Though this list of possibilities is good as far as it goes, it is nevertheless not quite complete, for there is at least one other way in which a person might come to own an immovable, namely, accession.

a. Acquisition by Acquisitive Prescription

What the plaintiff must show in order to prove that he acquired ownership via acquisitive prescription depends, naturally enough, on the kind of prescription on which he relies—ordinary or extraordinary. If it is ordinary, then he need only show possession for thirty years. If it is extraordinary, then he must show possession under just title and in good faith for ten years.

b. Acquisition "From a Previous Owner"

Though it is easy enough to understand what it means to prove that one acquired ownership by acquisitive prescription, it is not immediately clear what it means to prove that one acquired ownership "from a previous owner." As it turns out, there are several possibilities.

1) The Possibilities (via "Chains of Title" to Previous Owners)

a) Acquisition From a Previous Acquisitive Prescriber

One way in which the petitory plaintiff might meet this burden is to show that his title ultimately emanated from someone else who had acquired ownership via acquisitive prescription. This possibility is reflected in the statement of the plaintiff's burden of proof found in **LSA-C.C. Art. 531** and **LSA-C.C.P. Art. 3653(1)**, both of which state that the plaintiff carries his burden if he proves that he "acquired ownership from a previous owner." An ancestor-in-title who had acquired ownership via acquisitive prescription would, of course, qualify as a "previous owner." Thus, if the plaintiff can show (1) that someone else acquired ownership of the thing through acquisitive prescription and (2) that his own chain of title can be traced back, on the face of the public records, to that "someone else," then the plaintiff will prevail.

b) Acquisition From a Sovereign

1] GENERAL RULE

Another way in which the petitory plaintiff might meet his burden is to show that his title ultimately emanated from some "sovereign," that is, from a government that, by virtue of its sovereignty, originally owned the immovable in question. In the Louisiana context, there are only three possibilities: the kingdom of France, the kingdom of Spain, and the United States. In the famous (some would say "infamous") case of *Pure Oil Co. v. Skinner*,[3] the Louisiana Supreme Court ruled that to make this showing, the plaintiff had to prove, from the face of the public records, that he has an unbroken chain of title that can be traced all the way back to one of these sovereigns, in other words, that between the sovereign's original title and his own there are no "gaps." To say that this burden is difficult to meet is to engage in understatement. Thanks to the dismal state of older land records in many parts of Louisiana, most landowners, if they were to be forced to trace their chains of title as far back as possible, would find gaps in their titles and, therefore, would be unable to meet the burden.

2] EXCEPTION: THE "COMMON AUTHOR" RULE

The harshness of the general rule is mitigated somewhat by an important exception thereto, known as the "common author" rule. The source of the exception is **LSA-C.C. Art. 532**: "[w]hen the titles of the parties are traced to a common author, he is presumed to be the previous owner." A "common author" is a person who, on the face of the public records, transferred title to the thing first to one of the parties or to the ancestor-in-title of one of the parties and then, at another time, transferred title to the thing to the other party or the ancestor-in-title of the other party. It is important to note that this rule works in tandem with, not in opposition to, the rule of **LSA-C.C. Art. 531**, according to which one may prove perfect title by showing that one acquired the thing from a "previous owner." **Art. 532**, by virtue of the fiction that the common author was a "previous owner," supplies a "previous owner" for purposes of **Art. 531**, thereby providing what may be regarded as an evidentiary "short cut" to proving perfect title.

3. 294 So. 2d 797 (La. 1974).

Simply because the "common author" rule applies in a given case does not mean, without more, that the petitory plaintiff will necessarily prevail. As comment (a) to **Art. 532** indicates, the "plaintiff may recover against another in possession upon proof that his title is the more ancient from the common ancestor." Thus, to prevail, the plaintiff must show not only that he and the defendant share a common author, but also that this common author transferred title to the plaintiff's ancestor-in-title or the plaintiff before he transferred it to the defendant's ancestor-in-title or the defendant, in other words, that his chain-of-title from the common author is older.[4]

c) "Better title"

Where the defendant's possessory situation does not meet the requirements of the first sentence of Article 531, the plaintiff in a petitory action need prove only a "better title" to prevail. Civ. Code art. 531, § 2; Code Civ. Proc. art. 3463(2). According to the jurisprudence, "[a]s a general rule, the more ancient title prevails", in other words, "older is better." But this, according to at least one commentator, is a bit of an over-generalization. "It is not hard to imagine a dispute in which both parties offer less than perfect titles, but the better title is of more recent origin."[5] One example is where the newer title is "clearer." Imagine a case in which the description of the immovable contained in the title documents in one chain of title might be so vague that one could not say with certainty that the immovable in question was included therein but the description of the immovable contained in the title documents in the other chain of title was so specific that it is certain that the immovable in question is included therein. In such a case, we would say that the latter title is "clearer" and further, that, even if it was the newer title, it was nevertheless "better" than the older one.

---

4. A common bit of nonsense that instructors see in answers to questions on final examinations in the Property Law course goes something like this: "If the parties have a 'common author,' then the plaintiff need only prove 'better title,' not 'perfect title,' and older is better." The basis for this poppycock is easy enough to understand. When the student studies "perfect title," which he studies first, he learns that if the parties have a common author, then the party with the "older" chain of title prevails. Then, when he later studies "better title" (see below), he learns that the party with "older" chain of title prevails (at least usually). Attempting to (over-)simplify matters for ease of understanding and memorization, the student then collapses the one rule into the other. In the end, this technical error rarely leads the student to wrong conclusions, but it *is* a technical error nonetheless.

5. Camille B. Poché, *Better Title: An Examination of the Burden of Proof in Louisiana Petitory Actions*, 67 Tul. L. Rev. 511, 538-39 (1992).

B. Relationship to the Possessory Action

Like many other jurisdictions within the French civil law tradition, Louisiana has historically discouraged parties from trying issues of "possession" and issues of "ownership" in the same proceeding. The means of pursuing this end have been two-fold: (1) penalize the possessory action plaintiff if he "cumulates" that action with a petitory action; and (2) penalize the possessory action defendant if he asserts that he is the owner, whether in his answer to the possessory action petition or in either a reconventional demand or a separate suit. Though current Louisiana law evidences the same aversion to trying issues of possession and ownership together, the penalties it imposes are quite mild in comparison to those that were imposed by former law.

1. Against the Plaintiff (the Rule of "Noncumulation")

LSA-C.C.P. Art. 3657(A) declares that "[t]he plaintiff shall not cumulate the possessory action with... the petitory action" in the same suit or plead them in the alternative. If he does so, the possessory action does not automatically "abate" (that is, will not automatically be dismissed), as would have been the case under former law, but the defendant "may object... by asserting a dilatory exception." ***Id.*** If the defendant files such a dilatory exception, then the court, in its discretion, "may order separate trials or may order the plaintiff to elect which action he desires to pursue." ***Id.* cmt. (b).** But if the defendant does not, then "the objection of improper cumulation is waived." ***Id.***[6]

2. Against the Defendant

"When the defendant in a possessory action asserts title in himself, in the alternative or otherwise," he "does not thereby [either] convert the possessory action into a petitory action or judicially confess the possession of the plaintiff," as would have been the case under former law. **LSA-C.C.P. Art. 3657(B).** Instead, the only consequence of such an act is that "the defendant's assertions of title shall be considered [as evidence] in defense of the possessory action," but "only for the [limited]

6. Nevertheless, the possessory action will automatically abate if the plaintiff, instead of cumulating the action with a petitory action, brings a separate petitory action while the possessory action is pending. **LSA-C.C.P. Art. 3657(A), sent. 3.**

purposes stated in Article 3661(B)." ***Id.*** There are only three such purposes: to prove (1) that the defendant had *animus domini*; (2) the extent of the defendant's possession; and (3) the length of time of the defendant's possession. **LSA-C.C.P. Art. 3661(B)(1)–(3).**

Should the defendant wish to pursue a petitory action in response to the possessory action, he faces a number of restrictions. First, he is absolutely prohibited from asserting such an action by way of a reconventional demand in the possessory action. **LSA-C.C.P. Art. 3657(C), sent. 1.** Second, though he may assert such an action by way of a separate suit, if he does so, then he thereby "judicially confesses the possession of the plaintiff in the possessory action." ***Id.* sent. 2.** To "judicially confess" a person's "possession" is to admit that that person both (1) is in possession and (2) has the right to possess.

II. The Boundary Action

The petitory action is not the only kind of real action within which ownership interests in immovables may be vindicated. Another possibility, curiously enough, is the boundary action. I say "curiously enough" because the boundary action was not, in fact, *designed* to resolve issues of immovable ownership. To the contrary, its purpose is to resolve so-called "boundary disputes" between the putative owners of contiguous lands. Nevertheless, ownership issues sometimes—indeed, almost inevitably—get raised in and therefore must be resolved in such actions. That is because, in most cases, it is impossible to fix the boundary between two contiguous lands without first raising and resolving those questions.

A. Definitions

Before we descend into the details of the law of boundary actions, we first need to define some of the fundamental concepts in terms of which that law is cast. There are two such terms: boundaries and boundary markers.

1. Boundaries

A boundary is "a line of separation between contiguous lands." **LSA-C.C. Art. 784, sent. 1.** In other words, it is the (abstract, geometrical) dividing line between adjacent estates.

2. Boundary Markers

A boundary marker is "a natural or artificial object that marks on the ground the line of separation of contiguous lands." **LSA-C.C. Art. 784, sent. 2.** Obviously, the "marker" is something different from the "boundary" itself.

B. Scope

The boundary action is designed to settle "boundary disputes." These disputes are of two kinds.

1. Fixing Markers

The boundary action can be used not only to determine an uncertain or disputed line of separation, but to determine the proper location of a certain and undisputed line of separation. According to **LSA-C.C. Art. 785, par. 1, cl. 2**, "[t]he fixing of the boundary... may also involve the placement of markers on the ground, if markers were never placed, were wrongly placed, or are no longer to be seen." **LSA-C.C. Art. 796** adds that "[w]hen visible boundaries have been erroneously placed by one of the contiguous owners ..., the error may be rectified by the court...."

2. Fixing Boundaries

Far and away the more common kind of boundary dispute, however, is that in which the line of separation is itself "uncertain or disputed." **LSA-C.C. Art. 785, par. 1, cl. 1.** Disputes of this kind can be broken down into four categories: those arising from (1) vague property descriptions in the title of one, the other, or both parties; (2) overlapping property descriptions in the parties' respective titles; (3) "shifting" boundaries due to acquisitive prescription, where one party has possessed beyond the land described in his title and into the land described in the other party's title; and (4) cases where one or even both of the neighbors never had a title at all, but each claims to have possessed the land up to a certain boundary marker.

C. Prerequisites

1. Prerequisites Relative to the Thing

Not every conceivable "line of separation" dispute gives rise to a boundary action. Rather, the action is available only with respect to certain specified kinds of things that bear a certain specified spatial relation to each other. First, the action lies only if the dispute concerns the boundaries between "lands." Second, the action lies only if these lands are "contiguous." According to the Oxford English Dictionary, contiguous means "touching, in actual contact, next in space; meeting at a common boundary, bordering, adjoining."

In most circumstances, it's easy enough to tell whether any two "lands" are "contiguous." But that is not always the case. Imagine, first, that the two tracts of land are separated by a river. If that river is navigable, then the tracts are not contiguous, because the bottom of the river belongs to the State. But if the river is not navigable, then the tracts are contiguous, for the bottom of the river belongs to the neighbors themselves out to the mid-line of the river. Imagine, next, that the two tracts of land are separated by a highway. If that highway is publicly owned, in other words, owned by the State or one of its political subdivisions, then the tracts are not contiguous. But if that highway is privately owned, then the tracts are contiguous, for the road belongs to whichever neighbor owns the land on which it was built.

2. Prerequisites Relative to the Person

Not everyone who might wish to do so may bring a boundary action. According to **LSA-C.C. Art. 786**, "[t]he boundary may be fixed upon the demand of an owner or of one who possesses as owner. It may also be fixed upon the demand of a usufructuary...." There are, then, at least three categories of potential plaintiffs: (1) owner, (2) one who possesses as owner, and (3) usufructuary.

Though the significance of the first and last of these terms—owner and usufructuary—is pretty clear, the significance of the second—one who possesses as owner—may not be. This phrase undoubtedly includes "possessors" in the ordinary sense of the word. By the same token, it almost assuredly excludes "precarious possessors." This inference is confirmed by **LSA-C.C. Art. 787**, which provides that if a lessee needs a boundary action to protect his interest, he needs to get the lessor—the true possessor—to bring it for him.

One question that the text of the article leaves unanswered is whether the list of potential plaintiffs set out in **Art. 787** is exhaustive or merely illustrative. According to one noted authority, Professor Yiannopoulos, the answer is "merely illustrative." In his treatise he states that "Article

786... mentions only a usufructuary but this is an illustration; the provision ought to be applied to all persons having real rights in immovable property."[7] If that is so, then the holder of a predial servitude, a right of use, a habitation, or conceivably even a mortgage or a privilege, could be entitled to bring the action.

D. Rules of Determination

How is it that the court is supposed to go about fixing the boundary in a boundary action? To answer the question intelligently, we need to distinguish between what might be termed the general rule, on the one hand, and its corollaries or particular applications, on the other.

1. In General

The basis upon which the court is supposed to fix the boundary in a boundary action is established by **LSA-C.C. Art. 792**: "The court shall fix the boundary according to the ownership of the parties; if neither party proves ownership, the boundary shall be fixed according to limits established by possession." So, the court is to fix the boundary on the basis of ownership, if that is possible, or possession, if it is not.

Does that mean that the parties to a boundary action must raise the issue of ownership and try, to the extent they can, to prove their ownership of the disputed area? What if, for their own reasons, neither or at least one of the parties wants to raise the issue, preferring, instead, that the case be disposed of on the basis of possession alone? Is that permissible?

Art. 792 does not, itself, answer these questions. The answer, to the extent there is one, lies in **LSA-R.S. 13:4231**, which sets out Louisiana's rule of *res judicata*. That statute provides that "a valid and final judgment is conclusive between the same parties... [as to] all causes of action existing at the time of final judgment arising out of the transaction or occurrence that is the subject matter of the litigation." Each party's potential ownership claim, if any, it seems safe to say, is among the causes of action that arise out of the transaction or occurrence that gives rise to the boundary action in the first place. **Sec. 4231**, then, provides the par-

7. A.N. Yiannopoulos, Property § 286, *in* 2 La. Civ. Law Treatise 570 (2001).

ties to a boundary action with a powerful incentive to raise and adjudicate the issue of ownership. If you don't "use it," then, by virtue of that article, you "lose it."

2. *For Particular Situations*

a) Where Both Parties Rely on Title

In many boundary action cases, both parties purport to rely on their respective titles (as opposed to acquisitive prescription) to make their cases. Each contends, in essence, that his title is superior to the other's.

The Civil Code itself provides only minimal guidance to courts in assessing such claims. According to sentence two of **LSA-C.C. Art. 793**, "[w]hen the parties trace their titles to a common author preference shall be given to the more ancient title."

This rule is helpful as far as it goes. But what of cases in which the contestants do *not* trace their titles to a common author? To sort out which of two competing titles is superior in such cases, our courts have developed a number of guidelines. The most important is what is known as the "order of preference of calls," where "calls" simply means "elements of a property description." As the Louisiana Supreme Court noted in *Meyers v. Comegys*,

> the legal guides for determining a question of boundary, or the location of a land line, in the order of their importance and value, are: (1) Natural monuments; (2) artificial monuments; (3) distances; (4) courses; and (5) quantity. But the controlling consideration is the intention of the party or parties.[8]

This means, as one court of appeal has noted, that "[i]dentification of land by acreage or quantity is the lowest ranking of all; enumerated standards in describing property and other measurements, including description by metes and bounds, control over the acreage designation."[9] Another important guideline is this: if the property description includes or at least references a plat map, the location of the boundary as indicated in that map will control over other calls.[10]

---

8. 147 La. 851, 857, 83 So. 307, 309 (1920).

9. Sutton v. Montegut, 570 So. 2d 841, 846 (La. App. 5th Cir. 1990).

10. *Id.*

b) Where (at Least) One Party Relies on Acquisitive Prescription

It is also possible that at least one of the parties to a boundary action may purport to rely on acquisitive prescription rather than his title to make his case. In such an instance, that party's claim, in essence, is that the boundary between his property and that of his neighbor has effectively "shifted" in his favor as a result of his having possessed part of the land that was originally within his neighbor's title. This is the very possibility contemplated by **LSA-C.C. Art. 794**, which, as we have seen, permits particular successors claiming acquisitive prescription to "boundary tack":

> When a party proves acquisitive prescription, the boundary shall be fixed according to limits established by prescription rather than titles. If a party and his ancestors in title possessed for thirty years without interruption, within visible bounds, more land than their title called for, the boundary shall be fixed along these bounds.[11]

In such a case, the party relying on acquisitive prescription is entitled to a judgment recognizing what is, in effect, a "new" boundary.

---

11. It is worth noting that long-term acquisitive prescription (acquisitive prescription of 30 years) is the only possibility here. If the plaintiff claims that the boundary shifted due to prescription, he tacitly admits that the land in question was originally outside his boundary, in other words, that he did not originally have title to it. One who has no title at all certainly lacks "just title", and without just title, short-term acquisitive prescription (acquisitive prescription of 10 years) is precluded.

SUB-CHAPTER B

Movables

I. Basis for the Action

It is a curious fact that neither the Civil Code nor the Code of Civil Procedure nor any other Louisiana legislation establishes a means whereby the owner of a movable may obtain vindication of his ownership interest. That has not, however, stopped our courts from making a way. Borrowing from French court practice, much as they once borrowed the *actio de in rem verso*—the action for recovery of unjustified enrichment—before Louisiana codified its law on the subject, the courts have embraced the so-called "revendicatory action" (also spelled "revindicatory") for this purpose.

II. Burden of Proof

"The plaintiff in the revendicatory action has the burden of proof of his ownership, and if he fails to carry this burden his claim is dismissed." **LSA-C.C. Art. 526 cmt. (c).** This follows from the rule of **LSA-C.C. Art. 530, par. 1, sent. 1**: "[t]he possessor of a corporeal movable is presumed to be its owner."

There are many ways in which the plaintiff might meet this burden. Proof of acquisition of the thing through an unbroken chain of transactions to one who can be proved to have been the original owner would certainly do the trick. But so could proof of occupancy, acquisitive prescription, or accession.

The plaintiff might also be able to get some assistance from the rules found in **LSA-C.C. Art. 530**, at least if he is the current possessor or was a former possessor of the thing:

> The possessor of a corporeal movable is presumed to be its owner. The previous possessor of a corporeal movable is presumed to have been its owner during the period of his possession.

> These presumptions do not avail against a previous possessor who was dispossessed as a result of loss or theft.

As the author of the comment to this article observes, the article creates a "rebuttable presumption [of] ownership in favor of the *present* possessor" (emphasis added). In his treatise, Professor Yiannopoulos has shed still further light on the operation of the presumptions established by the article. But to appreciate the explanation fully, one must understand that in all but the rarest of cases the defendant will be the *current* possessor and the plaintiff the *previous* possessor (if a possessor at all). Here's the explanation:

> The defendant may always rely on the presumption of Article 530(1), first sentence, according to which the present possessor of a movable is presumed to be its owner. The plaintiff may rebut this presumption on proof that he was prior possessor and that he lost the possession of the movable as a result of loss or theft. In such a case, [the] plaintiff may rely on the presumption of Article 530(1), second sentence, according to which the prior possessor of a corporeal movable is presumed to have been owner during the period of his possession. The burden then shifts and the defendant, in order to be allowed to retain the movable, must prove that the plaintiff was never its owner, or, if he was, he lost his ownership. If the plaintiff cannot prove that he lost the possession of the movable as a result of loss or theft, he may not rely on the presumption of prior possession and ownership.[12]

Thus, the upshot of **Art. 530** seems to be that, at least where neither party has positive, convincing proof of his ownership, the current possessor will prevail unless the prior possessor can prove that his possession ended because he lost the thing or it was stolen from him.

---

12. YIANNOPOULOS, *supra* note 6, § 353, at 700.

Table of Legislation

CIVIL CODE BOOK 2

Things and the Different Modifications of Ownership

Title 1. Things.

Chapter 1. Division of Things.

Section 1. General Principles.

Art. 448.

Division of things.

Things are divided into common, public, and private; corporeals and incorporeals; and movables and immovables. (Acts 1978, No. 728, § 1.)

Art. 449.

Common things.

Common things may not be owned by anyone. They are such as the air and the high seas that may be freely used by everyone conformably with the use for which nature has intended them. (Acts 1978, No. 728, § 1.)

Art. 450.

Public things.

Public things are owned by the state or its political subdivisions in their capacity as public persons.

Public things that belong to the state are such as running waters, the waters and bottoms of natural navigable water bodies, the territorial sea, and the seashore.

Public things that may belong to political subdivisions of the state are such as streets and public squares. (Acts 1978, No. 728, § 1.)

Art. 451.

Seashore.

Seashore is the space of land over which the waters of the sea spread in the highest tide during the winter season. (Acts 1978, No. 728, § 1.)

Art. 452.

Public things and common things subject to public use.

Public things and common things are subject to public use in accordance with applicable laws and regulations. Everyone has the right to fish in the rivers, ports, roadsteads, and harbors, and the right to land on the seashore, to fish, to shelter himself, to moor ships, to dry nets, and the like, provided that he does not cause injury to the property of adjoining owners.

The seashore within the limits of a municipality is subject to its police power, and the public use is governed by municipal ordinances and regulations. (Acts 1978, No. 728, § 1.)

Art. 453.

Private things.

Private things are owned by individuals, other private persons, and by the state or its political subdivisions in their capacity as private persons. (Acts 1978, No. 728, § 1.)

Art. 454.

Freedom of disposition by private persons.

Owners of private things may freely dispose of them under modifications established by law. (Acts 1978, No. 728, § 1.)

Art. 455.

Private things subject to public use.

Private things may be subject to public use in accordance with law or by dedication. (Acts 1978, No. 728. § 1.)

Art. 456.

Banks of navigable rivers or streams.

The banks of navigable rivers or streams are private things that are subject to public use.

The bank of a navigable river or stream is the land lying between the ordinary low and the ordinary high stage of the water. Nevertheless, when there is a levee in proximity to the water, established according to law, the levee shall form the bank. (Acts 1978, No. 728, § 1.)

Art. 457.

Roads; public or private.

A road may be either public or private.

A public road is one that is subject to public use. The public may own the land on which the road is built or merely have the right to use it.

A private road is one that is not subject to public use. (Acts 1978, No. 728, § 1.)

Art. 458.

Works obstructing the public use.

Works built without lawful permit on public things, including the sea, the seashore, and the bottom of natural navigable waters, or on the banks of navigable rivers, that obstruct the public use may be removed at the expense of the persons who built or own them at the instance of the public authorities, or of any person residing in the state.

The owner of the works may not prevent their removal by alleging prescription or possession. (Acts 1978, No. 728, § 1.)

Art. 459.

Building encroaching on public way.

A building that merely encroaches on a public way without preventing its use, and which cannot be removed without causing substantial damage to its owner, shall be permitted to remain. If it is demolished from any cause, the owner shall be bound to restore to the public the part of the way upon which the building stood. (Acts 1978, No. 728, § 1.)

Art. 460.

Construction of navigation facilities on public places by port commissions or municipalities.

Port commissions of the state, or in the absence of port commissions having jurisdiction, **municipalities** may, within the limits of their respective jurisdictions, construct and maintain on public places, in beds of natural navigable water bodies, and on their banks or shores, works necessary for public utility, including buildings, wharves, and other facilities for the mooring of vessels and the loading or discharging of cargo and passengers. (Acts 1978, No. 728, § 1.)

Art. 461.

Corporeals and incorporeals.

Corporeals are things that have a body, whether animate or inanimate, and can be felt or touched.

Incorporeals are things that have no body, but are comprehended by the understanding, such as the rights of inheritance, servitudes, obligations, and right of intellectual property. (Acts 1978, No. 728, § 1.)

Section 2. Immovables.

Art. 462.

Tracts of land.

Tracts of land, with their component parts, are immovables. (Acts 1978, No. 728, § 1.)

Art. 463.

Component parts of tracts of land.

Buildings, other constructions permanently attached to the ground, standing timber, and unharvested crops or ungathered fruits of trees, are component parts of a tract of land when they belong to the owner of the ground. (Acts 1978, No. 728, § 1.)

Art. 464.

Buildings and standing timber as separate immovables.

Buildings and standing timber are separate immovables when they belong to a person other than the owner of the ground. (Acts 1978, No. 728, § 1.)

Art. 465.

Things incorporated into an immovable.

Things incorporated into a tract of land, a building, or other construction, so as to become an integral part of it, such as building materials, are its component parts. (Acts 1978, No. 728, § 1.)

Art. 466.

Component parts of a building or other construction.

Things that are attached to a building and that, according to prevailing usages, serve to complete a building of the same general type, without regard to its specific use, are its component parts. Component parts of this kind may include doors, shutters, gutters, and cabinetry, as well as plumbing, heating, cooling, electrical, and similar systems.

Things that are attached to a construction other than a building and that serve its principal use are its component parts.

Other things are component parts of a building or other construction if they are attached to such a degree that they cannot be removed without substantial damage to themselves or to the building or other construction. (Acts 2006, No. 765, § 1; Acts 2008, No. 632, § 1 eff. July 1, 2008.)

Art. 467.

Immovables by declaration.

The owner of an immovable may declare that machinery, appliances, and equipment owned by him and placed on the immovable, other than his private residence, for its service and improvement are deemed to be its component parts. The declaration shall be filed for registry in the conveyance records of the parish in which the immovable is located. (Acts 1978, No. 728, § 1.)

Art. 468.

Deimmobilization.

Component parts of an immovable so damaged or deteriorated that they can no longer serve the use of lands or buildings are deimmobilized.

The owner may deimmobilize the component parts of an immovable by an act translative of ownership and delivery to acquirers in good faith.

In the absence of rights of third persons, the owner may deimmobilize things by detachment or removal. (Acts 1978, No. 728, § 1. Amended by Acts 1979, No. 180, § 2.)

Art. 469.

Transfer or encumbrance of immovable.

The transfer or encumbrance of an immovable includes its component parts. (Acts 1978, No. 728, § 1. Amended by Acts 1979, No. 180, § 2.)

Art. 470.

Incorporeal immovables.

Rights and actions that apply to immovable things are incorporeal immovables. Immovables of this kind are such as personal servitudes established on immovables, predial servitudes, mineral rights, and petitory or possessory actions. (Acts 1978, No. 728, § 1.)

Section 3. Movables.

Art. 471.

Corporeal movables.

Corporeal movables are things, whether animate or inanimate, that normally move or can be moved from one place to another. (Acts 1978, No. 728, § 1.)

Art. 472.

Building materials.

Materials gathered for the erection of a new building or other construction, even though deriving from the demolition of an old one, are movables until their incorporation into the new building or after construction.

Materials separated from a building or other construction for the purpose of repair, addition, or alteration to it, with the intention of putting them back, remain immovables. (Acts 1978, No. 728, § 1.)

Art. 473.

Incorporeal movables.

Rights, obligations, and actions that apply to a movable thing are incorporeal movables. Movables of this kind are such as bonds, annuities, and interests or shares in entities possessing juridical personality.

Interests or shares in a juridical person that owns immovables are considered as movables as long as the entity exists; upon its dissolution, the right of each individual to a share in the immovables is an immovable. (Acts 1978, No. 728, § 1.)

Art. 474.

Movables by anticipation.

Unharvested crops and ungathered fruits of trees are movables by anticipation when they belong to a person other than the landowner. When encumbered with security rights of third persons, they are movables by anticipation insofar as the creditor is concerned.

The landowner may, by act translative of ownership or by pledge, mobilize by anticipation unharvested crops and ungathered fruits of trees that belong to him. (Acts 1978, No. 728, § 1.)

Art. 475.

Things not immovable.

All things, corporeal or incorporeal, that the law does not consider as immovables, are movables. (Acts 1978, No. 728, § 1.)

Chapter 2. Rights in Things.

Art. 476.

Rights in things.

One may have various rights in things:

1. Ownership;
2. Personal and predial servitudes; and
3. Such other real rights as the law allows. (Acts 1978, No. 728, § 1.)

Title 2. Ownership.

Chapter 1. General Principles.

Art. 477.

Ownership; content.

Ownership is the right that confers on a person direct, immediate, and exclusive authority over a thing. The owner of a thing may use, enjoy, and dispose of it within the limits and under the conditions established by law. (Acts 1979, No. 180, § 1; Acts 1995, No. 640, § 1, eff. Jan. 1, 1996; HR 17, 1998 1st Ex. Sess.; HCR 13, 1998 R.S.; Acts 2020, No. 20, § 1.)

Art. 478.

Resolutory condition; real right in favor of other person.

The right of ownership may be subject to a resolutory condition, and it may be burdened with a real right in favor of another person as allowed by law. The ownership of a thing burdened with a usufruct is designated as naked ownership. (Acts 1979, No. 180, § 1.)

Art. 479.

Necessity of a person.

The right of ownership may exist only in favor of a natural person or a juridical person. (Acts 1979, No. 180, § 1.)

Art. 480.

Co-ownership.

Two or more persons may own the same thing in indivision, each having an undivided share. (Acts 1979, No. 180, § 1.)

Art. 481.

Ownership and possession distinguished.

The ownership and the possession of a thing are distinct. Ownership exists independently of any exercise of it and may not be lost by nonuse.

Ownership is lost when acquisitive prescription accrues in favor of an adverse possessor. (Acts 1979, No. 180, § 1.)

Art. 482.

Accession.

The ownership of a thing includes by accession the ownership of everything that it produces or is united with it, either naturally or artificially, in accordance with the following provisions. (Acts 1979, No. 180, § 1.)

Chapter 2. Right of Accession.

Section 1. Ownership of Fruits.

Art. 483.

Ownership of fruits by accession.

In the absence of rights of other persons, the owner of a thing acquires the ownership of its natural and civil fruits. (Acts 1979, No. 180, § 1.)

Art. 484.

Young of animals.

The young of animals belong to the owner of the mother of them. (Acts 1979, No. 180, § 1.)

Art. 485.

Fruits produced by a third person; reimbursement.

When fruits that belong to the owner of a thing by accession are produced by the work of another person, or from seeds sown by him, the owner may retain them on reimbursing such person his expenses. (Acts 1979, No. 180, § 1.)

Art. 486.

Possessor's right to fruits.

A possessor in good faith acquires the ownership of fruits he has gathered. If he is evicted by the owner, he is entitled to reimbursement of expenses for fruits he was unable to gather.

A possessor in bad faith is bound to restore to the owner the fruits he has gathered, or their value, subject to his claim for reimbursement of expenses. (Acts 1979, No. 180, § 1.)

Art. 487.

Possessor in good faith; definition.

For purposes of accession, a possessor is in good faith when he possesses by virtue of an act translative of ownership and does not know of any defects in his ownership. He ceases to be in good faith when these defects are made known to him or an action is instituted against him by the owner for the recovery of the thing. (Acts 1979, No. 180, § 1.)

Art. 488.

Products; reimbursement of expenses.

Products derived from a thing as a result of diminution of its substance belong to the owner of that thing. When they are reclaimed by the owner, a possessor in good faith has the right to reimbursement of his expenses. A possessor in bad faith does not have this right. (Acts 1979, No. 180, § 1.)

Art. 489.

Apportionment of fruits.

In the absence of other provisions, one who is entitled to the fruits of a thing from a certain time or up to a certain time acquires the ownership of natural fruits gathered during the existence of his right, and a part of the civil fruits proportionate to the duration of his right. (Acts 1979, No. 180, § 1.)

Section 2.
Accession in Relation to Immovables.

Art. 490.

Accession above and below the surface.

Unless otherwise provided by law, the ownership of a tract of land carries with it the ownership of everything that is directly above or under it.

The owner may make works on, above, or below the land as he pleases, and draw all the advantages that accrue from them, unless he is restrained by law or by rights of others. (Acts 1979, No. 180, § 1.)

Art. 491.

Buildings, other constructions, standing timber, and crops.

Buildings, other constructions permanently attached to the ground, standing timber, and unharvested crops or ungathered fruits of trees may belong to a person other than the owner of the ground. Nevertheless, they are presumed to belong to the owner of the ground, unless separate ownership is evidenced by an instrument filed for registry in the conveyance records of the parish in which the immovable is located. (Acts 1979, No. 180, § 1.)

Art. 492.

Separate ownership of part of a building.

Separate ownership of a part of a building, such as a floor, an apartment, or a room, may be established only by a juridical act of the owner of the entire building when and in the manner expressly authorized by law. (Acts 1979, No. 180, § 1.)

Art. 493.

Ownership of improvements.

Buildings, other constructions permanently attached to the ground, and plantings made on the land of another with his consent belong to him who made them. They belong to the owner of the ground when they are made without his consent.

When the owner of buildings, other constructions permanently attached to the ground, or plantings no longer has the right to keep them on the land of another, he may remove them subject to his obligation to restore the property to its former condition. If he does not remove them within ninety days after written demand, the owner of the land may, after the ninetieth day from the date of mailing the written demand, appropriate ownership of the improvements by providing an additional written notice by certified mail, and upon receipt of the certified mail by the owner of the improvements, the owner of the land obtains ownership of the improvements and owes nothing to the owner of the improvements. Until such time as the owner of the land appropriates the improvements, the improvements shall remain the property of he who made them and he shall be solely responsible for any harm caused by the improvements.

When buildings, other constructions permanently attached to the ground, or plantings are made on the separate property of a spouse with community assets or with separate assets of the other spouse and when such improvements are made on community property with the separate assets of a spouse, this Article does not apply. The rights of the spouses are governed by Articles 2366, 2367, and 2367.1. (Acts 1984, No. 933, § 1; Acts 2003, No. 715, § 1.)

Art. 493.1.

Ownership of component parts.

Things incorporated in or attached to an immovable so as to become its component parts under Articles 465 and 466 belong to the owner of the immovable. (Acts 1984, No. 933, § 1.)

Art. 493.2.

Loss of ownership by accession; claims of former owner.

One who has lost the ownership of a thing to the owner of an immovable may have a claim against him or against a third person in accordance with the following provisions. (Acts 1984, No. 933, § 1.)

Art. 494.

Constructions by landowner with materials of another.

When the owner of an immovable makes on it constructions, plantings, or works with materials of another, he may retain them, regardless of his good or bad faith, on reimbursing the owner of the materials their current value and repairing the injury that he may have caused to him. (Acts 1979, No. 180, § 1.)

Art. 495.

Things incorporated in, or attached to, an immovable with the consent of the owner of the immovable.

One who incorporates in, or attaches to, the immovable of another, with his consent, things that become component parts of the immovable under Articles 465 and 466, may, in the absence of other provisions of law or juridical acts, remove them subject to his obligation of restoring the property to its former condition.

If he does not remove them after demand, the owner of the immovable may have them removed at the expense of the person who made them or elect to keep them and pay, at his option, the current value of the materials and of the workmanship or the enhanced value of the immovable. (Acts 1979, No. 180, § 1.)

Art. 496.

Constructions by possessor in good faith.

When constructions, plantings, or works are made by a possessor in good faith, the owner of the immovable may not demand their demolition and removal. He is bound to keep them and at his option to pay to the possessor either the cost of the materials and of the workmanship, or their current value, or the enhanced value of the immovable. (Acts 1979, No. 180, § 1.)

Art. 497.

Constructions by bad faith possessor.

When constructions, plantings, or works are made by a bad faith possessor, the owner of the immovable may keep them or he may demand their demolition and removal at the expense of the possessor, and, in addition, damages for the injury that he may have sustained. If he does not demand demolition and removal, he is bound to pay at his option either the current value of the materials and of the workmanship of the separable improvements that he has kept or the enhanced value of the immovable. (Acts 1979, No. 180, § 1.)

Art. 498.

Claims against third persons.

One who has lost the ownership of a thing to the owner of an immovable may assert against third persons his rights under Articles 493, 493.1, 494, 495, 496, or 497 when they are evidenced by an instrument filed for registry in the appropriate conveyance or mortgage records of the parish in which the immovable is located. (Acts 1979, No. 180, § 1. Acts 1984, No. 933, § 1.)

Art. 499.

Alluvion and dereliction.

Accretion formed successively and imperceptibly on the bank of a river or stream, whether navigable or not, is called alluvion. The alluvion belongs to the owner of the bank, who is bound to leave public that portion of the bank which is required for the public use.

The same rule applies to dereliction formed by water receding imperceptibly from a bank of a river or stream. The owner of the land situated at the edge of the bank left dry owns the dereliction. (Acts 1979, No. 180, § 1.)

Art. 500.

Shore of the sea or of a lake.

There is no right to alluvion or dereliction on the shore of the sea or of lakes. (Acts 1979, No. 180, § 1.)

Art. 501.

Division of alluvion.

Alluvion formed in front of the property of several owners is divided equitably, taking into account the extent of the front of each property prior to the formation of the alluvion in issue. Each owner is entitled to a fair proportion of the area of the alluvion and a fair proportion of the new frontage on the river, depending on the relative values of the frontage and the acreage. (Acts 1979, No. 180, § 1.)

Art. 502.

Sudden action of waters.

If a sudden action of the waters of a river or stream carries away an identifiable piece of ground and unites it with other lands on the same or on the opposite bank, the ownership of the piece of ground so carried away is not lost. The owner may claim it within a year, or even later, if the owner of the bank with which it is united has not taken possession. (Acts 1979, No. 180, § 1.)

Art. 503.

Island formed by river opening a new channel.

When a river or stream, whether navigable or not, opens a new channel and surrounds riparian land making it an island, the ownership of that land is not affected. (Acts 1979, No. 180, § 1.)

Art. 504.

Ownership of abandoned bed when river changes course.

When a navigable river or stream abandons its bed and opens a new one, the owners of the land on which the new bed is located shall take by way of indemnification the abandoned bed, each in proportion to the quantity of land that he lost.

If the river returns to the old bed, each shall take his former land. (Acts 1979, No. 180, § 1.)

Art. 505.

Islands and sandbars in navigable rivers.

Islands, and sandbars that are not attached to a bank, formed in the beds of navigable rivers or streams, belong to the state. (Acts 1979, No. 180, § 1.)

Art. 506.

Ownership of beds of nonnavigable riversor streams.

In the absence of title or prescription, the beds of nonnavigable rivers or streams belong to the riparian owners along a line drawn in the middle of the bed. (Acts 1979, No. 180, § 1.)

Section 3.
Accession in Relation to Movables.

Art. 507.

Accession as between movables.

In the absence of other provisions of law or contract, the consequences of accession as between movables are determined according to the following rules. (Acts 1979, No. 180, § 1.)

Art. 508.

Things principal and accessory.

Things are divided into principal and accessory. For purposes of accession as between movables, an accessory is a corporeal movable that serves the use, ornament, or complement of the principal thing.

In the case of a principal thing consisting of a movable construction permanently attached to the ground, its accessories include things that would constitute its component parts under Article 466 if the construction were immovable. (Amended by Acts 2008, No. 632, § 1, eff. Jan. 1, 2008.)

Art. 509.

Value or bulk as a basis to determine principal thing.

In case of doubt as to which is a principal thing and which is an accessory, the most valuable, or the most bulky if value is nearly equal, shall be deemed to be principal. (Acts 1979, No. 180, § 1.)

Art. 510.

Union of a principal and an accessory thing.

When two corporeal movables are united to form a whole, and one of them is an accessory of the other, the whole belongs to the owner of the principal thing. The owner of the principal thing is bound to reimburse the owner of the accessory its value. The owner of the accessory may demand that it be separated and returned to him, although the separation may cause some injury to the principal thing, if the accessory is more valuable than the principal and has been used without his knowledge. (Acts 1979, No. 180, § 1.)

Art. 511.

Ownership of new thing made with materials of another.

When one uses materials of another to make a new thing, the thing belongs to the owner of the materials, regardless of whether they may be given their earlier form. The owner is bound to reimburse the value of the workmanship.

Nevertheless, when the value of the workmanship substantially exceeds that of the materials, the thing belongs to him who made it. In this case, he is bound to reimburse the owner of the materials their value. (Acts 1979, No. 180, § 1.)

Art. 512.

Effect of bad faith.

If the person who made the new thing was in bad faith, the court may award its ownership to the owner of the materials. (Acts 1979, No. 180, § 1.)

Art. 513.

Use of materials of two owners; separation or co-ownership.

When one used partly his own materials and partly the materials of another to make a new thing, unless the materials can be conveniently separated, the thing belongs to the owners of the materials in indivision. The share of one is determined in proportion to the value of his materials and of the other in proportion to the value of his materials and workmanship. (Acts 1979, No. 180, § 1.)

Art. 514.

Mixture of materials.

When a new thing is formed by the mixture of materials of different owners, and none of them may be considered as principal, an owner who has not consented to the mixture may demand separation if it can be conveniently made.

If separation cannot be conveniently made, the thing resulting from the mixture belongs to the owners of the materials in indivision. The share of each is determined in proportion to the value of his materials.

One whose materials are far superior in value in comparison with those of any one of the others, may claim the thing resulting from the mixture. He is then bound to reimburse the others the value of their materials. (Acts 1979, No. 180, § 1.)

Art. 515.

Recovery of materials or value in lieu of ownership.

When an owner of materials that have been used without his knowledge for the making of a new thing acquires the ownership of that thing, he may demand that, in lieu of the ownership of the new thing, materials of the same species, quantity, weight, measure and quality or their value be delivered to him. (Acts 1979, No. 180, § 1.)

Art. 516.

Liability for unauthorized use of a movable.

One who uses a movable of another, without his knowledge, for the making of a new thing may be liable for the payment of damages. (Acts 1979, No. 180, § 1.)

Chapter 3. Transfer of Ownership by Agreement.

Art. 517.

Voluntary transfer of ownership of an immovable.

The ownership of an immovable is voluntarily transferred by a contract between the owner and the transferee that purports to transfer the ownership of the immovable. The transfer of ownership takes place between the parties by the effect of the agreement and is not effective against third persons until the contract is filed for registry in the conveyance records of the parish in which the immovable is located.

(Acts 1979, No. 180, § 1; Acts 2005, No. 169, § 2, eff. Jan. 1, 2006; Acts 2005 1st Ex. Sess., No. 13, § 1, eff. Nov. 29, 2005.)

Art. 518.

Voluntary transfer of the ownership of a movable.

The ownership of a movable is voluntarily transferred by a contract between the owner and the transferee that purports to transfer the ownership of the movable.

Unless otherwise provided, the transfer of ownership takes place as between the parties by the effect of the agreement and against third persons when the possession of the movable is delivered to the transferee.

When possession has not been delivered, a subsequent transferee to whom possession is delivered acquires ownership provided he is in good faith. Creditors of the transferor may seize the movable while it is still in his possession. (Acts 1984, No. 331, § 2, eff. Jan. 1, 1985.)

Art. 519.

Transfer of action for recovery of movable.

When a movable is in the possession of a third person, the assignment of the action for the recovery of that movable suffices for the transfer of its ownership. (Acts 1979, No. 180, § 1.)

Art. 520.

Transfer of ownership by merchant.

Except as otherwise provided by legislation, a transferee in good faith and for fair value acquires ownership of a corporeal movable from a transferor who is not the owner only if the transferor has possession of the thing with consent of the owner, is a merchant customarily selling similar things, and transfers the thing in the regular course of the transferor's business. (Acts 2023, No. 401, § 1.)

Art. 521.

Lost or stolen thing.

One who has possession of a lost or stolen thing may not transfer its ownership to another. For purposes of this Chapter, a thing is stolen when one has taken possession of it without the consent of its owner. A thing is not stolen when the owner delivers it or transfers its ownership to another as a result of fraud. (Acts 1979, No. 180, § 1.)

Art. 522.

Transfer of ownership by owner under annullable title.

A transferee of a corporeal movable in good faith and for fair value retains the ownership of the thing even though the title of the transferor is annulled on account of a vice of consent. (Acts 1979, No. 180, § 1.)

Art. 523.

Good faith; definition.

An acquirer of a corporeal movable is in good faith for purposes of this Chapter unless he knows, or should have known, that the transferor was not the owner. (Acts 1979, No.180, § 1.)

Art. 524.

Recovery of lost or stolen things.

The owner of a lost or stolen movable may recover it from a possessor who bought it in good faith at a public auction or from a merchant customarily selling similar things on reimbursing the purchase price.

The former owner of a lost, stolen, or abandoned movable that has been sold by authority of law may not recover it from the purchaser. (Acts 1979, No. 180, § 1.)

Art. 525.

Registered movables.

Movables required by law to be registered are subject to the provisions of this Chapter. (Acts 1979, No. 180, § 1; Acts 2023, No. 401, § 1.)

Chapter 4. Protection of Ownership.

Art. 526.

Recognition of ownership; recovery of the thing.

The owner of a thing is entitled to recover it from anyone who possesses or detains it without right and to obtain judgment recognizing his ownership and ordering delivery of the thing to him. (Acts 1979, No. 180, § 1.)

Art. 527.

Necessary expenses.

The evicted possessor, whether in good or in bad faith, is entitled to recover from the owner compensation for necessary expenses incurred for the preservation of the thing and for the discharge of private or public burdens. He is not entitled to recover expenses for ordinary maintenance or repairs. (Acts 1979, No. 180, § 1.)

Art. 528.

Useful expenses.

An evicted possessor in good faith is entitled to recover from the owner his useful expenses to the extent that they have enhanced the value of the thing. (Acts 1979, No. 180, § 1.)

Art. 529.

Right of retention.

The possessor, whether in good or in bad faith, may retain possession of the thing until he is reimbursed for expenses and improvements which he is entitled to claim. (Acts 1979, No. 180, § 1.)

Art. 530.

Presumption of ownership of movable.

The possessor of a corporeal movable is presumed to be its owner. The previous possessor of a corporeal movable is presumed to have been its owner during the period of his possession.

These presumptions do not avail against a previous possessor who was dispossessed as a result of loss or theft. (Acts 1979, No. 180, § 1.)

Art. 531.

Proof of ownership of immovable.

One who claims the ownership of an immovable against another in possession must prove that he has acquired ownership from a previous owner or by acquisitive prescription. If neither party is in possession, he need only prove a better title. (Acts 1979, No. 180, § 1.)

Art. 532.

Common author.

When the titles of the parties are traced to a common author, he is presumed to be the previous owner. (Acts 1979, No. 180, § 1.)

Title 3.
Personal Servitudes.

Chapter 1. Kinds of Servitudes.

Art. 533.

Kinds of servitudes.

There are two kinds of servitudes: personal servitudes and predial servitudes. (Acts 1976, No. 103, § 1.)

Art. 534.

Personal servitude.

A personal servitude is a charge on a thing for the benefit of a person. There are three sorts of personal servitudes: usufruct, habitation, and rights of use. (Acts 1976, No. 103, § 1.)

Chapter 2. Usufruct.

Section 1.
General Principles.

Art. 535.

Usufruct.

Usufruct is a real right of limited duration on the property of another. The features of the right vary with the nature of the things subject to it as consumables or nonconsumables. (Acts 1976, No. 103, § 1.)

Art. 536.

Consumable things.

Consumable things are those that cannot be used without being expended or consumed, or without their substance being changed, such as money, harvested agricultural products, stocks of merchandise, foodstuffs, and beverages. (Acts 1976, No.103, § 1.)

Art. 537.

Nonconsumable things.

Nonconsumable things are those that may be enjoyed without alteration of their substance, although their substance may be diminished or deteriorated naturally by time or by the use to which they are applied, such as lands, houses, shares of stock, animals, furniture, and vehicles. (Acts 1976, No. 103, § 1.)

Art. 538.

Usufruct of consumable things.

If the things subject to the usufruct are consumables, the usufructuary becomes owner of them. He may consume, alienate, or encumber them as he sees fit. At the termination of the usufruct he is bound either to pay to the naked owner the value that the things had at the commencement of the usufruct or to deliver to him things of the same quantity and quality. (Acts 1976, No. 103, § 1; Acts 2010, No. 881, § 1.)

Art. 539.

Usufruct of nonconsumable things.

If the things subject to the usufruct are nonconsumables, the usufructuary has the right to possess them and to derive the utility, profits, and advantages that they may produce, under the obligation of preserving their substance.

He is bound to use them as a prudent administrator and to deliver them to the naked owner at the termination of the usufruct. (Acts 1976, No. 103, § 1.)

Art. 540.

Nature of usufruct.

Usufruct is an incorporeal thing. It is movable or immovable according to the nature of the thing upon which the right exists. (Acts 1976, No. 103, § 1.)

Art. 541.

Divisibility of usufruct.

Usufruct is susceptible to division, because its purpose is the enjoyment of advantages that are themselves divisible. It may be conferred on several persons in divided or undivided shares, and it may be partitioned among the usufructuaries. (Acts 1976, No. 103, § 1.)

Art. 542.

Divisibility of naked ownership.

The naked ownership may be partitioned subject to the rights of the usufructuary. (Acts 1976, No. 103, § 1.)

Art. 543.

Partition of the property in kind or by licitation.

When property is held in indivision, a person having a share in full ownership may demand partition of the property in kind or by licitation, even though there may be other shares in naked ownership and usufruct.

A person having a share in naked ownership only or in usufruct only does not have this right, unless a naked owner of an undivided share and a usufructuary of that share jointly demand partition in kind or by licitation, in which event their combined shares shall be deemed to constitute a share in full ownership. (Acts 1983, No. 535, § 1.)

Art. 544.

Methods of establishing usufruct; things susceptible of usufruct.

Usufruct may be established by a juridical act either inter vivos or mortis causa, or by operation of law. The usufruct created by juridical act is called conventional; the usufruct created by operation of law is called legal.

Usufruct may be established on all kinds of things, movable or immovable, corporeal or incorporeal. (Acts 1976, No. 103, § 1.)

Art. 545.

Modifications of usufruct.

Usufruct may be established for a term or under a condition, and subject to any modification consistent with the nature of usufruct.

The rights and obligations of the usufructuary and of the naked owner may be modified by agreement unless modification is prohibited by law or by the grantor in the act establishing the usufruct. (Acts 1976, No. 103, § 1.)

Art. 546.

Usufruct in favor of successive usufructuaries.

Usufruct may be established in favor of successive usufructuaries. (Acts 1976, No.103, § 1.)

Art. 547.

Usufruct in favor of several usufructuaries.

When the usufruct is established in favor of several usufructuaries, the termination of the interest of one usufructuary inures to the benefit of those remaining, unless the grantor has expressly provided otherwise. (Acts 1976, No. 103, § 1.)

Art. 548.

Existence of usufructuaries.

When the usufruct is established by an act inter vivos, the usufructuary must exist or be conceived at the time of the execution of the instrument. When the usufruct is established by an act mortis causa, the usufructuary must exist or be conceived at the time of the death of the testator. (Acts 1976, No. 103, § 1.)

Art. 549.

Capacity to receive usufruct.

Usufruct may be established in favor of a natural person or a juridical person. (Acts 1976, No. 103, § 1; Acts 2010, No. 881, § 1.)

Section 2.
Rights of the Usufructuary.

Art. 550.

Right to all fruits.

The usufructuary is entitled to the fruits of the thing subject to usufruct according to the following articles. (Acts 1976, No. 103, § 1.)

Art. 551.

Kinds of fruits.

Fruits are things that are produced by or derived from another thing without diminution of its substance.

There are two kinds of fruits; natural fruits and civil fruits.

Natural fruits are products of the earth or of animals.

Civil fruits are revenues derived from a thing by operation of law or by reason of a juridical act, such as rentals, interest, and certain corporate distributions. (Acts 1976, No. 103, § 1.)

Art. 552.

Corporate distributions.

A cash dividend declared during the existence of the usufruct belongs to the usufructuary. A liquidation dividend or a stock redemption payment belongs to the naked owner subject to the usufruct.

Stock dividends and stock splits declared during the existence of the usufruct belong to the naked owner subject to the usufruct.

A stock warrant and a subscription right declared during the existence of the usufruct belong to the naked owner free of the usufruct. (Acts 1976, No. 103, § 1.)

Art. 553.

Voting of shares of stock and other rights.

The usufructuary has the right to vote shares of stock in corporations and to vote or exercise similar rights with respect to interests in other juridical persons, unless otherwise provided. (Acts 1976, No. 103, § 1; Acts 2010, No. 881, § 1.)

Art. 554.

Commencement of the right to fruits.

The usufructuary's right to fruits commences on the effective date of the usufruct. (Acts 1976, No. 103, § 1.)

Art. 555.

Nonapportionment of natural fruits.

The usufructuary acquires the ownership of natural fruits severed during the existence of the usufruct. Natural fruits not severed at the end of the usufruct belong to the naked owner. (Acts 1976, No. 103, § 1.)

Art. 556.

Apportionment of civil fruits.

The usufructuary acquires the ownership of civil fruits accruing during the existence of the usufruct.

Civil fruits accrue day by day and the usufructuary is entitled to them regardless of when they are received. (Acts 1976, No. 103, § 1.)

Art. 557.

Possession and use of the things.

The usufructuary takes the things in the state in which they are at the commencement of the usufruct. (Acts 1976, No. 103, § 1.)

Art. 558.

Improvements and alterations.

The usufructuary may make improvements and alterations on the property subject to the usufruct at his cost and with the written consent of the naked owner. If the naked owner fails or refuses to give his consent, the usufructuary may, after notice to the naked owner and with the approval of the court, make at his cost those improvements and alterations that a prudent administrator would make. (Acts 1976, No. 103, § 1; Acts 2010, No. 881, § 1.)

Art. 559.

Accessories.

The right of usufruct extends to the accessories of the thing at the commencement of the usufruct. (Acts 1976, No. 103, § 1.)

Art. 560.

Trees, stones, and other materials.

The usufructuary may cut trees growing on the land of which he has the usufruct and take stones, sand, and other materials from it, but only for his use or for the improvement or cultivation of the land. (Acts 1976, No. 103, § 1.)

Art. 561.

Mines and quarries.

The rights of the usufructuary and of the naked owner in mines and quarries are governed by the Mineral Code. (Acts 1976, No. 103, § 1.)

Art. 562.

Usufruct of timberlands.

When the usufruct includes timberlands, the usufructuary is bound to manage them as a prudent administrator. The proceeds of timber operations that are derived from proper management of timberlands belong to the usufructuary. (Acts 1976, No. 103, § 1.)

Art. 563.

Alluvion.

The usufruct extends to the increase to the land caused by alluvion or dereliction. (Acts 1976, No. 103, § 1.)

Art. 564.

Treasure.

The usufructuary has no right to the enjoyment of a treasure found in the property of which he has the usufruct. If the usufructuary has found the treasure, he is entitled to keep one-half of it as finder. (Acts 1976, No. 103, § 1.)

Art. 565.

Predial servitudes.

The usufructuary has a right to the enjoyment of predial servitudes due to the estate of which he has the usufruct. When the estate is enclosed within other lands belonging to the grantor of the usufruct, the usufructuary is entitled to a gratuitous right of passage. (Acts 1976, No. 103, § 1.)

Art. 566.

Actions.

The usufructuary may institute against the naked owner or third persons all actions that are necessary to insure the possession, enjoyment, and preservation of his right. (Acts 1976, No. 103, § 1.)

Art. 567.

Contracts affecting the usufructuary's liability.

The usufructuary may lease, alienate, or encumber his right. All such contracts cease of right at the end of the usufruct.

If the usufructuary leases, alienates, or encumbers his right, he is responsible to the naked owner for the abuse that the person with whom he has contracted makes of the property.(Acts 1976, No. 103, § 1; Acts 2010, No. 881, § 1.)

Art. 568.

Disposition of nonconsumable things.

The usufructuary may not dispose of nonconsumable things unless the right to do so has been expressly granted to him. Nevertheless, he may dispose of corporeal movables that are gradually and substantially impaired by use, wear, or decay, such as equipment, appliances, and vehicles, provided that he acts as a prudent administrator.

The right to dispose of a nonconsumable thing includes the rights to lease, alienate, and encumber the thing. It does not include the right to alienate by donation inter vivos, unless that right is expressly granted. (Acts 1976, No. 103, § 1; Acts 1986, No. 203, § 1; Acts 2010, No. 881, § 1.)

Art. 568.1.

Donation and alienation.

If a thing subject to the usufruct is donated inter vivos by the usufructuary, he is obligated to pay the naked owner at the termination of the usufruct the value of the thing as of the time of the donation. If a thing subject to the usufruct is otherwise alienated by the usufructuary, the usufruct attaches to any money or other property received by the usufructuary. The property received shall be classified as consumable or nonconsumable in accordance with the provisions of this Title, and the usufruct shall be governed by those provisions subject to the terms of the act establishing the orifginal usufruct. If, at the time of the alienation, the value of the property received by the usufructuary is less than the value of the thing alienated, the usufructuary is bound to pay the difference to the naked owner at the termination of the usufruct. (Acts 2010, No. 881, § 1.)

Art. 568.2.

Right to lease.

The right to dispose of a nonconsumable thing includes the right to lease the thing for a term that extends beyond the termination of the usufruct. If, at the termination of the usufruct, the thing remains subject to the lease, the usufructuary is accountable to the naked owner for any diminution in the value of the thing at the time attributable to the lease. (Acts 2010, No. 881, § 1.)

Art. 568.3.

Requirement to remove encumbrance.

If, at the termination of the usufruct, the thing subject to the usufruct is burdened by an encumbrance established by the usufructuary to secure an obligation, the usufructuary is bound to remove the encumbrance. (Acts 2010, No. 881, § 1.)

Art. 569.

Duties with regard to things gradually or totally impaired.

If the usufructuary has not disposed of corporeal movables that are by their nature impaired by use, wear, or decay, he is bound to deliver them to the owner in the state in which they may be at the end of the usufruct.

The usufructuary is relieved of this obligation if the things are entirely worn out by normal use, wear, or decay. (Acts 1976, No. 103, § 1; Acts 2010, No. 881, § 1.)

Section 3.
Obligations of the Usufructuary.

Art. 570.

Inventory.

The usufructuary shall cause an inventory to be made of the property subject to the usufruct. In the absence of an inventory the naked owner may prevent the usufructuary's entry into possession of the property.

The inventory shall be made in accordance with the rules established in Articles 3131 through 3137 of the Code of Civil Procedure. (Acts 1976, No. 103, § 1.)

Art. 571.

Security.

The usufructuary shall give security that he will use the property subject to the usufruct as a prudent administrator and that he will faithfully fulfill all the obligations imposed on him by law or by the act that established the usufruct unless security is dispensed with. If security is required, the court may order that it be provided in accordance with law. (Acts 1976, No. 103, § 1; Acts 2004, No. 158, § 1, eff. Aug. 15, 2004.)

Art. 572.

Amount of security.

The security shall be in the amount of the total value of the property subject to the usufruct.

The court may increase or reduce the amount of the security, on proper showing, but the amount shall not be less than the value of the movables subject to the usufruct. (Acts 1976, No. 103, § 1.)

Art. 573.

Dispensation of security by operation of law.

A. Security is dispensed with when any of the following occur:

(1) A person has a legal usufruct under Civil Code Article 223 or 3252.

(2) A surviving spouse has a legal usufruct under Civil Code Article 890 unless the naked owner is not a child of the usufructuary or if the naked owner is a child of the usufructuary and is also a forced heir of the decedent the naked owner may obtain security but only to the extent of his legitime.

(3) A parent has a legal usufruct under Civil Code Article 891 unless the naked owner is not a child of the usufructuary.

(4) A surviving spouse has a legal usufruct under Civil Code Article 2434 unless the naked owner is a child of the decedent but not a child of the usufructuary.

B. A seller or donor of property under reservation of usufruct is not required to give security. (Acts 1976, No. 103, § 1; Acts 2004, No. 158, § 1, eff. Aug. 15, 2004; Acts 2010, No. 881, § 1.)

Art. 574.

Delay in giving security.

A delay in giving security does not deprive the usufructuary of the fruits derived from the property since the commencement of the usufruct. (Acts 1976, No. 103, § 1; Acts 2010, No. 881, § 1.)

Art. 575.

Failure to give security.

If the usufructuary does not give security, the court may order that the property be delivered to an administrator appointed in accordance with Articles 3111 through 3113 of the Code of Civil Procedure for administration on behalf of the usufructuary. The administration terminates if the usufructuary gives security. (Acts 1976, No. 103, § 1; Acts 2010, No. 881, § 1.)

Art. 576.

Standard of care.

The usufructuary is answerable for losses resulting from his fraud, default, or neglect. (Acts 1976, No. 103, § 1.)

Art. 577.

Liability for repairs.

The usufructuary is responsible for ordinary maintenance and repairs for keeping the property subject to the usufruct in good order, whether the need for these repairs arises from accident or *force majeure*, the normal use of things, or his fault or neglect.

The naked owner is responsible for extraordinary repairs, unless they have become necessary as a result of the usufructuary's fault or neglect in which case the usufructuary is bound to make them at his cost. (Acts 1976, No. 103, § 1. Amended by Acts 1979, No. 157, § 1; Acts 2010, No. 881, § 1.)

Art. 578.

Ordinary and extraordinary repairs.

Extraordinary repairs are those for the reconstruction of the whole or of a substantial part of the property subject to the usufruct. All others are ordinary repairs. (Acts 1976, No. 103, § 1.)

Art. 579.

Rights of action for repairs.

During the existence of the usufruct, the naked owner may compel the usufructuary to make the repairs for which the usufructuary is responsible.

The usufructuary may not compel the naked owner to make the extraordinary repairs for which the owner is responsible. If the naked owner refuses to make them, the usufructuary may do so, and he shall be reimbursed without interest by the naked owner at the end of the usufruct. (Acts 1976, No. 103, § 1.)

Art. 580.

Reimbursement for necessary repairs.

If, after the usufruct commences and before the usufructuary is put in possession, the naked owner incurs necessary expenses or makes repairs for which the usufructuary is responsible, the naked owner has the right to claim the cost from the usufructuary and may retain the possession of the things subject to the usufruct until he is paid. (Acts 1976, No. 103, § 1; Acts 2010, No. 881, § 1.)

Art. 581.

Liability for necessary expenses.

The usufructuary is answerable for all expenses that become necessary for the preservation and use of the property after the commencement of the usufruct. (Acts 1976, No. 103, § 1; Acts 2010, No. 881, § 1.)

Art. 582.

Abandonment of usufruct.

The usufructuary may release himself from the obligation to make repairs by abandoning the usufruct or, with the approval of the court, a portion thereof, even if the owner has instituted suit to compel him to make repairs or bear the expenses of them, and even if the usufructuary has been cast in judgment.

He may not release himself from the charges of the enjoyment during the period of his possession, nor from accountability for the damages that he, or persons for whom he is responsible, may have caused. (Acts 1976, No. 103, § 1.)

Art. 583.

Ruin from accident, force majeure, *or age.*

A. Neither the usufructuary nor the naked owner is bound to restore property that has been totally destroyed through accident, *force majeure*, or age.

B. If the naked owner elects to restore the property or to make extraordinary repairs, he shall do so within reasonable time and in the manner least inconvenient and onerous for the usufructuary. (Acts 1976, No. 103, § 1; Acts 2010, No. 881, § 1.)

Art. 584.

Periodic charges.

The usufructuary is bound to pay the periodic charges, such as property taxes, that may be imposed during his enjoyment of the usufruct. (Acts 1976, No. 103, § 1; Acts 2010, No. 881, § 1.)

Art. 585.

Extraordinary charges.

The usufructuary is bound to pay the extraordinary charges that may be imposed, during the existence of the usufruct, on the property subject to it. If these charges are of a nature to augment the value of the property subject to the usufruct, the naked owner shall reimburse the usufructuary at the end of the usufruct only for the capital expended. (Acts 1976, No. 103, § 1.)

Art. 586.

Liability for debts; usufruct inter vivos.

When the usufruct is established inter vivos, the usufructuary is not liable for debts of the grantor, but if the debt is secured by an encumbrance of the thing subject to the usufruct, the thing may be sold for the payment of the debt.

(Acts 1976, No. 103, § 1; Acts 2010, No. 881, § 1.)

Art. 587.

Liability for debts; usufruct established mortis causa.

When the usufruct is established mortis causa, the usufructuary is not liable for estate debts, but the property subject to the usufruct may be sold for the payment of estate debts, in accordance with the rules provided for the payment of the debt of an estate in Book III of this Code. (Acts 1976, No. 103, § 1; Acts 2010, No. 881, § 1.)

Art. 588.

Discharge of debt on encumbered property; usufruct established inter vivos.

When property subject to a usufruct established inter vivos is encumbered to secure a debt before the commencement of the usufruct, the usufructuary may advance the funds needed to discharge the indebtedness. If he does so, the naked owner shall reimburse the usufructuary, without interest, at the termination of the usufruct, for the principal of the debt the usufructuary has discharged, and for any interest the usufructuary has paid that had accrued on the debt before the commencement of the usufruct. (Acts 1976, No. 103, § 1; Acts 2010, No. 881, § 1.)

Art. 589.

Discharge of debt on encumbered property by mortis causa usufructuary.

If the usufructuary of a usufruct established mortis causa advances funds to discharge an estate debt charged to the property subject to the usufruct, the naked owner shall reimburse the usufructuary, without interest, at the termination of the usufruct, but only to the extent of the principal of the debt he has discharged and for any interest he has paid that had accrued on the debt before the commencement of the usufruct. (Acts 1976, No. 103, § 1; Acts 2010, No. 881, § 1.)

Art. 590.

Encumbered property; discharge of debt on encumbered property by naked owner.

If the usufructuary fails or refuses to advance the funds needed to discharge a debt secured by property subject to the usufruct, or an estate debt that is charged to the property subject to the usufruct, the naked owner may advance the funds needed. If he does so, the naked owner may demand that the usufructuary pay him interest during the period of the usufruct. If the naked owner does not advance the funds, he may demand that all or part of the property be sold as needed to discharge the debt. (Acts 1976, No. 103, § 1; Acts 2010, No. 881, § 1.)

Art. 591.

Continuation of usufruct after sale of property.

If property subject to the usufruct is sold to pay an estate debt, or a debt of the grantor, the usufruct attaches to any proceeds of the sale of the property that remain after payment of the debt. (Acts 1976, No. 103, § 1; Acts 2010, No. 881, § 1.)

Art. 592.

Multiple usufructuaries; contribution to payment of estate debts.

If there is more than one usufructuary of the same property, each contributes to the payment of estate debts that are charged to the property in propertion to his enjoyment of the property. If one or more of the usufructuaries fails to advance his share, those of them who advance the funds shall have the right to recover the funds they advance from those who do not advance their shres. (Acts 1976, No. 103, § 1; Acts 2010, No. 881, § 1.)

Art. 593.

Discharge of legacy of annuity.

Unless there is a governing testamentary disposition, the legacy of an annuity that is chargeable to property subject to a usufruct is payable first from the fruits and products of the property subject to the usufruct and then from the property itself. (Acts 1976, No. 103, § 1; Acts 1990, No. 706, § 1; Acts 2010, No. 881, § 1.)

Art. 594.

Court costs; expenses of litigation.

Court costs in actions concerning the property subject to the usufruct are taxed in accordance with the rules of the Code of Civil Procedure. Expenses of litigation other than court costs are apportioned between usufructuaries and naked owners in accordance with the following Articles. (Acts 1976, No. 103, § 1; Acts 2010, No. 881, § 1.)

Art. 595.

Expenses of litigation; legal usufruct.

Parents who have a legal usufruct of the property of their children are bound for expenses of litigation concerning that property, in the same manner as if they were owners of it; but reimbursement may be ordered by the court at the termination of the usufruct in cases in which inequity might otherwise result. (Acts 1976, No. 103, § 1.)

Art. 596.

Expenses of litigation; conventional usufruct.

Conventional usufructuaries are bound for expenses of litigation with third persons concerning the enjoyment of the property. Expenses of litigation with third persons concerning both the enjoyment and the ownership are divided equitably between the usufructuary and the naked owner. Expenses of litigation between the usufructuary and the naked owner are borne by the person who has incurred them. (Acts 1976, No. 103, § 1.)

Art. 597.

Liability of the usufructuary for servitudes.

The usufructuary who loses a predial servitude by nonuse or who permits a servitude to be acquired on the property by prescription is responsible to the naked owner. (Acts 1976, No. 103, § 1.)

Art. 598.

Duty to give information to owner.

If, during the existence of the usufruct, a third person encroaches on the immovable property or violates in any other way the rights of the naked owner, the usufructuary must inform the naked owner. When he fails to do so, he shall be answerable for the damages that the naked owner may suffer. (Acts 1976, No. 103, § 1.)

Art. 599.

Usufruct of a herd of animals.

When the usufruct includes a herd of animals, the usufructuary is bound to use it as a prudent administrator and, from the increase of the herd, replace animals that die. If the entire herd perishes without the fault of the usufructuary, the loss is borne by the naked owner. (Acts 1976, No. 103, § 1.)

Art. 600.

Disposition of animals.

The usufructuary may dispose of individual animals of the herd, subject to the obligation to deliver to the naked owner at the end of the usufruct the value that the animals had at the time of disposition.

The usufructuary may also dispose of the herd or of a substantial part thereof, provided that he acts as a prudent administrator. In such a case, the proceeds are subject to the provisions of Article 618. (Acts 1976, No. 103, § 1.)

Art. 601.

Removal of improvements.

The usufructuary may remove all improvements he has made, subject to the obligation of restoring the property to its former condition. He may not claim reimbursement from the owner for improvements that he does not remove or that cannot be removed. (Acts 1976, No. 103, § 1; Acts 2010, No. 881, § 1.)

Art. 602.

Set off against damages.

The usufructuary may set off against damages due to the owner for the destruction or deterioration of the property subject to the usufruct the value of improvements that cannot be removed, provided they were made in accordance with Article 558. (Acts 1976, No. 103, § 1.)

Section 4.
Rights and Obligations of the Naked Owner.

Art. 603.

Disposition of the naked ownership; alienation or encumbrance of the property.

The naked owner may dispose of the naked ownership, but he can not thereby affect the usufruct. (Acts 1976, No. 103, § 1; Acts 2010, No. 881, § 1.)

Art. 604.

Servitudes.

The naked owner may establish real rights on the property subject to the usufruct, provided that they may be exercised without impairing the usufructuary's rights. (Acts 1976, No. 103, § 1; Acts 2010, No. 881, § 1.)

Art. 605.

Toleration of the enjoyment.

The naked owner must not interfere with the rights of the usufructuary. (Acts 1976, No. 103, § 1.)

Art. 606.

Improvements.

The naked owner may not make alterations or improvements on the property subject to the usufruct. (Acts 1976, No. 103, § 1.)

Section 5.
Termination of Usufruct.

Art. 607.

Death of the usufructuary.

The right of usufruct expires upon the death of the usufructuary. (Acts 1976, No. 103, § 1.)

Art. 608.

Dissolution of legal entity; thirty year limitation.

A usufruct established in favor of a juridical person terminates if the juridical person is dissolved or liquidated, but not if the juridical person is converted, merged or consolidated into a successor juridical person. In any event, a usufruct in favor of a juridical person shall terminate upon the lapse of thirty years from the date of the commencement of the usufruct. This Article shall not apply to a juridical person in its capacity as the trustee of a trust. (Acts 1976, No. 103, § 1; Acts 2010, No. 881, § 1.)

Art. 609.

Termination of legacy of revenues.

A legacy of revenues from specified property is a kind of usufruct and terminates upon death of the legatee unless a shorter period has been expressly stipulated. (Acts 1976, No. 103, § 1.)

Art. 610.

Usufruct for a term or under condition.

A usufruct established for a term or subject to a condition terminates upon the expiration of the term or the happening of the condition. (Acts 1976, No. 103, § 1.)

Art. 611.

Term; transfer of usufruct to another person.

When the usufructuary is charged to restore or transfer the usufruct to another person, his right terminates when the time for restitution or delivery arrives. (Acts 1976, No. 103, § 1.)

Art. 612.

Term; third person reaching a certain age.

A usufruct granted until a third person reaches a certain age is a usufruct for a term. If the third person dies, the usufruct continues until the date the deceased would have reached the designated age. (Acts 1976, No. 103, § 1.)

Art. 613.

Loss, extinction, or destruction of property.

The usufruct of nonconsumables terminates by the permanent and total loss, extinction, or destruction through accident, *force majeure* or decay of the property subject to the usufruct. (Acts 1976, No. 103, § 1; Acts 2010, No. 881, § 1.)

Art. 614.

Fault of a third person.

When any loss, extinction, or destruction of property subject to usufruct is attributable to the fault of a third person, the usufruct does not terminate but attaches to any claim for damages and the proceeds therefrom. (Acts 1976, No. 103, § 1.)

Art. 615.

Change of the form of property.

When property subject to usufruct changes form without an act of the usufructuary, the usufruct does not terminate even though the property may no longer serve the use for which it was originally destined.

When property subject to usufruct is converted into money or other property without an act of the usufructuary, as in a case of expropriation of an immovable or liquidation of a corporation, the usufruct terminates as to the property converted and attaches to the money or other property received by the usufructuary. (Acts 1976, No. 103, § 1; Acts 2010, No. 881, § 1.)

Art. 616.

Sale or exchange of the property; taxes.

When property subject to usufruct is sold or exchanged, whether in an action for partition or by agreement between the usufructuary and the naked owner or by a usufructuary who has the power to dispose of nonconsumable property, the usufruct terminates as to the nonconsumable property sold or exchanged, but as provided in Article 568.1, the usufrust attaches to the money or other property received by the usufructuary, unless the parties agree otherwise. Any tax or expense incurred as the result of the sale or exchange of property subject shall be paid from the proceeds of the sale or exchange, and shall be deducted from the amount due by the usufructuary to the naked owner at the termination of the usufruct. (Acts 1983, No. 525, § 1; Acts 2010, No. 881, § 1.)

Art. 617.

Proceeds of insurance.

When proceeds of insurance are due on account of loss, extinction, or destruction of property subject to usufruct, the usufruct attaches to the proceeds. If the usufructuary or the naked owner has separately insured his interest only, the proceeds belong to the insured party. (Acts 1976, No. 103, § 1.)

Art. 618.

Security of proceeds.

In cases governed by Articles 614, 615, 616, and the first sentence of Article 617, the naked owner may demand, within one year from receipt of the proceeds by the usufructuary, that the usufructuary give security for the proceeds. If such a demand is made, and the parties cannot agree, the nature of the security shall be determined by the court. This Article does not apply to corporeal movables referred to in the second sentence of Article 568, or to property disposed of by the usufructuary pursuant to the power to dispose of nonconsumables if the grantor of the usufruct has dispensed with the security. (Acts 1976, No. 103, § 1; Acts 2010, No. 881, § 1.)

Art. 619.

Changes made by the testator.

A usufruct by donation mortis causa is not considered as revoked merely because the testator has made changes in the property after the date of his testament. The effect of the legacy is determined by application of the rules contained in the title: Of donations inter vivos and mortis causa. (Acts 1976, No. 103, § 1; Acts 2010, No. 881, § 1.)

Art. 620.

Sale of the property or of the usufruct.

Usufruct terminates by the enforcement of an encumbrance established upon the property prior to the creation of the usufruct to secure a debt. The usufructuary may have an action against the grantor of the usufruct or against the naked owner under the provisions established in Section 3 of this Chapter.

The judicial sale of the usufruct by creditors of the usufructuary deprives the usufructuary of his enjoyment of the property but does not terminate the usufruct. (Acts 1976, No. 103, § 1; Acts 2010, No. 881, § 1.)

Art. 621.

Prescription of nonuse.

A usufruct terminates by the prescription of nonuse if neither the usufructuary nor any other person acting in his name exercises the right during a period of ten years. This applies whether the usufruct has been constituted on an entire estate or on a divided or undivided part of an estate. (Acts 1976, No. 103, § 1.)

Art. 622.

Confusion of usufruct and naked ownership.

A usufruct terminates by confusion when the usufruct and the naked ownership are united in the same person.

The usufruct does not terminate if the title by which the usufruct and the naked ownership were united is annulled for some previously existing defect or some vice inherent in the act. (Acts 1976, No. 103, § 1.)

Art. 623.

Abuse of the enjoyment; consequences.

The usufruct may be terminated by the naked owner if the usufructuary commits waste, alienates things without authority, neglects to make ordinary repairs, or abuses his enjoyment in any other manner. (Acts 1976, No. 103, § 1; Acts 2010, No. 881, § 1.)

Art. 624.

Security to prevent termination.

In the cases covered by the preceding Article, the court may decree termination of the usufruct or decree that the property be delivered to the naked owner on the condition that he shall pay to the usufructuary a reasonable annuity until the end of the usufruct. The amount of the annuity shall be based on the value of the usufruct.

The usufructuary may prevent termination of the usufruct or delivery of the property to the naked owner by giving security to insure that he will take appropriate corrective measures within a period fixed by the court. (Acts 1976, No. 103, § 1; Acts 2010, No. 881, § 1.)

Art. 625.

Intervention by creditors of the usufructuary.

A creditor of the usufructuary may intervene and may prevent termination of the usufruct and delivery of the property to the naked owner by offering to repair the damages caused by the usufructuary and by giving security for the future. (Acts 1976, No. 103, § 1; Acts 2010, No. 881, § 1.)

Art. 626.

Renunciation; rights of creditors.

A usufruct terminates by an express written renunciation.

A creditor of the usufructuary may cause to be annulled a renunciation made to his prejudice. (Acts 1976, No. 103, § 1.)

Art. 627.

Right of retention.

Upon termination of the usufruct, the usufructuary or his heirs have the right to retain possession of the property until reimbursed for all expenses and advances for which they have recourse against the owner or his heirs. (Acts 1976, No. 103, § 1.)

Art. 628.

Consequences of termination; usufruct of nonconsumables.

Upon termination of a usufruct of nonconsumables for a cause other than total and permanent destruction of the property, full ownership is restored. The usufructuary or his heirs are bound to deliver the property to the owner with its accessories and fruits produced since the termination of the usufruct.

If property has been lost or deteriorated through the fault of the usufructuary, the owner is entitled to the value the property otherwise would have had at the termination of the usufruct. (Acts 1976, No. 103, § 1.)

Art. 629.

Consequences of termination; usufruct of consumables.

At the termination of a usufruct of consumables, the usufructuary is bound to deliver to the owner things of the same quantity and quality or the value they had at the commencement of the usufruct. (Acts 1976, No. 103, § 1.)

Chapter 3. Habitation.

Art. 630.

Habitation.

Habitation is the nontransferable real right of a natural person to dwell in the house of another. (Acts 1976, No. 103, § 1.)

Art. 631.

Establishment and extinction.

The right of habitation is established and extinguished in the same manner as the right of usufruct. (Acts 1976, No. 103, § 1.)

Art. 632.

Regulation by title.

The right of habitation is regulated by the title that establishes it. If the title is silent as to the extent of habitation, the right is regulated in accordance with Articles 633 through 635. (Acts 1976, No. 103, § 1.)

Art. 633.

Persons residing in the house.

A person having the right of habitation may reside in the house with his family, although not married at the time the right was granted to him. (Acts 1976, No. 103, § 1.)

Art. 634.

Extent of right of habitation.

A person having the right of habitation is entitled to the exclusive use of the house or of the part assigned to him, and, provided that he resides therein, he may receive friends, guests, and boarders. (Acts 1976, No. 103, § 1.)

Art. 635.

Degree of care; duty to restore the property.

A person having the right of habitation is bound to use the property as a prudent administrator and at the expiration of his right to deliver it to the owner in the condition in which he received it, ordinary wear and tear excepted. (Acts 1976, No. 103, § 1.)

Art. 636.

Taxes, repairs, and other charges.

When the person having the right of habitation occupies the entire house, he is liable for ordinary repairs, for the payment of taxes, and for other annual charges in the same manner as the usufructuary.

When the person having the right of habitation occupies only a part of the house, he is liable for ordinary repairs to the part he occupies and for all other expenses and charges in proportion to his enjoyment. (Acts 1976, No. 103, § 1.)

Art. 637.

Nontransferable and nonheritable right.

The right of habitation is neither transferable nor heritable. It may not be alienated, let, or encumbered. (Acts 1976, No. 103, § 1.)

Art. 638.

Duration of habitation.

The right of habitation terminates at the death of the person having it unless a shorter period is stipulated. (Acts 1976, No. 103, § 1.)

Chapter 4. Rights of Use.

Art. 639.

Right of use.

The personal servitude of right of use confers in favor of a person a specified use of an estate less than full enjoyment. (Acts 1976, No. 103, § 1.)

Art. 640.

Content of the servitude.

The right of use may confer only an advantage that may be established by a predial servitude. (Acts 1976, No. 103, § 1.)

Art. 641.

Persons having the servitude.

A right of use may be established in favor of a natural person or a legal entity. (Acts 1976, No. 103, § 1.)

Art. 642.

Extent of the servitude.

A right of use includes the rights contemplated or necessary to enjoyment at the time of its creation as well as rights that may later become necessary, provided that a greater burden is not imposed on the property unless otherwise stipulated in the title. (Acts 1976, No. 103, § 1.)

Art. 643.

Transferable right.

The right of use is transferable unless prohibited by law or contract. (Acts 1976, No. 103, § 1.)

Art. 644.

Heritable right.

A right of use is not extinguished at the death of the natural person or at the dissolution of any other entity having the right unless the contrary is provided by law or contract. (Acts 1976, No. 103, § 1.)

Art. 645.

Regulation of the servitude.

A right of use is regulated by application of the rules governing usufruct and predial servitudes to the extent that their application is compatible with the rules governing a right of use servitude. (Acts 1976, No. 103, § 1.)

Title 4. Predial Servitudes.

Chapter 1. General Principles.

Art. 646.

Predial servitude; definition.

A predial servitude is a charge on a servient estate for the benefit of a dominant estate. The two estates must belong to different owners. (Acts 1977, No. 514, § 1.)

Art. 647.

Benefit to dominant estate.

There must be a benefit to the dominant estate. The benefit need not exist at the time the servitude is created; a possible convenience or a future advantage suffices to support a servitude.

There is no predial servitude if the charge imposed cannot be reasonably expected to benefit the dominant estate. (Acts 1977, No. 514, § 1.)

Art. 648.

Contiguity or proximity of the estates.

Neither contiguity nor proximity of the two estates is necessary for the existence of a predial servitude. It suffices that the two estates be so located as to allow one to derive some benefit from the charge on the other. (Acts 1977, No. 514, § 1.)

Art. 649.

Nature; incorporeal immovable.

A predial servitude is an incorporeal immovable. (Acts 1977, No. 514, § 1.)

Art. 650.

Inseparability of servitude.

A. A predial servitude is inseparable from the dominant estate and passes with it. The right of using the servitude cannot be alienated, leased, or encumbered separately from the dominant estate.

B. The predial servitude continues as a charge on the servient estate when ownership changes. (Acts 1977, No. 514, § 1; Acts 2004, No. 821, § 2, eff. Jan. 1, 2005.)

Art. 651.

Obligations of the owner of the servient estate.

The owner of the servient estate is not required to do anything. His obligation is to abstain from doing something on his estate or to permit something to be done on it. He may be required by convention or by law to keep his estate in suitable condition for the exercise of the servitude due to the dominant estate. A servitude may not impose upon the owner of the servient estate or his successors the obligation to pay for a fee or other charge on the occasion of an alienation, lease, or encumbrance of the servient estate. (Acts 1977, No. 514, § 1; Acts 2010, No. 938, § 1.)

Art. 652.

Indivisibility of servitude.

A predial servitude is indivisible. An estate cannot have upon another estate part of a right of way, or of view, or of any other servitude, nor can an estate be charged with a part of a servitude.

The use of a servitude may be limited to certain days or hours; when limited, it is still an entire right. A servitude is due to the whole of the dominant estate and to all parts of it; if this estate is divided, every acquirer of a part has the right of using the servitude in its entirety. (Acts 1977, No. 514, § 1.)

Art. 653.

Division of advantages.

The advantages resulting from a predial servitude may be divided, if they are susceptible of division. (Acts 1977, No. 514, § 1.)

Art. 654.

Kinds of predial servitudes.

Predial servitudes may be natural, legal, and voluntary or conventional. Natural servitudes arise from the natural situation of estates; legal servitudes are imposed by law; and voluntary or conventional servitudes are established by juridical act, prescription, or destination of the owner. (Acts 1977, No. 514, § 1.)

Chapter 2. Natural Servitudes.

Art. 655.

Natural drainage.

An estate situated below is the servient estate and is bound to receive the surface waters that flow naturally from a dominant estate situated above unless an act of man has created the flow. (Acts 1977, No. 514, § 1; Acts 2017, No. 105, § 1, eff. June 12, 2017.)

Art. 656.

Obligations of the owners.

The owner of the servient estate situated below may not do anything to prevent the flow of the water. The owner of the dominant estate situated above may not do anything to render the servitude more burdensome. (Acts 1977, No. 514, § 1; Acts 2017, No. 105, § 1, eff. June 12, 2017.)

Art. 657.

Estate bordering on running water.

The owner of an estate bordering on running water may use it as it runs for the purpose of watering his estate or for other purposes. (Acts 1977, No. 514, § 1.)

Art. 658.

Estate through which water runs.

The owner of an estate through which water runs, whether it originates there or passes from lands above, may make use of it while it runs over his lands. He cannot stop it or give it another direction and is bound to return it to its ordinary channel where it leaves his estate. (Acts 1977, No. 514, § 1.)

Chapter 3. Legal Servitudes.

Section 1. Limitations of Ownership.

Art. 659.

Legal servitudes; notion.

Legal servitudes are limitations on ownership established by law for the benefit of the general public or for the benefit of particular persons. (Acts 1977, No. 514, § 1.)

Art. 660.

Keeping buildings in repair.

The owner is bound to keep his buildings in repair so that neither their fall nor that of any part of their materials may cause damage to a neighbor or to a passerby. However, he is answerable for damages only upon a showing that he knew or, in the exercise of reasonable care, should have known of the vice or defect which caused the damage, that the damage could have been prevented by the exercise of reasonable care, and that he failed to exercise such reasonable care. Nothing in this Article shall preclude the court from the application of the doctrine of res ipsa loquitur in an appropriate case. (Acts 1977, No. 514, § 1; Acts 1996, 1st Ex. Sess., No. 1, § 1, eff. April 16, 1996.)

Art. 661.

Building in danger of falling.

When a building or other construction is in danger of falling a neighbor has a right of action to compel the owner to have it properly supported or demolished. When the danger is imminent the court may authorize the neighbor to do the necessary work for which he shall be reimbursed by the owner. (Acts 1977, No. 514, § 1.)

Art. 662.

Building near a wall.

One who builds near a wall, whether common or not, is bound to take all necessary precautions to protect his neighbor against injury. (Acts 1977, No. 514, § 1.)

Art. 663.

Projections over boundary.

A landowner may not build projections beyond the boundary of his estate. (Acts 1977, No. 514, § 1.)

Art. 664.

Rain drip from roof.

A landowner is bound to fix his roof so that rainwater does not fall on the ground of his neighbor. (Acts 1977, No. 514, § 1.)

Art. 665.

Legal public servitudes.

Servitudes imposed for the public or common utility relate to the space which is to be left for the public use by the adjacent proprietors on the shores of navigable rivers and for the making and repairing of levees, roads, and other public or common works. Such servitudes also exist on property necessary for the building of levees and other water control structures on the alignment approved by the U.S. Army Corps of Engineers as provided by law, including the repairing of hurricane protection levees.

All that relates to this kind of servitude is determined by laws or particular regulations. (Acts 2006, No. 776, § 1, eff. Aug. 15, 2006.)

Art. 666.

River road; substitution if destroyed or impassable.

He who from his title as owner is bound to give a public road on the border of a river or stream, must furnish another without any compensation, if the first be destroyed or carried away.

And if the road be so injured or inundated by the water, without being carried away, that it becomes impassable, the owner is obliged to give the public a passage on his lands, as near as possible to the public road, without recompense therefor.

Art. 667.

Limitations on use of property.

Although a proprietor may do with his estate whatever he pleases, still he cannot make any work on it, which may deprive his neighbor of the liberty of enjoying his own, or which may be the cause of any damage to him. However, if the work he makes on his estate deprives his neighbor of enjoyment or causes damage to him, he is answerable for damages only upon a showing that he knew or, in the exercise of reasonable care, should have known that his works would cause damage, that the damage could have been prevented by the exercise of reasonable care, and that he failed to exercise such reasonable care. Nothing in this Article shall preclude the court from the application of the doctrine of res ipsa loquitur in an appropriate case. Nonetheless, the proprietor is answerable for damages without regard to his knowledge or his exercise of reasonable care, if the damage is caused by an ultrahazardous activity. An ultrahazardous activity as used in this Article is strictly limited to pile driving or blasting with explosives. (Acts 1996, 1st Ex. Sess., No. 1, § 1, eff. April 16, 1996.)

Art. 668.

Inconvenience to neighbor.

Although one be not at liberty to make any work by which his neighbor's buildings may be damaged, yet every one has the liberty of doing on his own ground whatsoever he pleases, although it should occasion some inconvenience to his neighbor.

Thus he who is not subject to any servitude originating from a particular agreement in that respect, may raise his house as high as he pleases, although by such elevation he should darken the lights of his neighbors's [neighbor's] house, because this act occasions only an inconvenience, but not a real damage.

Art. 669.

Regulation of inconvenience.

If the works or materials for any manufactory or other operation, cause an inconvenience to those in the same or in the neighboring houses, by diffusing smoke or nauseous smell, and there be no servitude established by which they are regulated, their sufferance must be determined by the rules of the police, or the customs of the place.

Art. 670.

Encroaching building.

When a landowner constructs in good faith a building that encroaches on an adjacent estate and the owner of that estate does not complain within a reasonable time after he knew or should have known of the encroachment, or in any event complains only after the construction is substantially completed the court may allow the building to remain. The owner of the building acquires a predial servitude on the land occupied by the building upon payment of compensation for the value of the servitude taken and for any other damage that the neighbor has suffered. (Acts 1977, No. 514, § 1.)

Art. 671.

Destruction of private property to arrest fire.

Governing bodies of parishes and municipalities are authorized to adopt regulations determining the mode of proceeding to prevent the spread of fire by the destruction of buildings.

When private property is so destroyed in order to combat a conflagration, the owner shall be indemnified by the political subdivision for his actual loss. (Acts 1977, No. 514, § 1.)

Art. 672.

Other legal servitudes.

Other legal servitudes relate to common enclosures, such as common walls, fences and ditches, and to the right of passage for the benefit of enclosed estates. (Acts 1977, No. 514, § 1.)

Section 2. Common Enclosures.

Art. 673.

Common wall servitude.

A landowner who builds first may rest one-half of a partition wall on the land of his neighbor, provided that he uses solid masonry at least as high as the first story and that the width of the wall does not exceed eighteen inches, not including the plastering which may not be more than three inches in thickness. (Acts 1977, No. 514, § 1.)

Art. 674.

Contribution by neighbor.

The wall thus raised becomes common if the neighbor is willing to contribute one-half of its cost. If the neighbor refuses to contribute, he preserves the right to make the wall common in whole or in part, at any time, by paying to the owner one-half of the current value of the wall, or of the part that he wishes to make common. (Acts 1977, No. 514, § 1.)

Art. 675.

Presumption of common wall.

A wall that separates adjoining buildings and is partly on one estate and partly on another is presumed to be common up to the highest part of the lower building unless there is proof to the contrary. (Acts 1977, No. 514, § 1.)

Art. 676.

Adjoining wall.

When a solid masonry wall adjoins another estate, the neighbor has a right to make it a common wall, in whole or in part, by paying to its owner one-half of the current value of the wall, or of the part that he wishes to make common, and one-half of the value of the soil on which the wall is built. (Acts 1977, No. 514, § 1.)

Art. 677.

Rights and obligations of co-owners.

In the absence of a written agreement or controlling local ordinance the rights and obligations of the co-owners of a common wall, fence, or ditch are determined in accordance with the following provisions. (Acts 1977, No. 514, § 1.)

Art. 678.

Cost of repairs.

Necessary repairs to a common wall, including partial rebuilding, are to be made at the expense of those who own it in proportion to their interests. (Acts 1977, No. 514, § 1.)

Art. 679.

Abandonment of common wall.

The co-owner of a common wall may be relieved of the obligation to contribute to the cost of repairs by abandoning in writing his right to use it, if no construction of his is actually supported by the common wall. (Acts 1977, No. 514, § 1.)

Art. 680.

Rights in common walls.

The co-owner of a common wall may use it as he sees fit, provided that he does not impair its structural integrity or infringe on the rights of his neighbor. (Acts 1977, No. 514, § 1.)

Art. 681.

Opening in common wall.

The co-owner of a common wall may not make any opening in the wall without the consent of his neighbor. (Acts 1977, No. 514, § 1.)

Art. 682.

Raising the height of common wall.

A co-owner may raise the height of a common wall at his expense provided the wall can support the additional weight. In such a case, he alone is responsible for the maintenance and repair of the raised part. (Acts 1977, No. 514, § 1.)

Art. 683.

Neighbor's right to make the raised part common.

The neighbor who does not contribute to the raising of the common wall may at any time cause the raised part to become common by paying to its owner one-half of its current value. (Acts 1977, No. 514, § 1.)

Art. 684.

Enclosures.

A landowner has the right to enclose his land. (Acts 1977, No. 514, § 1.)

Art. 685.

Common fences.

A fence on a boundary is presumed to be common unless there is proof to the contrary. When adjoining lands are enclosed, a landowner may compel his neighbors to contribute to the expense of making and repairing common fences by which the respective lands are separated.

When adjoining lands are not enclosed, a landowner may compel his neighbors to contribute to the expense of making and repairing common fences only as prescribed by local ordinances. (Acts 1977, No. 514, § 1.)

Art. 686.

Common ditches.

A ditch between two estates is presumed to be common unless there be proof to the contrary.

Adjoining owners are responsible for the maintenance of a common ditch. (Acts 1977, No. 514, § 1.)

Art. 687.

Trees, bushes, and plants on the boundary.

Trees, bushes, and plants on the boundary are presumed to be common unless there be proof to the contrary.

An adjoining owner has the right to demand the removal of trees, bushes, or plants on the boundary that interfere with the enjoyment of his estate, but he must bear the expense of removal. (Acts 1977, No. 514, § 1.)

Art. 688.

Branches or roots of trees, bushes, or plants on neighboring property.

A landowner has the right to demand that the branches or roots of a neighbor's trees, bushes, or plants, that extend over or into his property be trimmed at the expense of the neighbor.

A landowner does not have this right if the roots or branches do not interfere with the enjoyment of his property. (Acts 1977, No. 514, § 1.)

Section 3. Right of Passage.

Art. 689.

Enclosed estate; right of passage.

The owner of an estate that has no access to a public road or utility may claim a right of passage over neighboring property to the nearest public road or utility. He is bound to compensate his neighbor for the right of passage acquired and to indemnify his neighbor for the damage he may occasion.

New or additional maintenance burdens imposed upon the servient estate or intervening lands resulting from the utility servitude shall be the responsibility of the owner of the dominant estate. (Acts 1977, No. 514, § 1; Acts 2012, No. 739, § 1.)

Art. 690.

Extent of passage.

The right of passage for the benefit of an enclosed estate shall be suitable for the kind of traffic or utility that is reasonably necessary for the use of that estate. (Acts 1977, No. 514, § 1; Acts 2012, No. 739, § 1.)

Art. 691.

Constructions.

The owner of the enclosed estate may construct on the right-of-way the type of road, utility, or railroad reasonably necessary for the exercise of the servitude.

The utility crossing shall be constructed in compliance with all appropriate and applicable federal and state standards so as to mitigate all hazards posed by the passage and the particular conditions of the servient estate and intervening lands. (Acts 1977, No. 514, § 1; Acts 2012, No. 739, § 1.)

Art. 692.

Location of passage.

The owner of the enclosed estate may not demand the right of passage or the right-of-way for the utility anywhere he chooses. The passage generally shall be taken along the shortest route from the enclosed estate to the public road or utility at the location least injurious to the intervening lands.

The location of the utility right-of-way shall coincide with the location of the servitude of passage unless an alternate location providing access to the nearest utility is least injurious to the servient estate and intervening lands.

The court shall evaluate and determine that the location of the servitude of passage or utility shall not affect the safety of the operations or significantly interfere with the operations of the owner of the servient estate or intervening lands prior to the granting of the servitude of passage or utility. (Acts 1977, No. 514, § 1; Acts 2012, No. 739, § 1.)

Art. 693.

Enclosed estate; voluntary act.

If an estate becomes enclosed as a result of a voluntary act or omission of its owner, the neighbors are not bound to furnish a passage to him or his successors. (Acts 1977, No. 514, § 1.)

Art. 694.

Enclosed estate; voluntary alienation or partition

When in the case of partition, or a voluntary alienation of an estate or of a part thereof, property alienated or partitioned becomes enclosed, passage shall be furnished gratuitously by the owner of the land on which the passage was previously exercised, even if it is not the shortest route to the public road or utility, and even if the act of alienation or partition does not mention a servitude of passage. (Acts 1977, No. 514, § 1; Acts 2012, No. 739, § 1.)

Art. 695.

Relocation of servitude.

The owner of the enclosed estate has no right to the relocation of this servitude after it is fixed. The owner of the servient estate has the right to demand relocation of the servitude to a more convenient place at his own expense, provided that it affords the same facility to the owner of the enclosed estate. (Acts 1977, No. 514, § 1.)

Art. 696.

Prescriptibility of action for indemnity.

The right for indemnity against the owner of the enclosed estate may be lost by prescription. The accrual of this prescription has no effect on the right of passage. (Acts 1977, No. 514, § 1.)

Art. 696.1.

Utility

As used in this Section, a utility is a service such as electricity, water, sewer, gas, telephone, cable television, and other commonly used power and communication networks required for the operation of an ordinary household or business. (Acts 2012, No. 739, § 1.)

Chapter 4. Conventional or Voluntary Servitudes.

Section 1. Kinds of Conventional Servitudes.

Art. 697.

Right to establish predial servitudes; limitations.

Predial servitudes may be established by an owner on his estate or acquired for its benefit.

The use and extent of such servitudes are regulated by the title by which they are created, and, in the absence of such regulation, by the following rules. (Acts 1977, No. 514, § 1.)

Art. 698.

Property susceptible of servitudes.

Predial servitudes are established on, or for the benefit of, distinct corporeal immovables. (Acts 1977, No. 514, § 1.)

Art. 699.

Examples of predial servitudes.

The following are examples of predial servitudes:

Rights of support, projection, drip, drain, or of preventing drain, those of view, of light, or of preventing view or light from being obstructed, of raising buildings or walls, or of preventing them from being raised, of passage, of drawing water, of aqueduct, of watering animals, and of pasturage. (Acts 1977, No. 514, § 1.)

Art. 700.

Servitude of support.

The servitude of support is the right by which buildings or other constructions of the dominant estate are permitted to rest on a wall of the servient estate.

Unless the title provides otherwise, the owner of the servient estate is bound to keep the wall fit for the exercise of the servitude, but he may be relieved of this charge by abandoning the wall. (Acts 1977, No. 514, § 1.)

Art. 701.

Servitude of view.

The servitude of view is the right by which the owner of the dominant estate enjoys a view; this includes the right to prevent the raising of constructions on the servient estate that would obstruct the view. (Acts 1977, No. 514, § 1.)

Art. 702.

Prohibition of view.

The servitude of prohibition of view is the right of the owner of the dominant estate to prevent or limit openings of view on the servient estate. (Acts 1977, No. 514, § 1.)

Art. 703.

Servitude of light.

The servitude of light is the right by which the owner of the dominant estate is entitled to make openings in a common wall for the admission of light; this includes the right to prevent the neighbor from making an obstruction. (Acts 1977, No. 514, § 1.)

Art. 704.

Prohibition of light.

The servitude of prohibition of light is the right of the owner of the dominant estate to prevent his neighbor from making an opening in his own wall for the admission of light or that limits him to certain lights only. (Acts 1977, No. 514, § 1.)

Art. 705.

Servitude of passage.

The servitude of passage is the right for the benefit of the dominant estate whereby persons, animals, utilities, or vehicles are permitted to pass through the servient estate. Unless the title provides otherwise, the extent of the right and the mode of its exercise shall be suitable for the kind of traffic or utility necessary for the reasonable use of the dominant estate. (Acts 1977, No. 514, § 1; Acts 2012, No. 739, § 1.)

Art. 706.

Servitudes; affirmative or negative.

Predial servitudes are either affirmative or negative.

Affirmative servitudes are those that give the right to the owner of the dominant estate to do a certain thing on the servient estate. Such are the servitudes of right of way, drain, and support.

Negative servitudes are those that impose on the owner of the servient estate the duty to abstain from doing something on his estate. Such are the servitudes of prohibition of building and of the use of an estate as a commercial or industrial establishment. (Acts 1977, No. 514, § 1.)

Art. 707.

Servitudes; apparent or nonapparent.

Predial servitudes are either apparent or nonapparent. Apparent servitudes are those that are perceivable by exterior signs, works, or constructions; such as a roadway, a window in a common wall, or an aqueduct.

Nonapparent servitudes are those that have no exterior sign of their existence; such as the prohibition of building on an estate or of building above a particular height. (Acts 1977, No. 514, § 1.)

Section 2.
Establishment of Predial Servitudes by Title.

Art. 708.

Establishment of predial servitude.

The establishment of a predial servitude by title is an alienation of a part of the property to which the laws governing alienation of immovables apply. (Acts 1977, No. 514, § 1.)

Art. 709.

Mandatary.

A mandatary may establish a predial servitude if he has an express and special power to do so. (Acts 1977, No. 514, § 1.)

Art. 710.

Naked owner.

The naked owner may establish a predial servitude that does not infringe on the rights of the usufructuary or that is to take effect at the termination of the usufruct. The consent of the usufructuary is required for the establishment of any other predial servitude. (Acts 1977, No. 514, § 1.)

Art. 711.

Usufructuary.

The usufructuary may not establish on the estate of which he has the usufruct any charges in the nature of predial servitudes. (Acts 1977, No. 514, § 1.)

Art. 712.

Owner for a term or under condition.

A person having ownership subject to a term or the happening of a condition may establish a predial servitude, but it ceases with his right. (Acts 1977, No. 514, § 1.)

Art. 713.

Purchaser with reservation of redemption.

A purchaser under a reserved right of redemption may establish a predial servitude on the property, but it ceases if the seller exercises his right of redemption. (Acts 1977, No. 514, § 1.)

Art. 714.

Co-owner; servitude on entire estate.

A predial servitude on an estate owned in indivision may be established only with the consent of all the co-owners.

When a co-owner purports to establish a servitude on the entire estate, the contract is not null; but, its execution is suspended until the consent of all co-owners is obtained. (Acts 1977, No. 514, § 1.)

Art. 715.

Exercise of Servitude.

A co-owner who has consented to the establishment of a predial servitude on the entire estate owned in indivision may not prevent its exercise on the ground that the consent of his co-owner has not been obtained.

If he becomes owner of the whole estate by any means which terminates the indivision, the predial servitude to which he has consented burdens his property. (Acts 1977, No. 514, § 1.)

Art. 716.

Servitude on undivided part.

When a co-owner has consented to the establishment of a predial servitude on his undivided part only, the consent of the other co-owners is not required, but the exercise of the servitude is suspended until his divided part is determined at the termination of the state of indivision. (Acts 1977, No. 514, § 1.)

Art. 717.

Partition in kind.

If the estate owned in indivision is partitioned in kind, the servitude established by a co-owner on his undivided part burdens only the part allotted to him. (Acts 1977, No. 514, § 1.)

Art. 718.

Partition by licitation.

If the estate is partitioned by licitation and the co-owner who consented to the establishment of the predial servitude acquires the ownership of the whole, the servitude burdens the entire estate as if the co-owner had always been sole owner. If the entire estate is adjudicated to any other person the right granted by the co-owner is extinguished. (Acts 1977, No. 514, § 1.)

Art. 719.

Successor of the co-owner.

Except as provided in Article 718, the successor of the co-owner who has consented to the establishment of a predial servitude, whether on the entire estate owned in indivision or on his undivided part only, occupies the same position as his ancestor. If he becomes owner of a divided part of the estate the servitude burdens that part, and if he becomes owner of the whole the servitude burdens the entire estate. (Acts 1977, No. 514, § 1.)

Art. 720.

Additional servitudes.

The owner of the servient estate may establish thereon additional servitudes, provided they do not affect adversely the rights of the owner of the dominant estate. (Acts 1977, No. 514, § 1.)

Art. 721.

Servitude on mortgaged property.

A predial servitude may be established on mortgaged property. If the servitude diminishes the value of the estate to the substantial detriment of the mortgagee, he may demand immediate payment of the debt.

If there is a sale for the enforcement of the mortgage the property is sold free of all servitudes established after the mortgage. In such a case, the acquirer of the servitude has an action for the restitution of its value against the owner who established it. (Acts 1977, No. 514, § 1.)

Art. 722.

Modes of establishment.

Predial servitudes are established by all acts by which immovables may be transferred. Delivery of the act of transfer or use of the right by the owner of the dominant estate constitutes tradition. (Acts 1977, No. 514, § 1.)

Art. 723.

Servitudes on public things.

Predial servitudes may be established on public things, including property of the state, its agencies and political subdivisions. (Acts 1977, No. 514, § 1.)

Art. 724.

Multiple dominant or servient estates.

A predial servitude may be established on several estates for the benefit of one estate. One estate may be subjected to a servitude for the benefit of several estates. (Acts 1977, No. 514, § 1.)

Art. 725.

Reciprocal servitudes.

The title that establishes a servitude for the benefit of the dominant estate may also establish a servitude on the dominant estate for the benefit of the servient estate. (Acts 1977, No. 514, § 1.)

Art. 726.

Servitude on after-acquired property.

Parties may agree to establish a predial servitude on, or for the benefit of, an estate of which one is not then the owner. If the ownership is acquired, the servitude is established.

Parties may agree that a building not yet built will be subjected to a servitude or that it will have the benefit of a servitude when it is built. (Acts 1977, No. 514, § 1.)

Art. 727.

Servitude on part of an estate.

A predial servitude may be established on a certain part of an estate, if that part is sufficiently described. (Acts 1977, No. 514, § 1.)

Art. 728.

Limitation of use.

The use of a predial servitude may be limited to certain times. Thus, the rights of drawing water and of passage may be confined to designated hours. (Acts 1977, No. 514, § 1.)

Art. 729.

Conventional alteration of legal or natural servitude.

Legal and natural servitudes may be altered by agreement of the parties if the public interest is not affected adversely. (Acts 1977, No. 514, § 1.)

Art. 730.

Interpretation of servitude.

Doubt as to the existence, extent, or manner of exercise of a predial servitude shall be resolved in favor of the servient estate. (Acts 1977, No. 514, § 1.)

Art. 731.

Charge expressly for the benefit of an estate.

A charge established on an estate expressly for the benefit of another estate is a predial servitude although it is not so designated. (Acts 1977, No. 514, § 1.)

Art. 732.

Interpretation in the absence of express declaration.

When the act does not declare expressly that the right granted is for the benefit of an estate or for the benefit of a particular person, the nature of the right is determined in accordance with the following rules. (Acts 1977, No. 514, § 1.)

Art. 733.

Interpretation; benefit of dominant estate.

When the right granted be of a nature to confer an advantage on an estate, it is presumed to be a predial servitude. (Acts 1977, No. 514, § 1.)

Art. 734.

Interpretation; convenience of a person.

When the right granted is merely for the convenience of a person, it is not considered to be a predial servitude, unless it is acquired by a person as owner of an estate for himself, his heirs and assigns. (Acts 1977, No. 514, § 1.)

Section 3. Acquisition of Conventional Servitudes for the Dominant Estate.

Art. 735.

Persons acquiring servitude.

A predial servitude may be acquired for the benefit of the dominant estate by the owner of that estate or by any other person acting in his name or in his behalf. (Acts 1977, No. 514, § 1.)

Art. 736.

Capacity to acquire servitude.

An incompetent may acquire a predial servitude for the benefit of his estate without the assistance of the administrator of his patrimony or of his tutor or curator. (Acts 1977, No. 514, § 1.)

Art. 737.

Renunciation of servitude by owner of dominant estate.

The owner of the dominant estate may renounce the contract by which a predial servitude was acquired for the benefit of his estate, if he finds the contract onerous, and if the contract was made without his authority or while he was incompetent. (Acts 1977, No. 514, § 1.)

Art. 738.

No revocation by grantor.

The grantor may not revoke the servitude on the ground that the person who acquired it for the benefit of the dominant estate was not the owner, that he was incompetent, or that he lacked authority. (Acts 1977, No. 514, § 1.)

Art. 739.

Acquisition by title only.

Nonapparent servitudes may be acquired by title only, including a declaration of destination under Article 741. (Acts 1977, No. 514, § 1. Amended by Acts 1978, No. 479, § 1.)

Art. 740.

Modes of acquisition of servitudes.

Apparent servitudes may be acquired by title, by destination of the owner, or by acquisitive prescription. (Acts 1977, No. 514, § 1.)

Art. 741.

Destination of the owner.

Destination of the owner is a relationship established between two estates owned by the same owner that would be a predial servitude if the estates belonged to different owners.

When the two estates cease to belong to the same owner, unless there is express provision to the contrary, an apparent servitude comes into existence of right and a nonapparent servitude comes into existence if the owner has previously filed for registry in the conveyance records of the parish in which the immovable is located a formal declaration establishing the destination. (Acts 1977, No. 514, § 1. Amended by Acts 1978, No. 479, § 1.)

Art. 742.

Acquisitive prescription.

The laws governing acquisitive prescription of immovable property apply to apparent servitudes. An apparent servitude may be acquired by peaceable and uninterrupted possession of the right for ten years in good faith and by just title; it may also be acquired by uninterrupted possession for thirty years without title or good faith. (Acts 1977, No. 514, § 1.)

Art. 743.

Accessory rights.

Rights that are necessary for the use of a servitude are acquired at the time the servitude is established. They are to be exercised in a way least inconvenient for the servient estate. (Acts 1977, No. 514, § 1.)

Section 4.
Rights of the Owner of the Dominant Estate.

Art. 744.

Necessary works; cost of repairs.

The owner of the dominant estate has the right to make at his expense all the works that are necessary for the use and preservation of the servitude. (Acts 1977, No. 514, § 1.)

Art. 745.

Right to enter into the servient estate.

The owner of the dominant estate has the right to enter with his workmen and equipment into the part of the servient estate that is needed for the construction or repair of works required for the use and preservation of the servitude. He may deposit materials to be used for the works and the debris that may result, under the obligation of causing the least possible damage and of removing them as soon as possible. (Acts 1977, No. 514, § 1.)

Art. 746.

Exoneration from responsibility by abandonment of the servient estate.

If the act establishing the servitude binds the owner of the servient estate to make the necessary works at his own expense, he may exonerate himself by abandoning the servient estate or the part of it on which the servitude is granted to the owner of the dominant estate. (Acts 1977, No. 514, § 1.)

Art. 747.

Division of dominant estate.

If the dominant estate is divided, the servitude remains due to each part, provided that no additional burden is imposed on the servient estate. Thus, in case of a right of passage, all the owners are bound to exercise that right through the same place. (Acts 1977, No. 514, § 1.)

Art. 748.

Noninterference by the owner of servient estate.

The owner of the servient estate may do nothing tending to diminish or make more inconvenient the use of the servitude.

If the original location has become more burdensome for the owner of the servient estate, or if it prevents him from making useful improvements on his estate, he may provide another equally convenient location for the exercise of the servitude which the owner of the dominant estate is bound to accept. All expenses of relocation are borne by the owner of the servient estate. (Acts 1977, No. 514, § 1.)

Art. 749.

Extent and manner of use of servitude when title is silent.

If the title is silent as to the extent and manner of use of the servitude, the intention of the parties is to be determined in the light of its purpose. (Acts 1977, No. 514, § 1.)

Art. 750.

Location of servitude when the title is silent.

If the title does not specify the location of the servitude, the owner of the servient estate shall designate the location. (Acts 1977, No. 514, § 1.)

Section 5. Extinction of Predial Servitudes.

Art. 751.

Destruction of dominant or of servient estate.

A predial servitude is extinguished by the permanent and total destruction of the dominant estate or of the part of the servient estate burdened with the servitude. (Acts 1977, No. 514, § 1.)

Art. 752.

Reestablishment of things.

If the exercise of the servitude becomes impossible because the things necessary for its exercise have undergone such a change that the servitude can no longer be used, the servitude is not extinguished; it resumes its effect when things are reestablished so that they may again be used, unless prescription has accrued. (Acts 1977, No. 514, § 1.)

Art. 753.

Prescription for nonuse.

A predial servitude is extinguished by nonuse for ten years. (Acts 1977, No. 514, § 1.)

Art. 754.

Commencement of nonuse.

Prescription of nonuse begins to run for affirmative servitudes from the date of their last use, and for negative servitudes from the date of the occurrence of an event contrary to the servitude.

An event contrary to the servitude is such as the destruction of works necessary for its exercise or the construction of works that prevent its exercise. (Acts 1977, No. 514, § 1.)

Art. 755.

Obstacle to servitude.

If the owner of the dominant estate is prevented from using the servitude by an obstacle that he can neither prevent nor remove, the prescription of nonuse is suspended on that account for a period of up to ten years. (Acts 1977, No. 514, § 1.)

Art. 756.

Failure to rebuild dominant or servient estate.

If the servitude cannot be exercised on account of the destruction of a building or other construction that belongs to the owner of the dominant estate, prescription is not suspended. If the building or other construction belongs to the owner of the servient estate, the preceding article applies. (Acts 1977, No. 514, § 1)

Art. 757.

Sufficiency of acts by third persons.

A predial servitude is preserved by the use made of it by anyone, even a stranger, if it is used as appertaining to the dominant estate. (Acts 1977, No. 514, § 1.)

Art. 758.

Imprescriptibility of natural servitudes.

The prescription of nonuse does not run against natural servitudes. (Acts 1977, No. 514, § 1.)

Art. 759.

Partial use.

A partial use of the servitude constitutes use of the whole. (Acts 1977, No. 514, § 1. Art.)

Art. 760.

More extensive use than title.

A more extensive use of the servitude than that granted by the title does not result in the acquisition of additional rights for the dominant estate unless it be by acquisitive prescription. (Acts 1977, No. 514, § 1.)

Art. 761.

Use of accessory right.

The use of a right that is only accessory to the servitude is not use of the servitude. (Acts 1977, No. 514, § 1.)

Art. 762.

Use by co-owner.

If the dominant estate is owned in indivision, the use that a co-owner makes of the servitude prevents the running of prescription as to all.

If the dominant estate is partitioned, the use of the servitude by each owner preserves it for his estate only. (Acts 1977, No. 514, § 1.)

Art. 763.

Minority or other disability.

The prescription of nonuse is not suspended by the minority or other disability of the owner of the dominant estate. (Acts 1977, No. 514, § 1.)

Art. 764.

Burden of proof of use.

When the prescription of nonuse is pleaded, the owner of the dominant estate has the burden of proving that he or some other person has made use of the servitude as appertaining to his estate during the period of time required for the accrual of the prescription. (Acts 1977, No. 514, § 1.)

Art. 765.

Confusion.

A predial servitude is extinguished when the dominant and the servient estates are acquired in their entirety by the same person. (Acts 1977, No. 514, § 1.)

Art. 766.

Resolutory condition.

When the union of the two estates is made under resolutory condition, or if it cease by legal eviction, the servitude is suspended and not extinguished. (Acts 1977, No. 514, § 1.)

Art. 767.

Acceptance of succession; confusion.

Until a successor has formally or informally accepted a succession, confusion does not take place. If the successor renounces the succession, the servitudes continue to exist. (Acts 1977, No. 514, § 1; Acts 2001, No. 572, § 1.)

Art. 768.

Confusion; separate and community property.

Confusion does not take place between separate property and community property of the spouses. Thus, if the servient estate belongs to one of the spouses and the dominant estate is acquired as a community asset, the servitude continues to exist. (Acts 1977, No. 514, § 1.)

Art. 769.

Irrevocability of extinction by confusion.

A servitude that has been extinguished by confusion may be reestablished only in the manner by which a servitude may be created. (Acts 1977, No. 514, § 1.)

Art. 770.

Abandonment of servient estate.

A predial servitude is extinguished by the abandonment of the servient estate, or of the part on which the servitude is exercised. It must be evidenced by a written act. The owner of the dominant estate is bound to accept it and confusion takes place. (Acts 1977, No. 514, § 1.)

Art. 771.

Renunciation of servitude.

A predial servitude is extinguished by an express and written renunciation by the owner of the dominant estate. (Acts 1977, No. 514, § 1.)

Art. 772.

Renunciation by owner.

A renunciation of a servitude by a co-owner of the dominant estate does not discharge the servient estate, but deprives him of the right to use the servitude. (Acts 1977, No. 514, § 1.)

Art. 773.

Expiration of time or happening of condition.

A predial servitude established for a term or under a resolutory condition is extinguished upon the expiration of the term or the happening of the condition. (Acts 1977, No. 514, § 1.)

Art. 774.

Dissolution of the right of the grantor.

A predial servitude is extinguished by the dissolution of the right of the person who established it. (Acts 1977, No. 514, § 1.)

Title 5. Building Restrictions.

Art. 775.

Building restrictions.

Building restrictions are charges imposed by the owner of an immovable in pursuance of a general plan governing building standards, specified uses, and improvements. The plan must be feasible and capable of being preserved. (Acts 1977, No. 170, § 1.)

Art. 776.

Establishment.

Building restrictions may be established only by juridical act executed by the owner of an immovable or by all the owners of the affected immovables. Once established, building restrictions may be amended or terminated as provided in this Title. (Acts 1977, No. 170, § 1; Acts 1999, No. 309, § 1, eff. June 16, 1999.)

Art. 777.

Nature and regulation.

Building restrictions are incorporeal immovables and real rights likened to predial servitudes. They are regulated by application of the rules governing predial servitudes to the extent that their application is compatible with the nature of building restrictions. (Acts 1977, No. 170, § 1.)

Art. 778.

Affirmative duties.

Building restrictions may impose on owners of immovables affirmative duties that are reasonable and necessary for the maintenance of the general plan. Building restrictions may not impose upon the owner of an immovable or his successors the obligation to pay a fee or other charge on the occasion of an alienation, lease or encumbrance of the immovable. (Acts 1977, No. 170, § 1; Acts 2010, No. 938, § 1.)

Art. 779.

Injunctive relief.

Building restrictions may be enforced by mandatory and prohibitory injunctions without regard to the limitations of Article 3601 of the Code of Civil Procedure. (Acts 1977, No. 170, § 1.)

Art. 780.

Amendment and termination of building restrictions.

Building restrictions may be amended, whether such amendment lessens or increases a restriction, or may terminate or be terminated, as provided in the act that establishes them. In the absence of such provision, building restrictions may be amended or terminated for the whole or a part of the restricted area by agreement of owners representing more than one-half of the land area affected by the restrictions, excluding streets and street rights-of-way, if the restrictions have been in effect for at least fifteen years, or by agreement of both owners representing two-thirds of the land area affected and two-thirds of the owners of the land affected by the restrictions, excluding streets and street rights-of-way, if the restrictions have been in effect for more than ten years. (Acts 1977, No. 170, § 1. Amended by Acts 1980, No. 310, § 1. Acts 1983, No. 129, § 1; Acts 1999, No. 309, § 1, eff. June 16, 1999.)

Art. 781.

Termination; liberative prescription.

No action for injunction or for damages on account of the violation of a building restriction may be brought after two years from the commencement of a noticeable violation. After the lapse of this period, the immovable on which the violation occurred is freed of the restriction that has been violated. (Acts 1977, No.170, § 1.)

Art. 782.

Abandonment of plan or of restriction.

Building restrictions terminate by abandonment of the whole plan or by a general abandonment of a particular restriction. When the entire plan is abandoned the affected area is freed of all restrictions; when a particular restriction is abandoned, the affected area is freed of that restriction only. (Acts 1977, No. 170, § 1.)

Art. 783.

Matters of interpretation and application.

Doubt as to the existence, validity, or extent of building restrictions is resolved in favor of the unrestricted use of the immovable. The provisions of the Louisiana Condominium Act, the Louisiana Timesharing Act, and the Louisiana Home owners Association Act shall supersede any and all provisions of this Title in the event of a conflict. (Acts 1977, No. 170, § 1; Acts 1999, No. 309, § 1, eff. June 16, 1999.)

Title 6. Boundaries.

Chapter 1. General Provisions.

Art. 784.

Boundary; marker.

A boundary is the line of separation between contiguous lands. A boundary marker is a natural or artificial object that marks on the ground the line of separation of contiguous lands. (Acts 1977, No. 169, § 1.)

Art. 785.

Fixing of the boundary.

The fixing of the boundary may involve determination of the line of separation between contiguous lands, if it is uncertain or disputed; it may also involve the placement of markers on the ground, if markers were never placed, were wrongly placed, or are no longer to be seen.

The boundary is fixed in accordance with the following rules. (Acts 1977, No. 169, § 1.)

Art. 786.

Persons who may compel fixing of boundary.

The boundary may be fixed upon the demand of an owner or of one who possesses as owner. It may also be fixed upon the demand of a usufructuary but it is not binding upon the naked owner unless he has been made a party to the proceeding. (Acts 1977, No. 169, § 1.)

Art. 787.

Lessee may compel lessor.

When necessary to protect his interest, a lessee may compel the lessor to fix the boundary of the land subject to the lease. (Acts 1977, No. 169, § 1.)

Art. 788.

Imprescriptibility of the right.

The right to compel the fixing of the boundary between contiguous lands is imprescriptible. (Acts 1977, No. 169, § 1.)

Art. 789.

Fixing of boundary judicially or extrajudicially.

The boundary may be fixed judicially or extrajudicially. It is fixed extrajudicially when the parties, by written agreement, determine the line of separation between their lands with or without reference to markers on the ground. (Acts 1977, No. 169, § 1.)

Art. 790.

Costs.

When the boundary is fixed extrajudicially costs are divided equally between the adjoining owners in the absence of contrary agreement. When the boundary is fixed judicially court costs are taxed in accordance with the rules of the Code of Civil Procedure. Expenses of litigation not taxed as court costs are borne by the person who has incurred them. (Acts 1977, No. 169, § 1.)

Art. 791.

Liability for unauthorized removal of markers.

When the boundary has been marked judicially or extrajudicially, one who removes boundary markers without court authority is liable for damages. He may also be compelled to restore the markers to their previous location. (Acts 1977, No. 169, § 1.)

Chapter 2. Effect of Titles, Prescription, or Possession.

Art. 792.

Fixing of boundary according to ownership or possession.

The court shall fix the boundary according to the ownership of the parties; if neither party proves ownership, the boundary shall be fixed according to limits established by possession. (Acts 1977, No. 169, § 1.)

Art. 793.

Determination of ownership according to titles.

When both parties rely on titles only, the boundary shall be fixed according to titles. When the parties trace their titles to a common author preference shall be given to the more ancient title. (Acts 1977, No. 169, § 1.)

Art. 794.

Determination of ownership according to prescription.

When a party proves acquisitive prescription, the boundary shall be fixed according to limits established by prescription rather than titles. If a party and his ancestors in title possessed for thirty years without interruption, within visible bounds, more land than their title called for, the boundary shall be fixed along these bounds. (Acts 1977, No. 169, § 1.)

Art. 795.

Effect of boundary agreement.

When the boundary is fixed extrajudicially, the agreement of the parties has the effect of a compromise. (Acts 1977, No. 169, § 1.)

Art. 796.

Error in the location of markers; rectification.

When visible markers have been erroneously placed by one of the contiguous owners alone, or not in accordance with a written agreement fixing the boundary, the error may be rectified by the court unless a contiguous owner has acquired ownership up to the visible bounds by thirty years possession. (Acts 1977, No. 169, § 1.)

Title 7. Ownership in Indivision.

Art. 797.

Ownership in indivision; definition.

Ownership of the same thing by two or more persons is ownership in indivision. In the absence of other provisions of law or juridical act, the shares of all co-owners are presumed to be equal. (Acts 1990, No. 990, § 1, eff. Jan. 1, 1991.)

Art. 798.

Right to fruits and products.

Co-owners share the fruits and products of the thing held in indivision in proportion to their ownership.

When fruits or products are produced by a co-owner, other co-owners are entitled to their shares of the fruits or products after deduction of the costs of production. (Acts 1990, No. 990, § 1, eff. Jan. 1, 1991.)

Art. 799.

Liability of a co-owner.

A co-owner is liable to his co-owner for any damage to the thing held in indivision caused by his fault. (Acts 1990, No. 990, § 1, eff. Jan. 1, 1991.)

Art. 800.

Preservation of the thing.

A co-owner may without the concurrence of any other co-owner take necessary steps for the preservation of the thing that is held in indivision. (Acts 1990, No. 990, § 1, eff. Jan. 1, 1991.)

Art. 801.

Use and management by agreement.

The use and management of the thing held in indivision is determined by agreement of all the co-owners. (Acts 1990, No. 990, § 1, eff. Jan. 1, 1991.)

Art. 802.

Right to use the thing.

Except as otherwise provided in Article 801, a co-owner is entitled to use the thing held in indivision according to its destination, but he cannot prevent another co-owner from making such use of it. As against third persons, a co-owner has the right to use and enjoy the thing as if he were the sole owner. (Acts 1990, No. 990, § 1, eff. Jan. 1, 1991.)

Art. 803.

Use and management of the thing in the absence of agreement.

When the mode of use and management of the thing held in indivision is not determined by an agreement of all the co-owners and partition is not available, a court, upon petition by a co-owner, may determine the use and management. (Acts 1990, No. 990, § 1, eff. Jan. 1, 1991.)

Art. 804.

Substantial alterations or improvements.

Substantial alterations or substantial improvements to the thing held in indivision may be undertaken only with the consent of all the co-owners.

When a co-owner makes substantial alterations or substantial improvements consistent with the use of the property, though without the express or implied consent of his co-owners, the rights of the parties shall be determined by Article 496. When a co-owner makes substantial alterations or substantial improvements inconsistent with the use of the property or in spite of the objections of his co-owners, the rights of the parties shall be determined by Article 497. (Acts 1990, No. 990, § 1, eff. Jan. 1, 1991.)

Art. 805.

Disposition of undivided share.

A co-owner may freely lease, alienate, or encumber his share of the thing held in indivision. The consent of all the co-owners is required for the lease, alienation, or encumbrance of the entire thing held in indivision. (Acts 1990, No. 990, § 1, eff. Jan. 1, 1991.)

Art. 806.

Expenses of maintenance and management.

A co-owner who on account of the thing held in indivision has incurred necessary expenses, expenses for ordinary maintenance and repairs, or necessary management expenses paid to a third person, is entitled to reimbursement from the other co-owners in proportion to their shares.

If the co-owner who incurred the expenses had the enjoyment of the thing held in indivision, his reimbursement shall be reduced in proportion to the value of the enjoyment. (Acts 1990, No. 990, § 1, eff. Jan. 1, 1991.)

Art. 807.

Right to partition; exclusion by agreement.

No one may be compelled to hold a thing in indivision with another unless the contrary has been provided by law or juridical act.

Any co-owner has a right to demand partition of a thing held in indivision. Partition may be excluded by agreement for up to fifteen years, or for such other period as provided in R.S. 9:1702 or other specific law. (Acts 1990, No. 990, § 1, eff. Jan. 1, 1991; Acts 1991, No. 349, § 1.)

Art. 808.

Partition excluded.

Partition of a thing held in indivision is excluded when its use is indispensable for the enjoyment of another thing owned by one or more of the co-owners. (Acts 1990, No. 990, § 1, eff. Jan. 1, 1991.)

Art. 809.

Judicial and extrajudicial partition.

The mode of partition may be determined by agreement of all the co-owners. In the absence of such an agreement, a co-owner may demand judicial partition. (Acts 1990, No. 990, § 1, eff. Jan. 1, 1991.)

Art. 810.

Partition in kind.

The court shall decree partition in kind when the thing held in indivision is susceptible to division into as many lots of nearly equal value as there are shares and the aggregate value of all lots is not significantly lower than the value of the property in the state of indivision. (Acts 1990, No. 990, § 1, eff. Jan. 1, 1991.)

Art. 811.

Partition by licitation or by private sale.

When the thing held in indivision is not susceptible to partition in kind, the court shall decree a partition by licitation or by private sale and the proceeds shall be distributed to the co-owners in proportion to their shares. (Acts 1990, No. 990, § 1, eff. Jan. 1, 1991.)

Art. 812.

Effect of partition on real rights.

When a thing held in indivision is partitioned in kind or by licitation, a real right burdening the thing is not affected. (Acts 1990, No. 990, § 1, eff. Jan. 1, 1991.)

Art. 813.

Partition in kind.

When a thing is partitioned in kind, a real right that burdens the share of a co-owner attaches to the part of the thing allotted to him. (Acts 1990, No. 990, § 1, eff. Jan. 1, 1991.)

Art. 814.

Rescission of partition for lesion.

An extrajudicial partition may be rescinded on account of lesion if the value of the part received by a co-owner is less by more than one-fourth of the fair market value of the portion he should have received. (Acts 1990, No. 990, § 1, eff. Jan. 1, 1991.)

Art. 815.

Partition by licitation.

When a thing is partitioned by licitation, a mortgage, lien, or privilege that burdens the share of a co-owner attaches to his share of the proceeds of the sale. (Acts 1990, No. 990, § 1, eff. Jan. 1, 1991.)

Art. 816.

Partition in kind; warranty.

When a thing is partitioned in kind, each co-owner incurs the warranty of a vendor toward his co-owners to the extent of his share. (Acts 1990, No. 990, § 1, eff. Jan. 1, 1991.)

Art. 817.

Imprescriptibility of action.

The action for partition is imprescriptible. (Acts 1990, No. 990, § 1, eff. Jan. 1, 1991.)

Art. 818.

Other rights held in indivision.

The provisions governing co-ownership apply to other rights held in indivision to the extent compatible with the nature of those rights. (Acts 1990, No. 990, § 1, eff. Jan. 1, 1991.)

Arts. 819 to 822. [*Repealed.*]

Repealed by Acts 1977, No. 514, § 1.

Arts. 823 to 855. [*Repealed.*]

Repealed by Acts 1977, No. 170, § 1.

Arts. 856 to 869. [*Repealed.*]

Repealed by Acts 1977, No. 169, § 1.

Title 23. Occupancy and Possession.

Chapter 1. Occupancy.

Art. 3412.

Occupancy.

Occupancy is the taking of possession of a corporeal movable that does not belong to anyone. The occupant acquires ownership the moment he takes possession. (Acts 1982, No. 187, § 1, eff. Jan. 1, 1983.)

Art. 3413.

Wild animals, birds, fish, and shellfish.

Wild animals, birds, fish, and shellfish in a state of natural liberty either belong to the state in its capacity as a public person or are things without an owner. The taking of possession of such things is governed by particular laws and regulations.

The owner of a tract of land may forbid entry to anyone for purposes of hunting or fishing, and the like. Nevertheless, despite a prohibition of entry, captured wildlife belongs to the captor. (Acts 1982, No. 187, § 1, eff. Jan. 1, 1983.)

Art. 3414.

Loss of ownership of wildlife.

If wild animals, birds, fish, or shellfish recover their natural liberty, the captor loses his ownership unless he takes immediate measures for their pursuit and recapture. (Acts 1982, No. 187, § 1, eff. Jan. 1, 1983.)

Art. 3415.

Wildlife in enclosures.

Wild animals or birds within enclosures, and fish or shellfish in an aquarium or other private waters, are privately owned.

Pigeons, bees, fish, and shellfish that migrate into the pigeon house, hive, or pond of another belong to him unless the migration has been caused by inducement or artifice. (Acts 1982, No. 187, § 1, eff. Jan. 1, 1983.)

Art. 3416.

Tamed wild animals.

Tamed wild animals and birds are privately owned as long as they have the habit of returning to their owner. They are considered to have lost the habit when they fail to return within a reasonable time. In such a case, they are considered to have recovered their natural liberty unless their owner takes immediate measures for their pursuit and recapture. (Acts 1982, No. 187, § 1, eff. Jan. 1, 1983.)

Art. 3417.

Domestic animals.

Domestic animals that are privately owned are not subject to occupancy. (Acts 1982, No. 187, § 1, eff. Jan. 1, 1983.)

Art. 3418.

Abandoned things.

One who takes possession of an abandoned thing with the intent to own it acquires ownership by occupancy. A thing is abandoned when its owner relinquishes possession with the intent to give up ownership. (Acts 1982, No. 187, § 1, eff. Jan. 1, 1983.)

Art. 3419.

Lost things.

One who finds a corporeal movable that has been lost is bound to make a diligent effort to locate its owner or possessor and to return the thing to him.

If a diligent effort is made and the owner is not found within three years, the finder acquires ownership. (Acts 1982, No. 187, § 1, eff. Jan. 1, 1983.)

Art. 3420.

Treasure.

One who finds a treasure in a thing that belongs to him or to no one acquires ownership of the treasure. If the treasure is found in a thing belonging to another, half of the treasure belongs to the finder and half belongs to the owner of the thing in which it was found.

A treasure is a movable hidden in another thing, movable or immovable, for such a long time that its owner cannot be determined. (Acts 1982, No. 187, § 1, eff. Jan. 1, 1983.)

Chapter 2. Possession.

Section 1.
Notion and Kinds of Possession.

Art. 3421.

Possession.

Possession is the detention or enjoyment of a corporeal thing, movable or immovable, that one holds or exercises by himself or by another who keeps or exercises it in his name.

The exercise of a real right, such as a servitude, with the intent to have it as one's own is quasi-possession. The rules governing possession apply by analogy to the quasipossession of incorporeals. (Acts 1982, No. 187, § 1, eff. Jan. 1, 1983.)

Art. 3422.

Nature of possession; right to possess.

Possession is a matter of fact; nevertheless, one who has possessed a thing for over a year acquires the right to possess it. (Acts 1982, No. 187, § 1, eff. Jan. 1, 1983.)

Art. 3423.

Rights of possessors.

A possessor is considered provisionally as owner of the thing he possesses until the right of the true owner is established. (Acts 1982, No. 187, § 1, eff. Jan. 1, 1983.)

Section 2.
Acquisition, Exercise, Retention, and Loss of Possession.

Art. 3424.

Acquisition of possession.

To acquire possession, one must intend to possess as owner and must take corporeal possession of the thing. (Acts 1982, No. 187, § 1, eff. Jan. 1, 1983.)

Art. 3425.

Corporeal possession.

Corporeal possession is the exercise of physical acts of use, detention, or enjoyment over a thing. (Acts 1982, No. 187, § 1, eff. Jan. 1, 1983.)

Art. 3426.

Constructive possession.

One who possesses a part of an immovable by virtue of a title is deemed to have constructive possession within the limits of his title. In the absence of title, one has possession only of the area he actually possesses. (Acts 1982, No. 187, § 1, eff. Jan. 1, 1983.)

Art. 3427.

Presumption of intent to own the thing.

One is presumed to intend to possess as owner unless he began to possess in the name of and for another. (Acts 1982, No. 187, § 1, eff. Jan. 1, 1983.)

Art. 3428.

Acquisition of possession through another.

One may acquire possession of a thing through another who takes it for him and in his name. The person taking possession must intend to do so for another. (Acts 1982, No. 187, § 1, eff. Jan. 1, 1983.)

Art. 3429.

Exercise of possession by another.

Possession may be exercised by the possessor or by another who holds the thing for him and in his name. Thus, a lessor possesses through his lessee. (Acts 1982, No. 187, § 1, eff. Jan. 1, 1983.)

Art. 3430.

Juridical persons.

A juridical person acquires possession through its representatives. (Acts 1982, No. 187, § 1, eff. Jan. 1, 1983.)

Art. 3431.

Retention of possession; civil possession.

Once acquired, possession is retained by the intent to possess as owner even if the possessor ceases to possess corporeally. This is civil possession. (Acts 1982, No. 187, § 1, eff. Jan. 1, 1983.)

Art. 3432.

Presumption of retention of possession.

The intent to retain possession is presumed unless there is clear proof of a contrary intention. (Acts 1982, No. 187, § 1, eff. Jan. 1, 1983.)

Art. 3433.

Loss of possession.

Possession is lost when the possessor manifests his intention to abandon it or when he is evicted by another by force or usurpation. (Acts 1982, No. 187, § 1, eff. Jan. 1, 1983.)

Art. 3434.

Loss of the right to possess.

The right to possess is lost upon abandonment of possession. In case of eviction, the right to possess is lost if the possessor does not recover possession within a year of the eviction.

When the right to possess is lost, possession is interrupted. (Acts 1982, No. 187, § 1, eff. Jan. 1, 1983.)

Section 3. Vices of Possession.

Art. 3435.

Vices of possession.

Possession that is violent, clandestine, discontinuous, or equivocal has no legal effect. (Acts 1982, No. 187, § 1, eff. Jan. 1, 1983.)

Art. 3436.

Violent, clandestine, discontinuous, and equivocal possession.

Possession is violent when it is acquired or maintained by violent acts. When the violence ceases, the possession ceases to be violent. Possession is clandestine when it is not open or public, discontinuous when it is not exercised at regular intervals, and equivocal when there is ambiguity as to the intent of the possessor to own the thing. (Acts 1982, No. 187, § 1, eff. Jan. 1, 1983.)

Section 4. Precarious Possession.

Art. 3437.

Precarious possession.

The exercise of possession over a thing with the permission of or on behalf of the owner or possessor is precarious possession. (Acts 1982, No. 187, § 1, eff. Jan. 1, 1983.)

Art. 3438.

Presumption of precariousness.

A precarious possessor, such as a lessee or a depositary, is presumed to possess for another although he may intend to possess for himself. (Acts 1982, No. 187, § 1, eff. Jan. 1, 1983.)

Art. 3439.

Termination of precarious possession.

A co-owner, or his universal successor, commences to possess for himself when he demonstrates this intent by overt and unambiguous acts sufficient to give notice to his co-owner.

Any other precarious possessor, or his universal successor, commences to possess for himself when he gives actual notice of this intent to the person on whose behalf he is possessing. (Acts 1982, No. 187, § 1, eff. Jan. 1, 1983.)

Art. 3440.

Protection of precarious possession.

Where there is a disturbance of possession, the possessory action is available to a precarious possessor, such as a lessee or a depositary, against anyone except the person for whom he possesses. (Acts 1982, No. 187, § 1, eff. Jan. 1, 1983.)

Section 5.
Transfer, Tacking, and Proof of Possession.

Art. 3441.

Transfer of possession.

Possession is transferable by universal title or by particular title. (Acts 1982, No. 187, § 1, eff. Jan. 1, 1983.)

Art. 3442.

Tacking of possession.

The possession of the transferor is tacked to that of the transferee if there has been no interruption of possession. (Acts 1982, No. 187, § 1, eff. Jan. 1, 1983.)

Art. 3443.

Presumption of continuity of possession.

One who proves that he had possession at different times is presumed to have possessed during the intermediate period. (Acts 1982, No. 187, § 1, eff. Jan. 1, 1983.)

Art. 3444.

Possessory action.

Possession of immovables is protected by the possessory action, as provided in Articles 3655 through 3671 of the Code of Civil Procedure.

Possession of movables is protected by the rules of the Code of Civil Procedure that govern civil actions. (Acts 1982, No. 187, § 1, eff. Jan. 1, 1983.)

Title 24. Prescription.

Chapter 1. General Principles.

Section 1. Prescription.

Art. 3445.

Kinds of prescription.

There are three kinds of prescription: acquisitive prescription, liberative prescription, and prescription of nonuse. (Acts 1982, No. 187, § 1, eff. Jan. 1, 1983.)

Art. 3446.

Acquisitive prescription.

Acquisitive prescription is a mode of acquiring ownership or other real rights by possession for a period of time. (Acts 1982, No. 187, § 1, eff. Jan. 1, 1983.)

Art. 3447.

Liberative prescription.

Liberative prescription is a mode of barring of actions as a result of inaction for a period of time. (Acts 1982, No. 187, § 1, eff. Jan. 1, 1983.)

Art. 3448.

Prescription of nonuse.

Prescription of nonuse is a mode of extinction of a real right other than ownership as a result of failure to exercise the right for a period of time. (Acts 1982, No. 187, § 1, eff. Jan. 1, 1983.)

Art. 3449.

Renunciation of prescription.

Prescription may be renounced only after it has accrued. (Acts 1982, No. 187, § 1, eff. Jan. 1, 1983.)

Art. 3450.

Express or tacit renunciation.

Renunciation may be express or tacit. Tacit renunciation results from circumstances that give rise to a presumption that the advantages of prescription have been abandoned.

Nevertheless, with respect to immovables, renunciation of acquisitive prescription must be express and in writing. (Acts 1982, No. 187, § 1, eff. Jan. 1, 1983.)

Art. 3451.

Capacity to renounce.

To renounce prescription, one must have capacity to alienate. (Acts 1982, No. 187, § 1, eff. Jan. 1, 1983.)

Art. 3452.

Necessity for pleading prescription.

Prescription must be pleaded. Courts may not supply a plea of prescription. (Acts 1982, No. 187, § 1, eff. Jan. 1, 1983.)

Art. 3453.

Rights of creditors and other interested parties.

Creditors and other persons having an interest in the acquisition of a thing or in the extinction of a claim or of a real right by prescription may plead prescription, even if the person in whose favor prescription has accrued renounces or fails to plead prescription. (Acts 1982, No. 187, § 1, eff. Jan. 1, 1983.)

Art. 3454.

Computation of time.

In computing a prescriptive period, the day that marks the commencement of prescription is not counted. Prescription accrues upon the expiration of the last day of the prescriptive period, and if that day is a legal holiday, prescription accrues upon the expiration of the next day that is not a legal holiday. (Acts 1982, No. 187, § 1, eff. Jan. 1, 1983.)

Art. 3455.

Computation of time by months.

If the prescriptive period consists of one or more months, prescription accrues upon the expiration of the day of the last month of the period that corresponds with the date of the commencement of prescription, and if there is no corresponding day, prescription accrues upon the expiration of the last day of the period. (Acts 1982, No. 187, § 1, eff. Jan. 1, 1983.)

Art. 3456.

Computation of time by years.

If a prescriptive period consists of one or more years, prescription accrues upon the expiration of the day of the last year that corresponds with the date of the commencement of prescription. (Acts 1982, No. 187, § 1, eff. Jan. 1, 1983.)

Art. 3457.

Prescription established by legislation only.

There is no prescription other than that established by legislation. (Acts 1982, No. 187, § 1, eff. Jan. 1, 1983.)

Section 2. Peremption.

Art. 3458.

Peremption; effect.

Peremption is a period of time fixed by law for the existence of a right. Unless timely exercised, the right is extinguished upon the expiration of the peremptive period. (Acts 1982, No. 187, § 1, eff. Jan. 1, 1983.)

Art. 3459.

Application of rules of prescription.

The provisions on prescription governing computation of time apply to peremption. (Acts 1982, No. 187, § 1, eff. Jan. 1, 1983.)

Art. 3460.

Peremption need not be pleaded.

Peremption may be pleaded or it may be supplied by a court on its own motion at any time prior to final judgment. (Acts 1982, No. 187, § 1, eff. Jan. 1, 1983.)

Art. 3461.

Renunciation, interruption, or suspension ineffective.

Peremption may not be renounced, interrupted, or suspended. (Acts 1982, No. 187, § 1, eff. Jan. 1, 1983.)

Chapter 2. Interruption and Suspension of Prescription.

Section 1. Interruption of Prescription.

Art. 3462.

Interruption by filing of suit or by service of process.

Prescription is interrupted when the owner commences action against the possessor, or when the obligee commences action against the obligor, in a court of competent jurisdiction and venue. If action is commenced in an incompetent court, or in an improper venue, prescription is interrupted only as to a defendant served by process within the prescriptive period. (Acts 1982, No. 187, § 1, eff. Jan. 1, 1983.)

Art. 3463.

Duration of interruption; abandonment or discontinuance of suit.

A. An interruption of prescription resulting from the filing of a suit in a competent court and in the proper venue or from service of process within the prescriptive period continues as long as the suit is pending.

B. Interruption is considered never to have occurred if the plaintiff abandons the suit, voluntarily dismisses the suit at any time either before the defendant has made any appearance of record or thereafter, or fails to prosecute the suit at the trial. The dismissal of a suit pursuant to a compromise does not constitute a voluntary dismissal. (Acts 1982, No. 187, § 1, eff. Jan. 1, 1983; Acts 1999, No. 1263, § 2, eff. Jan. 1, 2000; Acts 2018, No. 443, § 1; Acts 2021, No. 414, § 1.)

Art. 3464.

Interruption by acknowledgment.

Prescription is interrupted when one acknowledges the right of the person against whom he had commenced to prescribe. (Acts 1982, No. 187, § 1, eff. Jan. 1, 1983.)

Art. 3465.

Interruption of acquisitive prescription.

Acquisitive prescription is interrupted when possession is lost.

The interruption is considered never to have occurred if the possessor recovers possession within one year or if he recovers possession later by virtue of an action brought within the year. (Acts 1982, No. 187, § 1, eff. Jan. 1, 1983.)

Art. 3466.

Effect of interruption.

If prescription is interrupted, the time that has run is not counted. Prescription commences to run anew from the last day of interruption. (Acts 1982, No. 187, § 1, eff. Jan. 1, 1983.)

Section 2. Suspension of Prescription.

Art. 3467.

Persons against whom prescription runs.

Prescription runs against all persons unless exception is established by legislation. (Acts 1982, No. 187, § 1, eff. Jan. 1, 1983.)

Art. 3468.

Incompetents.

Prescription runs against absent persons and incompetents, including minors and interdicts, unless exception is established by legislation. (Acts 1983, No. 173, § 3, eff. Jan. 1, 1984; Acts 1991, No. 107, § 1.)

Art. 3469.

Suspension of prescription.

Prescription is suspended as between: the spouses during marriage, parents and children during minority, tutors and minors during tutorship, and curators and interdicts during interdiction, and caretakers and minors during minority.

A "caretaker" means a person legally obligated to provide or secure adequate care for a child, including a tutor, guardian, or legal custodian.

Art. 3470.

Prescription during delays for inventory; vacant succession.

Prescription runs during the delay the law grants to a successor for making an inventory and for deliberating. Nevertheless, it does not run against a beneficiary successor with respect to his rights against the succession.

Prescription runs against a vacant succession even if an administrator has not been appointed. (Acts 1982, No. 187, § 1, eff. Jan. 1, 1983.)

Art. 3471.

Limits of contractual freedom.

A juridical act purporting to exclude prescription, to specify a longer period than that established by law, or to make the requirements of prescription more onerous, is null. (Acts 1982, No. 187, § 1, eff. Jan. 1, 1983.)

Art. 3472.

Effect of suspension.

The period of suspension is ot counted toward accrual of prescription. Prescription commences to run again upon the termination of the period of suspension. (Acts 1982, No. 187, § 1, eff. Jan. 1, 1983.)

Art. 3472.1.

Emergency suspension of prescription and peremption.

Notwithstanding any other provision of the law or any provision of an executive order or proclamation, in the event the governor, in response to a state of emergency or disaster, issues an executive order or proclamation pursuant to R.S. 29:721 through 775 that purports to suspend or extend liberative prescriptive or peremptive periods in all or part of the state, the executive order or proclamation shall have the effect of suspending only those liberative prescriptive or peremptive periods that would have otherwise accrued during the period of time specified in the order or proclamation or, if no period of time is specified, during the duration of the effectiveness of the executive order or proclamation. Upon the termination of the period of suspension, liberative prescription or peremption commences to run again and accrues upon the earlier of thirty days after the expiration of the period of suspension or in accordance with the period of time as calculated pursuant to Article 3472. (Acts 2020, 1st Ex. Sess., No. 3, § 1, eff. June 25, 2020; Acts 2022, No. 469, § 1.)

Chapter 3. Acquisitive Prescription.

Section 1. Immovables: Prescription of Ten Years in Good Faith and Under Just Title.

Art. 3473.

Prescription of ten years.

Ownership and other real rights in immovables may be acquired by the prescription of ten years. (Acts 1982, No. 187, § 1, eff. Jan. 1, 1983.)

Art. 3474.

Incompetents.

This prescription runs against absent persons and incompetents, including minors and interdicts. (Acts 1982, No. 187, § 1, eff. Jan. 1, 1983; Acts 1991, No. 107, § 1.)

Art. 3475.

Requisites.

The requisites for the acquisitive prescription of ten years are: possession of ten years, good faith, just title, and a thing susceptible of acquisition by prescription. (Acts 1982, No. 187, § 1, eff. Jan. 1, 1983.)

Art. 3476.

Attributes of possession.

The possessor must have corporeal possession, or civil possession preceded by corporeal possession, to acquire a thing by prescription.

The possession must be continuous, uninterrupted, peaceable, public, and unequivocal. (Acts 1982, No. 187, § 1, eff. Jan. 1, 1983.)

Art. 3477.

Precarious possessor; inability to prescribe.

Acquisitive prescription does not run in favor of a precarious possessor or his universal successor. (Acts 1982, No. 187, § 1, eff. Jan. 1, 1983.)

Art. 3478.

Termination of precarious possession; commencement of prescription.

A co-owner, or his universal successor, may commence to prescribe when he demonstrates by overt and unambiguous acts sufficient to give notice to his co-owner that he intends to possess the property for himself. The acquisition and recordation of a title from a person other than a co-owner thus may mark the commencement of prescription.

Any other precarious possessor, or his universal successor, may commence to prescribe when he gives actual notice to the person on whose behalf he is possessing that he intends to possess for himself. (Acts 1982, No. 187, § 1, eff. Jan. 1, 1983.)

Art. 3479.

Particular successor of precarious possessor.

A particular successor of a precarious possessor who takes possession under an act translative of ownership possesses for himself, and prescription runs in his favor from the commencement of his possession. (Acts 1982, No. 187, § 1, eff. Jan. 1, 1983.)

Art. 3480.

Good faith.

For purposes of acquisitive prescription, a possessor is in good faith when he reasonably believes, in light of objective considerations, that he is owner of the thing he possesses. (Acts 1982, No. 187, § 1, eff. Jan. 1, 1983.)

Art. 3481.

Presumption of good faith.

Good faith is presumed. Neither error of fact nor error of law defeats this presumption. This presumption is rebutted on proof that the possessor knows, or should know, that he is not owner of the thing he possesses. (Acts 1982, No. 187, § 1, eff. Jan. 1, 1983.)

Art. 3482.

Good faith at commencement of prescription.

It is sufficient that possession has commenced in good faith; subsequent bad faith does not prevent the accrual of prescription of ten years. (Acts 1982, No. 187, § 1, eff. Jan. 1, 1983.)

Art. 3483.

Just title.

A just title is a juridical act, such as a sale, exchange, or donation, sufficient to transfer ownership or another real right. The act must be written, valid in form, and filed for registry in the conveyance records of the parish in which the immovable is situated. (Acts 1982, No. 187, § 1, eff. Jan. 1, 1983.)

Art. 3484.

Transfer of undivided part of an immovable.

A just title to an undivided interest in an immovable is such only as to the interest transferred. (Acts 1982, No. 187, § 1, eff. Jan. 1, 1983.)

Art. 3485.

Things susceptible of prescription.

All private things are susceptible of prescription unless prescription is excluded by legislation. (Acts 1982, No. 187, § 1, eff. Jan. 1, 1983.)

Section 2.
Immovables: Prescription of Thirty Years.

Art. 3486.

Immovables; prescription of thirty years.

Ownership and other real rights in immovables may be acquired by the prescription of thirty years without the need of just title or possession in good faith. (Acts 1982, No. 187, § 1, eff. Jan. 1, 1983.)

Art. 3487.

Restriction as to extent of possession.

For purposes of acquisitive prescription without title, possession extends only to that which has been actually possessed. (Acts 1982, No. 187, § 1, eff. Jan. 1, 1983.)

Art. 3488.

Applicability of rules governing prescription of ten years.

The rules governing acquisitive prescription of ten years apply to the prescription of thirty years to the extent that their application is compatible with the prescription of thirty years. (Acts 1982, No. 187, § 1, eff. Jan. 1, 1983.)

Section 3.
Movables: Acquisitive Prescription of Three Years or Ten Years.

Art. 3489.

Movables; acquisitive prescription.

Ownership and other real rights in movables may be acquired either by the prescription of three years or by the prescription of ten years. (Acts 1982, No. 187, § 1, eff. Jan. 1, 1983.)

Art. 3490.

Prescription of three years.

One who has possessed a movable as owner, in good faith, under an act sufficient to transfer ownership, and without interruption for three years, acquires ownership by prescription. (Acts 1982, No. 187, § 1, eff. Jan. 1, 1983.)

Art. 3491.

Prescription of ten years.

One who has possessed a movable as owner for ten years acquires ownership by prescription. Neither title nor good faith is required for this prescription. (Acts 1982, No. 187, § 1, eff. Jan. 1, 1983.)

Chapter 4. Liberative Prescription.

Section 1. One Year Prescription.

Art. 3492.

Delictual actions.

Delictual actions are subject to a liberative prescription of one year. This prescription commences to run from the day injury or damage is sustained. It does not run against minors or interdicts in actions involving permanent disability and brought pursuant to the Louisiana Products Liability Act or state law governing product liability actions in effect at the time of the injury or damage. (Acts 1992, No. 621, § 1.)

Art. 3493.

Damage to immovable property; commencement and accrual of prescription.

When damage is caused to immovable property, the one year prescription commences to run from the day the owner of the immovable acquired, or should have acquired, knowledge of the damage. (Acts 1983, No. 173, § 1, eff. Jan. 1, 1984.)

Section 1-A. Two-Year Prescription.

Art. 3493.10.

Delictual actions; two-year prescription; criminal act.

Delictual actions which arise due to damages sustained as a result of an act defined as a crime of violence under Chapter 1 of Title 14 of the Louisiana Revised Statutes of 1950 are subject to a liberative prescription of two years. This prescription commences to run from the day injury or damage is sustained. (Acts 1999, No. 832, § 1.)

Section 2. Three Year Prescription.

Art. 3494.

Actions subject to a three-year prescription.

The following actions are subject to a liberative prescription of three years:

(1) An action for the recovery of compensation for services rendered, including payment of salaries, wages, commissions, tuition fees, professional fees, fees and emoluments of public officials, freight, passage, money, lodging, and board;

(2) An action for arrearages of rent and annuities;

(3) An action on money lent;

(4) An action on an open account; and

(5) An action to recover underpayments or overpayments of royalties from the production of minerals, provided that nothing herein applies to any payments, rent, or royalties derived from state-owned properties. (Acts 1986, No. 1031, § 1.)

Art. 3495.

Commencement and accrual of prescription.

This prescription commences to run from the day payment is exigible. It accrues as to past due payments even if there is a continuation of labor, supplies, or other services. (Acts 1983, No. 173, § 1, eff. Jan. 1, 1984.)

Art. 3496.

Action against attorney for return of papers.

An action by a client against an attorney for the return of papers delivered to him for purposes of a law suit is subject to a liberative prescription of three years. This prescription commences to run from the rendition of a final judgment in the law suit or the termination of the attorney-client relationship. (Acts 1983, No. 173, § 1, eff. Jan. 1, 1984.)

Art. 3496.1.

Action against a person for abuse of a minor.

An action against a person for abuse of a minor is subject to a liberative prescriptive period of three years. This prescription commences to run from the day the minor attains majority, and this prescription, for all purposes, shall be suspended until the minor reaches the age of majority. This prescriptive period shall be subject to any exception of peremption provided by law. (Acts 1992, No. 322, § 1.)

Section 3. Five Year Prescription.

Art. 3497.

Actions subject to a five year prescription.

The following actions are subject to a liberative prescription of five years: An action for annulment of a testament;

An action for the reduction of an excessive donation;

An action for the rescission of a partition and warranty of portions; and.

An action for damages for the harvesting of timber without the consent of the owner.

This prescription is suspended in favor of minors, during minority. (Acts 1983, No. 173, § 1, eff. Jan. 1, 1984; Acts, 2009, No. 107, § 1.)

Art. 3497.1.

Actions for arrearages of spousal support or of installment payments for contributions made to a spouse's education or training.

An action to make executory arrearages of spousal support or installment payments awarded for contributions made by one spouse to the education or training of the other spouse is subject to a liberative prescription of five years. (Acts 1984, No. 147, § 1, eff. June 25, 1984; Acts 1990, No. 1008, § 3, eff. Jan. 1, 1991; Acts 1997, No. 605, § 1, eff. July 3, 1997.)

Art. 3498.

Actions on negotiable and nonnegotiable instruments.

Actions on instruments, whether negotiable or not, and on promissory notes, whether negotiable or not, are subject to a liberative prescription of five years. This prescription commences to run from the day payment is exigible. (Acts 1993, No. 901, §§ 1 and 2, eff. July 1, 1993; Acts 1993, No. 948, §§ 6 and 9, eff. June 25, 1993.)

Section 4. Ten Year Prescription.

Art. 3499.

Personal action.

Unless otherwise provided by legislation, a personal action is subject to a liberative prescription of ten years. (Acts 1983, No. 173, § 1, eff. Jan. 1, 1984.)

Art. 3500.

Action against contractors and architects.

An action against a contractor or an architect on account of defects of construction, renovation, or repair of buildings and other works is subject to a liberative prescription of ten years. (Acts 1983, No. 173, § 1, eff. Jan. 1, 1984.)

Art. 3501.

Prescription and revival of money judgments.

A money judgment rendered by a trial court of this state is prescribed by the lapse of ten years from its signing if no appeal has been taken, or, if an appeal has been taken, it is prescribed by the lapse of ten years from the time the judgment becomes final.

An action to enforce a money judgment rendered by a court of another state or a possession of the United States, or of a foreign country, is barred by the lapse of ten years from its rendition; but such a judgment is not enforceable in this state if it is prescribed, barred by the statute of limitations, or is otherwise unenforceable under the laws of the jurisdiction in which it was rendered.

Any party having an interest in a money judgment may have it revived before it prescribes, as provided in Article 2031 of the Code of Civil Procedure. A judgment so revived is subject to the prescription provided by the first paragraph of this Article. An interested party may have a money judgment rendered by a court of this state revived as often as he may desire. (Acts 1983, No. 173, § 1, eff. Jan. 1, 1984.)

Art. 3501.1.

Actions for arrearages of child support.

An action to make executory arrearages of child support is subject to a liberative prescription of ten years. (Acts 1997, No. 605, § 1, eff. July 3, 1997.)

Section 5. Thirty Year Prescription.

Art. 3502.

Action for the recognition of a right of inheritance.

An action for the recognition of a right of inheritance and recovery of the whole or a part of a succession is subject to a liberative prescription of thirty years. This prescription commences to run from the day of the opening of the succession. (Acts 1983, No. 173, § 1, eff. Jan. 1, 1984.)

Section 6.
Interruption and Suspension of Liberative Prescription.

Art. 3503.

Solidary obligors.

When prescription is interrupted against a solidary obligor, the interruption is effective against all solidary obligors and their successors.

When prescription is interrupted against a successor of a solidary obligor, the interruption is effective against other successors if the obligation is indivisible. If the obligation is divisible, the interruption is effective against other successors only for the portions for which they are bound. (Acts 1983, No. 173, § 1, Jan. 1, 1984.)

Art. 3504.

Surety.

When prescription is interrupted against the principal debtor, the interruption is effective against his surety. (Acts 1983, No. 173, § 1, eff. Jan 1, 1984.)

Art. 3505. [*Repealed.*]

Repealed by Acts 1982, No. 187, § 2, effective January 1, 1983.

Miscellaneous

Art. 7.

Laws for the preservation of the public interest.

Persons may not by their juridical acts derogate from laws enacted for the protection of the public interest. Any act in derogation of such laws is an absolute nullity. (Acts 1987, No. 124, § 1, effective January 1, 1988.)

Art. 876.

Kinds of successors.

There are two kinds of successors corresponding to the two kinds of succession described in the preceding articles:

Testate successors, also called legatees.

Intestate successors, also called heirs. (Acts 1981, No. 919, § 1, eff. Jan. 1, 1982.)

Art. 888.

Succession rights of descendants.

Descendants succeed to the property of their ascendants. They take in equal portions and by heads if they are in the same degree. They take by roots if all or some of them succeed by representation. (Acts 1981, No. 919, § 1, eff. Jan. 1, 1982.)

Art. 889.

Devolution of community property.

If the deceased leaves no descendants, his surviving spouse succeeds to his share of the community property. (Acts 1981, No. 919, § 1, eff. Jan. 1, 1982.)

Art. 890.

Usufruct of surviving spouse.

If the deceased spouse is survived by descendants, the surviving spouse shall have a usufruct over the decedent's share of the community property to the extent that the decedent has not disposed of it by testament. This usufruct terminates when the surviving spouse dies or remarries, whichever occurs first. (Acts 1981, No. 919, § 1. Amended by Acts 1982, No. 445, § 1; Acts 1990, No. 1075, § 1, eff. July 27, 1990; Acts 1996, 1st Ex. Sess., No. 77, § 1.)

Art. 936.

Continuation of the possession of decedent.

The possession of the decedent is transferred to his successors, whether testate or intestate, and if testate, whether particular, general, or universal legatees.

A universal successor continues the possession of the decedent with all its advantages and defects, and with no alteration in the nature of the possession.

A particular successor may commence a new possession for purposes of acquisitive prescription. (Acts 1997, No. 1421, § 1, eff. July 1, 1999.)

Art. 1300.

Limited or conditional prohibition against partition by donor.

But a donor or testator can order that the effects given or bequeathed by him, be not divided for a certain time, or until the happening of a certain condition. But if the time fixed exceed five years, or if the condition do not happen within that term, from the day of the donation or of the opening of the succession, the judge, at the expiration of this term of five years, may order the partition, if it is proved to him that the coheirs can not agree among themselves, or differ as to the administration of the common effects.

Art. 1301.

Testator's right to prohibit partition during minority of heirs.

If the father or other ascendant orders by his will that no partition shall be made among his minor children or minor grandchildren inheriting from him, during the time of their minority, this prohibition must be observed, until one of the children or grandchildren comes of age, and demands the partition.

Art. 1520.

Prohibited substitutions, definitions.

A disposition that is not in trust by which a thing is donated in full ownership to a first donee, called the institute, with a charge to preserve the thing and deliver it to a second donee, called the substitute, at the death of the institute, is null with regard to both the institute and the substitute. (Amended by Acts 1962, No. 45, § 1; Acts 2001, No. 825, § 1.)

Art. 1541.

Form required for donations.

A donation inter vivos shall be made by authentic act under the penalty of absolute nullity, unless otherwise expressly permitted by law. (Acts 2008, No. 204, § 1, eff. Jan. 1, 2009.)

Art. 1543.

Manual gift.

The donation inter vivos of a corporeal movable may also be made by delivery of the thing to the donee without any other formality. (Acts 2008, No. 204, § 1, eff. Jan. 1, 2009.)

Art. 1550.

Form for donation of certain incorporeal movables.

The donation or the acceptance of a donation of an incorporeal movable of the kind that is evidenced by a certificate, document, instrument, or other writing, and that is transferable by endorsement or delivery, may be made by authentic act or by compliance with the requirements otherwise applicable to the transfer of that particular kind of incorporeal movable.

In addition, an incorporeal movable that is investment property, as that term is defined in Chapter 9 of the Louisiana Commercial Laws, may also be donated by a writing signed by the donor that evidences donative intent and directs the transfer of the property to the donee or his account or for his benefit. Completion of the transfer to the donee or his account or for his benefit shall constitute acceptance of the donation. (Acts 2008, No. 204, § 1, eff. Jan. 1, 2009.)

Art. 1570.

Testaments; form.

A disposition mortis causa may be made only in the form of a testament authorized by law. (Acts 1997, No. 1421, § 1, eff. July 1, 1999.)

Art. 1574.

Forms of testaments.

There are two forms of testaments: olographic and notarial. (Acts 1997, No. 1421, § 1, eff. July 1, 1999.)

Art. 1575.

Olographic testament.

A. An olographic testament is one entirely written, dated, and signed in the handwriting of the testator. Although the date may appear anywhere in the testament, the testator must sign the testament at the end of the testament. If anything is written by the testator after his signature, the testament shall not be invalid and such writing may be considered by the court, in its discretion, as part of the testament. The olographic testament is subject to no other requirement as to form. The date is sufficiently indicated if the day, month, and year are reasonably ascertainable from information in the testament, as clarified by extrinsic evidence, if necessary.

B. Additions and deletions on the testament may be given effect only if made by the hand of the testator. (Acts 1997, No. 1421, § 1, eff. July 1, 1999; Acts 2001, No. 824, § 1.)

Art. 1576.

Notarial testament.

A notarial testament is one that is executed in accordance with the formalities of Articles 1577 through 1580.1. (Acts 1997, No. 1421, § 1, eff. July 1, 1999; Acts 1999, No. 745, § 1, eff. July 1, 1999.)

Art. 1585.

Universal legacy.

A universal legacy is a disposition of all of the estate, or the balance of the estate that remains after particular legacies. A universal legacy may be made jointly for the benefit of more than one legatee without changing its nature. (Acts 1997, No. 1421, § 1, eff. July 1, 1999.)

Art. 1586.

General legacy.

A general legacy is a disposition by which the testator bequeaths a fraction or a certain proportion of the estate, or a fraction or certain proportion of the balance of the estate that remains after particular legacies. In addition, a disposition of property expressly described by the testator as all, or a fraction or a certain proportion of one of the following categories of property, is also a general legacy: separate or community property, movable or immovable property, or corporeal or incorporeal property. This list of categories is exclusive. (Acts 1997, No. 1421, § 1, eff. July 1, 1999.)

Art. 1587.

Particular legacy.

A legacy that is neither general nor universal is a particular legacy. (Acts 1997, No. 1421, § 1, eff. July 1, 1999.)

Art. 1756.

Obligations; definition.

An obligation is a legal relationship whereby a person, called the obligor, is bound to render a performance in favor of another, called the obligee. Performance may consist of giving, doing, or not doing something. (Acts 1984, No. 331, § 1, eff. Jan. 1, 1985.)

Art. 1763.

Definition.

A real obligation is a duty correlative and incidental to a real right. (Acts 1984, No. 331, § 1, eff. Jan. 1, 1985.)

Art. 1764.

Effects of real obligation.

A real obligation is transferred to the universal or particular successor who acquires the movable or immovable thing to which the obligation is attached, without a special provision to that effect.

But a particular successor is not personally bound, unless he assumes the personal obligations of his transferor with respect to the thing, and he may liberate himself of the real obligation by abandoning the thing. (Acts 1984, No. 331, § 1, eff. Jan. 1, 1985.)

Art. 1833.

Authentic act.

A. An authentic act is a writing executed before a notary public or other officer authorized to perform that function, in the presence of two witnesses, and signed by each party who executed it, by each witness, and by each notary public before whom it was executed. The typed or hand-printed name of each person shall be placed in a legible form immediately beneath the signature of each person signing the act.

B. To be an authentic act, the writing need not be executed at one time or place, or before the same notary public or in the presence of the same witnesses, provided that each party who executes it does so before a notary public or other officer authorized to perform that function, and in the presence of two witnesses and each party, each witness, and each notary public signs it. The failure to include the typed or handprinted name of each person signing the act shall not affect the validity or authenticity of the act.

C. If a party is unable or does not know how to sign his name, the notary public must cause him to affix his mark to the writing. (Acts 1984, No. 331, § 1, eff. Jan. 1, 1985; Acts 2003, No. 965, § 1, eff. Jan. 1, 2005.)

Art. 1839.

Transfer of immovable property.

A transfer of immovable property must be made by authentic act or by act under private signature. Nevertheless, an oral transfer is valid between the parties when the property has been actually delivered and the transferor recognizes the transfer when interrogated on oath.

An instrument involving immovable property shall have effect against third persons only from the time it is filed for registry in the parish where the property is located. (Acts 1984, No. 331, § 1, eff. Jan. 1, 1985.)

Art. 1909.

Onerous contracts.

A contract is onerous when each of the parties obtains an advantage in exchange for his obligation. (Acts 1984, No. 331, § 1, eff. Jan. 1, 1985.)

Art. 1910.

Gratuitous contracts.

A contract is gratuitous when one party obligates himself towards another for the benefit of the latter, without obtaining any advantage in return. (Acts 1984, No. 331, § 1, eff. Jan. 1, 1985.)

Art. 1966.

No obligation without cause.

An obligation cannot exist without a lawful cause. (Acts 1984, No. 331, § 1, eff. Jan. 1, 1985.)

Art. 1968.

Unlawful cause.

The cause of an obligation is unlawful when the enforcement of the obligation would produce a result prohibited by law or against public policy.

Examples of obligations with unlawful causes include those that arise from gaming, gambling, and wagering not authorized by law. (Acts 1984, No. 331, § 1, eff. Jan. 1, 1985; Acts 2019, No. 106, § 1.)

Art. 1971.

Freedom of parties.

Parties are free to contract for any object that is lawful, possible, and determined or determinable. (Acts 1984, No. 331, § 1, eff. Jan. 1, 1985.)

Art. 2030.

Absolute nullity of contracts.

A contract is absolutely null when it violates a rule of public order, as when the object of a contract is illicit or immoral. A contract that is absolutely null may not be confirmed.

Absolute nullity may be invoked by any person or may be declared by the court on its own initiative. (Acts 1984, No. 331, § 1, eff. Jan. 1, 1985.)

Art. 2031.

Relative nullity of contracts.

A contract is relatively null when it violates a rule intended for the protection of private parties, as when a party lacked capacity or did not give free consent at the time the contract was made. A contract that is only relatively null may be confirmed.

Relative nullity may be invoked only by those persons for whose interest the ground for nullity was established, and may not be declared by the court on its own initiative. (Acts 1984, No. 331, § 1, effective January 1, 1985.)

Art. 2053.

Nature of contract, equity, usages, conduct of the parties, and other contracts between same parties.

A doubtful provision must be interpreted in light of the nature of the contract, equity, usages, the conduct of the parties before and after the formation of the contract, and of other contracts of a like nature between the same parties. (Acts 1984, No. 331, § 1, eff. Jan. 1, 1985.)

Art. 2339.

Fruits and revenues of separate property.

The natural and civil fruits of the separate property of a spouse, minerals produced from or attributable to a separate asset, and bonuses, delay rentals, royalties, and shutin payments arising from mineral leases are community property. Nevertheless, a spouse may reserve them as his separate property as provided in this Article.

A spouse may reserve them as his separate property by a declaration made in an authentic act or in an act under private signature duly acknowledged. A copy of the declaration shall be provided to the other spouse prior to filing of the declaration.

As to the fruits and revenues of immovables, the declaration is effective when a copy is provided to the other spouse and the declaration is filed for registry in the conveyance records of the parish in which the immovable property is located. As to fruits of movables, the declaration is effective when a copy is provided to the other spouse and the declaration is filed for registry in the conveyance records of the parish in which the declarant is domiciled. (Acts 1979, No. 709, § 1; Amended by Acts 1980, No. 565, § 2; Acts 2008, No. 855, § 1.)

Art. 2369.1.

Application of co-ownership provisions.

After termination of the community property regime, the provisions governing co-ownership apply to former community property, unless otherwise provided by law or by juridical act.

When the community property regime terminates for a cause other than death or judgment of declaration of death of a spouse, the following Articles also apply to former community property until a partition, or the death or judgment of declaration of death of a spouse. (Acts 1990, No. 991, § 1; Acts 1995, No. 433, § 1.)

Art. 2432.

Right to marital portion.

When a spouse dies rich in comparison with the surviving spouse, the surviving spouse is entitled to claim the marital portion from the succession of the deceased spouse. (Acts 1979, No. 710, § 1.)

Art. 2434.

Quantum.

The marital portion is one-fourth of the succession in ownership if the deceased died without children, the same fraction in usufruct for life if he is survived by three or fewer children, and a child's share in such usufruct if he is survived by more than three children. In no event, however, shall the amount of the marital portion exceed one million dollars. (Acts 1979, No. 710, § 1; Acts 1987, No. 289, § 1.)

Art. 2440.

Sale of immovable, method of making.

A sale or promise of sale of an immovable must be made by authentic act or by act under private signature, except as provided in Article 1839. (Acts 1993, No. 841, § 1, eff. Jan. 1, 1995.)

Art. 2442.

Recordation of sale of immovable to affect third parties.

The parties to an act of sale or promise of sale of immovable property are bound from the time the act is made, but such an act is not effective against third parties until it is filed for registry according to the laws of registry. (Acts 1993, No. 841, § 1, eff. Jan. 1, 1995; Acts 2005, No. 169, § 2, eff. Jan. 1, 2006; Acts 2005 1st Ex. Sess., No. 13, § 1, eff. Nov. 29, 2005.)

Art. 2467.

Transfer of risk.

The risk of loss of the thing sold owing to a fortuitous event is transferred from the seller to the buyer at the time of delivery.

That risk is so transferred even when the seller has delivered a nonconforming thing, unless the buyer acts in the manner required to dissolve the contract. (Acts 1993, No. 841, § 1, eff. Jan. 1, 1995.)

Art. 2475.

Seller's obligations of delivery and warranty.

The seller is bound to deliver the thing sold and to warrant to the buyer ownership and peaceful possession of, and the absence of hidden defects in, that thing. The seller also warrants that the thing sold is fit for its intended use. (Acts 1993, No. 841, § 1, eff. Jan. 1, 1995.)

Art. 2477.

Methods of making delivery.

Delivery of an immovable is deemed to take place upon execution of the writing that transfers its ownership.

Delivery of a movable takes place by handing it over to the buyer. If the parties so intend delivery may take place in another manner, such as by the seller's handing over to the buyer the key to the place where the thing is stored, or by negotiating to him a document of title to the thing, or even by the mere consent of the parties if the thing sold cannot be transported at the time of the sale or if the buyer already has the thing at that time. (Acts 1993, No. 841, § 1, eff. Jan. 1, 1995.)

Art. 2481.

Incorporeals, method of making delivery.

Delivery of incorporeal movable things incorporated into an instrument, such as stocks and bonds, takes place by negotiating such instrument to the buyer. Delivery of other incorporeal movables, such as credit rights, takes place upon the transfer of those movables. (Acts 1993, No. 841, § 1, eff. Jan. 1, 1995.)

Art. 2589.

Rescission for lesion beyond moiety.

The sale of an immovable may be rescinded for lesion when the price is less than one half of the fair market value of the immovable. Lesion can be claimed only by the seller and only in sales of corporeal immovables. It cannot be alleged in a sale made by order of the court.

The seller may invoke lesion even if he has renounced the right to claim it. (Acts 1993, No. 841, § 1, eff. Jan. 1, 1995.)

Art. 2659.

Application of general rules of sale.

The giving in payment is governed by the rules of the contract of sale, with the differences provided for in this Chapter. (Acts 1993, No. 841, § 1, eff. Jan. 1, 1995.)

Art. 2664.

Application of the rules of sale.

The contract of exchange is governed by the rules of the contract of sale, with the differences provided in this Title. (Acts 2010, No. 186, § 1.)

Art. 2668.

Contract of lease defined.

Lease is a synallagmatic contract by which one party, the lessor, binds himself to give to the other party, the lessee, the use and enjoyment of a thing for a term in exchange for a rent that the lessee binds himself to pay.

The consent of the parties as to the thing and the rent is essential but not necessarily sufficient for a contract of lease. (Acts 2004, No. 821, § 1, eff. Jan. 1, 2005.)

Art. 2673.

The thing.

All things, corporeal or incorporeal, that are susceptible of ownership may be the object of a lease, except those that cannot be used without being destroyed by that very use, or those the lease of which is prohibited by law. (Acts 2004, No. 821, § 1, eff. Jan. 1, 2005.)

Art. 2891.

Loan for use; definition.

The loan for use is a gratuitous contract by which a person, the lender, delivers a nonconsumable thing to another, the borrower, for him to use and return. (Acts 2004, No. 743, § 1, eff. Jan. 1, 2005.)

Art. 2904.

Loan for consumption; definition.

The loan for consumption is a contract by which a person, the lender, delivers consumable things to another, the borrower, who binds himself to return to the lender an equal amount of things of the same kind and quality. (Acts 2004, No. 743, § 1, eff. Jan. 1, 2005.)

Art. 2926.

Deposit; definition.

A deposit is a contract by which a person, the depositor, delivers a movable thing to another person, the depositary, for safekeeping under the obligation of returning it to the depositor upon demand. (Acts 2003, No. 491, § 1, eff. Jan. 1, 2004.)

Art. 3133.

Liability of an obligor for his obligations.

Whoever is personally bound for an obligation is obligated to fulfill it out of all of his property, movable and immovable, present and future. (Acts 2014, No. 281, § 1, eff. Jan. 1, 2015.)

Art. 3134.

Ratable treatment of creditors.

In the absence of a preference authorized or established by legislation, an obligor's property is available to all his creditors for the satisfaction of his obligations, and the proceeds of its sale are distributed ratably among them. (Acts 2014, No. 281, § 1, eff. Jan. 1, 2015.)

Art. 3141.

Pledge defined.

Pledge is a real right established by contract over property of the kind described in Article 3142 to secure performance of an obligation. (Acts 2014, No. 281, § 1, eff. Jan. 1, 2015.)

Art. 3142.

Property susceptible of pledge.

The only things that may be pledged are the following:

(1) A movable that is not susceptible of encumbrance by security interest.

(2) The lessor's rights in the lease of an immovable and its rents.

(3) Things made susceptible of pledge by law. (Acts 2014, No. 281, § 1, eff. Jan. 1, 2015.)

Art. 3278.

Mortgage defined.

Mortgage is a nonpossessory right created over property to secure the performance of an obligation. (Acts 1991, No. 652, § 1, eff. Jan. 1, 1992.)

Art. 3279.

Rights created by mortgage.

Mortgage gives the mortgagee, upon failure of the obligor to perform the obligation that the mortgage secures, the right to cause the property to be seized and sold in the manner provided by law and to have the proceeds applied toward the satisfaction of the obligation in preference to claims of others. (Acts 1991, No. 652, § 1, eff. Jan. 1, 1992.)

Art. 3286.

Property susceptible of mortgage.

The only things susceptible of mortgage are:

(1) A corporeal immovable with its component parts.

(2) A usufruct of a corporeal immovable.

(3) A servitude of right of use with the rights that the holder of the servitude may have in the buildings and other constructions on the land.

(4) The lessee's rights in a lease of an immovable with his rights in the buildings and other constructions on the immovable.

(5) Property made susceptible of conventional mortgage by special law. (Acts 1991, No. 652, § 1, eff. Jan. 1, 1992; Acts 1992, No. 649, § 1, eff. July 1, 1993; Acts 1993, No. 948, § 6, eff. June 25, 1993.)

Art. 3506.

General definitions of terms.

Whenever the terms of law, employed in this Code, have not been particularly defined therein, they shall be understood as follows:

1. The masculine gender comprehends the two sexes, whenever the provision is not one, which is evidently made for one of them only: Thus, the word man or men includes women; the word son or sons includes daughters; the words he, his and such like, are applicable to both males and females.

2. The singular is often employed to designate several persons or things: the heir, for example, means the heirs, where there are more than one.

3. Abandoned.—In the context of a father or mother abandoning his child, abandonment is presumed when the father or mother has left his child for a period of at least twelve months and the father or mother has

failed to provide for the child's care and support, without just cause, thus demonstrating an intention to permanently avoid parental responsibility.

4. Repealed by Acts 1999, No. 503, § 1.

5. Assigns.—Assigns means those to whom rights have been transmitted by particular title; such as sale, donation, legacy, transfer or cession.

6. and 7. Repealed by Acts 1999, No. 503, § 1.

8. Children.—Under this name are included those persons born of the marriage, those adopted, and those whose filiation to the parent has been established in the manner provided by law, as well as descendants of them in the direct line. A child born of marriage is a child conceived or born during the marriage of his parents or adopted by them. A child born outside of marriage is a child conceived and born outside of the marriage of his parents.

9. to 11. Repealed by Acts 1999, No. 503, § 1.

12. Family.—Family in a limited sense, signifies father, mother, and children. In a more extensive sense, it comprehends all the individuals who live under the authority of another, and includes the servants of the family. It is also employed to signify all the relations who descend from a common root.

13. to 22. Repealed by Acts 1999, No. 503, § 1.

23. Repealed by Acts 1987, No. 125, § 2, eff. Jan. 1, 1988.

24. to 27. Repealed by Acts 1999, No. 503, § 1.

28. Successor.—Successor is, generally speaking, the person who takes the place of another. There are in law two sorts of successors: the universal successor, such as the heir, the universal legatee, and the general legatee; and the successor by particular title, such as the buyer, donee or legatee of particular things, the transferee. The universal successor represents the person of the deceased, and succeeds to all his rights and charges. The particular successor succeeds only to the rights appertaining to the thing which is sold, ceded or bequeathed to him.

29. to 31. Repealed by Acts 1999, No. 503, § 1.

32. Third Persons.—With respect to a contract or judgment, third persons are all who are not parties to it. In case of failure, third persons are, particularly, those creditors of the debtor who contracted with him without knowledge of the rights which he had transferred to another. (Paragraph (8) amended by Acts 1979, No. 607, § 1 and Acts 1981, No. 919, § 2, eff. Jan. 1, 1982; Paragraph (12) amended by Acts 1979, No. 711, § 1; Acts 1987, No. 125, § 2, eff. Jan. 1, 1988; Acts 1990, No. 989, § 7, eff.

Jan. 1, 1991; Acts 1991, No. 923, § 1, eff. Jan. 1, 1992; Acts 1997, No. 1317, § 1, eff. July 15, 1997; Acts 1997, No. 1421, § 2, eff. July 1, 1999; Acts 1999, No. 503, § 1; Acts 2004, No.26, § 1, eff. Aug. 15, 2004.)

Code of Civil Procedure

Art. 3651.

Petitory action.

The petitory action is one brought by a person who claims the ownership of, but who does not have the right to possess, immovable property or a real right therein, against another who is in possession or who claims the ownership thereof adversely, to obtain judgment recognizing the plaintiff's ownership. (Amended by Acts 1981, No. 256, § 1; Acts 2023, No. 421, § 2.)

Art. 3652.

Same; parties; venue.

A. A petitory action may be brought by a person who claims the ownership of only an undivided interest in the immovable property or real right therein, or whose asserted ownership is limited to a certain period which has not yet expired, or which may be terminated by an event which has not yet occurred.

B. A lessee or other person who occupies the immovable property or enjoys the real right therein under an agreement with the person who claims the ownership thereof adversely to the plaintiff may be joined in the action as a defendant.

C. A petitory action shall be brought in the venue provided by Article 80(A)(1), even when the plaintiff prays for judgment for the fruits and revenues of the property, or for damages. (Amended by Acts 1981, No. 256, § 1; Acts 2010, No. 185, § 1.)

Art. 3653.

Same; proof of title; immovable.

A. To obtain a judgment recognizing his ownership of immovable property or real right therein, the plaintiff in a petitory action shall:

(1) Prove that he has acquired ownership from a previous owner or by acquisitive prescription, if the court finds that the defendant has been in possession for one year after having commenced possession in good faith and with just title or that the defendant has been in possession for ten years.

(2) Prove a better title thereto than the defendant in all other cases.

B. When the titles of the parties are traced to a common author, the common author is presumed to be the previous owner. (Amended by Acts 1981, No. 256, § 1; Acts 2023, No. 421, § 2.)

Art. 3654.

Proof of title in action for declaratory judgment, concursus, expropriation, or similar proceeding.

When the issue of ownership of immovable property or of a real right therein is presented in an action for a declaratory judgment, or in a concursus, expropriation, or similar proceeding, or when the issue of the ownership of funds that are deposited in the registry of the court and that belong to the owner of the immovable property or of the real right therein is so presented, the court shall render judgment as follows:

(1) If the party who would be entitled to the possession of the immovable property or real right therein in a possessory action has been in possession for one year after having commenced possession in good faith and with just title or has been in possession for ten years, the court shall render judgment in favor of that party, unless the adverse party proves that he would be entitled to a judgment recognizing his ownership in a petitory action under Article 3653(A)(1).

(2) In all other cases, the court shall render judgment in favor of the party who proves better title to the immovable property or real right therein. (Amended by Acts 1981, No. 256, § 1; Acts 2023, No. 421, § 2.)

Art. 3655.

Possessory action.

The possessory action is one brought by the possessor or precarious possessor of immovable property or of a real right therein to be maintained in his possession of the property or enjoyment of the right when he has been disturbed, or to be restored to the possession or enjoyment thereof when he has been evicted. (Amended by Acts 1981, No. 256, § 1; Acts 2023, No. 421, § 2.)

Art. 3656.

Same; parties; venue.

A. A possessory action may be brought by one who possesses for himself. A person entitled to the use or usufruct of immovable property, and one who owns a real right therein, possesses for himself. A possessory action may also be brought by a precarious possessor against anyone except the person for whom he possesses.

B. The possessory action shall be brought against the person who caused the disturbance, and in the venue provided by Article 80(A)(1), even when the plaintiff prays for a judgment for the fruits and revenues of the property, or for damages. (Acts 2010, No. 185, § 1; Acts 2023, No. 421, § 2.)

Art. 3657.

Same; cumulation with petitory action or declaratory judgment action; reconventional demand or separate suit asserting ownership or title.

A. The plaintiff shall not cumulate the possessory action with either the petitory action or a declaratory judgment action to determine ownership. If the plaintiff does so, the possessory action does not abate, but the defendant may object to the cumulation by asserting a dilatory exception. If, before executory judgment in the possessory action, the plaintiff institutes the petitory action or a declaratory judgment action in a separate suit, the possessory action abates.

B. When the defendant in a possessory action asserts title in himself, in the alternative or otherwise, the defendant does not thereby convert the possessory action into a petitory action or judicially confess the possession of the plaintiff in the possessory action, but the defendant's assertions of title shall be considered in defense of the possessory action only for the purposes stated in Article 3661(B).

C. Unless the plaintiff in the possessory action seeks an adjudication of his ownership, the defendant shall not file a reconventional demand asserting a petitory action or declaratory judgment action to determine ownership. If, before executory judgment in a possessory action, the defendant therein institutes a petitory action or a declaratory judgment action to determine ownership in a separate suit he files against the plaintiff in the possessory action, the defendant in the possessory action judicially confesses the possession of the plaintiff in the possessory action. (Acts 2023, No. 421, § 2.)

Art. 3658.

Same; requisites

To maintain the possessory action the plaintiff shall allege and prove all of the following:

(1) The plaintiff had possession or precarious possession of the immovable property or real right therein at the time the disturbance occurred.

(2) The plaintiff and his ancestors in title, or the person for whom the plaintiff possesses precariously and that person's ancestors in title, had such possession quietly and without interruption for more than a year immediately prior to the disturbance, unless evicted by force or fraud.

(3) The disturbance was one in fact or in law, as defined in Article 3659.

(4) The possessory action was instituted within a year of the disturbance. (Amended by Acts 1981, No. 256, § 1; Acts 2023, No. 421, § 2.)

Art. 3659.

Same; disturbance in face and in law defined.

A. Disturbances of possession that give rise to the possessory action are of two kinds: disturbance in fact and disturbance in law.

B. A disturbance in fact is an eviction, or any other physical act that prevents the possessor of immovable property or of a real right therein from enjoying his possession quietly, or that throws any obstacle in the way of that enjoyment.

C. A disturbance in law is the occurrence or existence of any of the following adversely to the possessor of immovable property or a real right therein:

(1) The execution, recordation, or registry, after the possessor or his ancestors in title acquired the right to possess, of any instrument that

asserts or implies a right of ownership or right to the possession of the immovable property or a real right therein.

(2) The continuing existence of record of any instrument that asserts or implies a right of ownership or right to the possession of the immovable property or a real right therein, unless the instrument was recorded before the possessor and his ancestors in title commenced possession.

(3) Any other claim or pretension of ownership or right to the possession of the immovable property or a real right therein, whether written or oral, except when asserted in an action or proceeding. (Amended by Acts 1981, No. 256, § 1; Acts 2023, No. 421, § 2.)

Art. 3660.

Same; possession.

A. A person is in possession of immovable property or of a real right therein, within the intendment of the articles of this Chapter, when the person has the corporeal possession thereof, or civil possession thereof preceded by corporeal possession by him or his ancestors in title, and possesses for himself or precariously for another, whether in good or bad faith, or even as a usurper.

B. Subject to the provisions of Articles 3656 and 3664, a person who claims the ownership of immovable property or of a real right therein possesses through his lessee, through another who occupies the property or enjoys the right under an agreement with him or his lessee, or through a person who has the use or usufruct thereof to which his right of ownership is subject. (Amended by Acts 1981, No. 256, § 1; Acts 2023, No. 421, § 2.)

Art. 3661.

Same; title not at issue; limited admissibility of evidence of title.

A. In the possessory action, the ownership or title of the parties to the immovable property or real right therein is not at issue.

B. No evidence of ownership or title to the immovable property or real right therein shall be admitted except to prove any of the following:

(1) The possession thereof by a party as owner.

(2) The extent of the possession thereof by a party and his ancestors in title.

(3) The length of time in which a party and his ancestors in title have had possession thereof. (Amended by Acts 1981, No. 256, § 1; Acts 2023, No. 421, § 2.)

Art. 3662.

Same; relief that may be granted successful plaintiff in judgment; appeal.

A. A judgment rendered for the plaintiff in a possessory action shall:

(1) Recognize the plaintiff's right to the possession of the immovable property or real right therein, and restore him to possession thereof if he has been evicted, or maintain him in possession thereof if the disturbance has not been an eviction.

(2) Order the defendant to assert his adverse claim of ownership of the immovable property or real right therein in a petitory action to be filed within sixty days after the date the judgment becomes executory, or be precluded thereafter from asserting the ownership thereof, if the plaintiff has prayed for this relief and this relief is not precluded by Paragraph B of this Article.

(3) Award the plaintiff the damages to which he is entitled and for which he has prayed.

B. A judgment in a possessory action shall not grant the relief described in Subparagraph (A)(2) of this Article against the state or against a defendant who appeared in the action only through an attorney appointed to represent him under Article 5091.

C. A suspensive appeal from the judgment rendered in a possessory action may be taken within the delay provided in Article 2123, and a devolutive appeal may be taken from the judgment only within thirty days of the applicable date provided in Article 2087(A). (Amended by Acts 1981, No. 256, § 1; Acts 2010, No. 185, § 1; Acts 2023, No. 421, § 2.)

Art. 4607.

Partition by licitation or by private sale.

When a partition is to be made by licitation, the sale shall be conducted at public auction and after the advertisements required for judicial sales under execution. When a partition is to be made at private sale without the consent of all co-owners, the sale shall be for not less than the appraised value of the property, and documents required pursuant to a court order shall be executed on behalf of the absentee or nonconsenting co-owner by a court-appointed representative, who may be a co-owner, after the advertisements required for judicial sales under execution are made. All counsel of record, including curators appointed to represent absentee defendants, and persons appearing in proper person shall be given notice of the sale date. At any time prior to the sale, the parties may agree upon a nonjudicial partition. (Acts 1990, No. 832, § 1; Acts 2020, No. 281, § 2, eff. June 11, 2020; Acts 2021, No. 27, § 2, eff. June 1, 2021.)

Mineral Code

Art. 190.

Usufructuary of land entitled to enjoyment of mines or quarries worked; exception.

A. If a usufruct of land is that of parents during marriage, or any other legal usufruct, or if there is no provision including the use and enjoyment of mineral rights in a conventional usufruct, the usufructuary is entitled to the use and enjoyment of the landowner's rights in minerals as to mines or quarries actually worked at the time the usufruct was created.

B. If a usufruct of land is that of a surviving spouse, whether legal or conventional, and there is no contrary provision in the instrument creating the usufruct, the usufructuary is entitled to the use and enjoyment of the landowner's rights in minerals, whether or not mines or quarries were actually worked at the time the usufruct was created. However, the rights to which the usufructuary is thus entitled shall not include the right to execute a mineral lease without the consent of the naked owner.

Added by Acts 1974, No. 50, § 1, eff. Jan. 1, 1975. Amended by Acts 1986, No. 245, § 1.

Art. 191.

When oil and gas wells and lignite operations considered open mines.

A. As applied to oil and gas, the principle stated in Article 190 means that if at the time a usufruct is created minerals are being produced from the land or other land unitized therewith, or if there is present on the land or other land unitized therewith, a well shown by surface production test to be capable of producing in paying quantities, the usufructuary is entitled to the use and enjoyment of the landowner's rights in minerals as to all pools penetrated by the well or wells in question.

B. As applied to lignite or another form of coal, the principle stated in Article 190 means that if at the time a usufruct is created the land has been included in a mining plan, the usufructuary is entitled to the use and enjoyment of the landowner's rights in minerals as to all seams proposed to be developed in the mining plan provided the following requirements are satisfied:

(1) Lignite or another form of coal has been discovered as a result of acts committed on the land or due to acts providing a reasonable basis of proof of the discovery of the mineral.

(2) A mining plan for the ultimate production of lignite or other forms of coal, together with a permit issued by the responsible government official, is filed in the conveyance records of the parish or parishes in which the land is located.

(3) Actual mining operations have begun on land included in the plan, although such operations need not be conducted on the land subject to the usufruct.

Added by Acts 1974, No. 50, § 1, eff. Jan. 1, 1975. Amended by Acts 1982, No. 780, § 1.

Art. 196.

Obligations of naked owner arising from enjoyment of rights in minerals.

In enjoying the right recognized by Article 195, the naked owner is entitled to use only so much of the surface of the land as is reasonably necessary for his operations, but he is responsible to the usufructuary or those holding rights under him for the value of such use and for all damaged caused by the naked owner's mining activities or operations. If the activities or operations are conducted by one to whom the naked owner has granted a mineral servitude, the naked owner and his grantee are liable in solido for damages suffered by the usufructuary or those holding rights under him.

Revised Statutes

9:5804.

Immovable property of municipal corporation.

Any municipal corporation owning alienable immovable property may prevent the running of prescription acquirendi causa against it in favor of any third possessor, by recording a notice with the clerk of court of the parish where the property is situated, or with the register of conveyances in the Parish of Orleans insofar as property in that parish is concerned. This notice shall contain a description of the property and a declaration that it is public property belonging to the municipality and the recording shall suspend the running of prescription during the time the ownership of the property shall remain vested in the name of the municipality.

The recordation of the written act by which a municipal corporation shall acquire alienable immovable property likewise shall be deemed sufficient notice in order to suspend the term of prescription.

33:5051.

Platting land into squares or lots before sale; filing map of land; limitations on dedications.

A. Whenever the owner of any real estate desires to lay off the same into squares or lots with streets or alleys between the squares or lots and with the intention of selling or offering for sale any of the squares or lots, he shall, before selling any square or lot or any portion of same:

(1) Cause the real estate to be surveyed and platted or subdivided by a licensed land surveyor into lots or blocks, or both, each designated by number.

(2) Set monuments at all of the corners of every lot and block thereof.

(3) Write the lot designation on the plat or map, and cause it to be made and filed in the office of the keeper of notarial records of the parish wherein the property is situated and copied into the conveyance record book of such parish, and a duplicate thereof filed with the assessor of the parish, a correct map of the real estate so divided.

B. The map referenced in Subsection A of this Section shall contain the following:

(1) The section, township, and range in which such real estate or subdivision thereof lies according to government survey.

(2) The dimensions of each square in feet, feet and inches, or meters.

(3) The designation of each lot or subdivision of a square and its dimensions in feet, feet and inches, or meters.

(4) The name of each street and alley and its length and width in feet, feet and inches, or meters.

(5) The name or number of each square or plat dedicated to public use.

(6) A certificate of the parish surveyor or any other licensed land surveyor of this state approving said map and stating that the same is in accordance with the provisions of this Section and with the laws and ordinances of the parish in which the property is situated.

(7) A formal dedication made by the owner or owners of the property or their duly authorized agent of all the streets, alleys, and public squares or plats shown on the map to public use.

C. Formal dedication of property as a road, street, alley, or cul-de-sac shall impose no responsibility on the political subdivision in which the property is located until:

(1) The dedication is formally and specifically accepted by the political subdivision through a written certification that the road, street, alley, or cul-de-sac is in compliance with all standards applicable to construction set forth in ordinances, regulations, and policies of the political subdivision, which certification may be made directly on the map which contains the dedication; or

(2) The road, street, alley, or cul-de-sac is maintained by the political subdivision.

48:491.

Public Roads.

A. All roads or streets in this state that are opened, laid out, or appointed by virtue of any act of the legislature or by virtue of an order of any parish governing authority in any parish, or any municipal governing authority in any municipality shall be public roads or streets, as the case may be.

B. (1)(a) All roads and streets in this state which have been or hereafter are kept up, maintained, or worked for a period of three years by the authority of a parish governing authority within its parish, or by the authority of a municipal governing authority within its municipality, shall be public roads or streets, as the case may be, if there is actual or constructive knowledge of such work by adjoining landowners exercising reasonable concern over their property.

(b) Actual or constructive knowledge is presumed if prior to or during the work the public body notifies the last known adjoining landowners of same by written notice by certified or registered mail, return receipt requested. When such notice is given more than two years and ten months from commencement of such work, it shall suspend the foregoing prescription for sixty days.

(c) Actual or constructive knowledge is conclusively presumed within all parishes and municipalities, except as otherwise provided by R.S. 48:491(B)(3), if the total period of such maintenance is four years or more, unless prior thereto and within sixty days of such actual or constructive knowledge, the prescription is interrupted or suspended in any manner provided by law.

(2) When a local governing authority for any reason decides to dispose of any road, street, or property used for right-of-way purposes which was originally donated to the authority or its ancestor in title, the property shall revert to the original donor or his heirs or assigns. The authority shall notify the donor or his heirs of its intention to donate the property by sending written notice via certified mail, return receipt requested, to the donor or his heirs at his last known address. The notice shall inform the donor or his heirs or his assigns of the authority's intention to have the land revert and provide him ninety days from receipt in which to respond. If, upon the expiration of the ninety-day period, no response has been received by the authority, it shall dispose of the property in accordance with applicable law. In the donation deed from the authority to the donor or his heirs or his assigns, the authority shall reserve rights of passage for landowners who own property contiguous to the property to be reverted.

(3) Repealed by Acts 2003, No. 204, § 1.

C. All roads or streets made on the front of their respective tracts of lands by individuals when the lands have their front on any of the rivers or bayous within this state shall be public roads when located outside of municipalities and shall be public streets when located inside of municipalities.

D. Notwithstanding any other provisions of law to the contrary, any road or street used by the public is a public road or street provided it is designated as such by the local governing authority, and it shall be within the discretion of the local governing authority to maintain the road up to a private drive; however, no road or street on private property shall be designated as a public road unless ownership is transferred or the right of way is given to the local governing authority.

49:3.

Ownership of waters within boundaries.

The State of Louisiana owns in full and complete ownership the waters of the Gulf of Mexico and of the arms of the Gulf and the beds and shores of the Gulf and the arms of the Gulf, including all lands that are covered by the waters of the Gulf and its arms either at low tide or high tide, within the boundaries of Louisiana.

Constitution

Art. 12 § 13.

Prescription against state.

Prescription shall not run against the state in any civil matter, unless otherwise provided in this constitution or expressly by law.

Topical Table of Cases

I. Things
  A. Public v. private things
    1. **Public things as a matter of law: waterbodies and related lands**
      a. **Territorial sea and seashore**
        Milne v. Girodeau, 12 La. 324 (1838)
        Buras v. Salinovich, 154 La. 594, 97 So. 748 (1923)
      b. **Navigable rivers and streams**
        State v. Two O'Clock Bayou Land Co., 365 So. 2d 1174 (La. App. 3d Cir. 1978)
        Wemple v. Eastham, 150 La. 247, 90 So. 637 (1922)
        Warner v. Clarke, 232 So. 2d 99 (La. App. 2d Cir. 1970)
        Parm v. Shumate, 513 F.3d 135 (5th Cir. 2007)
      c. **Lakes**
        State v. Placid Oil Co., 300 So. 2d 154 (La. 1973)
      d. **Canals**
        Vermilion Corp. v. Vaughn, 356 So. 2d 551 (La. App. 3d Cir. 1978)
    2. **Public things as a matter of fact**
      a. **Public v. private capacity**
        City of New Iberia v. Romero, 391 So. 2d 548 (La. App. 3d Cir. 1980)
      b. **Dedication to public use**
        Cenac v. PAWRA, 851 So. 2d 1006 (La. 2003)
        Martin v. Cheramie, 264 So. 2d 285 (La. App. 4th Cir. 1972)

B. Immovables v. movables

1. Immovables

a. Tracts of land

Landry v. Leblanc, 416 So. 2d 247 (La. App. 3d Cir. 1982)

b. Buildings

PHAC Services v. Seaways Int'l, Inc., 403 So. 2d 1199 (La. 1981)

c. Integral parts

In re Receivership of Augusta Sugar Co., 134 La. 971, 64 So. 870 (1914)

d. Attachments

Equibank v. IRS, 749 F.2d 1176 (5th Cir. 1985)

American Bank & Trust Co. v. Shel-Boze, Inc., 527 So. 2d 1052 (La. App. 1st Cir. 1988)

e. De-immobilization; separate immovables

Folse v. Triche, 113 La. 915, 37 So. 875 (1904)

Brown v. Hodge-Hunt Lumber Co, 162 La. 635, 110 So. 886 (1926)

Willetts Wood Products Co. v. Concordia Land & Timber Co., 169 La. 240, 124 So. 841 (1929)

2. Movables

Beard v. Duralde, 23 La. Ann. 284 (1871)

C. Corporeals v. incorporeals

Miller, Succession of, 405 So. 2d 812 (La. 1981)

South Central Bell Telephone Co. v. Barthelemy, 643 So. 2d 1240 (La. 1994)

D. Fruits v. products

Gueno v. Medlenka, 238 La. 1081, 117 So. 2d 817 (1960)

II. Possession

A. Acquisition of possession

1. *Corpus*

Manson Realty Co. v. Plaisance, 196 So. 2d 555 (La. App. 4th Cir. 1967)

2. *Animus domini*

Harper v. Willis, 383 So. 2d 1299 (La. App. 3d Cir. 1980)

B. Precarious possession

Falgoust v. Inness, 163 So. 429 (La. App. Orl. Cir. 1935)

C. Acquisition, maintenance, and loss of possession

Ellis v. Prevost, 19 La. 251 (1841)

Souther v. Domingue, 238 So. 2d 264 (La. App. 3d Cir. 1970)

Evans v. Dunn, 458 So. 2d 650 (La. App. 3d Cir. 1984)

Whitley v. Texaco, Inc, 434 So. 2d 96 (La. App. 5th Cir. 1983)

D. Effects of possession

1. Presumption of ownership

Peloquin v. Calcasieu Parish Police Jury, 367 So. 2d 1246 (La. App. 3d Cir. 1979)

2. Judicial protection of possession: possessory action

Mire v. Crowe, 439 So. 2d 517 (La. App. 1st Cir. 1983)

3. Acquisition of ownership: acquisitive prescription

a. In general

1) Suspension

Corsey v. State Department of Corrections, 375 So. 2d 1319 (La. 1979)

2) Interruption: eviction

Richard v. Comeaux, 260 So. 2d 350 (La. App. 1st Cir. 1972)

Liner v. LL&E Co., 319 So.2d 766 (La. 1975)

3) Renunciation

Harmon v. Harmon, 308 So. 2d 524 (La. App. 3d Cir. 1975)

b. Of immovables

1) Unabridged (long-term)

Cortinas v. Peters, 224 La. 9, 68 So. 2d 739 (1953)

Humble v. Dewey, 215 So. 2d 378 (La. App. 3d Cir. 1968)

Franks Petroleum, Inc. v. Babineaux, 446 So. 2d 862 (La. App. 2d Cir. 1984)

Noel v. Jumonville, 245 La. 324, 158 So.2d 179 (1963)

Brown v. Wood, 451 So. 2d 569 (La. App. 2d Cir. 1984)

2) **Abridged (short-term)**

a) **Just title**

Wilkie v. Cox, 222 So. 2d 85 (La. App. 3d Cir.), cert denied 254 La. 470, 223 So. 2d 873 (1969)

b) **Good faith**

Board of Comm'rs v. S.D. Hunter Foundation, 354 So. 2d 156 (La. 1977)

Malone v. Fowler, 228 So. 2d 500 (La. App. 3d Cir. 1969)

Phillips v. Parker, 483 So. 2d 972 (La. 1986)

Lacour v. Sanders, 442 So. 2d 1280 (La. App. 3d Cir. 1983)

c) **Delay: tacking**

Bartlett v. Calhoun, 412 So. 2d 597 (La. 1982)

III. **Principal real rights**

A. **Ownership**

1. **Acquisition of ownership**

Autocephalous Greek-Orthodox Church v. Goldberg & Feldman Fine Arts, 717 F. Supp. 1374 (S.D. Ind. 1989)

2. **Extent: accession**

a. **Fruits and products**

Elder v. Ellerbe, 135 La. 990, 66 So. 337 (1914)

Harang v. Bowie Lumber Co., 145 La. 95, 81 So. 769 (1919)

b. **Immovables**

1) **Ownership**

Marcellous v. David, 252 So. 2d 178 (La. App. 3d Cir. 1971)

Graffagnino v. Lifestyles, Inc., 402 So. 2d 742 (La. App. 4th Cir. 1981)

Guzzetta v. Texas Pipe Line Co., 485 So. 2d 508 (La. 1986)

Britt Builders, Inc. v. Brister, 618 So .2d 899 (La. App. 1st Cir. 1993)

2) **Reciprocal rights: reimbursement**

Voiers v. Atkins Bros., 113 La. 303, 36 So. 974 (1903)

Sanders v. Jackson, 192 So. 2d 654 (La. App. 3d Cir. 1966)

3. **Judicial protection of ownership**

a. **Immovables: petitory action**

1) **Title in general**

Sutton v. Montegut, 570 So. 2d 841 (La. App. 5th Cir. 1990)

2) **Standards of proof**

a) **Perfect title**

Deselle v. Bonnette, 251 So. 2d 68 (La. App. 3d Cir. 1971)

Pure Oil v. Skinner, 294 So. 2d 797 (La. 1974)

b) **Better title**

Kelso v. Lange, 421 So.2d 973 (La. App. 3d Cir. 1982); writ denied 426 So. 2d 174 (La. 1983)

b. **Movables: revendicatory action**

Songbyrd v. Bearsville Records, Inc., 104 F.3d 773 (5th Cir. 1997)

B. **Co-ownership**

Leblanc v. Scurto, 173 So. 2d 322 (La. App. 1st Cir. 1965)

Miller, Succession of, 674 So. 2d 441 (La. 1981)

Ben Glazer Co. v. Tharp-Sontheimer-Tharp, Inc, 491 So. 2d 722 (La. App. 4th Cir. 1986)

C. **Dismemberments of ownership (servitudes)**

1. **Predial servitudes**

a. **Natural**

Broussard v. Cormier, 154 La. 877, 98 So. 403 (1923)

Poole v. Guste, 261 La. 1110, 262 So.2d 339 (1972)

b. **Legal**

1) **Neighborhood**

Higgins Oil & Fuel Co. v. Guaranty Oil Co., 145 La. 233, 82 So. 206 (1919)

Yokum v. 615 Bourbon Street, LLC, 977 So. 2d 859 (La. 2008)

2) **Enclosed estates**

Stuckey v. Collins, 464 So. 2d 346 (La. App. 2d Cir. 1985)

c. Conventional

1) Creation

a) Title

Langevin v. Howard, 363 So. 2d 1209 (La. App. 2d Cir. 1978)

b) Acquisitive prescription

Palomeque v. Prudhomme, 664 So. 2d 88 (La. 1995)

Boudreaux v. Cummings, 138 So. 3d 798 (La. 2014)

c) Destination of the owner

Alexander v. Boghel, 4 La. 312 (1832)

730 Bienville Partners, Ltd. v. First National Bank, 596 So. 2d 836 (La. App. 4th Cir. 1992)

2) Effects

a) Servient estate's duty of non-interference

Hymel v. St. John the Baptist Parish School Board, 303 So. 2d 588 (La. App. 4th Cir. 1974)

Ryan v. Southern Natural Gas Co., 879 F.2d 162 (5th Cir. 1989)

b) Judicial protection of predial servitudes

Louisiana Irrigation & Mill Co. v. Pousson, 262 La. 973, 265 So.2d 756 (1972)

Kizer v. Lilly, 471 So. 2d 716 (La. 1985)

3) Extinction: prescription of non-use

Vincent v. Meaux, 325 So. 2d 346 (La. App. 3d Cir. 1975)

Tilley v. Lowery, 511 So. 2d 1245 (La. App. 2d Cir. 1987)

Ashland Oil Co. v. Palo Alto, Inc., 615 So. 2d 971 (La. App. 1st Cir. 1993)

Thompson v. Meyers, 34 La. Ann. 615 (1882)

Powers v. Foucher, 12 Mart. (O.S.) 70 (1822)

2. Personal servitudes: usufruct

a. Classification

1) Nonconsumables v. consumables

Leury v. Mayer, 122 La. 486, 47 So. 839 (1908)

2) Legal v. conventional

a) Legal

Norsworthy v. Succession of Norsworthy, 704 So. 2d 953 (La. App. 2d Cir. 1997)

b) Conventional

Goode, Succession of, 425 So. 2d 673 (La. 1982)

Smith v. Nelson, 121 La. 170, 46 So. 200 (1908)

b. Effects: rights and duties of the usufructuary

Kennedy v. Kennedy, 699 So. 2d 351 (La. 1997)

Crain, Succession of, 450 So. 2d 1374 (La. App. 1st Cir. 1984)

c. Termination

Bond v. Green, 401 So. 2d 639 (La. App. 3d Cir. 1981)

Kimball v. Standard Fire Ins. Co., 578 So. 2d 546 (La. App. 3d Cir. 1991)

Watson v. Federal Land Bank of Jackson, 606 So. 2d 920 (La. App. 3d Cir. 1992)

Index

[References are to pages.]

A

Abridged Acquisitive Prescription of Immovables

Generally, 135
Bad faith, evidence of
  Generally, 142
  Errors of fact
    Generally, 142
    Clouds on title in public records, 144
    Errors of law, 145
    Public records and clouds, 144
    Quitclaim deeds, 143
Delay
  Junction of possessions, 146
  Length, 146
  Possessions, junction of, 146
Good faith
  Procedural matters
    Evidence of bad faith (See subhead: Bad faith, evidence of)
    Presumption of good faith, 141
  Substantive matters
    Definition, 140
    Nature, 141
    Timing, 141
Juridical Act, 136
Just title
  Generally, 135
  Elements derived from general principles
    Not absolutely null, 138
    Not putative, 139
    Not subject to still-pending suspensive condition, 139
  Elements enumerated in Article 3483
    Juridical Act, 136
    Proper form, 137
    Recorded title, 138
    Translative Act (See subhead: Translative Act)
    Written title, 137
Translative Act
  Definition, 136
  Distinctions
    Acts generative of merely personal (credit) rights, 137
    Declarative Acts, 136

Abridged Acquisitive Prescription of Movables

Generally, 147
Act translative of ownership, 148
Delay
  Junction of possessions, 149

Length, 149
Possessions, junction of, 149
Good faith, 148

Acquisition in Conventional Servitudes
Generally, 228
Acquisitive prescription, by
Domain, 234
Modes, 234
Requirements
Good faith, 236
Just title, 236
Possession (See subhead: Possession for acquisitive prescription)
Destination, by
Definition, 237
Manner of creation
Generally, 238
Apparent servitudes, 238
Nonapparent servitudes, 238
Possession for acquisitive prescription
Constitutive elements
Animus domini, 235
Corpus, 235
Quasi-possession, 234
Re the Act, 228
Re the grantee
Capacity, 232
Who can receive, 232
Re the grantor
Capacity to grant, 231
Power to grant, 231
Who can grant
Co-owner of servient estate, 229
Owner of servient estate, 229
Possessor, 230
Prescriber of servient estate, 230
Usufructuary of servient estate, 230
Title, by
Domain, 228
Formal requirements
Exception, 233
General rule, 233
Requirements, 228
Re the Act, 228
Re the grantor (See subhead: Re the grantor)
Substantive requirements
Re the Act, 228
Re the grantee (See subhead: Re the grantee)
Re the grantor (See subhead: Re the Grantor)

Acquisitive Prescription
Abridged
Immovables (See Abridged Acquisitive Prescription of Immovables)
Movables (See Abridged Acquisitive Prescription of Movables)
Basic principles
Generally, 117
Interruption of prescription (See subhead: Interruption of prescription)
Lapse of time, calculation of
Accrual, 117
Commencement, 117
Renunciation of prescription (See subhead: Renunciation of prescription)
Suspension of prescription (See subhead: Suspension of prescription)
Causes for suspension
Exceptions
Generally, 122

Certain "fiduciary" relationships, 122
Contra non valentem, 123
Familial relationships, 122
"Fiduciary" relationships, 122
Registered immovables of municipalities, 123
General rule, 122
Civil interruption
Generally, 120
Acknowledgement, 121
Owner, by, 120
Possessor, by, 121
Suit, 120
Constitutive elements of acquisitive prescription
Generally, 135
Delay (See subhead: Delay)
Immovables (See Immovable Things)
Movables (See Movable Things)
Possession, 129
Thing susceptible of acquisition by prescription (See subhead: Thing susceptible of acquisition by prescription)
Contrast, definition by
Differences
Domain, 116
Necessity of possession, 116
Prescription, varieties of, 115
Similarities, 116
Varieties of prescription, 115
Conventional servitudes, in (See Acquisition in Conventional Servitudes, subhead: Acquisitive prescription, by)
Co-possessors, by, 187
Definition
Contrast, by (See subhead: Contrast, definition by)
Exposition, by, 115
Delay
Continuation of possessions
Generally, 130
Spatial extent of joined possession (See subhead: Spatial extent of joined possession)
General principles, 130
Tacking of possessions
Generally, 130
Spatial extent of joined possession (See subhead: Spatial extent of joined possession)
Effects of acquisitive prescription, 126
Elements common to all modes of acquisitive prescription (See subhead: Constitutive elements of acquisitive prescription)
Immovables (See Immovable Things)
Interruption of prescription
Definition, 118
Effect of interruption, 121
Varieties
Generally, 118
Civil interruption (See subhead: Civil interruption)
Natural interruption (See subhead: Natural interruption)
Lapse of time, calculation of
Accrual, 117
Commencement, 117
Mode of acquiring ownership, as, 43
Movables (See Movable Things)
Natural interruption
Generally, 119

Abandonment, 119
Eviction, 119
Personal servitudes, 252
Possession
Generally, 129
Spatial extent of joined possession (See subhead: Spatial extent of joined possession)
Renunciation of prescription
Attributes, 124
Definition, 124
Effect of renunciation, 126
Form
Generally, 125
Immovables, 125
Movables, 125
Time of renunciation, 125
Spatial extent of joined possession
Generally, 131
Particular successors
Boundary tacking, 133
Exception, 133
General rule, 132
No tacking beyond title, 132
Spatially unrestricted tacking, 132
Universal successors, 132
Suspension of prescription
Causes for suspension (See subhead: Causes for suspension)
Definition, 122
Effect of suspension, 124
Thing susceptible of acquisition by prescription
Generally, 127
Common things, 128
Private things
Exception, 128
General rule, 128
Public things, 128

Adjunction, Accession with Respect to Movables
Definition, 173
Ownership, 175
Prerequisites
Generally, 173
Principal and accessory
Generally, 174
Bulk, 174
Function, 174
Value, 174
Whole, 175
Remedies
Accessory, owner of
Damages, 176
Reimbursement, 176
Return, separation and, 176
Separation and return, 176
Principal, owner of, 175

Artificial Accession
Generally, 158
Remedial rules
Generally, 162
Owner of original immovable consented to production or union of new thing
Improvements, consented-to, 162
INATs, consented-to, 163
Owner of original immovable did not consent to production or union of new thing
Generally, 165
Bad faith, good faith versus, 166
Domain, 165
Good faith versus bad faith, 166
Preliminary matter, 166
Rules, 168

Union accomplished by contributor using things that did not belong to owner
Ownership rules
Improvements, accession of, 159
INATs, accession of, 161
Remedial rules (See subhead: Remedial rules)
Union accomplished *by owner* using things that belonged to another
Ownership rules, 170
Reimbursement rules, 170

B

Boundary Action
Definitions
Boundary, 287
Boundary markers, 288
Prerequisites
Relative to the thing, 288
Relative to the person, 289
Rules of determination
Generally, 290
Title relied on by parties, 291
Acquisitive prescription relied on by party, 291
Scope
Boundaries, fixing, 288
Markers, fixing, 288

Building Restrictions
Alteration
Amendment
Juridical act terms, per, 277
Suppletive law, 277
Termination
Abandonment, 279
Juridical act, 278
Prescription of non-use, 278
Characterization, 273
Classification, 273
Creation
General plan of development, 275
Means, 274
Definition, 272
Enforcement, 276
Interpretation, 276
Termination (see Alteration)

C

Common and Noncommon Things
Definitions, 12
Illustrations, 12
Significance, 12

Composite Things
(See Single and Composite Things)

Conservatory Acts
Co-owned thing itself, rights in, 191

Consumables and Nonconsumables
Definition, 51
Distinction, nature of criterion for, 52
Illustrations, 51
In property law, 52
Nominate contracts, 53
Outside property law, 53
Significance
In property law, 52
Nominate contracts, 53
Outside property law, 53
Usufruct
Effects of, 52
Nature of, 52
Usufruct of consumable and nonconsumables
Abusus, 253
Fruits, 255
Naked owner during usufruct, 261
Termination, 269, 270

Conventional Servitudes
Acquisition (See Acquisition in Conventional Servitudes)
Delay for prescription of nonuse
  Generally, 242
  Commencement of delay, 242
  Contract, alteration of delay by, 243
  Interruption, 242
  Suspension, 242
Effects
  Dominant estate, owner of, 238
  Servient estate, owner of, 239
Extinction
  Abandonment, 244
  Confusion, 244
  Destruction, 240
  Nonuse
    Generally, 241
    Burden of proof, 244
    Delay (See subhead: Delay for prescription of nonuse)
    Procedural incidents, 244
    What is "use", 241
    Who can use, 242
  Renunciation, 245
Subclassification
  Generally, 227
  Affirmative v. negative, 227
  Apparent v. nonapparent, 227
  Evidence of charge on servient estate, 227
  Nature of charge on servient estate, 227
  Negative, affirmative v., 227
  Nonapparent, apparent v., 227

Co-Owners, Rights Of
Co-owned thing itself, rights in
  Alterations, improvements and, 192
  Conservatory Acts, 191
  Fruits, 189
  Improvements and alterations, 192
  Ordinary maintenance and repair, 192
  Repair, ordinary maintenance and, 192
  Use
    Agreement, use defined by, 191
    Equal use, 190
Co-owner's share of co-owned thing
  Alienation, 193
  Lease, 194
  Personal rights, creation of, 194
  Real rights, creation of
    Generally, 193
    Accessory real rights, 193
    Principal real rights less than ownership, 193
    Servitudes, 193

Corporeal Immovables
Declaration, by, 41
Definition, 28
Nature, varieties by
  All tracts of land, 28
  Attachments to buildings and immovable constructions
    Definition, 37
    Matter of fact, attachments as, 38
    Matter of law, attachments as, 38
  Immovable constructions, other, 37
  Land, all tracts of, 28
  Man-made structures, certain
    Classifications, 28
    Differentiation, 28
    Enumeration, 28
    Prerequisites to immovability (See subhead: Prerequisites to immovability)

Matter of law, attachments as
Buildings, to, 38
Other immovable constructions, 40
Of buildings, 37
Of tracts of land, 35
Prerequisites to immovability (See subhead: Prerequisites to immovability)
Vegetation, certain
Classifications (See subhead: Vegetation classification)
Differentiation, enumeration and (See subhead: Vegetation classification)
Enumeration and differentiation (See subhead: Vegetation classification)
Ungathered fruits, 32
Unharvested crops, 32
Prerequisites to immovability
Buildings, 29
Constructions, other
Generally, 30
Belongs to owner of ground, 30
Permanently attached to ground, 30
Standing timber, 33
Ungathered fruits, 32
Unharvested crops, 32
Varieties
Declaration, by, 41
Nature, by (See subhead: Nature, varieties by)
Vegetation classification
Generally, 31
Standing timber
Generally, 31
Not cut down, 31
Rooted in soil, 31
Timber, 31

Corporeal Movables
Definition, 42
Illustrations, 42
Occupancy, 108

Corporeal Things
Definition, 46
Scope of possession, 69
Significance
Generally, 47
Outside property law, 48
Property law, 47

D

Dismemberments of Ownership
(See Servitudes)

F

Fructus
(See Fruits)

Fruits
Generally, 53
Accession of, 180
Allocation, 254
Civil fruits, 54, 254
Community property, 58
Complications
Generally, 54
Natural fruits versus natural products
Minerals, 54
Timber, 56
Definition, 254
Definitions, 53
Illustrations
Civil fruits, 54
Natural fruits, 54
In property law
Accession, 57
Dismemberments of ownership, 57
Modes of acquiring ownership, 57

Ownership of unconsented-to production, 57
Usufruct, 57
Matrimonial regimes law, 58
Natural fruits, 54, 254
Rights in co-owned thing itself, 189
Significance
Community property, 58
In property law (See subhead: In property law)
Matrimonial regimes law, 58
Substantive rights with respect to, 97
Ungathered fruits, 32

I

Immovable Things
Abridged acquisitive prescription (See Abridged Acquisitive Prescription of Immovables)
Corporeal immovables (See Corporeal Immovables)
Definitions, 27
Significance (See Movable Things, subhead: Significance)
Unabridged acquisitive prescription, 135

Improvements Versus INATs
Accession with respect to immovables
Ownership, 61
Remedies (See subhead: Remedies)
Definitions, 60
Distinction, nature of criterion of, 61
Illustrations, 60
Ownership, 61
Property law
Ownership, 61
Remedies (See subhead: Remedies)
Remedies
Generally, 62
Consented-to improvements, 63
Consented-to INATs, 63
Unconsented-to improvements and INATs, 62
Significance
Ownership, 61
Remedies (See subhead: Remedies)
Subclassifications
Consented-to improvements and INATs, 61
Unconsented-to improvements and INATs, 61

INATs
(See Improvements Versus INATs)

Incorporeal Immovables
Definition, 41
Illustrations, 41

Incorporeal Movables
Definition, 42
Illustrations, 42

Incorporeal Things
Generally, 69
Definitions, 46
Significance (See Corporeal Things, subhead: Significance)

J

Judicial Protection of Possession
Generally, 99
Ownership, protection compared, 286
Possessory action
Prerequisites to possessory action (See Prerequisites to Possessory Action)
Proper parties plaintiff

Precarious possessors, 106
True possessors, 106
Scope, 100
Prerequisites to possessory action (See Prerequisites to Possessory Action)

Juridical Act
Generally, 136
Abridged acquisitive prescription, 136
Acquisition of usufruct
Contractual and testamentary
Freedom, 247
Interpretation, 249
General exposition, 247
Contrary provision in
Generally, 199
Act creating indivision, 199
Convention among co-owners, 200
Division mandated by, 189
Transfer by co-owners, 198

L
Legal Servitudes
Common enclosures
Generally, 221
Ditches, 222
Fences, 222
Plants, removal of, 222
Walls, 221
Enclosed estates
Indemnity
Exception, 225
General rule, 224
Location of passage (See subhead: Passage, location of)
Passage, location of (See subhead: Passage, location of)
Right of passage, entitlement to
Exception, 224
General rule, 223
Encroaching buildings, 220
Indemnity
Exception, 225
General rule, 224
Legal "public" servitudes, 218
Loss of right, 226
Neighborhood, obligations of, 219
Obligations of neighborhood, 219
Passage, location of
Exceptions
Other, 226
Voluntary alienation, resulting from, 226
General rule, 225
Right of passage, entitlement to
Exception, 224
General rule, 223

M
Mélange, Accession with Respect to Movables
Definition, 179
Ownership, 179
Prerequisites, 179
Remedies
Damages, replacement and, 180
Reimbursement, 180
Replacement and damages, 180

Mere Products
Accession of, 181
Complications (See Fruits, subhead: Complications prescription, by)
Definitions, 53
Illustrations, 53
Significance (See Fruits, subhead: Significance)

Modified Ownership
(See Ownership in Indivision)

Movable Things
Generally, 42
Abridged acquisitive prescription (See Abridged Acquisitive Prescription of Movables)
Corporeal immovables (See Corporeal Immovables)
Corporeal movables (See Corporeal Immovables)
  Definition, 42
  Illustrations, 42
Definitions, 27
Incorporeal movables
  Definition, 42
  Illustrations, 42
Property law
  Accessory real rights, 44
  Effectivity *vis-à-vis* third persons, 43
  Modes of acquiring ownership
    Accession, 43
    Acquisitive prescription, 43
  Mortgage, 44
  Objects, 44
  Pledge, 44
  Servitudes, 44
  Transfer of ownership, 43
Revendicatory action (See Revendicatory (Revindicatory) Action)
Significance
  Lesion, 45
  Obligations
    Donation *inter vivos*, 45
    Sale, 44
  Property law (See subhead: Property law)
  Sales, 45
Unabridged acquisitive prescription, 147

N

Natural Accession
Generally, 171
Abandoned bed, 173
Alluvion and dereliction
  Generally, 171
  Along lake or seashore, 172
  Along river or stream, 172
Avulsion, 172
Dereliction, alluvion and (See subhead: Alluvion and dereliction)
Islands from new channels, 172
Islands on beds, 173

Natural Navigable Water Bodies
Generally, 16
Bottoms
  Generally, 17
  Definition of bottom
    Lakes, of, 18
    Rivers, of, 17
    Streams, of, 17
  Streams/rivers and lakes, distinction between, 17

Natural Servitudes
Generally, 218
Drain, right of (See subhead: Right of drain)
Right of drain
  Definition, 218
  Duties, rights and, 218
  Rights and duties, 218
Right to use running water, 218
Running water, right to use, 218

Noncommon Things
(See Common and Noncommon Things)

Nonconsumables
(See Consumables and Nonconsumables)

O

Occupancy
Constitutive elements
Generally, 107
Corporeal movable, 108
Possession, 107
Thing that has no owner (See subhead: Thing that has no owner)
Co-possessors, by, 187
Definition, 107
Quasi-occupancy (See Quasi-Occupancy)
Thing that has no owner
Domestic animals, 110
Things that, though once owned, have ceased to be owned
Abandoned things, 110
Wild animals, 111
Things that have never been owned
Generally, 108
Common things, constituents of, 108
Constituents of certain common things, 108
Domestic animal, 110
Wild animal (See Wild Animal)
Wild animal (See Wild Animal)

Ownership
Accession
Explication (See subhead: Explication of accession)
Regimes of accession (See subhead: Regimes of accession)
Constitutive elements
Generally, 153
Abusus
Generally, 154
Juridical disposition, 154
Physical disposition, 154
Characteristics
Generally, 155
Absolute, 155
Exclusive, 155
Perpetual, 155
Fructus, 154
Usus, 154
Definition, 153
Explication of accession
Definition, 156
Prerequisites, 157
Types of rules, 157
Varieties, 156
Immovables, accession with respect to
Preliminary matters
Distinctive prerequisites, 158
Nature of rules, 158
Rules
Artificial accession (See Artificial Accession)
Natural accession (See Natural Accession)
Indivision, ownership in (See Ownership in Indivision)
Movables, accession with respect to
Adjunction (See Adjunction, Accession with Respect to Movables)
Fruits, accession of, 180
Mélange (See Mélange, Accession with Respect to Movables)
Mere products, 181
Transformation (See Transformation, Accession with Respect to Movables)
Regimes of accession
Generally, 158

Immovables, accession with respect to (See subhead: Immovables, accession with respect to)

Ownership in Indivision
Accession, improvements and alterations
Generally, 195
Ownership, 195
Remedies, 196
Creation
Generally, 185
Act of will, by
Bilateral Acts, 188
Dations en paiement, 188
Donations *inter vivos*, 188
Donations *mortis causa*, 188
Exchanges, 188
Sales, 188
Unilateral Acts, 188
Operation of law, by
Generally, 185
Acquisitive prescription by co-possessors, 187
Community, termination of, 186
Co-possessors, acquisitive prescription by, 187
Divorce and separation, 186
Intestate succession, 185
Materials, commingling or mixture of, 186
Occupancy and quasi-occupancy by co-possessors, 187
Quasi-occupancy by co-possessors, occupancy and, 187
Quasi-occupancy of treasure, 187
Separation, divorce and, 186
Termination of community, 186
Treasure, quasi-occupancy of, 187
Definition
Generally, 183
Ownership, 183
Same thing, 184
Two or more persons, 184
Division of shares
Exceptions
Generally, 189
Juridical Act, division mandated by, 189
Law, division mandated by, 189
General rule, 188
Domain, 185
Rights of co-owners (See Co-Owners, Rights of)
Shares, division of (See subhead: Division of shares)
Termination of co-ownership (See Termination of Co-Ownership)

P

Personal Servitudes
Habitation, 270
Right of use, 271
Usufruct (See Usufruct)

Petitory Action
Acquisitive prescription, acquisition by, 283
Burden of proof
Better title, 285
Common author rule, 284
Perfect title ("title good against the world), 283
Previous owner, acquisition from, 283
Possessary action, compared, 286

Relationship to the possessory action
- Defendant, against, 286
- Plaintiff, against, 286
- Rule of noncumulation, 286

Possession
Generally, 67
Acquisition of possession
- Generally, 75
- Derivative possession
  - Generally, 77
  - Particular succession, via, 79
  - Universal succession, via, 78
- Original possession
  - Generally, 76
  - Vicarious *animus*, 76
  - Vicarious *corpus*, 76

Actual possession
- Definition of, 74
- Modes of proving, 75

Animus
- Burden of proof, 72
- Presumptions, 72
- Procedural matters, 72
- Substantive matters, 71

Concept of possession, 68
Conservation of possession
- Generally, 79
- Burden of proof, 81
- Presumption, 81
- Procedural matters, 81
- Substantive matters
  - *Animus domini*, 80
  - *Corpus*, 80

Constitutive elements of possession
- Generally, 70
- *Animus* (See subhead: *Animus*)
- *Corpus*, 70

Constructive possession
- Nature of, 74
- Requisites for, 74

Continuation of possession, 90
Corpus, 70, 76,80
Definitions, 68, 85
Detention
- Complex precarious possession
  - Co-ownership, 87
  - Servitude, 87
- Compound precarious possession
  - Co-ownership, 87
  - Servitude, 87
- Definition, 85
- Presumptions, 88
- Procedural matters, 88
- Simple precarious possession
  - *Commodatum*, 87
  - Deposit, 86
  - Lease, 86
  - Loan for use, 87
  - Pledge, 86
  - Possessory security right, 86
- Termination
  - Generally, 88
  - Borrowers, 89
  - Co-owners, 88
  - Depositaries, 89
  - Detainers, other, 89
  - Lessees, 89
  - Pledgees, 89
  - Servitude holders, 89

Effects of possession
- Presumption of ownership, 95
- Procedural rights, 95
- Substantive rights (See subhead: Substantive rights)

Extent of possession
- Generally, 73
- Without title
  - Actual possession, definition of, 74
  - Modes of proving actual possession, 75

Procedural matters, 75
Substantive matters, 74
With title
Nature of constructive possession, 74
Requisites for constructive possession, 74
Judicial protection of possession (See Judicial Protection of Possession)
Junction of possessions, 90
Loss of possession
Generally, 81
Animus alone, loss of, 83
Corpus alone, loss of
Generally, 82
Destruction, 83
Escape, 83
Eviction, 82
Usurpation, 82
Corpus and *animus,* loss of both, 82
Ownership, 67
Precarious possession (See subhead: Detention)
Presumption of ownership, 95
Procedural rights, 95
Scope of possession (See subhead: Things susceptible of possession)
Substantive rights
Accession
Generally, 96
Enhancements, rights with respect to, 97
Fruits and products, rights with respect to, 97
Improvements and INATs, 97
INATs, improvements and, 97
Products, rights with respect to, 97
Others, 97
"Right to possess"
Acquisition, 96
Loss, 96
Tacking of possessions, 90
Things susceptible of possession
Corporeal things, 69
Incorporeal things, 69
Private things, 69
Public things, 69
Vices of possession
Generally, 83
Clandestinity, 84
Discontinuity, 84
Equivocation, 85
Violence, 83

Possessory Action
(See Judicial Protection of Possession, subhead: Possessory action)

Predial Servitudes
Characteristics
Indivisibility, 216
Inseparability
Dominant estate, from, 216
Servient estate, from, 215
Classifications
Generally, 217
Conventional servitudes (See Conventional Servitudes)
Legal servitudes (See Legal Servitudes)
Natural servitudes (See Natural Servitudes)
Definitions
Generally, 207
Estate (See subhead: Estate)
Dominant estate
Benefit of, 211
Definition, 209
Estate
Generally, 207

Dominant estate, 209
Separate ownership of estates, 214
Servient, 208
Limitations, 217
Nature, 215
Separate ownership of estates, 214
Servient estate
Charge on, 209
Definition, 208

Prerequisites to Possessory Action
Generally, 100
Action within one year of disturbance, 105
Disturbance in fact or in law
Generally, 101
Definition and varieties
Generally, 101
Eviction, 101
Mere disturbance, 101
Eviction, 101
Mere disturbance, 101
Necessity, 101
Fact, disturbance in (See subhead: Disturbance in fact or in law)
Law, disturbance in (See subhead: Disturbance in fact or in law)
Possession at time of disturbance, 104
Time of disturbance, possession at, 104
Uninterrupted possession for one year prior to disturbance
Elements of requirement, 104
Eviction by force, 105
Eviction by fraud, 105
Exception to requirement
Generally, 104
Eviction by force, 105
Eviction by fraud, 105
Force, eviction by, 105
Fraud, eviction by, 105
Force, eviction by, 105
Fraud, eviction by, 105
Requirement, elements of, 104

Private Things
Generally, 19
Duration of insusceptibility of private ownership, 26
Public things compared (See Public Things, subhead: Private things compared)
Subclassifications
Private persons, private things of, 20
Public persons, private things of, 19

Property Law
Generally, 3, 8
Patrimonial rights, 4
Real rights, 4
Rights
Generally, 4
Patrimonial rights, 4
Real rights, 4
Technical meaning
Generally, 3
Rights (See subhead: Rights)
Things, 4

Public Things
Generally, 13
Duration of insusceptibility of private ownership, 26
Matter of fact, public things as
Criteria, 15
Definition, 14
Illustrations, 18
Public things as a matter of law and, distinction between, 26
Matter of law, public things as
Criteria, 15
Definitions, 14

Illustrations
Generally, 16
Running waters, 16
Public things as a matter of fact and, distinction between, 26
Seashore, 18
Territorial sea, 18
Preliminary investigation, 13
Private capacity, public versus, 13
Private things, public use of
Dedication, subject to public use by, 23
Subject to public use by law
Generally, 22
"General" servitude of public use, 22
"Levee" servitude of public use, 23
"River road" servitude of public use, 23
Private things compared
Private ownership, susceptibility of
Generally, 20
Ease of disposal, 20
Susceptibility of (adverse) possession, 21
Vulnerability to prescription, 21
"Public use," susceptibility of
Private things (See subhead: Private things, public use of)
Public things, 21
Public versus private capacity, 13

Q

Quasi-Occupancy
Co-possessors, 187
Definition, 111
Lost things, quasi-occupancy of
Definition by exposition, 113
Requirement
Diligent effort, 113
Three years' possession, 114
Treasure, quasi-occupancy of
Allocation, rules of, 114
Creation, 187
Definition, 114
Requirements, 114
Lost things, quasi-occupancy of (See subhead: Lost things, quasi-occupancy of)
Varieties
Treasure, quasi-occupancy of (See subhead: Treasure, quasi-occupancy of)

R

Revendicatory (Revindicatory) Action
Generally, 293
Burden of proof, 293
Presumptions, 293

S

Servitudes
Predial servitudes (See Predial Servitudes)

Single and Composite Things
Accession, 59
Definitions, 58
Illustrations, 58
Immovables
Encumbrance of, 59
Transfer of, 59
Mortgage, 59
Movables, 59
Obligations law, property and, 59
Ownership, 59
Property and obligations law, 59
Property law, 59
Sales, 59
Significance

Accession, 59
Immovables
Encumbrance of, 59
Transfer of, 59
Mortgage, 59
Movables, 59
Obligations law, property and, 59
Ownership, 59
Property and obligations law, 59
Property law, 59
Sales, 59

T

Termination of Co-Ownership
Generally, 198
Contrary provision in juridical act
Generally, 199
Act creating indivision, 199
Convention among co-owners, 200
Juridical act of transfer by co-owners, 198
Loss of thing, 198
Partition
Exceptions
Contrary provision in juridical act (See subhead: Contrary provision in juridical act)
Contrary provision of law, 200
General rule, 199
Interests of co-owners
Kind, in, 204
Licitation, by, 204
Localization, 204
Interests of third parties
Co-owned thing, 204
Co-owner's share, 205
Juridical nature
Conventional, 200
Judicial, 200
Legal, 200
Modes
Generally, 200
Kind, in, 201
Sale, by, 201
Thing, loss of, 198

Things
Generally, 9
Common and noncommon things (See Common and Noncommon Things)
Corporeal things (See Corporeal Things)
Immovable things (See Immovable Things)
Incorporeal things (See Incorporeal Things)
Loss of, 198
Movable things (See Movable Things)
Noncommon things (See Common and Noncommon Things)
Private things (See Private Things)
Public things (See Public Things)

Transformation, Accession with Respect to Movables
Definition, 176
"Labor only" transformation
Definition, 177
Ownership, 178
Prerequisites, 177
Remedies
Damages, replacement and, 178
Reimbursement, 178
Replacement and damages, 178
"Labor plus capital" transformation
Definition, 176
Ownership, 177

Prerequisites, 176
Remedies
Damages, replacement and, 177
Reimbursement, 177
Replacement and damages, 177
Varieties
"Labor only" transformation (See subhead: subhead: "Labor only" transformation)
"Labor plus capital" transformation (See subhead: "Labor plus capital" transformation)

Translative Act
(*See* Abridged Acquisitive Prescription of Immovables, subhead: Translative Act)

U

Unabridged Acquisitive Prescription
Immovables, 135
Movables, 147

Unilateral Acts
Ownership in indivision, 188

Usufruct
Acquisition
Acquisitive prescription, by, 252
Juridical act, by (See subhead: Juridical act, acquisition by)
Operation of law, by (See subhead: Operation of law, acquisition by)
Allocation of fruits
Generally, 254
Civil fruits, 254
Natural fruits, 254
Definitions, 245
Duties of usufructuary during usufruct
Charges, 260
Inventory, 257
Preservation, 260
Prudent administrator, 261
Repairs, 259
Security (See subhead: Security, usufructuary post)
Effects of
Naked owner during the usufruct, rights and duties of
Consumables, usufruct of, 261
Nonconsumables, usufruct of, 261
Partition powers (See subhead: Partition powers)
Usufructuary during usufruct
Duties of (See subhead: Duties of usufructuary during usufruct)
Rights of (See subhead: Rights of usufructuary during usufruct)
Juridical act, acquisition by, general exposition
Generally, 247
Contractual and testamentary freedom, 247
Contractual and testamentary interpretation, 249
Operation of law, acquisition by
Generally, 251
Marital portion usufruct, 252
Spousal usufruct, 251
Partition powers
Absolute, 263
Naked ownership, partition of, 263
Underlying thing, partition of, 263
Usufruct, partition of, 262
Rights of usufructuary during usufruct

Generally, 253
Thing subject to usufruct (See subhead: Thing subject to usufruct)
Usufruct itself, rights with respect, 257
Right to use usufruct of nonconsumables
Generally, 255
Prudent administrator, duty to act as, 255
Restrictions
Changes in destination, restriction on, 256
Improvements, restriction on, 255
Other physical alterations, restriction on, 255
Security, usufructuary post
Exceptions
Generally, 258
Amount of security, 259
Form of security, 259
General rule, 258
Termination
Causes of termination
Abuse, 268
Burdened thing, transformation of, 266
"Death" of usufructuary, 264
Destruction of underlying thing, 264
Forced sale of burdened thing, 269
Nonuse, prescription of, 269
Waste, 268
Consequences of termination
Consumables, usufruct of, 270
Nonconsumables, usufruct of, 269
Thing subject to usufruct
Abusus
Consumables, usufruct of, 253
Nonconsumables, usufruct of, 253
Disposition
Consumables, usufruct of, 253
Nonconsumables, usufruct of, 253
Fruits
Generally, 253
Allocation (See subhead: Allocation of fruits)
Definition, 254
Use
Generally, 255
Consumables, usufruct of, 255
Nonconsumables, usufruct of (See subhead: Right to use usufruct of nonconsumables)
Varieties, 246

W

Water Bodies, Natural Navigable
(See Natural Navigable Water Bodies)

Wild Animal
Generally, 108, 111
Definition
Contrast, by, 109
Exposition, by, 109
Natural liberty, never deprived of
Generally, 109
Enclosed wild animals, 110
Wild animals that have been captured, 110
Wild animals that have been tamed, 110